2019 MINUTES OF THE GENERAL ASSEMBLY CUMBERLAND PRESBYTERIAN CHURCH

Office of the General Assembly

Cumberland Presbyterian Church

August 2019

8207 Traditional Place
Cordova (Memphis), Tennessee 38016

©2019 Office of the General Assembly, CPC

All Rights Reserved. No part of this book may be reproduced or transmitted in any form or by any means, electronic or mechanical, including photocopying, recording, or by any information storage or retrieval system, without permission in writing from the publisher. For information address Office of the General Assembly, Cumberland Presbyterian Center, 8207 Traditional Place, Cordova (Memphis), Tennessee, 38016-7414.

Published by the Communications Ministry Team of the Cumberland Presbyterian Church and distributed by Cumberland Presbyterian Resources of the Discipleship Ministry Team, CPC.

The Discipleship Ministry Team of the Ministry Council of the Cumberland Presbyterian Church is the successor organization to the Board of Christian Education of the Cumberland Presbyterian Church.

Funded, in part, by your contributions to Our United Outreach.

First Edition 2019

ISBN: 978-1-945929-25-0

Vision of Ministry

Biblically-based and Christ-centered
    born out of a specific sense of mission,
    the Cumberland Presbyterian Church strives to be true to its heritage:
    to be open to God's reforming spirit,
    to work cooperatively with the larger Body of Christ,
    and to nurture the connectional bonds that make us one.
The Cumberland Presbyterian Church seeks—to be the hands and feet of Christ in witness and service to the world and, above all, the Cumberland Presbyterian Church lives out the love of God to the glory of Jesus Christ.

TABLE OF CONTENTS

Vision of Ministry .... Title Page
Program 3
Commissioners 5
Youth Advisory Delegates 6
Committees and Abbreviations 6
Committee Meeting Rooms 6
Committee Assignments 7
Referrals to Committees 8
Recommendations at a Glance 9
Assembly Meetings and Officers 10
Bylaws of General Assembly Corporation 13
Memorial Roll of Ministers 23
Living General Assembly Moderators 24
Membership of Boards and Agencies 25

Reports
    Moderator 33
    Stated Clerk 36
    Ministry Council 42
    Board of Stewardship, Foundation and Benefits 50
    Board of the Historical Foundation 76
    Board of Trustees of Memphis Theological Seminary 85
    OUO Committee 95
    Commission on Chaplains and Military Personnel 97
    Permanent Judiciary Committee 99
    Nominating Committee 101
    Place of Meeting Committee 104
    Unified Committee on Theology and Social Concerns 105
    Unification Task Force 107
    Board of Trustees of Bethel University 113
    Board of Trustees of the Cumberland Presbyterian Children's Home 114
    Joint Committee on Amendments 117
    Evaluation Committee 119

Memorials 126

Agency Budgets 129

General Assembly Minutes 142

Audits
    Denomination Center Agencies 152
    Bethel University 214
    CP Children's Home 265
    Memphis Theological Seminary 285

Appendices 312

Church Calendar .... Inside Back Cover

PROGRAM SCHEDULE

Assembly Meetings: Von Braun Convention Center
CPC General Assembly Office: North Hall (upstairs, Salon 10)
CPC Women's Ministry Office: North Hall, East Hallway
CPCA GA Office: South Hall, Meeting Room 3
Retiring Moderator: The Reverend Jay Earheart-Brown, West Tennessee Presbytery
Co-Hosts: Robert Donnell Presbytery (CPC) and Huntsville Presbytery (CPCA)
Co-Pastor Hosts: The Reverend Cardelia Howell-Diamond, Robert Donnell Presbytery (CPC) and
   The Reverend Terence Haley, Huntsville Presbytery (CPCA)
Co-Worship Directors: The Reverend Mitchell Walker (CPCA) and The Reverend Joy Warren (CPC)
Music Director: Elder Victor Garth, Mt Zion CPCA
Exhibits & Bookstore: East Hall 3
Ministry Exchange: North Hall 2 (Tuesday and Wednesday)

SUNDAY, JUNE 9, 2019

Location	Time	Event	
Hotel Lobby	1:00 p.m.	Welcome table	Embassy Suites
Convention Center	3-5:00 p.m.	GA Office open for Commissioner/YAD check-in	
		Registration for Women's Ministry Convention	
		Setup displays	
	7:30 p.m.	Joint Opening GA Worship/Communion Service	North Hall 2 & 3
		(An offering will be received)	

FIRST DAY - MONDAY, JUNE 10, 2019

	8:00 a.m.	Orientation for Commissioners/Youth Advisory Delegates	
			South Hall, Ballroom 1
		Orientation for Committee Chairs and Co-Chairs	
		(Commissioner/YAD packets may be picked up before or after the orientation session.)	
	9:00 a.m.	Women's Ministry Registration (open until 5:00 p.m.)	
			North Hall, East Hallway
	10:00 a.m.	Joint Opening Devotion	North Hall 2 & 3
		Welcome, Pastor Host, Local Officials	
		Joint UTF presentation	
	12:00 p.m.	CP Women's Ministry Regional Council Luncheon	South Hall, Ballroom 1
	2:00 p.m.	Opening GA Business Session	North Hall 2 & 3
		Constitution of the CPC General Assembly	
		Adoption of the Agenda	
		Report of the Credentials Committee	
		Election of Moderator	
		Election of Vice-Moderator	
		Presentation by the Stated Clerk, Mike Sharpe	
		Communications	
		Corrections to Preliminary Minutes	
		Committee Appointments and Referrals to Committees	
		Introduction of Board and Agency Representatives	
	3:00 p.m.	Break	
	3:30 p.m.	Committees to Meet	various locations
CPCA Center &	5:00 p.m.	Joint Moderator & Women's Ministry Reception	
Church Street CPCA		(come and go – hors d'oeuvres)	
226 Church Street		Open House at the CPCA Center & Church Street CPCA	
	6:00 p.m.	Dinner Break	
Convention Center	7:00 p.m.	Joint Committees to Meet	
		various locations	
		CP Women's Ministry/National Missionary Society Gathering	
			South Hall, Ballroom 1

SECOND DAY - TUESDAY, JUNE 11, 2019

7:00 - 9 a.m.	Joint Fun Run & Walk	Big Springs Int'l Park
8:00 a.m.	Convention Registration (continues)	North Hall, East Hallway
9:30 a.m.	CP Women's Ministry Convention Convenes	North Hall 1
10:00 a.m.	GA Committee Meetings (devotions in committees)	various locations
12:00 p.m.	CPCA National Missionary Society Luncheon	South Hall, Ballroom 1
2:00 p.m.	CP Women's Ministry Reconvenes	North Hall 1
5:30 p.m.	Bethel University Dinner	South Hall, Ballroom 1

EVENING PROGRAM

7:00 p.m.	Committee Meetings	various locations
8:30 p.m.	Joint Reception Honoring Women in Ministry	South Hall, Ballroom 1

THIRD DAY - WEDNESDAY, JUNE 12, 2019

8:00 a.m.	Joint Devotions/Presentations (led by National Missionary Society)	North Hall 3
9:00 a.m.	Women's Ministry Convention	North Hall 1
9:30 a.m.	GA Committees Meet	various locations
12:00 p.m.	MTS/PAS Luncheon	South Hall, Ballroom 1
2:00 p.m.	Women's Ministry Convention	North Hall 1
5:00 p.m.	Conclusion of Committee Meetings	various locations
5:30 p.m.	CP Children's Home Dinner	South Hall, Ballroom 1

EVENING PROGRAM

7:00 p.m.	Evening Worship/Program (Soul Shop – Training on suicidal desperation among Adolescents sponsored by DMT)	North Hall 2 & 3

FOURTH DAY - THURSDAY, JUNE 13, 2019

8:30 a.m.	Devotional - (led by Youth Advisory Delegate)	North Hall 2 & 3
9:00 a.m.	Break	
9:00 a.m.	Women's Ministry Convention	North Hall 1
9:30 a.m.	General Assembly Business	North Hall 2 & 3
	Commissioning Service for Missionaries	
12:00 noon	Lunch Break	
	Cumberland Presbyterian Women's Luncheon	East Hall 2
2:00 p.m.	General Assembly Business	North Hall 2 & 3
5:00 p.m.	Dinner Break	
	Take Down Displays	

EVENING PROGRAM

7:00 p.m.	General Assembly Business (as needed)	

Closing Devotion: Led by Worship Director

(In the event that business is not concluded on Thursday,
the closing worship will be at the conclusion
of business on Friday morning.)

COMMISSIONERS
to the
ONE HUNDRED EIGHTY-EIGHTH GENERAL ASSEMBLY

PRESBYTERY	MINISTER	COMMITTEE	ELDER	COMMITTEE
Andes (2)	Joaquin Orozco	J	Cesar Restrepo	TSC/UTF
Arkansas (2)	Bobby Coleman	J	Kim Virden	C/HF
	Michael Suttle	C/HF	Nadine Rail	J
Cauca Valley (4)	Wilfrido Quinones	TSC/UTF	Leticia Ceballos	J
	Rodrigo Torres	J	Liliana Manzano	TSC/UTF
Choctaw (1)	Virginia Espinoza	TSC/UTF	Jimmie Scott	C/HF
Columbia (2)	Todd Gaskill	J	Jonathan Bates	HE/CH
	Jason Mikel	TSC/UTF	Sally Sain	S/E/OUO
Covenant (3)	Victor Hassell	J	Casey Easley	C/HF
	Daniel Hopkins	C/HF	Randall Hooper	S/E/OUO
	David LeNeave	S/E/OUO	Roger McCuiston	MC
Cumberland (3)	James Byrd	HE/CH	Dianna Clark	TSC/UTF
	Chris Darland	S/E/OUO	Edna Hobbs	C/HF
	Steve Delashmit	MC	April Whitmer	MC
Cumberland East Coast (1)	Jin Soo Park	MC		
Del Cristo (2)	Shelia O'Mara	HE/CH		
	Nate Mathews	S/E/OUO		
East Tennessee (3)	Tammy Greene	J	Don Bird	S/E/OUO
	Mark Hester	MC	Jerry Godolphin	MC
	Alfonzo Marquez	TSC/UTF	Tom Witmer	J
Emaus (1)	Zenobia Rivera	TSC/UTF	Lina Maria Velasquez	J
Grace (3)	Derek Jacks	HE/CH	Hue Bell	HE/CH
	Luke Lawson	MC	Jim Phillips	J
	David Linski	S/E/OUO	Norris Ray	C/HF
Hong Kong (2)			IP Shun-Tak Andy	MC
			KWOK Chor Wo	MC
Hope (1)	Jimmy Peyton	HE/CH	Tommy Word	HE/CH
Japan (2)	Ichiro Wada	MC)		
Missouri (1)	Kevin Vanderlaan	C/HF	Larry Nottingham	TSC/UTF
Murfreesboro (3)	Mark Barron	TSC/UTF	Frances Hobbs	HE/CH
	Michael Clark	J	Dale McDaniel	TSC/UTF
	Christian Smith	S/E/OUO	Kathy Roberts	J
Nashville (3)	Lisa Cook	C/HF	Randy Gannon	S/E/OUO
	Steve Jones	HE/CH	Paul Hyde	TSC/UTF
	Teresa Shauf	MC	Becky Urrutia	HE/CH
North Central (2)	Eduardo Montoya	TSC/UTF	Mary Gard	J
	Kevin Small	HE/CH	Debra Shanks	C/HF
Red River (3)	Judy Madden	HE/CH	Toby Thomason	J
	Allan Mink	S/E/OUO	Vince Wilson	HE/CH
	Linda Snelling	TSC/UTF		
Robert Donnell (1)	Brian Tanck	S/E/OUO	Tammy Norris	S/E/OUO
Tenn./Georgia (2)	Courtney Krueger	MC	Mike McCormack	C/HF
	Phillip Layne	C/HF	Delbert Secrest	S/E/OUO
Trinity (2)	Fredy Diaz	C/HF	Lezlie Daniel	MC
	Mary Kathryn Kirkpatrick	S/E/OUO	Brian Martin	TSC/UTF
West Tennessee (5)	Jay Earheart-Brown	C/HF	Valerie Fowlkes	J
	Tiffany McClung	HE/CH	Mark Maddox	MC
	Don McCurley	J	Debbie Marston	HE/CH
	Brittany Meeks	S/E/OUO	Marshall Moss	C/HF
	Michael Qualls	MC		

YOUTH ADVISORY DELEGATES
to the
ONE HUNDRED EIGHTY-SIXTH GENERAL ASSEMBLY

(Each Presbytery is eligible to send two Youth Advisory Delegates)

PRESBYTERY	DELEGATE	COMMITTEE
Arkansas	Hannah Davis	MC
	Sarah Davis	S/E/OUO
Choctaw	(no youth delegate)	
Columbia	Aaron Way	MC
Covenant	Victoria Hassell	HE/CH
Cumberland	Isaac Embry	C/HF
del Cristo	(no youth delegate)	
East Tennessee	Brandon Smith	J
	Anna Wood	HE/CH
Emaus	Sara Sofia Alfonso	MC
Grace	Hayden Bell	S/E/OUO
	Daniel Fowler	HE/CH
Hope	McKenzie Cornelius	TSC/UTF
Japan	(no youth delegate)	
Missouri	Olivia Pruitt	S/E/OUO
	Nathaniel Wood	MC
Murfreesboro	Chandler Anderson	MC
	Gregory Oliver	C/HF
Nashville	(no youth delegate)	
North Central	Colten Lash	HE/CH
	Noah Jenkins	J
Red River	Chase DeWees	TSC/UTF
	Robert Rush	J
Robert Donnell	Nyah Anderson	S/E/OUO
	Zanna Howell-Diamond	C/HF
Tennessee Georgia	(no youth delegate)	
Trinity	Sofia Triana	C/HF
	Darcie Webb	TSC/UTF
West Tennessee	Grace Holland	TSC/UTF
	Will Suiter	J

COMMITTEES ABBREVIATIONS AND MEETING ROOMS

ABBREV.	COMMITTEE	MEETING ROOMS
C/HF	Chaplains/Historical Foundation	South Hall, Meeting Room 2
HE/CH	Higher Education/Children's Home	South Hall, Ballroom 4
J	Judiciary	South Hall, Ballroom 3
MC	Ministry Council	South Hall, Ballroom 5
S/E/OUO	Stewardship/Elected Officers/Our United Outreach	South Hall, Meeting Room 1
TSC/UTF	Theology & Social Concerns/Unification Task Force	South Hall, Ballroom 2

COMMITTEE ASSIGNMENTS

1. **CHAPLAINS/HISTORICAL FOUNDATION** *(South Hall, Meeting Room 2)*
   Chair: Reverend Lisa Cook   **Co-Chair:** Reverend Fredy Diaz
   Ministers: Lisa Cook, Fredy Diaz, Jay Earheart-Brown, Daniel Hopkins, Phillip Layne, Michael Suttle, Kevin Vanderlaan
   Elders: Casey Easley, Edna Hobbs, Mike McCormack, Marshall Moss, Ray Norris, Jimmy Scott, Debra Shanks, Kim Virden
   Youth Advisory Delegates: Isaac Embry, Zanna Howell-Diamond, Gregory Oliver, Sofia Triana

2. **HIGHER EDUCATION/CHILDREN'S HOME** *(South Hall, Ballroom 4)*
   Chair: Elder Debbie Marston   **Co-Chair:** Reverend Jimmy Peyton
   Ministers: James Bird, Derek Jacks, Steve Jones, Judy Madden, Tiffany McClung, Shelia O'Mara, Jimmy Peyton, Kevin Small
   Elders: Jonathan Bates, Hue Bell, Frances Hobbs, Debbie Marston, Becky Urrutia, Vince Wilson, Tommy Word
   Youth Advisory Delegates: Daniel Fowler, Victoria Hassell, Colten Lash, Anna Wood

3. **JUDICIARY** *(South Hall, Ballroom 3)*
   Chair: Reverend Bobby Coleman   **Co-Chair:** Reverend Tammy Greene
   Ministers: Michael Clark, Bobby Coleman, Todd Gaskill, Tammy Greene, Victor Hasell, Don McCurley, Joaquin Orozco, Rodrigo Torres
   Elders: Leticia Cellabos, Valeria Fowlkes, Mary Gard, Jim Phillips, Kathy Roberts, Nadine Rail, Toby Thomason, Tom Witmer
   Youth Advisory Delegates: Noah Jenkins, Brandon Smith, Robert Rush, Will Suiter

4. **MINISTRY COUNCIL** *(South Hall, Ballroom 5)*
   Chair: Reverend Mark Hester   **Co-Chair:** Elder Lezlie Daniel
   Ministers: Steve Delashmit, Mark Hester, Courtney Krueger, Luke Lawson, Jin Soo Park, Michael Qualls, Theresa Shauf, Ichiro Wada
   Elders: IP Shunk-Tak Andy, Lezlie Daniel, Jerry Godolphin, Mark Maddox, Roger McCuiston, April Whitmer, KWOK Chor Wo
   Youth Advisory Delegates: Sara Sofia Alfonso, Chandler Anderson, Hannah Davis, Aaron Way, Nathaniel Wood

5. **STEWARDSHIP/ELECTED OFFICERS/OUR UNITED OUTREACH** *(South Hall, Meeting Room 1)*
   Chair: Reverend Mary Katherine Kirkpatrick   **Co-Chair:** Elder Randy Gannon
   Ministers: Chris Darland, Mary Katherine Kirkpatrick, David LeNeave, David Linski, Nate Mathews, Brittany Meeks, Alan Mink, Christian Smith, Brian Tanck
   Elders: Don Bird, Randy Gannon, Randall Hooper, Tammy Norris, Sally Sain, Delbert Secrest
   Youth Advisory Delegates: Nyah Anderson, Hayden Bell, Sarah Davis, Olivia Pruitt

6. **THEOLOGY & SOCIAL CONCERNS/UNIFICATION TASK FORCE** *(South Hall, Ballroom 2)*
   Chair: Reverend Linda Snelling   **Co-Chair:** Reverend Eduardo Montoya
   Ministers: Mark Barron, Virginia Espinoza, Alfonso Marquez, Jason Mikel, Eduardo Montoya, Wilfrido Quinones, Zenobia Rivera, Linda Snelling
   Elders: Dianna Clark, Paul Hyde, Liliana Manzano, Brian Martin, Dale McDaniel, Larry Nottingham, Cesar Restrepo
   Youth Advisory Delegates: McKenzie Cornelius, Chase DeWees, Grace Holland, Darcie Webb

7. **CREDENTIALS:**
   Chair: Reverend Virginia Espinoza
   Co-Chair: Elder Larry Nottingham
   Member: Elder Sally Sain
   Youth Advisory Delegate: Noah Jenkins

REFERRALS TO COMMITTEES

Referrals to the Committee on Chaplains/Historical Foundation
Page **Report**
- 76 The Report of the Board of Trustees of the Historical Foundation
- 97 The Report of the Commission on Military Chaplains and Personnel
- 122 The Report of the Evaluation Committee, Part II (Recommendations 7-11)

Referrals to the Committee on Children's Home/Higher Education
Page **Report**
- 85 The Report of the Board of Trustees of Memphis Theological Seminary
- 113 The Report of the Board of Trustees of Bethel University
- 114 The Report of the Board of Trustees of the Cumberland Presbyterian Children's Home
- 119 The Report of the Evaluation Committee, Part I (Recommendations 1-6)
- 126 The Memorial from Missouri Presbytery Regarding the Program of Alternate Studies
- 126 The Memorial from Missouri Presbytery Regarding the Requirements for Recognition of Ordination

Referrals to the Committee on Judiciary
Page **Report**
- 99 The Report of the Permanent Committee on Judiciary
- 117 The Report of the Joint Committee on Amendments
- 128 The Memorial from Nashville Presbytery Regarding Sacrament of Baptism

Referrals to the Committee on Ministry Council
Page **Report**
- 42 The Report of the Ministry Council,
- 127 The Memorial from Presbytery del Cristo Regarding A Denominational Day of Prayer and Fasting

Referrals to the Committee on Stewardship/Elected Officers
Page **Report**
- 33 The Report of the Moderator
- 36 The Report of the Stated Clerk
- 50 The Report of the Board of Stewardship, Foundation and Benefits
- 95 The Report of the Our United Outreach Committee
- 104 The Report of the Place of Meeting Committee
- 129 Line Item Budgets Submitted by General Assembly Agencies

Referrals to the Committee on Theology and Social Concerns/Unification Task Force
Page **Report**
- 105 The Report of the Unified Committee on Theology and Social Concerns
- 107 The Report of the Unification Task Force

RECOMMENDATIONS AT A GLANCE

Report of the Moderator
Page 33 Recommendation 1
34 Recommendation 2

Report of the Stated Clerk
Page 38 Recommendation 1

Report of the Ministry Council
Page 47 Recommendations 1-2
48 Recommendations 3-4

Report of the Board of Stewardship, Foundation and Benefits
(No Recommendations)

Report of the Board of Trustees of the Historical Foundation
Page 82 Recommendation 1

Report of the Board of Trustees of Memphis Theological Seminary
Page 88 Recommendation 1
90 Recommendation 2
93 Recommendation 3

Report of the Our United Outreach Committee
Page 95 Recommendation 1
96 Recommendation 2

Report of the Commission on Chaplains and Military Personnel
Page 97 Recommendations 1-2

Report of the Permanent Judiciary Committee
(No Recommendations)

Report of the Place of Meeting Committee
(No Recommendations)

Report of the Unified Committee on Theology and Social Concerns
Page 105 Recommendation 1

Report of the Unification Task Force
Page 112 Recommendation 1

Report of the Board of Trustees of Bethel University
(No Recommendations)

Report of the Board of Trustees of the CP Children's Home
(No Recommendations)

Report of the Joint Committee on Amendments
Page 117 Recommendation 1

Report of the Evaluation Committee
Page 119 Recommendation 1
120 Recommendations 2-6
121 Recommendation 7
123 Recommendations 8-11

Memorials
(Page 126-128)

Budgets of General Assembly Board/Agencies
(Pages 129-137)

ASSEMBLY MEETINGS AND OFFICERS

Historical Review of the Stated Meetings and Officers of:

THE CUMBERLAND PRESBYTERY, 1810-1813

Date	Place	Moderator	Clerk	Members
1810, February	Sam McAdow's House, Dickson Co., TN	Samuel McAdow	Young Ewing	3
1810, March 20	Ridge Meeting-House, Sumner Co., TN.	Samuel McAdow	Young Ewing	14
1810, October 23	Lebanon Meeting-House	Finis Ewing	Young Ewing	16
1811, March 19	Big Spring, Wilson Co., TN	Robert Bell	Young Ewing	19
1811, October 9	Ridge Meeting-House	Thomas Calhoun	David Foster	23
1812, April 7	Suggs Creek Meeting-House	Hugh Kirkpatrick	James B. Porter	28
1812, November 3	Lebanon, KY	Finis Ewing	Hugh Kirkpatrick	22
1813, April 6	Beech Meeting-House, Sumner Co. TN	Robert Bell	James B. Porter	34

THE CUMBERLAND SYNOD, 1813-1828

Date	Place	Moderator	Clerk	Members
1813, October 5	Beech Meeting-House	William McGee	Finis Ewing	13
1814, April 5	Suggs Creek	David Foster	James B. Porter	27
1815, October 17	Beech Meeting-House	William Barnett	David Foster	15
1816, October 15	Free Meeting-House, TN	Thomas Calhoun	David Foster	22
1817, October 21	Mt. Moriah, KY	Robert Donnell	Hugh Kirkpatrick	27
1818, October 20	Big Spring, TN	Finis Ewing	Robert Bell	27
1819, October 19	Suggs Creek, TN	Samuel King	William Barnett	24
1820, October 17	Russellville, KY	Thomas Calhoun	William Moore	30
1821, Third Tues. in Oct.	Russellville, KY	Minutes not recorded		
1822, October 15	Beech Meeting-House	James B. Porter	David Foster	47
1823, October 21	Russellville, KY	John Barnett	Aaron Alexander	48
1824, October 19	Cane Creek, TN	Samuel King	William Moore	68
1825, October 18	Princeton, KY	William Barnett	Hiram McDaniel	76
1826, Third Tues. in Oct.	Russellville, KY	Minutes not recorded		
1827, November 20	Russellville, KY	James S. Guthrie	Laban Jones	63
1828, October 21	Franklin, TN	Hiram A. Hunter	Richard Beard	94

THE GENERAL ASSEMBLY, 1829-

Date	Place	Moderator	Clerk	Members
1829, May 19	Princeton, KY	Thomas Calhoun	F. R. Cossitt	26
1830, May 18	Princeton, KY	James B. Porter	F. R. Cossitt	36
1831, May 17	Princeton, KY	Alex Chapman	F. R. Cossitt	34
1832, May 15	Nashville, TN	F. R. Cossitt	F. R. Cossitt	36
1833, May 21	Nashville, TN	Samuel King	F. R. Cossitt	35
1834, May 20	Nashville, TN	Thomas Calhoun	James Smith	48
1835, May 19	Princeton, KY	Sam King	James Smith	42
1836, May 17	Nashville, TN	Reuben Burrow	James Smith	43
1837, May 16	Lebanon, TN	Robert Donnell	James Smith	49
1838, May 15	Princeton, KY	Hiram A. Hunter	James Smith	47
1840, May 19	Elkton, KY	Reuben Burrow	James Smith	55
1841, May 18	Owensboro, KY	William Ralston	C. G. McPherson	56
1842, May 17	Owensboro, KY	Milton Bird	C. G. McPherson	57
1843, May 16	Owensboro, KY	A. M. Bryan	C. G. McPherson	68
1845, May 20	Lebanon, TN	Richard Beard	C. G. McPherson	95
1846, May 19	Owensboro, KY	M. H. Bone	C. G. McPherson	86
1847, May 18	Lebanon, Ohio	Hiram A. Hunter	C. G. McPherson	71
1848, May 16	Memphis, TN	Milton Bird	C. G. McPherson	100
1849, May 16	Princeton, KY	John L. Smith	C. G. McPherson	75
1850, May 21	Clarksville, TN	Reuben Burrow	Milton Bird	102
1851, May 20	Pittsburgh, PA	Milton Bird	Milton Bird	71
1852, May 18	Nashville, TN	David Lowry	Milton Bird	107
1853, May 17	Princeton, KY	H. S. Porter	Milton Bird	108
1854, May 16	Memphis, TN	Isaac Shook	Milton Bird	112
1855, May 15	Lebanon, TN	M. H. Bone	Milton Bird	101
1856, May 15	Louisville, KY	Milton Bird	Milton Bird	99
1857, May 21	Lexington, MO	Carson P. Reed	Milton Bird	106
1858, May 20	Huntsville, AL	Felix Johnson	Milton Bird	124
1859, May 19	Evansville, IN	T. B. Wilson	Milton Bird	131
1860, May 17	Nashville, TN	S. G. Burney	Milton Bird	168
1861, May 16	St. Louis, MO	A. E. Cooper	Milton Bird	51
1862, May 15	Owensboro, KY	P. G. Rea	Milton Bird	58
1863, May 21	Alton, IL	Milton Bird	Milton Bird	73
1864, May 19	Lebanon, OH	Jesse Anderson	Milton Bird	65
1865, May 18	Evansville, IN	Hiram Douglas	Milton Bird	78
1866, May 17	Owensboro, KY	Richard Beard	Milton Bird	155
1867, May 16	Memphis, TN	J. B. Mitchell	Milton Bird	176
1868, May 21	Lincoln, IL	G. W. Mitchell	Milton Bird	184
1869, May 20	Murfreesboro, TN	S. T. Anderson	Milton Bird	173
1870, May 19	Warrensburg, MO	J. C. Provine	Milton Bird	167

Date	Place	Moderator	Clerk	Members
1871, May 18	Nashville, TN	J. B. Logan	Milton Bird	173
1872, May 16	Evansville, IN	C. H. Bell	Milton Bird	182
1873, May 15	Huntsville, AL	J. W. Poindexter	John Frizzell	165
1874, May 21	Springfield, MO	T. C. Blake	John Frizzell	185
1875, May 20	Jefferson, TX	W. S. Campbell	John Frizzell	169
1876, May 18	Bowling Green, KY	J. M. Gill	John Frizzell	184
1877, May 17	Lincoln, IL	A. B. Miller	John Frizzell	171
1878, May 16	Lebanon, TN	D. E. Bushnell	John Frizzell	205
1879, May 15	Memphis, TN	J. S. Grider	John Frizzell	143
1880, May 20	Evansville, IN	A. Templeton	John Frizzell	194
1881, May 19	Austin, TX	W. J. Darby	John Frizzell	187
1882, May 18	Huntsville, AL	S. H. Buchanan	John Frizzell	188
1883, May 17	Nashville, TN	A. J. McGlumphey	T. C. Blake	204
1884, May 15	McKeesport, PA	John Frizzell	T. C. Blake	148
1885, May 21	Bentonville, AR	G. T. Stainback	T. C. Blake	185
1886, May 20	Sedalia, MO	E. B. Crisman	T. C. Blake	193
1887, May 19	Covington, OH	Nathan Green	T. C. Blake	187
1888, May 17	Waco, TX	W. H. Black	T. C. Blake	217
1889, May 16	Kansas City, MO	J. M. Hubbert	T. C. Blake	217
1890, May 15	Union City, TN	E. G. McLean	T. C. Blake	220
1891, May 21	Owensboro, KY	E. F. Beard	T. C. Blake	213
1892, May 19	Memphis, TN	W. T. Danley	T. C. Blake	229
1893, May 18	Little Rock, AR	W. S. Ferguson	T. C. Blake	226
1894, May 17	Eugene, OR	F. R. Earle	T. C. Blake	167
1895, May 16	Meridian, MS	M. B. DeWitt	T. C. Blake	208
1896, May 21	Birmingham, AL	A. W. Hawkins	J. M. Hubbert	200
1897, May 20	Chicago, IL	H. S. Williams	J. M. Hubbert	224
1898, May 19	Marshall, MO	H. H. Norman	J. M. Hubbert	221
1899, May 18	Denver, CO	J. M. Halsell	J. M. Hubbert	181
1900, May 17	Chattanooga, TN	H. C. Bird	J. M. Hubbert	230
1901, May 16	West Point, MS	E. E. Morris	J. M. Hubbert	226
1902, May 15	Springfield, MO	S. M. Templeton	J. M. Hubbert	255
1903, May 21	Nashville, TN	R. M. Tinnon	J. M. Hubbert	247
1904, May 19	Dallas, TX	W. E. Settle	J. M. Hubbert	251
1905, May 18	Fresno, CA	J. B. Hail	J. M. Hubbert	249
1906, May 17	Decatur, IL	Ira Landrith	J. M. Hubbert	279
1906, May 24	Decatur, IL	J. L. Hudgins	T. H. Padgett	106
1907, May 17	Dickson, TN	A. N. Eshman	J. L. Goodknight	140
1908, May 21	Corsicana, TX	F. H. Prendergast	J. L. Goodknight	136
1909, May 20	Bentonville, AR	J. T. Barbee	J. L. Goodknight	142
1910, May 19	Dickson, TN	J. H. Fussell	J. L. Goodknight	144
1911, May 18	Evansville, IN	J. W. Duvall	J. L. Goodknight	109
1912, May 16	Warrensburg, MO	J. D. Lewis	J. L. Goodknight	119
1913, May 15	Bowling Green, KY	J. H. Milholland	J. L. Goodknight	112
1914, May 21	Wagoner, OK	F. A. Brown	J. L. Goodknight	105
1915, May 20	Memphis, TN	William Clark	D. W. Fooks	116
1916, May 18	Birmingham, AL	J. L. Price	D. W. Fooks	125
1917, May 17	Lincoln, IL	F. A. Seagle	D. W. Fooks	102
1918, May 16	Dallas, TX	C. H. Walton	D. W. Fooks	117
1919, May 15	Fayetteville, AR	J. H. Zwingle	D. W. Fooks	101
1920, May 15	McKenzie, TN	J. E. Cortner	D. W. Fooks	123
1921, May 19	Greenfield, MO	Judge John B. Tally	D. W. Fooks	108
1922, May 18	Greeneville, TN	Hugh S. McCord	D. W. Fooks	102
1923, May 17	Fairfield, IL	P. F. Johnson, D. D.	D. W. Fooks	105
1924, May 15	Austin, TX	D. M. McAnulty	D. W. Fooks	93
1925, May 21	Nashville, TN	W. E. Morrow	D. W. Fooks	114
1926, May 20	Columbus, MS	I. K. Floyd	D. W. Fooks	111
1927, May 19	Lakeland, FL	T. A. DeVore	D. W. Fooks	97
1928, May 21	Jackson, TN	J. L. Hudgins	D. W. Fooks	97
1929, May 16	Princeton, KY	H. C. Walton	D. W. Fooks	98
1930, May 15	Olney, TX	O. A. Barbee	D. W. Fooks	92
1931, May 21	Evansville, IN	J. L. Elliot	D. W. Fooks	98
1932, May 19	Chattanooga, TN	G. G. Halliburton	D. W. Fooks	104
1933, June 14	Memphis, TN	W. B. Cunningham	D. W. Fooks	94
1934, June 14	Springfield, MO	A. C. DeForest	D. W. Fooks	103
1935, June 13	McKenzie, TN	C. A. Davis	D. W. Fooks	104
1936, June 18	San Antonio, TX	E. K. Reagin	D. W. Fooks	100
1937, June 16	Knoxville, TN	George E. Coleman	D. W. Fooks	109
1938, June 16	Russellville, AR	D. D. Dowell	D. W. Fooks	117
1939, June 15	Marshall, MO	E. R. Ramer	D. W. Fooks	126
1940, June 13	Cookeville, TN	Keith T. Postlethwaite	D. W. Fooks	116
1941, June 19	Denton, TX	L. L. Thomas	D. W. Fooks	120
1942, June 18	McKenzie, TN	George W. Burroughs	D. W. Fooks	108
1943, June 17	Paducah, KY	A. A. Collins	D. W. Fooks	94
1944, June 15	Bowling Green, KY	I. M. Vaughn	D. W. Fooks	94
1945, May 31	Lewisburg, TN	S. T. Byars	Wayne Wiman	103
1946, June 13	Birmingham, AL	C. R. Matlock	Wayne Wiman	105
1947, June 12	Knoxville, TN	Morris Pepper	Wayne Wiman	108

Date	Place	Moderator	Clerk	Members
1948, June 17	Nashville, TN	Paul F. Brown	Wayne Wiman	105
1949, June 16	Muskogee, OK	Blake Warren	Wayne Wiman	109
1950, June 15	Los Angeles, CA	L. P. Turnbow	Wayne Wiman	98
1951, June 14	Longview, TX	John E. Gardner	Wayne Wiman	105
1952, June 12	Memphis, TN	Emery A. Newman	Wayne Wiman	120
1953, June 18	Gadsden, AL	Charles L. Lehning, Jr.	Wayne Wiman	107
1954, June 17	Dyersburg, TN	John S. Smith	Wayne Wiman	124
1955, June 16	Lubbock, TX	Ernest C. Cross	Shaw Scates	118
1956, June 21	Cookeville, TN	Hubert Morrow	Shaw Scates	118
1957, June 21	Evansville, IN	William T. Ingram, Jr.	Shaw Scates	119
1958, June 18	Birmingham, AL	Wayne Wiman	Shaw Scates	116
1959, June 17	Springfield, MO	Virgil T. Weeks	Shaw Scates	120
1960, June 15	Nashville, TN	Arleigh G. Matlock	Shaw Scates	130
1961, June 21	Florence, AL	Ollie W. McClung	Shaw Scates	126
1962, June 20	Little Rock, AR	Eugene L. Warren	Shaw Scates	126
1963, June 19	Austin, TX	Franklin Chesnut	Shaw Scates	117
1964, June 17	Chattanooga, TN	Vaughn Fults	Shaw Scates	123
1965, June 16	San Francisco, CA	Thomas Forester	Shaw Scates	114
1966, June 15	Memphis, TN	John W. Sparks	Shaw Scates	124
1967, June 21	Paducah, KY	Raymon Burroughs	Shaw Scates	123
1968, June 19	Oklahoma City, OK	Loyce S. Estes	Shaw Scates	115
1969, June 18	San Antonio, TX	J. David Hester	Shaw Scates	116
1970, June 17	Knoxville, TN	L. C. Waddle	Shaw Scates	116
1971, June 16	Jackson, TN	E. Thach Shauf	Shaw Scates	116
1972, June 19	Kansas City, MO	Claude D. Gilbert	Shaw Scates	110
1973, June 18	Ft. Worth, TX	Thomas H. Campbell	Shaw Scates	101
1974, June 17	Bowling Green, KY	David A. Brown	Shaw Scates	116
1975, June 16	McKenzie, TN	Roy E. Blakeburn	Shaw Scates	120
1976, June 21	Tulsa, OK	Hubert W. Covington	T. V. Warnick	115
1977, June 30	Tampa, FL	Fred W. Bryson	T. V. Warnick	122
1978, June 19	McKenzie, TN	Jose Fajardo	T. V. Warnick	120
1979, June 18	Albuquerque, NM	James C. Gilbert	T. V. Warnick	126
1980, June 16	Evansville, IN	Robert L. Hull	T. V. Warnick	126
1981, June 15	Denton, TX	W. Jean Richardson	T. V. Warnick	126
1982, June 21	Owensboro, KY	W. A. Rawlins	T. V. Warnick	124
1983, June 20	Birmingham, AL	Robert G. Forester	T. V. Warnick	127
1984, June 11	Chattanooga, TN	C. Ray Dobbins	T. V. Warnick	125
1985, June 17	Lexington, KY	Virgil H. Todd	Roy E. Blakeburn	125
1986, June 23	Odessa, TX	James W. Knight	Roy E. Blakeburn	125
1987, June 15	Louisville, KY	Wilbur S. Wood	Roy E. Blakeburn	125
1988, June 6	Tulsa, OK	Beverly St. John	Robert Prosser	119
1989, June 12	Knoxville, TN	William Rustenhaven, Jr.	Robert Prosser	96
1990, June 25	Ft. Worth, TX	Thomas D. Campbell	Robert Prosser	88
1991, June 24	Paducah, KY	Floyd T. Hensley, Jr.	Robert Prosser	106
1992, June 22	Jackson, TN	John David Hall	Robert Prosser	102
1993, June 21	Little Rock, AR	Robert M. Shelton	Robert Prosser	100
1994, June 20	Albuquerque, NM	Donald C. Alexander	Robert Prosser	100
1995, June 19	Nashville, TN	Clinton O. Buck	Robert Prosser	102
1996, June 17	Huntsville, AL	Merlyn A. Alexander	Robert Prosser	95
1997, April 11	Nashville, TN	Merlyn A. Alexander	Robert Prosser	80
1997, June 16	Louisville, KY	W. Lewis Wynn	Robert Prosser	95
1998, June 15	Chattanooga, TN	Masaharu Asayama	Robert Prosser	97
1999, June 21	Memphis, TN	Gwendolyn Roddye	Marjorie Shannon	96
2000, June 19	Bowling Green, KY	Bob G. Roberts	Robert D. Rush	96
2001, June 18	Odessa, TX	Randolph Jacob	Robert D. Rush	88
2002, June 17	Paducah, KY	Bert L. Owen	Robert D. Rush	95
2003, June 23	Knoxville, TN	Charles McCaskey	Robert D. Rush	96
2004, June 21	Irving, TX	Edward G. Sims	Robert D. Rush	87
2005, June 27	Franklin, TN	Linda H. Glenn	Robert D. Rush	91
2006, June 18	Birmingham, AL	Donald Hubbard	Robert D. Rush	87
2007, June 18	Hot Springs, AR	Frank Ward	Robert D. Rush	84
2007, December 7	Nashville, TN	Frank Ward	Robert D. Rush	62
2008, June 7	Japan	Jonathan Clark	Robert D. Rush	82
2009, June 15	Memphis, TN	Sam Suddarth	Robert D. Rush	86
2010, June 13	Dickson, TN	Boyce Wallace	Robert D. Rush	88
2011, June 20	Springfield, MO	Don M. Tabor	Michael Sharpe	82
2012, June 18	Florence, AL	Robert D. Rush	Michael Sharpe	90
2013, June 17	Murfreesboro, TN	Forest Prosser	Michael Sharpe	93
2014, June 16	Chattanooga, TN	Lisa Anderson	Michael Sharpe	80
2015, June 20	Colombia, South America	Michele Gentry	Michael Sharpe	91
2016, June 20	Nashville, Tennessee	Dwayne Tyus	Michael Sharpe	84
2017, June 19	Palm Harbor, Florida	David Lancaster	Michael Sharpe	77
2018, June 17	Norman, Oklahoma	Jay Earheart-Brown	Michael Sharpe	86
2019, June 10	Huntsville, Alabama	Shelia O'Mara	Michael Sharpe	89

BYLAWS

Bylaws of the Cumberland Presbyterian Church General Assembly Corporation
A Non-profit Religious Corporation Organized and Existing
Under the Laws of the State of Tennessee

ARTICLE 1-RELIGIOUS CORPORATION

1.01 Purpose. The Cumberland Presbyterian Church is a spiritual body comprised of a portion of the universal body of believers confessing Jesus Christ as Lord and Savior. As an ecclesiastical body, the Cumberland Presbyterian Church is a connectional Church which includes all of the judicatories of the Church. The highest judicatory of this ecclesiastical body is the General Assembly of the Cumberland Presbyterian Church (referred to in these Bylaws as "the Church"). This corporation has been formed to serve and support the Church by holding real and personal property of the Church, employing staff to serve the Church, and performing other secular and legal functions.

1.02 Ecclesiastical Authority Not Limited by Corporate Powers. The enumeration in state statutes or these Bylaws of specific powers which may be exercised by the Commissioners, Board of Directors, or the officers of the corporation when acting in their corporate capacity shall not limit their authority when acting in their ecclesiastical capacity for the Church.

1.03 Church Authorities. The doctrine of the Cumberland Presbyterian Church, expressed in the Confession of Faith, Constitution, Rules of Discipline, and Rules of Order of the Cumberland Presbyterian Church, shall have precedence over any inconsistent provision of these Bylaws.

ARTICLE 2-TERMINOLOGY

2.01 Delegates. The corporation's delegates shall be called "Commissioners."
2.02 General Assembly. A meeting of the Commissioners shall be called a "General Assembly."
2.03 President. The corporation's president shall be called the "Stated Clerk."
2.04 Ecumenical Representative. A person who is not a member of a Cumberland Presbyterian Chuch or presbytery but who supports the mission of a denominational entity and is elected to a term of service on that entity shall be called an "Ecumenical Representative."

ARTICLE 3-OFFICES

3.01 Location. The principal office of the corporation in the State of Tennessee shall be located in Shelby County, Tennessee. The corporation may have such other offices, either within or outside the State of Tennessee, as the General Assembly or the Board of Directors may direct from time to time.

ARTICLE 4–COMMISSIONERS

4.01 Commissioners. The Commissioners shall have the powers and authority described in the corporation's charter and these Bylaws. Included among them are the power to:

   a. Elect the elected members of the Board of Directors.
   b. Approve any amendment to the corporation's charter except an amendment to delete the names of the original directors; to change the name of the registered agent, or to change the address of the registered office;
   c. Elect and remove the Moderator, Stated Clerk, and the Engrossing Clerk.
   d. Fill vacancies on the corporation's various boards, agencies and committees, and on the boards of any subsidiaries;
   e. Approve the merger or dissolution of the corporation, or the sale of substantially all of the corporation's assets; and
   f. Transact such other business of the corporation as may properly come before any meeting of the Commissioners.

4.02 Selection of Commissioners: Number and Qualifications. Commissioners shall be selected by the presbyteries. A presbytery shall be entitled to send one minister and one elder for each 1,000, or fraction thereof, active members (including ordained clergy) in the presbytery. Each elder selected as a Commissioner must be serving as a member of a session at the time of the General Assembly at which he or she will serve. A Commissioner shall continue to serve until no longer qualified or until his or her successor is selected and qualified. The clerk of each presbytery shall certify the presbytery's duly elected commissioners, youth advisory delegates, and alternates to the Stated Clerk in a manner provided by the Stated Clerk.

4.03 Youth Advisory Delegates. Each presbytery may select not more than two youth advisory delegates who should be from 15 through 19 years of age. Advisory delegates may serve as members with full rights on General Assembly committees, but shall not vote as Commissioners.

4.04 Annual Meeting and Notice. The Commissioners shall meet annually at a date and time established by the General Assembly. The meeting shall be continued from day to day until adjournment. Written notice of the meeting shall be mailed to the stated clerks of all presbyteries and published in the Cumberland Presbyterian at least sixty (60) days prior to the proposed meeting.

4.05 Special Meetings and Notice. The Moderator, or in case of the Moderator's absence, death, or inability to act, the Stated Clerk, may with the written concurrence or at the written request of twenty Commissioners, ten of whom shall be ministers and ten elders, representing at least five presbyteries, call a special meeting of the Commissioners. If warranted by a change of circumstances, a called special meeting may be cancelled by the Moderator, or in case of the Moderator's absence, death, or inability to act, the Stated Clerk, with the written concurrence of at least ten of the Commissioners who requested or concurred in the call of the special meeting. Written notice of any special meeting shall be mailed to the stated clerks of all presbyteries, to all Commissioners, and to their alternates at least sixty (60) days prior to the meeting. The notice shall specify the particular business of the special meeting, and no other business shall be transacted.

4.06 Place of Meeting. The General Assembly may designate any place within or outside the state of Tennessee as the place for an annual meeting. If the Commissioners fail to designate a place for an annual meeting, or if an emergency requires the place to be changed, the Board of Directors may designate a place for the annual meeting. The Moderator or the Stated Clerk, as the case may be, when calling a special meeting shall designate the time and place of the meeting in the notice of the meeting.

4.07 Quorum. Any twenty or more Commissioners, of whom at least ten are ministers and ten elders, entitled to vote shall constitute a quorum at any General Assembly. When a quorum is once present to organize a meeting, business may continue to be conducted and votes taken despite the subsequent withdrawal of any Commissioner. A meeting may be adjourned despite the absence of a quorum.

4.08 Voting. Every Commissioner shall be entitled to one vote, which must be cast by the Commissioner in person; no proxies are permitted. All corporate actions shall be taken by majority vote except as otherwise provided by the corporation's parliamentary authority. Voting for members of the Board of Directors shall be non-cumulative.

ARTICLE 5-BOARD OF DIRECTORS

5.01 Authority. The Board of Directors shall manage the business and affairs of the corporation except for any power or authority which is reserved to the Commissioners or delegated to any other agency of the corporation. The Board of Directors is authorized to amend the corporation's charter only to delete the names of the original directors; to change the name of the registered agent; or to change the address of the registered office.

5.02 Composition of the Board of Directors. The Board of Directors shall consist of seven (7) members, who shall be the directors of the corporation. Six (6) members shall be elected by the Commissioners and the Stated Clerk shall serve by virtue of office. All members, whether elected or ex officio, shall have all of the privileges of office.

5.03 Qualification for Election. Each person elected to the Board of Directors shall be a natural person who is a person in good standing of a presbytery or local Cumberland Presbyterian Church. No two directors shall be from the same presbytery, provided, however, that a director who moves from one presbytery to another may continue to serve until the expiration of his or her term of office.

5.04 Election and Tenure. The elected members of the Board of Directors shall serve terms of three (3) years each. The terms shall be staggered so that two (2) directors shall be elected each year. Each person elected shall serve until his or her successor has been elected and qualified.

5.05 Action of Board in Emergency or By Default. If, for any reason, the General Assembly fails to fill a vacancy on the Board of Directors at the next General Assembly, then the Board of Directors may fill the vacancy by majority vote of the members then in office.

5.06 Meetings. The Board of Directors shall meet annually or more often at such time and place as it may set. Special meetings may be called by or at the request of the Stated Clerk or any three directors at any place, either within or outside the state of Tennessee.

5.07 Notice. Notice of any meeting shall be given at least five (5) days before the date of the meeting, except that notice by mail shall be given at least ten (10) days before the date of the meeting. Notice may be communicated in person; by telephone, fax, or electronic mail; or by first class mail or courier. Except as specifically provided by these Bylaws, neither the business to be transacted at nor the purpose of any special or regular meeting of the Board of Directors need be specified in the notice of the meeting.

5.08 Notice of Special Actions. Any meeting of the Board of Directors at which one or more of the following actions shall be considered must be preceded by seven (7) days written notice to each member that the matter will be voted upon, unless notice has been waived. Actions requiring such notice are: amendment or restatement of the corporate charter; approval of a plan of merger for the corporation; sale of all or substantially all of the corporation's assets; and dissolution of the corporation.

5.09 Officers of the Board of Directors. The Board of Directors may have such officers of the board as it may deem appropriate.

5.10 Quorum and Voting. A majority of the members shall constitute a quorum for the transaction of business at any meeting of the Board of Directors. When a quorum is once present to organize a meeting, it is not broken by the subsequent withdrawal of any of those present. A meeting may be adjourned despite the lack of a quorum. The vote of a majority of the members present at a meeting at which a quorum is present shall be the act of the Board of Directors unless a greater vote is specifically required by the Charter or the Bylaws.

5.11 Conference Meetings. Any or all the members of the Board of Directors or any committee designated by it may meet by means of conference telephone or similar communications equipment which permits all persons participating in the meeting to hear each other simultaneously. A member who participates in a meeting by such means is deemed to be present in person at the meeting.

5.12 Action by Written Consent. Whenever the members of the Board of Directors are required or permitted to take any action by vote, such action may be taken without a meeting on written consent, setting forth the action so taken and signed by all of the members entitled to vote,

5.13 Emergency Actions. If the Board of Directors determines by a vote of three-fourths of all its members that an emergency exists of such magnitude as to threaten the work of the whole Church, or of all boards and other agencies of the Church, and that the emergency requires action before the next meeting of the General Assembly, then the Board of Directors shall exercise the powers of the Commissioners in such emergency.

5.14 Compensation. Members of the Board of Directors shall receive no compensation in their capacity as members of the Board of Directors. Members may be paid their expenses, if any, of attendance at each meeting of the Board of Directors.

5.15 Removal of Directors. An elected member of the Board of Directors may be removed by the Commissioners for misfeasance or if he or she is no longer qualified to be elected to the Board of Directors.

ARTICLE 6-WAIVER OF NOTICE

6.01 Written Waiver. Any notice required to be given to any member of the Board of Directors or a Commissioner under these Bylaws, the Charter, or the laws of Tennessee may be waived. The waiver shall be in writing, signed (either before or after the event requiring notice) by the person entitled to the notice, and delivered to the corporation.

6.02 Waiver by Attendance. The attendance of a member of the Board of Directors or a Commissioner at any meeting shall constitute a waiver of notice of the meeting, unless the person attends a meeting for the express purpose of objecting to the transaction of any business because the meeting was not properly called or convened.

ARTICLE 7-MODERATOR AND VICE-MODERATOR

7.01 Nomination and Election. At the beginning of each annual meeting the General Assembly shall elect a Commissioner to serve as Moderator until the next annual meeting. Nominations for Moderator shall come from the floor. One nominating speech, not to exceed ten minutes, shall be permitted on behalf of each nominee. If there is more than one nominee, the election shall be conducted by written ballot. A committee appointed and supervised by the Stated Clerk shall receive the ballots, count them, and certify the election. If no nominee receives a majority of the votes cast, a run-off election shall be conducted. Only those leading nominees who together received a majority of the votes cast on the preceding ballot shall be included in the run-off election.

7.02 Nature of Office. The Moderator of the General Assembly is the ecclesiastical head of the Cumberland Presbyterian Church during the tenure of the office and a spiritual representative of the Cumberland Presbyterian Church wherever God leads. The Moderator receives a precious gift and great opportunity for service in the Church: the freedom to go anywhere and to listen to the mind, heart and spirit of the denomination and to speak with and to the Church. The office of Moderator has great honor and respect, and the person elected to the Office is a priest, prophet, and pastor of the Church at large. The Moderator prays with and for the work of the Spirit of God in the life of the denomination at every opportunity. The Moderator participates in the life and work of the Church as far as possible, and pays particular attention to ecumenical relations, especially with the Cumberland Presbyterian Church in America. Judicatories, congregations, and others are urged to invite the Moderator, and the Moderator is encouraged to attend meetings of Church entities and judicatories to observe the life and work of the Church at every level.

7.03 Duties and Privileges of Office.
  a. The Moderator shall preside at all meetings of the General Assembly.
  b. The Moderator shall appoint, with the consent of the General Assembly, such special committees as are needed;
  c. The Moderator shall serve as chairperson of the General Assembly Program Committee and as a member of the Place of Meeting Committee;
  d. The Moderator shall perform such other duties as may be assigned by the General Assembly.
  e. The Moderator shall serve as an advisory member of the Ministry Council during tenure in office.
  f. The Moderator shall observe the places and times God is calling the Church to service, assess the need for a Denominational response to God's call, and report items that concern the General Assembly.
  g. The Moderator shall wear the official cross and stoles of office during the term of office.

7.04 Expenses of Office. Any allowance budgeted by the General Assembly to offset the expenses of the Moderator shall be administered by the Stated Clerk. Persons issuing an invitation to the Moderator are encouraged to agree in advance on arrangements for the payment of travel expenses. Upon the Moderator's retirement from office, a gavel and a replica of the Moderator's cross shall be presented to the Moderator.

7.05 Vice-Moderator. The General Assembly shall elect a Vice-Moderator in like manner. The Vice-Moderator shall perform such duties as may be assigned by the Moderator of the General Assembly and perform the duties of the Moderator in the event of the Moderator's disability or absence from office for any reason.

7.06 Removal. The Moderator or Vice-Moderator may be removed by the General Assembly whenever in its judgment the removal would serve the best interests of the corporation.

ARTICLE 8-STATED CLERK

8.01 President. The Stated Clerk is the principal executive officer of the corporation and shall also have the titles of "president" and "treasurer".

8.02 Nomination and Election. The Nominating Committee may nominate the serving Stated Clerk for re-election. If the Nominating Committee declines to nominate the serving Stated Clerk for re-election, or if the Stated Clerk has vacated the office, resigned, or declined to be re-nominated, then the Corporate Board shall conduct a search for and nominate a candidate to the General Assembly. In either event, further nominations may be made by the Commissioners. The Commissioners shall elect the Stated Clerk by majority vote.

8.03 Term of Office. The Stated Clerk shall be elected to a term of four (4) years. The regular term of office begins on January 1 and ends on December 31. There is no limit on the number of terms which may be served by an individual Stated Clerk.

8.04 Duties. The Stated Clerk shall be concerned with the spiritual life of the Church and with maintaining and strengthening a united witness for the Church. The Stated Clerk shall also generally supervise and control the business affairs of the corporation and see that all orders and resolutions of the General Assembly are carried into effect. In fulfillment of these duties, the Stated Clerk shall:
  01. Have responsibility to provide for the orderly governance of the Church in accordance with the Constitution, Rules of Order and Rules of Discipline.
  02. Maintain records of the corporation and respond to requests for official records of General Assembly actions and interpretations of its actions.
  03. Represent the Church when an official of the General Assembly is needed.
  04. Represent the Cumberland Presbyterian Church in establishing and maintaining relations with other Churches, particulary those of the Presbyterian and Reformed tradition, and in addressing common concerns.
  05. Sign all documents on behalf of the corporation or the Cumberland Presbyterian Church.
  06. Represent the corporation or the Church in litigation or other legal matters affecting the Cumberland Presbyterian Church, including the selection and employment of legal counsel.
  07. Make suitable arrangements for General Assembly meetings, including researching possible meeting sites, contracting for facilities, and arranging space for committee meetings and sessions of the General Assembly;
  08. Provide for printing and other communication needs of the General Assembly while in session.
  09. Call meetings of the Place of Meeting Committee and the Program Committee.

10. Prepare and distribute an information form to be completed by Commissioners for the Moderator's use in making committee appointments.
11. Advise the Moderator in the appointment of committees.
12. In consultation with the Moderator, refer all matters to come before the next General Assembly; and provide copies of all such referrals to the Commissioners and advisory delegates before the General Assembly convenes.
13. Prepare and distribute preliminary minutes and an agenda for General Assembly meetings which shall provide time for the consideration of any appropriate business, including memorials from a judicatory or denominational entity delivered to the Stated Clerk in writing by April 30.
14. Supervise the recording and publication of minutes and a summary of actions taken by each General Assembly.
15. Make copies of General Assembly minutes available to ordained ministers, licentiates, candidates, commissioners, clerks of sessions, members of denominational entities, schools of the Church, synod, and presbytery clerks, to the Stated Clerk's exchanges and other interested persons in order to encourage lower judicatories and persons in the Church to implement the actions of the General Assembly.
16. File the minutes of each General Assembly with the Historical Foundation as a permanent record.
17. Maintain and update annually the Digest of the General Assembly actions.
18. Represent the Church at large on the Ministry Council.
19. Provide support services for the Moderator and all denominational entities.
20. Receive and make any appropriate response to communications to the Cumberland Presbyterian Church or General Assembly.
21. Maintain a name and address file on congregations, session clerks, pastors, and other leadership of congregations with statistical information about congregations, presbyteries, and synods.
22. Solicit, receive, publish, and disseminate annual reports from churches.
23. Review reports by denominational entities and assist them in complying with correct reporting and budgeting procedures and in avoiding duplication of work.
24. Hold, report annually, and distribute as authorized by the General Assembly or the Ministry Council the Contingency Fund and all other General Assembly Funds not entrusted to the care of a denominational entity.
25. Call the Judiciary Committee into session or by other means secure the advice of the committee on appropriate matters.
26. Communicate with presbyteries and synods on behalf of the General Assembly and attend their meetings from time to time.
27. Provide training for presbytery and synod clerks and orientations for General Assembly commissioners.
28. Generally perform duties as are prescribed in the Constitution or directed by the General Assembly.

8.05 Removal. The Stated Clerk may be removed by the General Assembly whenever in its judgment the removal would serve the best interests of the corporation.

ARTICLE 9-OTHER OFFICERS

9.01 Secretary. The chief executive officer of the Ministry Council shall, by virtue of office, be the secretary of the corporation, and shall in general perform all duties incident to the office of secretary.

9.02 Engrossing Clerk. The Engrossing Clerk shall be elected by the General Assembly to a term of four (4) years. The regular term of office begins on January 1 and ends on December 31. There is no limit on the number of terms which may be served by an individual Engrossing Clerk. The Engrossing Clerk shall serve as Stated Clerk pro tempore during the meeting of the General Assembly in the event the Stated Clerk is absent or unable to serve. The Engrossing Clerk shall perform such other duties as may from time to time be prescribed by the Board of Directors or the General Assembly.

9.03 Additional Officers. The corporation may have such additional officers as it may from time to time find necessary or appropriate.

ARTICLE 10-ORGANIZATION AND RELATIONSHIPS

10.01 Generally. The following are denominational entities related to the Cumberland Presbyterian Church:

01. Subsidiary corporations: Board of Stewardship, Foundation and Benefits of the

Cumberland Presbyterian Church; Memphis Theological Seminary of the Cumberland Presbyterian Church; Ministry Council of the Cumberland Presbyterian Church.
02. Related corporations: Bethel University; Cumberland Presbyterian Children's Home; Historical Foundation of the Cumberland Presbyterian Church and the Cumberland Presbyterian Church in America.
03. Commissions: Chaplains and Military Personnel.
04. Committees: Committee on Nominations; Joint Committee on Amendments; Judiciary, Our United Outreach; Place of Meeting Committee; Program Committee; Unified Committee on Theology and Social Concerns.

10.02 Election and Tenure. The following qualifications and rules relate to service on any denominational entity.
01. Unless elected as an Ecumenical Representative, no person shall be qualified to serve except a member in good standing in a presbytery or local congregation of the Cumberland Presbyterian Church.
02. No person who is employed in an executive capacity including Chief Executive, Vice-President, Team Leader, Director, or equivalent in the Cumberland Presbyterian Church is eligible to serve on a denominational entity. No employee of a denominational entity is eligible for service on the same denominational entity.
03. Each person shall be elected for a term of three years unless elected to fill the remainder of an unexpired term. However, if a person elected to serve on a denominational entity where residence in a particular synod is a qualification for election shall move to another synod while in office, the term to which he or she was elected shall terminate at the close of the next meeting of the General Assembly. When nominating persons to boards and agencies, priority consideration be given to persons whose individual life and/or church involvement demonstrates a commitment to support Our United Outreach.
04. Members of the Committee on Nominations may not be elected to a consecutive term. All other persons may serve up to three consecutive terms for a total not to exceed nine years in office.
05. A Cumberland Presbyterian who has served on any entity is not eligible to serve on the same entity (except for an authorized consecutive term) until at least two (2) years have elapsed since the conclusion of the previous service.
06. A Cumberland Presbyterian who is serving on any entity is not eligible to serve on another entity until at least one (1) year has elapsed since the conclusion of the previous service.
07. An Ecumenical Representative who is serving or has served on any entity is not eligible to serve on any other entity (except for an authorized consecutive term on the same entity) until at least one (1) year has elapsed since the conclusion of the previous service.

10.03 Resignation or Removal.
01. Any person serving on a denominational entity who is no longer qualified or eligible to serve shall be deemed to have resigned.
02. Any person serving on an incorporated denominational entity may resign by delivering written notice of resignation to the secretary or an executive officer of the denominational entity, who shall promptly report the resignation to the Stated Clerk. Any person serving on an unincorporated denominational entity may resign by delivering written notice of resignation to the Stated Clerk. A resignation is effective when delivered unless some other effective date is specified in the written resignation.
03. No member who continues to meet the standard requirements for election or appointment to any denominational entity shall be removed from office except for misfeasance. Removal of a person elected by the General Assembly shall be by vote of the General Assembly.

10.04 Board of Stewardship, Foundation and Benefits. The corporation shall elect the eleven (11) directors of the Board of Stewardship as provided in its charter.

10.05 Historical Foundation. The corporation shall elect six (6) of the twelve (12) directors of the Historical Foundation as provided in its charter. The corporation shall elect the directors of the Historical Foundation in such a manner that, immediately following any election, there shall be at least one (1) member from each synod and no person shall be elected if the election would cause two directors from the same presbytery to be serving simultaneously. The remaining six (6) directors shall be elected by the Cumberland Presbyterian Church in America.

10.06 Memphis Theological Seminary. The corporation shall elect the twenty-four (24) directors of Memphis Theological Seminary as provided in its charter. The corporation shall elect the directors in such a manner that, immediately following any election, there shall be eleven (11) directors who are members of denominations other than the Cumberland Presbyterian Church.

10.07 Ministry Council.
- 01. The corporation shall elect the fifteen (15) directors of the Ministry Council as provided in its charter.
- 02. The corporation shall elect the directors of the Ministry Council in such a manner that immediately following any election, there shall be three (3) directors from each synod; at least six (6) but no more than nine (9) directors who are ordained clergy; and no more than nine (9) directors of the same gender.
- 03. The Stated Clerk and Moderator shall be designated as Advisory Members to the board of directors of the Ministry Council. In addition, the corporation shall elect three (3) Youth Advisory Members who shall be between the ages of 15 - 17 be elected for 1-year terms, with eligibility for re-election for one additional term.

10.08 Commission on Chaplains and Military Personnel. The commission shall consist of three (3) members elected by the corporation.

ARTICLE 11-COMMITTEES

11.01 General. The corporation shall have the committees provided for in these Bylaws and such other standing or special committees as the General Assembly may create from time to time. Except as otherwise provided in these Bylaws, the Moderator, in consultation with the Stated Clerk, shall appoint all committees.

11.02 Committees of Commissioners and Youth Advisory Delegates. Prior to each General Assembly, the Moderator, in consultation with the Stated Clerk, shall organize the Commissioners and Youth Advisory Delegates into the following committees: Chaplains/Missions/Pastoral Development, Children's Home/Historical Foundation, Higher Education, Judiciary, Ministry Council/Communications/Discipleship, Stewardship/Elected Officers, and Theology and Social Concerns. Each committee shall consider such matters expected to come before the General Assembly as are referred to it by the Stated Clerk. Any denominational organization, the work of which is affected by a matter before a committee, shall be entitled to address the committee.

11.03 Committee on Nominations.
- 01. The committee shall consist of ten (10) persons elected by the corporation in such a manner that, immediately following any election, the committee shall have at least one minister and one lay person from each synod. It is preferred but not required that no two members shall be from the same presbytery.
- 02. Approximately one third of the members of the committee shall be elected each year by the General Assembly and shall serve one term not to exceed three years.
- 03. The committee shall meet not earlier than February 15 each year and shall nominate to the General Assembly qualified persons to fill all vacancies to be filled by vote of the General Assembly, including vacancies on the Committee on Nominations, unless another method of nomination is provided in these Bylaws. The report of the committee shall list the names of nominees, the presbytery if a minister, and the presbytery and the local congregation if a lay person. The Committee on Nominations shall be intentional in nominating persons who represent the global nature of the Church.
- 04. Presbyteries and synods and their moderators and stated clerks are requested to assist the Committee on Nominations by recommending persons for any position by providing the name and qualifications of the potential nominees to the Stated Clerk no later than February 1 on a form to be provided by the Stated Clerk. Nominations from the floor shall also be in order.
- 05. No person shall be nominated for election by the General Assembly unless the nominee has within the past year given his or her consent to the nomination.

11.04 Joint Committee on Amendments. The Judiciary Committee shall appoint as many as five of its members to act in committee with an equal number of members of the Judiciary Committee of the Cumberland Presbyterian Church in America. Upon the request of the General Assembly of the Cumberland Presbyterian Church or the General Assembly of the Cumberland Presbyterian Church in America, this Joint Committee shall prepare for the consideration of both general assemblies proposed amendments to the Confession of Faith, Catechism, Constitution, Rules of Discipline, Directory for Worship, and Rules of Order.

11.05 Judiciary Committee.
- 01. The committee shall consist of nine (9) persons elected by the corporation in such a manner that, immediately following any election, the committee shall have at least four members (4) who are ordained ministers and at least three (3) members who are licensed attorneys-at-law. The Stated Clerk shall be staff liaison to the committee,

attending its meetings and providing resources and counsel.
02. The committee shall meet at least annually upon the call of its chairperson or the Stated Clerk.
03. The committee shall provide advice and counsel to the Stated Clerk. Upon the written request of any judicatory or denominational entity made to the chairperson or Stated Clerk, the committee shall render an advisory opinion on matters of church law or procedure. The chairperson shall secure the views of all members of the committee and write the advisory opinion based on the majority view of the members. The committee shall not render legal opinions on matters of civil law nor otherwise engage in the practice of law.
04. At least one member of the committee shall attend each meeting of the General Assembly to advise with its officers and Commissioners on matters of church law or procedure. At the Moderator's request a member of the committee shall be available to advise the Moderator during the business sessions of the General Assembly.
05. The committee shall be a commission within the meaning of section 2.5 of the Rules of Discipline to hear and determine appeals from synods.
06. The committee shall have oversight of and responsibility for ecclesiastical decisions made by a body acting in the place of a presbytery with respect to mission work and mission fields. The oversight and responsibility exercised by the committee shall be the same as that exercised by a synod with respect to a presbytery under its care, specifically Constitution 8.5, a, b, and c

11.06 Our United Outreach Committee.
01. The committee shall consist of five (5) persons elected by the corporation in such a manner that, immediately following any election, the committee shall have one person from each synod. Seven (7) additional members will include a member of the Ministry Council, a member of the Corporate Board, a member of the Board of Stewardship, Foundation and Benefits, a member of the Board of Trustees of the Historical Foundation, and a Cumberland Presbyterian member of the Boards of Trustees of Bethel University, the Cumberland Presbyterian Children's Home, and Memphis Theological Seminary. The executives of the above named denominational entities shall serve as non-voting, Resource/Advocacy members. In addition, the corporation shall elect three (3) Youth Advisory members who shall be between the ages of 15-17 and be elected for one (1) year terms, with eligibility for re-election for one additional term.
02. The Office of the General Assembly will be responsible for the expenses of the representative of each synod. The represented denominational entities will be responsible for the expenses of their representatives and executives.

11.07 Place of Meeting. The committee shall consist of the Moderator, the Stated Clerk and a representative of the Cumberland Presbyterian Women's Ministries.

11.08 Program Committee. The committee shall consist of the Moderator, Stated Clerk, Director of Ministries, Assistant to the Stated Clerk who serves as secretary, the pastor of the host church, four elected representatives designated by the Ministry Council from among its ministry teams, and one representative designated by each of the following: Bethel University, Board of Stewardship, Foundation, and Benefits, Cumberland Presbyterian Children's Home, Historical Foundation, Memphis Theological Seminary, and the Cumberland Presbyterian Women's Ministry. The committee will begin planning for two years prior to the meeting of a particular General Assembly.

11.09 Unified Committee on Theology and Social Concerns. The committee shall consist of eight (8) members elected by the corporation, the Stated Clerk, and the President of Memphis Theological Seminary. At least one member of the committee other than the Seminary's president shall be a Cumberland Presbyterian member of the faculty of Memphis Theological Seminary.

ARTICLE 12-INDEMNIFICATION

12.01 Indemnification. The corporation shall indemnify any director, officer or employee who is, or is threatened to be, made a party to a completed, pending, or threatened action or proceeding from any liability arising from the director's, officer's or employee's official capacity with the corporation. This indemnification shall extend to the personal representation of a deceased person if the person would be entitled to indemnification under these Bylaws if living.

12.02 Costs and Expenses Covered by Indemnification. Indemnification provided under these Bylaws shall extend to the payment of a judgment, settlement, penalty, or fine, as well as attorney's fees, court costs, and other reasonable and necessary expenses incurred by the director or officer with respect to the action or proceeding.

12.03 Limitation on Indemnification. No indemnification shall be made to or on behalf of any

person if a judgment or other final adjudication adverse to that person establishes his or her liability:
- 01. for any breach of the duty of loyalty to the corporation;
- 02. for acts or omissions not in good faith or which involve intentional misconduct or a knowing violation of law; or
- 03. for any distribution of the assets of the corporation which is unlawful under Tennessee law.

ARTICLE 13-TRUSTEE FOR THE CORPORATION

13.01 Trustee. The Board of Stewardship, Foundation and Benefits of the Cumberland Presbyterian Church, a nonprofit corporation existing under the laws of the state of Tennessee, holds certain real property and other assets of the Church as trustee for the use and benefit of the Church. The Board of Stewardship may continue to hold such real property and other assets, but after the adoption of these Bylaws, it shall hold those assets as trustee for the use and benefit of the Cumberland Presbyterian Church General Assembly Corporation.

13.02 Other Assets. Other, additional property may from time to time be conveyed to the Board of Stewardship to be held by it as trustee for the corporation. All assets held by the Board of Stewardship as trustee for the corporation shall be held at the pleasure and direction of the General Assembly.

ARTICLE 14-PARLIAMENTARY AUTHORITY

14.01 Designation. The parliamentary authority of the corporation in all meetings shall be the latest revised edition of the Rules of Order as set out in the Confession of Faith and Government of the Cumberland Presbyterian Church. In matters not provided for in the Rules of Order, the parliamentary authority shall be Robert's Rules of Order, latest revised edition.

14.02 Standing Rules. The following shall be Standing Rules for meetings of the General Assembly and may be suspended as provided in the parlimentary authority. (see Rules of Order 8.34c)

Standing Rules

1. Unless otherwise determined by the General Assembly or by the Stated Clerk in the event of an emergency, the annual General Assembly shall meet on the third or fourth Monday of June at two o'clock in the afternoon to organize, elect a moderator and transact business, and shall close on Thursday or Friday of the same week.

2. Reports of all standing and special committees shall be considered in the order established by the Moderator in consultation with the Stated Clerk. Committee reports may be presented orally or in writing provided to all Commissioners and youth advisory delegates. Those presenting committee reports shall have the opportunity to make remarks and give explanation, such presentations not to exceed ten minutes unless time is extended by two-thirds vote taken without debate. All committee recommendations shall be submitted in writing.

3. All materials from denominational entities for consideration or action by a General Assembly shall be submitted to the Stated Clerk at least thirty (30) days before the meeting of General Assembly.

4. Resolutions and memorials proposed for adoption by individual commissioners rather than denominational entities or judicatories of the Cumberland Presbyterian Church shall be introduced no later than the close of business on the second day of a meeting of General Assembly, and, when introduced, shall be referred by the Moderator, in counsel with the Stated Clerk, to the appropriate committee or committees for report and recommendations to the Assembly.

ARTICLE 15-REPORTS AND AUDITS

15.01 Congregational Reports. Annually by December 1, the Stated Clerk shall send to session clerks statistical forms for reporting congregational data. Session clerks shall mail the completed forms to presbytery clerks by February 1. The presbytery clerk shall mail the composite statistical report for all congregations of a presbytery to the Stated Clerk by February 10.

15.02 Institutional Reports. In order to be considered for inclusion in the General Assembly budget, all denominational entities shall deliver to the Stated Clerk an annual report including a concise description of the organization's work during the previous year and a line item budget for the forthcoming year. Financial reports should be condensed as much as possible while conveying all essential information on the organization's operations. All denominational entities except academic institutions on a fiscal year are requested to maintain their books on a calendar year.

15.03 Reporting Schedule. An electronic copy and two written copies of the annual report signed by two officers of the organization shall be delivered to the Stated Clerk by March 15 each year. Organizations requesting funds from Our United Outreach shall submit multi-year program budgets to the Our United Outreach Committee.

15.04 Audits. Organizations and operations included in the General Assembly budget shall be audited annually by a certified public accountant. Copies of the auditor's report, including any recommendations for changes in the procedures relating to internal financial controls, shall be delivered to the Stated Clerk. Organizations with total receipts of $100,000 or less are not required to have an audit but shall submit their books and financial statements to the Stated Clerk annually.

15.05 Bonds. Each organization or person whose financial records are required to be audited shall have a fidelity bond in an amount adequate to protect all funds held by the organization or person.

ARTICLE 16-AMENDMENTS

16.01 Manner of Amendment. Except as provided below, these Bylaws may be amended or repealed only by the affirmative vote of two-thirds of the votes cast in a duly constituted meeting of the General Assembly. No portion of the Bylaws may be amended or repealed by the Board of Directors. Fair and reasonable notice of any proposed amendment shall be provided as required by state law.

16.02 Extraordinary Actions. In order to be effective the following actions must be approved by (1) the affirmative vote of two consecutive General Assemblies, or (2) a ninety percent (90%) vote of a single General Assembly.

    01. Terminating the existence of a denominational entity named in Bylaw 10.01
    02. Creating a new denominational entity other than a temporary committee or task force.
    03. Decreasing the Our United Outreach budget allocation to a denominational entity by more than 40% of the amount distributed to it during the previous calendar year; or
    04. Taking any other actions which would cause a drastic change in the mission or structure of the Cumberland Presbyterian Church.

MEMORIAL ROLL OF MINISTERS

IN MEMORY OF
MINISTERS LOST BY DEATH

NAME	PRESBYTERY	AGE	DATE
Ballow, Brent	Covenant	61	08/23/18
Bennett, Alfred J	Nashville	90	10/06/18
Blackburn, Samuel	Arkansas	84	10/19/18
Brooks, Wayne E	East Tennessee	72	03/10/19
Bynum, Ronald	Robert Donnell	87	04/28/18
Campbell, Coyle	Murfreesboro	79	11/10/18
Coleman, Don	West Tennessee	81	04/30/18
Cook, Carl	Arkansas	77	01/02/19
Dewhirst, Tim	Red River	71	04/14/18
Diamond, James	Murfreesboro	77	08/20/18
Ferree, Carol	Cumberland	69	01/11/19
Johnson, Beverly	East Tennessee	91	08/30/18
Keown, Gale	East Tennessee	92	11/20/18
Korb, Leon	North Central	93	05/02/19
Lambert, James	Robert Donnell	95	03/21/17
Lively, Louella	Covenant	93	09/30/18
McClanahan, Walter	West Tennessee	78	04/27/19
Montoya, David	Andes	63	01/20/19
Moore, Hillman C	Covenant	84	03/13/18
Moore, James R Sr	Grace	91	11/03/18
Mosley, Karen	West Tennessee	60	04/14/18
Norman, Maury	Nashville	97	01/10/19
Parish, Johnny	Nashville	59	01/26/18
Parsons, Hugh	Trinity	83	04/18/18
Perkins, William	Cumberland	85	01/08/18
Pope, Charles (Buddy)	Columbia	73	12/17/18
Ranson, Doris	Cumberland	86	05/12/18
Richardson, W Jean	East Tennessee	88	01/02/19
Rustenhaven, William (Bill) Jr	Trinity	88	02/01/19
Schott, Fred	Nashville	86	01/01/19
Shelton, Robert M	Red River	84	03/04/18
Sweet, Don	East Tennessee	91	02/03/19

LIVING GENERAL ASSEMBLY MODERATORS

2018—REV. JAY EARHEART-BROWN, 475 N Highland Street, Apt 9L, Memphis, TN 38122
2017—REV. DAVID LANCASTER, 426 Fuqua Road, Martin, TN 38237
2016—REV. DWAYNE TYUS, 426 Old Hickory Boulevard, Madison, TN 37115
2015—REV. MICHELE GENTRY, Urb San Jorge casa 28, Km 8 via a La Tebaida Armenia, Quindio, COLOMBIA, SA
2014—REV. LISA HALL ANDERSON, 1790 Faxon Avenue, Memphis, TN 38112
2013—REV. FOREST PROSSER, 1157 Mountain Creek Road, Chattanooga, TN 37405
2012—REV. ROBERT D. RUSH, 12935 Quail Park Drive, Cypress, TX 77429
2011—REV. DON M. TABOR, 9611 Mitchell Place, Brentwood, TN 37027
2009—ELDER SAM SUDDARTH, 206 Ha Le Koa Court, Smyrna, TN 37167
2007—REV. FRANK WARD, 8207 Traditional Place, Cordova, TN 38016
2006—REV. DONALD HUBBARD, 2128 Campbell Station Road, Knoxville, TN 37932
2005—REV. LINDA H. GLENN, 49 Mason Road, Threeway, TN 38343
2004—REV. EDWARD G. SIMS, 2161 N. Meadows Drive, Clarksville, TN 37043
2003—REV. CHARLES MCCASKEY, 679 Canter Lane, Cookeville, TN 38501
1999—ELDER GWENDOLYN G. RODDYE, 3728 Wittenham Drive, Knoxville, TN 37921
1998—REV. MASAHARU ASAYAMA, 3-15-9 Higashi, Kunitachi-shi, Tokyo, JAPAN
1996—REV. MERLYN A. ALEXANDER, 80 N. Hampton Lane, Jackson, TN 38305
1995—REV. CLINTON O. BUCK, PO Box 770068, Memphis, TN 38117
1992—REV. JOHN DAVID HALL, 109 Oddo Lane SE, Huntsville, AL 35802
1990—REV. THOMAS D. CAMPBELL, PO Box 315, Calico Rock, AR 72519

IN MEMORY OF:

Moderator of the 151st General Assembly
REV. W. JEAN RICHARDSON
Died January 2, 2019

Moderator of the 159th General Assembly
REV. WILLIAM RUSTENHAVEN, JR.
Died February 1, 2019

GENERAL ASSEMBLY OFFICERS

MODERATOR
THE REVEREND SHELIA O'MARA
PO Box 170
Gadsden, TN 38337
189thcpcgamoderator@gmail.com
(443)699-2321

VICE MODERATOR
THE REVEREND MICHAEL CLARK
2353 Blue Springs Road
Decherd, TN 37324
michael.clark@winchestercp.org
(931)967-2121

STATED CLERK AND TREASURER
THE REVEREND MICHAEL SHARPE
8207 Traditional Place
Cordova, TN 38016
(901)276-4572
FAX (901)272-3913
msharpe@cumberland.org

ENGROSSING CLERK
THE REVEREND VERNON SANSOM
7810 Shiloh Road
Midlothian, TX 76065
(972)825-6887
vernon@sansom.us

THE BOARD OF DIRECTORS OF THE GENERAL ASSEMBLY CORPORATION

(Members whose terms expire in 2020)
(2)REV. JOHN BUTLER, 501 Cherokee Drive, Campbellsville, KY 42718
    rev.butlerj8134@gmail.com
(2)MS. BETTY JACOB, PO Box 158, Broken Bow, OK 74728
    chocpres@pine-net.com

(Members whose terms expire in 2021)
(2)MS. CALOTTA EDSELL, 7044 Woodsong Cove, Germantown, TN 38138
    cedsell@hotmail.com
(2)REV. NORLAN SCRUDDER, 29688 S 534 Road, Park Hill, OK 74451
    ndscrudder@gmail.com

(Members whose terms expire in 2022)
(3)REV. BOBBY COLEMAN, 107 E Henson, Springdale, AR 72764
    bobby.coleman@gmail.com
(1)REV. RICKEY PAGE, 736 Rodney Drive, Nashville, TN 37205
    rickey.page@wncp.org

*Ecumenical Partners   +Cumberland Presbyterian Church in America

MINISTRY COUNCIL

(Members whose terms expire in 2020)
(3)REV. DONNY ACTON, 1413 Oakridge Drive, Birmingham, AL 35242
(1)REV. MICHAEL CLARK, 2353 Blue Springs Road, Dechard, TN 37324
(1)MR. DAVID CORREA, Calle 76 #87-14, Medellin, COLOMBIA, SOUTH AMERICA
(1)MS. SAMANTHA HASSELL, 510 N Main Street, Sturgis, KY 42459
(1)MS. CHARELLE WEBB, 3507 Pickering Lane, Pearland, TX 77584
(Members whose terms expire in 2021)
(3)MR. KENNETH BEAN, 1035 Stonewall Street N, McKenzie, TN 38201
(2)REV. KENNY BUTCHER, 403 Kalye Court, Mt Juliet, TN 37122
(2)REV. PHILLIP LAYNE, 10699 Griffith Highway, Whitwell, TN 37397
(2)MS. VICTORY MOORE, 17388 Chandlerville Road, Virginia, IL 62691
(1)MS. MELINDA REAMS, 10 W Azalea Lane, Russellville, AR 72802
(Members whose terms expire in 2022)
(2)MS. CARLA BELLIS, 19264 Law 2170, Aurora, MO 65605
(1)MS. DEBBIE HAYES, 69 Cactus Drive, Benton, KY 42025
(1)MR. TED SHIRAI, 25 Minami Kibogaoka, Asahi-ku, Yokohama, Kanagawa, JAPAN
(1)REV. TIM SMITH, 214 Jeffery Drive, Fayetteville, TN 37334
(2)REV. MIKE WILKINSON, 1504 Clear Brook Drive, Knoxville, TN 37922

YOUTH ADVISORY MEMBERS
(2)MS. SYDNEY HOLDER, 6589 County Road 747, Cullman, AL 35055
(2)MS. MADISON HOLLAND, 565 County Road 17, Scottsboro, AL 35768
(1)MS. LACEY YOUNG, 1211 Michael Drive, Alabaster, AL 35007

ADVISORY MEMBERS
REV. SHELIA O'MARA, PO Box 170, Gadsden, TN 38337
REV. MICHAEL SHARPE, 8207 Traditional Place, Cordova, TN 38016

COMMUNICATIONS MINISTRY TEAM

(Members whose terms expire in 2020)
(1)MS. FREDERICKA SILVEY-JOHNS, PO Box 234, Calico Rock, AR 72519
(3)MS. DUSTY LUTHY, 2026 Washington Street, Paducah, KY 42003
(Members whose terms expire in 2021)
(1)REV. NATHANIEL MATHEWS, 5240 114th Street Apt 1002, Lubbock, TX 79424
(Members whose terms expire in 2022)
(1)MS. JOYCE MCCULLOUGH, 238 Mortons Lake Road, Manchester, TN 37355
(1)REV. NEAL WILKINSON, 296 Sunset Drive, Lebanon, MO 65536

*Ecumenical Partners   +Cumberland Presbyterian Church in America

DISCIPLESHIP MINISTRY TEAM

(Members whose terms expire in 2020)
(3)MS. LE ILA DIXON, 4406 John Reagan Street, Marshall, TX 75672
(3)REV. DREW GRAY, 12304 Wickliffe Road, Kevil, KY 42053
(1)REV. BILLY PRICE, 12510 Buttermilk Road, Knoxville, TN 37932
(Members whose terms expire in 2021)
(3)MS. CANDY BARR, 3291 McLean Drive, Rogersville, AL 35652
(3)MS. RACHEL COOK, 210 Bynum Street, Scottsboro, AL 35768
(1)MR. EAN TAYLOR, 437 Peach Creek Crescent, Nashville, TN 37214
(Members whose terms expire in 2022)
(1)REV. JONATHAN BELLIS, 17246 Highway K, Aurora, MO 65605
(1)REV. ABBY PREVOST, 9111 County Road 747, Cullman, AL 35055
(2)REV. JESSE THORNTON, 2518 IL Highway 15, Fairfield, IL 62837

MISSIONS MINISTRY TEAM

(Members whose terms expire in 2021)
(1)MR. OLLIE MCCLUNG, 2912 Riverwood Lane, Birmingham, AL 35243
(1)MS. MARGIE SHANNON, 2307 Littlemore Drive, Cordova, TN 38016
(Members whose terms expire in 2022)
(3)REV. BRITTANY MEEKS, 710 N Avalon Street, Memphis, TN 38107
(1)MS. KAREN PATTEN, 5728 North Street, Bartlett, TN 38134
(1)MR. DEAN REICHENBACH, 615 Seaton Drive, Smithville, TN 37166
(3)REV. CHRIS WARREN, 906 Prince Lane, Murfreesboro, TN 37129

PASTORAL DEVELOPMENT MINISTRY TEAM

(Members whose terms expire in 2020)
(3)REV. AMBER CLARK, 2353 Blue Springs Road, Decherd, TN 37324
(Members whose terms expire in 2021)
(1)REV. LISA ANDERSON, 1790 Faxon Avenue, Memphis, TN 38112
(1)REV. PAUL FARHEART-BROWN, 510 City House Court, Apt 406, Memphis, TN 38103
(Members whose terms expire in 2022)
(3)REV. DUAWN MEARNS, 311 Chickasaw Drive, Ada, OK 74820
(3)REV. SANDRA SHEPHERD, 1432 Wexford Downs Lane, Nashville, TN 37211

GENERAL ASSEMBLY BOARD OF:

I. TRUSTEES OF BETHEL UNIVERSITY

(Members whose terms expire in 2019)
(2)MR. JEFF AMREIN, 11711 Paramont Way, Prospect, KY 40059
(3)*JUDGE BEN CANTRELL, 1485A Woodmont Boulevard, Nashville, TN 37215
(1)*MR. SCOTT CONGER, 143 Fawn Ridge Drive, Jackson, TN 38305
(3)+DR. ARMY DANIEL, 3125 Searcy Drive, Huntsville, AL 35810
(2)MR. BILL DOBBINS 5716 Quest Ridge Road, Franklin, TN 37064
(3)DR. ROBERT LOW, c/o New Prime, Inc., 2740 W Mayfair Avenue, Springfield, MO 65803
(1)*DR. BROCK MARTIN, 419 Browning Avenue, Huntingdon, TN 38344

(Members whose terms expire in 2020)
(1)DR. NANCY BEAN, PO Box 205, McKenzie, TN 38201
(3)*MS. LISA COLE, PO Box 198615, Nashville, TN 37219
(3)MR. CHESTER (CHET) DICKSON, 24 W Rivercrest Drive, Houston, TX 77042
(2)REV. NANCY MCSPADDEN, 2143 Grider Field Road, Pine Bluff, AR 71601
(3)DR. ED PERKINS, 721 Paris Street, McKenzie, TN 38201
(2)MR. KENNETH (KEN) D. QUINTON, 2912 Waller Omer Road, Sturgis, KY 42459
(1)MR. TOMMY SURBER, 825 Hico Road, McKenzie, TN 38201
(2)REV. ROBERT (BOB) WATKINS, 5405 Kacena Avenue, Marion, IA 52302

(Members whose terms expire in 2021)
(1)*MR. CLINTON FOX, 1820 South Boulevard, Houston, TX 77098
(3)+REV. ELTON C. HALL, SR., 305 Tiffton Circle, Hewitt, TX 76643
(1)MS. LINDA C. INGRAM, 203 Ballard Lane, Sparta, TN 38583
(3)MS. DEWANNA LATIMER, 193 Moses Drive, Jackson, TN 38305
(2)*DR. E. RAY MORRIS, PO Box 924628, Norcross, GA 30010
(2)MR. STEVE PERRYMAN, 535 Ranch Road, Rogersville, MO 65742
(1)REV. ROBERT TRUITT, 1238 Old Eastside Road, Burns, TN 37029

II. TRUSTEES OF CUMBERLAND PRESBYTERIAN CHILDREN'S HOME

(Members whose terms expire in 2019)
(1)MRS. CAROLYN HARMON, 4435 Newport Highway, Greeneville, TN 37743
(3)*MS. PATRICIA LONG, 525 E Oak Street, Aledo, TX 76008
(1)REV. JOYCE MERRITT, 3929 Snail Shell Cove, Rockvale, TN 37153
(1)MR JAY THOMAS, 3301 Cooperbranch E, Denton, TX 76209
(1)*MR. CAMERON MARONE, 6085 Water Street, Plano, TX 75024

(Members whose terms expire in 2020)
(1)MR. PETE CARTER, 306 Jackson Hills Drive, Maryville, TN 37804
(2)*MR. CHARLES W. HARRIS, 3293 Birch Avenue, Grapevine, TX 76051
(2)*MR. KNIGHT MILLER, 509 Brixham Park Drive, Franklin, TN 37069
(1)+REV. PERRYN RICE, 8525 Audelia Road, Dallas, TX 75238

(Members whose terms expire in 2021)
(3)MR. RICHARD DEAN, 2140 Cove Circle North, Gadsden, AL 35903
(1)BRIAN MARTIN, 614 CR 4608, Troup, TX 75789
(1)MRS. GUIN TYUS, 903 W Hickory Boulevard, Madison, TN 37115

(Members whose terms expire in 2021)
(1)*MR. BRIAN CARWRIGHT, 3218 Northwood Drive, Highland Village, TX 75077
(1)MR. SAM SUDDARTH, 206 Ha Le Koa Court, Smyrna, TN 37167
(1)*MR. MATTHEW WHITTEN, 3909 Fawn Drive, Denton, TX 76208

*Ecumenical Partners   +Cumberland Presbyterian Church in America

III. TRUSTEES OF HISTORICAL FOUNDATION

(Members whose terms expire in 2020)
(1)+MS. JACKIE COOPER, 4705 Indan Summer Drive, Nashville, TN 37207
(3)MR. MICHAEL FARE, 401 E Deanna Lane, Nixa, MO 65714
(3)+MS. DOROTHY M. HAYDEN, 3103 Carolina Avenue, Bessemer, AL 35020
(1)+REV. JOE HOWARD, III, 2903 Al Lipscomb Way, Dallas, TX 75215
(2)+MS. PAT WARD, 2620 Rabbit Lane, Madison, AL 35756

(Members whose terms expire in 2021)
(2)REV. LISA OLIVER, 110 Allen Drive, Hendersonville, TN 37075
(1)MS. KELLY SHANTON, 3932 W Beaver Creek Drive, Powell, TN 37849

(Members whose terms expire in 2022)
(2)MS. ROBIN MCCASKEY HUGHES, 1205 Olde Bridge Road, Edmond, OK 73034
(2)MS. ASHLEY LINDSEY, 403 College Street, Smiths Grove, KY 42171
(1)MS. MARTHA JO MIMS, 3011 Wolfe Road, Columbus, MS 39705
(2)+WILLIE LYNK, 932 Valley Square Road, Morganfield, KY 42437

IV. TRUSTEES OF MEMPHIS THEOLOGICAL SEMINARY OF THE CUMBERLAND PRESBYTERIAN CHURCH

(Members whose terms expire in 2020)
(2)REV. ANNE HAMES, 118 Paris Street, McKenzie, TN 38201
(1)+MS. VANESSA K. MIDGETT, 118 Thunderbird Drive, Huntsville, AL 35749
(1)REV. JASON MIKEL, 410 Ramblewood Lane, Nolensville, TN 37135
(1)*REV. JIMMY MOSBY, PO Box 45843, Little Rock, AR 72214
(1)REV. WES JOHNSON, 3151 Stillhouse Creek Drive SE, Atlanta, GA 30339
(1)*MR. REGINALD PORTER, JR., 4458 Whitepine Cove, Memphis, TN 38109
(1)*MS. ANNA ROBBINS, 2714 Lombard Avenue, Memphis, TN 38111
(1)REV. KIP RUSH, 516 Franklin Road, Brentwood, TN 37027

(Members whose terms expire in 2021)
(1)REV. DANIEL BARKLEY, 2732 Rexford Street, Hokes Bluff, AL 35903
(1)REV. RON FELL, PO Box 285, Fairfield, IL 62837
(1)REV. GLORIA VILLA DIAZ, 2425 Holly Hall Street B42, Houston, TX 77054
(1)REV. YOONG KIM, 225 Bayswater Drive, Suwanee, GA 30024
(1)REV. RIAN PUCKETT, 55 Ham Street, Batesville, AR 72501
(3)MS. SONDRA RODDY, 628 Mannington Place, Lexington, KY 40503
(3)*REV. MELVIN CHARLES SMITH, 1263 Haynes Street, Memphis, TN 38114
(3)*MS. LATISHA TOWNS, Regional One-The Med, 877 Jefferson Avenue, Memphis, TN 38103

(Members whose terms expire in 2022)
(1)MR. GREG ALLEN, 1138 Balbade Drive, Nashville, TN 37215
(1)REV. JILL CARR, PO Box 1547, Lebanon, MO 65536
(2)*MS. JANE ASHLEY FOLK, 4123 Chanwil Place, Memphis, TN 38117
(2)*REV. LARRY HILLIARD, 102 Johnson Street, Waveland, MS 39576
(1)MS. CHERYL LESLIE, 3374 Walnut Grove Road, Memphis, TN 38111
(1)*MS. LISANNE MARSHALL, 325 Meadow Grove Lane, Memphis, TN 38120
(1)*REV. KEITH NORMAN, 2835 Broad Avenue, Memphis, TN 38112
(2)*REV. DEBORAH SMITH, 584 E McLemore Avenue, Memphis, TN 38106

*Ecumenical Partners   +Cumberland Presbyterian Church in America

V. STEWARDSHIP, FOUNDATION AND BENEFITS

(Members whose terms expire in 2020)
(2)MR. RANDY DAVIDSON, PO Box 880, Ada, OK 74821
(1)REV. MARK HESTER, 763 Finn Long Road, Friendsville, TN 37737
(1)REV. GARY TUBB, 103 Forest Drive, Mountain Home, AR 72653
(1)REV. DWAYNE TYUS, 426 W Old Hickory Boulevard, Madison, TN 37115

(Members whose terms expire in 2021)
(1)MS. DEBBIE SHANKS, 3997 N 100th Street, Casey, IL 62420
(2)MR. JAMES SHANNON, 2307 Littlemore Drive, Cordova, TN 38016
(3)MR. MICHAEL ST. JOHN, 324 Carriage Place, Lebanon, MO 65536

(Members whose terms expire in 2022)
(2)REV. KEN BYFORD, 23746 Highway 9 N, Piedmont, AL 36272
(1)MRS. MARY JO RAY, 16 Nottingham Lane, Columbus, MS 39705
(2)MS. ANDREA SMITH, 1715 Water Cure Road, Winchester, TN 37398
(1)MR. OWEN SMITH, 119 Pine Island Drive, Marshall, TX 75672

GENERAL ASSEMBLY COMMISSIONS:

I. MILITARY CHAPLAINS AND PERSONNEL

(1) Term Expires in 2020–REV. CHARLES MCCASKEY, 679 Canter Lane, Cookeville, TN 38501
(2) Term Expires in 2021–REV. TONY JANNER, 104 Northwood Drive, McKenzie TN 38201
(1) Term Expires in 2022–REV. SHELIA O'MARA, PO Box 170, Gadsden, TN 38337

These three persons and the Stated Clerk represent the denomination as members of the Presbyterian Council for Chaplains and Military Personnel, 4125 Nebraska Avenue NW, Washington, DC 20016

GENERAL ASSEMBLY COMMITTEES

I. JUDICIARY

(Members whose terms expire in 2020)
(1)MS. PAMELA BROWN, 6400 North Grove Avenue, Warr Acres, OK 73012
    pambrownlaw@cox.net
(2)REV. HARRY CHAPMAN, 4908 El Picador Court SE, Rio Rancho, NM 87124
    wrightrev2gmail.com
(1)REV. GEOFFREY KNIGHT, 2119 Avalon Place, Houston, TX 77019
    geoff@cphouston.org

(Members whose terms expire in 2021)
(3)REV. ANNETTA CAMP, 2303 Mill Creek Road, Halls, TN 38040
    anetta@cumberlandchurch.com
(1)REV. JIM RATLIFF, 13 Hernando Drive, Cherokee Village, AR 72529
    kudzu8161@yahoo.com
(2)MR. BILL TALLY, 907 Tipperary Drive, Scottsboro, AL 35768
    wtally@scottsboro.org

*Ecumenical Partners   +Cumberland Presbyterian Church in America

(Members whose terms expire in 2022)
(2)MS. RACHEL MOSES, 1138 Blaine Avenue, Cookeville, TN 38501
coachrach@aol.com
(2)REV. JAN OVERTON, 3320 Pipe Line Road, Birmingham, AL 35243
jan@crestlinechurch.org
(1)REV. ROGER REID, 637 Colburn Drive, Lewisburg, TN 37091
drrtr@yahoo.com

II. JOINT COMMITTEE ON AMENDMENTS

The committee consists of five members of the Judiciary Committee of the Cumberland Presbyterian Church in America and the Cumberland Presbyterian Church.

III. NOMINATING

(Members whose terms expire in 2020)
(1)REV. BRIAN HAYES, 69 Cactus Drive, Benton, KY 42025
cprevbhayes@gmail.com
(1)MR. LEE HOLDER, 6589 County Road 747, Cullman, AL 35055
holder4bama@yahoo.com
(1)REV. TOM SPENCE, PO Box 802, Burns Flat, OK 73624
tomspence0302@gmail.com
(1)MS. JENANN LESLIE, 300 Henley Perry Drive, Marshall, TX 75670
jenann.leslie@gmail.com
(Members whose terms expire in 2021)
(1)MR. ETHAN MORGAN, 119 Mountain Top Lane, Cookeville, TN 38506
remorgan8@gmail.com
(1)REV. RANDY SHANNON, 30282 Highway H, Marshall, MO 65340
pastor_randy_shannon@yahoo.com
(Members whose terms expire in 2022)
(1)MS. ALLISON CARR, PO Box 1547 Lebanon, MO 65536
(1)MS. DIANN PHELPS, 4743 Happy Hollow Road, Hawesville, KY 42348
(1)REV. MICAIAH TANCK, 902 Tipperary Drive, Scottsboro, AL 35768
(1)REV. BRENT WILLS, 4607 E Richmond Shop, Lebanon, TN 37090

IV. OUR UNITED OUTREACH COMMITTEE

(Members whose terms expire in 2020)
(1)MS. MARY ANN COLE, 1726 Karen Circle, Bowling Green, KY 42104
(1)MR. MIKEL DAVIS, 102 Willow Wood Lane, Ovilla, TX 75154
(Members whose terms expire in 2021)
(1)MS. GWEN RODDYE, 3728 Wittenham Drive, Knoxville, TN 37921
(3)MS. ROBIN WILLS, 4607 E Richmond Shop Road, Lebanon, TN 37090
(Members whose terms expire in 2022)
(2)REV. BRUCE HAMILTON, 1037 Binns Drive, Monticello, AR 71655

YOUTH ADVISORY MEMBERS:
(1)MS. SIERRA ALEXANDER, 1014 Wren Street, Dyersburg, TN 38024
(1)MS. KAILEY SUNDSTROM, 309 Bryson Lane, Clarksville, TN 37043
(1)MR. NATE WOOD, 17246 Highway K, Aurora, MO 65605

V. PLACE OF MEETING

THE STATED CLERK OF THE GENERAL ASSEMBLY
THE MODERATOR OF THE GENERAL ASSEMBLY
A REPRESENTATIVE OF WOMEN'S MINISTRIES OF THE MISSIONS MINISTRY TEAM

VI. UNIFIED COMMITTEE ON THEOLOGY AND SOCIAL CONCERNS

(Members whose terms expire in 2020)
(1)+MS. SHARON COMBS, PO Box 122, Sturgis, KY 42459
    (270)860-4175
(1)+REV. EDMUND COX, 249 Mimosa Circle, Maryville, TN 37801
    edmundcox765@gmail.com
(2)+REV. NANCY FUQUA, 1963 County Road 406, Towncreek, AL 35672
    fuq23@bellsouth.net; (256)566-1226
(1)REV. RICHARD MORGAN, 1468 Williams Cove Road, Winchester, TN 37398
    icthuse3@gmail.com
(1)REV. LISA SCOTT, (address on file in GA office)
    lascott1979@att.net
(1)+REV. RICK WHITE, 124 Town West, Lorena, TX 76655
    rickwaco3@aol.com

(Members whose terms expire in 2021)
(1)REV. MITCH BOULTON, 80 Topsy Lane, Savannah, TN 38372
    steelermitch@gmail.com
(1)+REV. BOBBY HAWKINS, 220 S. Foxwell Street, Providence, KY 42450
    hawk49@bellsouth.net
(1)REV. MICHAEL QUALLS, 5355 June Cove, Horn Lake, MS 38637
    mqualls1@yahoo.com
(1)+MR. JAMES REYNOLDS, 128 Heritage Lane, Madison, ALabama 35758
    jwreyns@aol.com
(1)MS. MELISSA WILSON, 107 Hillwood Drive, Dickson, TN 37055
    milzwilz@yahoo.com

(Members whose terms expire in 2022)
(1)REV. VIRGINIA ESPINOZA, PO Box 132, Boswell, OK 74727
(1)REV. TERRA SISCO, 811 W Cheyenne Street, Marlow, OK 73055
(1)REV. JO WARREN, 811 Wall Street, Morrilton, AR 72110

President of Memphis Theological Seminary - Ex-officio Member

OTHER DENOMINATIONAL PERSONNEL
REPRESENTATIVES TO:

Caribbean and North American Area Council, World Communion of Reformed Churches:
STATED CLERK MICHAEL SHARPE, 8207 Traditional Place, Cordova, TN 38016

(Member whose terms expire in 2020)
(1)MS. SHERRY POTEET, PO box 313, Gilmer, TX 75644
    spoteet1@aol.com

*Ecumenical Partners   +Cumberland Presbyterian Church in America

THE REPORT OF THE MODERATOR

I. TRIBUTE TO FORMER VICE MODERATOR BUDDY POPE

I am deeply grateful for the opportunity given me to serve as Moderator of the 188th General Assembly of the Cumberland Presbyterian Church. I was honored to serve with Vice Moderator, Reverend Buddy Pope, of Columbia Presbytery. During the fall, Buddy attended several presbytery meetings in my place. We talked regularly to make sure that we were on the same page in representing the General Assembly to the larger church, and in listening to the needs and will of the church. I was deeply saddened to hear of Buddy's death, after an acute illness, late in 2018. I was able to attend the visitation and give my personal condolences to his wife and children, and to express appreciation for his service to his church. His family expressed to me how grateful Buddy was for the privilege of serving as Vice Moderator of the 188th General Assembly. Though he is not here to say so, I know that he would want me to let you know how humbled and thankful he was for the opportunity to serve in this office.

RECOMMENDATION 1: That the 189th General Assembly formally express its appreciation for the life, ministry, and service of Reverend Buddy Pope as Vice Moderator of the 188th General Assembly, and that the clerk be instructed to send notice of our appreciation to Buddy's family at his earliest convenience.

II. CONNECTIONALISM

I am deeply grateful for the gracious welcome I received in attending many Presbytery meetings, the meeting of the Ministry Council in August, and the Board of Stewardship in March. It is always encouraging to worship with Cumberland Presbyterians and to see the work of our church in its varied manifestations.

In my travels, I have sought to encourage our connectionalism as a church, a goal I expressed when I was nominated for office last spring. It is gratifying to see that connectionalism in action. On the other hand, it is always disappointing when we see some churches and ministers who do not take advantage of the strengths that such connections afford us all. In my own presbytery, I was shocked to learn that almost 40% of the churches failed to make a single contribution to our presbyterial budget in 2018. That is a sign of disaffection that we must all be working to overcome.

III. PROPOSED CONSTITUTIONAL AMENDMENT

In observing the work of the church, I have come to believe that our Constitution's description of advisory members is inadequate for several reasons. The current language, in section 3.0, Judicatories of the Church, reads as follows:

"3.07 Other ministers [who are not members of the body] who are present in a meeting of presbytery or synod may or may not be seated by action of the body as advisory members, which if granted gives them the privilege to speak to any matter before the body. Persons so seated shall be introduced to the presbytery or the synod by the moderator."

This is the only statement on the use of advisory members in the Constitution. In addition to this statement, the practice of presbyteries electing youth advisory delegates to the meeting of General Assembly is also spelled out in the Bylaws of the General Assembly Corporation, section 4.03. While the paragraph from the Constitution does a fairly reasonable job of describing long-standing practice in our denomination when it comes to middle judicatories, I don't think it is adequate for several reasons.

1. There is no recognition that visiting elders should be afforded the same courtesy as ministers. One of the geniuses of Presbyterian polity is its parity of ministry between ordained ministers and elders. There is no reason, in the courts of the church, to distinguish between them. When an elder, serving as a denominational official, attends presbytery or synod meetings to speak on behalf of the wider church, that person should be afforded the same respect and recognition as any visiting ordained minister.

2. The practice of youth advisory delegates, so beneficial to the work of the General Assembly for many years, should be encouraged at all levels of church judicatories, including local church sessions.

3. There is nothing in the Constitution that addresses the status of assistant and associate pastors with the session of the church they serve. Some Presbyterian denominations grant assistant pastors advisory status in the session, and associate pastors full voting membership on the session. In discussions, the actual practice is often that assistant and associate pastors are granted advisory membership on the session, but there is no provision that explicitly grants them that right.

4. In one presbytery I visited during the year, the stated clerk, who is an elder, is usually granted permission to speak as necessary at the beginning of each presbytery meeting, since the clerk is usually not a member of the body. At other presbytery meetings I have witnessed elders and lay persons who are making reports on behalf of the presbytery's boards and/or standing committees who have to request permission to speak. This should not be necessary for anyone representing one of the presbytery's standing boards or committees.

For all of the reasons outlined above, I would like to propose the following constitutional amendment to this meeting of General Assembly, to replace the current section 3.07 quoted above.

"3.07 Every judicatory of the church has the prerogative to seat persons as advisory members, with full privilege of speaking to any issue before the judicatory, but no vote. The following persons shall be granted advisory membership in the stated judicatory:

a. Presbytery approved and installed assistant and associate pastors will be advisory members of the session they serve.

b. Elected officers of any judicatory (stated clerk, engrossing clerk, treasurer, etc.) and official representatives from any standing committee or board of the judicatory will be advisory members of that judicatory, if they are not members of the body, without the need to request permission to speak.

The following persons may be approved as advisory members of a judicatory, but are not required to be seated as such. Persons so seated shall be introduced to the judicatory by the moderator:

a. In middle judicatories, visiting ordained Cumberland Presbyterian ministers from other presbyteries/synods.

b. In middle judicatories, visiting elders from other presbyteries/synods.

c. In any judicatory, youth advisory delegates elected to serve.

d. Representatives from higher judicatories.

e. Officers from the Cumberland Presbyterian Women's Ministry or other auxiliaries.

f. Attorneys employed by the judicatory.

g. Visiting ministers or leaders from other denominations with whom the judicatory is in partnership.

No judicatory should feel obligated to seat advisory members, but should grant this privilege in a way that serves the mission and ministry of the church. Persons who are not regular or advisory members of any judicatory may be granted permission to speak to the judicatory on majority vote or consent of the judicatory."

RECOMMENDATION 2: That the General Assembly approve the proposed amendment to substitute a new section 3.07 for the existing 3.07 in the Constitution of the CPC/CPCA, and that the proposed amendment be forwarded to the Joint Committee on Amendments for their review and counsel.

IV. GRATITUDE

I am grateful for the assistance of stated clerk Michael G. Sharpe, engrossing clerk Vernon Sansom, and assistant to the clerk Elizabeth Vaughn for their help in carrying out my duties at the 188th General Assembly, and over the past year. Their counsel and friendship was vital to any success I may have had.

I had the honor of serving my church through teaching and leading our seminary, Memphis Theological Seminary, for 21 years. In that time, I was blessed by relationships with colleagues and students and trustees and friends of the seminary who have enriched my life beyond measure. I continue to pray for the work of Memphis Theological Seminary, and for those who are now in position to lead our seminary into the future. If it hadn't been for my work and travels on behalf of Memphis Theological Seminary, I may never have had the opportunity to be elected moderator.

I owe a great debt of gratitude to the church I have been serving as pastor since September 1 of 2018. The elders and members of Faith Cumberland Presbyterian Church in Bartlett, Tennessee, have welcomed me into their community with open arms and provided me the encouragement and love I have needed over the past several months. They have been gracious to allow me time to serve in this role as moderator, and I look forward to serving alongside them, and building God's kingdom in our community, for many years to come.

Our two sons, Paul and Carter, are a daily inspiration to Mary and me. They are talented, caring, compassionate young men of faith who bring joy into our lives daily. Mary, my wife of almost 34 years, my companion and soul-mate, has been my rock for a long time, but no more so than over the past year. I am grateful beyond words for the freedom and encouragement she gives me to grow and develop and become all that God would have me be.

I pray that others may have their lives blessed as richly as mine has been throughout my life as a child, member, and minister of the Cumberland Presbyterian Church.

Respectfully submitted,
Jay Earheart-Brown
Moderator of the 188th General Assembly

THE REPORT OF THE STATED CLERK

I. THE OFFICE OF THE STATED CLERK

The Constitution, the Rules of Discipline, the Rules of Order, and the General Assembly Bylaws (found in the front of the General Assembly Minutes) list the many responsibilities for the person who holds the position of Stated Clerk, the primary task is to maintain and strengthen a united witness for the Church. The Stated Clerk shall also generally supervise and control the business affairs of the Corporation, and see that all directives of the General Assembly are implemented.

The Office of the General Assembly also provides budgeting, accounting, and support services for commissions, committees, agencies and task forces without executive assistance.

Additional services and activities provided through the office of the Stated Clerk this past year include:
- Providing assistance to the Unification Task Force and the Evaluation Committee.
- Developing and maintaining a web presence for the following General Assembly Committees/Commissions without staff: Nominating Committee, Unified Committee on Theology and Social Concerns, Commission on Military Chaplains and Personnel, Our United Outreach Committee and the Unification Task Force.
- Creation of spring and fall Denominational News Updates, a compilation of talking points obtained from each board and agency that may be shared by visiting denominational staff and the moderator when making visits to presbyteries and in other settings. The updates are also shared with presbytery clerks.
- Development of a Travel Chart, to assist with the coordination of travel plans by denominational staff to meetings of presbyteries. The travel chart is also shared with presbytery clerks.
- Hosted the annual conference for Presbytery and Synod Clerks.

A significant portion of the Stated Clerk's time has been spent responding to various judicial and legal questions affecting local churches and presbyteries. The Clerk is appreciative for advice provided to this office from both the Permanent Judiciary Committee and from Mr. Jamie Jordan who serves as legal counsel for the Office of the General Assembly.

The Stated Clerk is grateful to the Church for calling him to serve in this position and appreciates the support of the Church for the Office and for the person who holds this position.

II. STAFF

Ms. Elizabeth Vaughn serves as the Assistant to the Stated Clerk, a position that requires her to maintain accurate records of ministers, probationers, congregations, record income and expenses and to authorize payment of all items in the Office of the General Assembly budget. The Church is fortunate to have a person with such knowledge, efficiency and dedication to work. The Stated Clerk and the Assistant to the Stated Clerk are currently the only employees of the Office of the General Assembly.

Reverend Vernon Sansom continues to serves as Engrossing Clerk and is to be commended for the accuracy in recording the minutes of the General Assembly. Vernon also leads the orientation session for those who serve as chairperson and co-chairperson for each General Assembly appointed Committee and provides valuable assistance in the preparation of committee reports at each meeting of the General Assembly.

III. ECUMENICAL RELATIONSHIPS

The Cumberland Presbyterian Church has historically been involved in ecumenical relationships. Through co-operative ministries, chaplains for the military and veteran's hospitals are endorsed, migrant workers and persons in Appalachia are served, and missionaries are sent into a variety of countries. Through ecumenical partnerships disaster relief funds are distributed. Through working co-operatively church school and camping materials are developed. The Cumberland Presbyterian witness is more effective through participation with other Christians in these and various other ministries.

A. CUMBERLAND PRESBYTERIAN CHURCH IN AMERICA

The Cumberland Presbyterian Church in America and the Cumberland Presbyterian Church have one heritage, one Confession of Faith and share in several co-operative relationships and ministries such as the Historical Foundation, the United Board of Christian Discipleship, youth ministry, and the Unified Committee on Theology and Social Concerns. The Cumberland Presbyterian Church in America and the Cumberland Presbyterian Church also participate with other Reformed bodies in ministry. Although working through partnerships, the witness of the Cumberland Presbyterian Church in America and the Cumberland Presbyterian Church would be greatly enhanced through a union of the two denominations.

B. WORLD COMMUNION OF REFORMED CHURCHES

Both the Cumberland Presbyterian Church and the Cumberland Presbyterian Church in a America are members of World Communion of Reformed Churches (WCRC). The WCRC was formed in 2010 by a merger of the World Alliance of Reformed Churches and the Reformed Ecumenical Council. The WCRC represents approximately eighty million members of two hundred thirty denominations from one hundred seven countries, including Reformed, Congregationalists, Presbyterian and United Churches. Resources and updates from the World Communion of Reformed Churches are available on their website: (www.wcrc.ch).

Reverend Christopher Ferguson serves as general secretary of the WCRC and offices in Hanover, Germany where the headquarters for WCRC is located.

IV. THE CORPORATE BOARD

In the called meeting in December 2007, the General Assembly elected a new board of directors for the General Assembly Incorporation, thus the Corporate Board was formed. The responsibilities for the Corporate Board are listed in the General Assembly Bylaws, Article 5.

The Corporate Board met as needed by conference call this past year, actions included: appointment of the GA Evaluation Committee as directed by the 188th General Assembly.

The Center Interagency Team (CIT) comprised of the Center's Principle Executive Officers, continues to be responsible for oversight of the day-to-day maintenance and property needs at the Denominational Center. Current CIT members include: Mike Sharpe (Office of the General Assembly), Robert Heflin (Board of Stewardship, Foundation and Benefits), Susan Gore (Historical Foundation), and Edith Old (Ministry Council). The Shared Services budget covers the cost for maintaining the Center offices and property (see page 122).

V. COMMUNICATIONS

The Office of the General Assembly received memorials from the following Presbyteries: del Cristo, Missouri and Nashville (see pages 126-128 of the Preliminary Minutes) and have been referred to the appropriate General Assembly select committees for consideration.

A Petition from Arkansas Presbytery was received (see page 138), but because the petition presents the same question as one which remains within the control of the assembly (a referral from the 188th General Assembly re: Human Sexuality), the General Assembly Permanent Committee on Judiciary advised the clerk that it would not be in order for the Arkansas Petition to be considered by the General Assembly in its 2019 meeting (see page 99 of the Preliminary Minutes).

VI. ENDORSEMENTS FOR MODERATOR

The Reverend Shelia O'Mara, Presbytery del Cristo and the Reverend Michael Clark, Murfreesboro Presbytery have been endorsed as Moderator of the 189th General Assembly.

VII. MINUTES OF THE GENERAL ASSEMBLY

The Office of the General Assembly continues to make the minutes of the General Assembly available on a CD, and mailing them to persons requesting them. The resource center also prints and sells a few printed copies of the General Assembly Minutes each year. For information contact Matthew Gore, mhg@cumberland.org. It is permissible to download and print a copy of the minutes from the website (www.cumberland.org/gao).

VIII. STATISTICAL INFORMATION

The annual congregational report forms are sent to the session clerk on December 1, and due in the office of the Stated Clerk of the Presbytery on February 1, and all reports are to be in the Office of the General Assembly by February 10.

In 2018 a two hundred and two congregations failed to report, thus statistics are not accurate. The statistics for a non-reporting congregation may be several years old, but it is the latest information available. The General Assembly Office continues to shorten and simplify the reporting process. Efforts also continue to further simplify online reporting for those able to utilize the technology. Hard copies of the report forms will still be made available for those congregations who do not have access to the internet.

The 178th and 179th General Assembly directed "that each presbytery request that its Board of Missions or similar agency, as they minister to the needs of the churches within their presbyteries, remind the churches that it is important that they submit annual reports which are part of our history and offer assistance when needed in preparation of these reports." If a congregation fails to receive a report, a duplicate form can be requested from the Office of the General Assembly or one may be printed from the web site (www.cumberland.org/gao), and going to the section on congregational reports.

Compiled statistical information is available in the annual Yearbook available online (www.cumberland.org/gao) or in print format, available through Cumberland Resource Distribution – resources@cumberland.org (901-276-4581)

IX. CHURCH CALENDAR 2019-2020

The 182nd General Assembly, directed the Office of the General Assembly to be responsible for reporting the "Church Calendar" to the General Assembly for adoption. Listed below are the dates received from the Boards and Agencies of the denomination.

RECOMMENDATION 1: That the 189th General Assembly approve the following dates for the 2019-2020 Church Calendar:

CHURCH CALENDAR 2019-2020

July-2019
6	Children's Fest/Middle Schooler's Event, McKenzie, Tennessee
7	Outdoor Ministries Sunday
13	Program of Alternate Studies Graduation
13-27	PAS Summer Extension School, Bethel, McKenzie, Tennessee
16-20	Presbyterian Youth Triennium

August-2019
4	Bethel University Commencement
4-Sept 30	Christian Education Season
7-10	Youth Worker Retreat
18	MTS Fall Semester Begins *(tentative)*
18	Seminary/PAS Sunday
22	Bethel University Fall Semester Begins
25	MTS Fall Semester Begins *(tentative)*
28	MTS Opening convocation *(tentative)*
30	Bethel University Spring Convocation

September-2019
4	MTS Opening convocation *(tentative)*
8	Family Sunday
8	Senior Adult Sunday
12-15	Young Adult Ministry Council
15	Christian Service Recognition Sunday
15	International Day of Prayer and Action for Human Habitat
22	Seminary Sunday

October-2019
	Church Paper Month
	Clergy Appreciation Month

	Domestic Violence Awareness Month
6	Worldwide Communion Sunday
13	Pastor Appreciation Sunday
15	A Day at the Park
20	Native American Sunday

November-2019

	Any Sunday Loaves and Fishes Program
1	All Saints Day
3	World Community Sunday (Church Women United)
3	Bethel University Sunday
3	Stewardship Sunday
7-9	Symposium
10	Day of Prayer for People with Aids and Other Life-Threatening Illnesses
17	Bible Sunday
24	Christ the King Sunday

December-2019

	Any Sunday Gift to the King Offering
2	PAS Advisory Council
2-24	Advent in Church and Home
8	Bethel University Commencement
24	Christmas Eve
25	Christmas Day

January-2020

6	Epiphany
6	MTS Classes Begin
6-7	Stated Clerks' Conference
11	Human Trafficking Awareness Day
13	BU Spring Semester Begins
15	Deadline for receipt of 2019 Our United Outreach Contributions

February-2020

	Black History Month
1	Annual congregational reports due in General Assembly office
2	Denomination Day
2	Historical Foundation Offering
2	Souper Bowl Sunday
9	Our United Outreach Sunday
16	Youth Sunday
26	Ash Wednesday, the beginning of Lent
26–April 11	Lent to Easter

March-2020

	Women's History Month (USA)
6	World Day of Prayer (CWU)
15	Children's Home Sunday
23-29	National Farm Workers Awareness Week

April-2020

5	Palm/Passion Sunday
9	Maundy Thursday
10	Good Friday
12	Easter
19	Earth Day

May-2020

1	Friendship Day (Church Women United)
7	National Day of Prayer
9	Bethel University Commencement
16	MTS Closing Convocation & Graduation
24	Memorial Day Offering for Military Chaplains & Personnel for USA churches
31	Pentecost

31	World Missions Sunday
31	Stott-Wallace Missionary Offering

June-2020

7-12	General Assembly
8-12	CPWM Convention
14	Cumberland Presbyterian Church Ministries Sunday
21	Unification Sunday
28-July 3	Cumberland Presbyterian Youth Conference, Bethel University, McKenzie, Tennessee

July-2020

5	Outdoor Ministries Sunday
9-12	Americas Youth Gathering 2020
11	Children's Fest/Middle Schooler's Event, Cookeville, Tennessee
11	Program of Alternate Studies Graduation
11-25	PAS Summer Extension School, Bethel, McKenzie, Tennessee
18	Children's Fest/Middle Schooler's Event, Cookeville, Tennessee

August-2020

1	Bethel University Commencement
2-Sept 30	Christian Education Season
5-10	Asian Youth Gathering 2020
16	Seminary/PAS Sunday
17	Bethel University Fall Semester Begins
25	Bethel University Convocation
26	MTS Fall Semester Begins *(tentative)*
27	MTS Opening convocation *(tentative)*

September-2020

13	Family Sunday
13	Senior Adult Sunday
20	Christian Service Recognition Sunday
20	International Day of Prayer and Action for Human Habitat

October-2020

	Church Paper Month
	Clergy Appreciation Month
	Domestic Violence Awareness Month
4	Worldwide Communion Sunday
11	Pastor Appreciation Sunday
18	Native American Sunday
20	A Day at the Park

November-2020

	Any Sunday Loaves and Fishes Program
1	All Saints Day
1	Bethel University Sunday
1	Stewardship Sunday
6	World Community Day (Church Women United)
15	Day of Prayer for People with Aids and Other Life-Threatening Illnesses
15	Bible Sunday
22	Christ the King Sunday
29- Dec 24	Advent in Church and Home

December-2020

	Any Sunday Gift to the King Offering
7	PAS Advisory Council
13	Bethel University Commencement
24	Christmas Eve
25	Christmas Day

X. CONTINGENCY FUND

The Stated Clerk is to hold, distribute and report annually the General Assembly Contingency Fund (see Bylaws 8.04, #24). Below is a summary Contingency Fund Activity for the 2018 Calendar Year.

Summary of 2018 Activity

Balance Forward 1/1/2018 $ 50,825.69

Income in 2018:
    Our United Outreach/Contributions $ 11,946.26
    Interest   896.14
    Total Income: **$ 12,840.40**

Expenditures in 2018:
    Deposit for 2019 GA meeting $ 20,000.00
    Total Expenses: **$ 20,000.00**

Total Fund Balance as of 12/31/18 $ 43,666.09

*Restricted Funds:

    $ 4,100.00   The current balance designated by the 178th General Assembly to print the Catechism in the various languages represented in the church.

    1,011.51   Pastoral Development Ministry Team/General Assembly Ordination Task Force

Total Amount of *Restricted Funds: $ 5,111.51 (12/31/18)

Total Amount of Unrestricted Amount: $ 38,554.58 (12/31/18)

Total Fund Balance: $ 43,666.09 (12/31/18)

Respectfully submitted,
Michael Sharpe, Stated Clerk

THE REPORT OF THE MINISTRY COUNCIL

To the 189th General Assembly of the Cumberland Presbyterian Church meeting in session at the Embassy Suites and Conference Center, Huntsville, Alabama.

I. MINISTRY COUNCIL

A. INTRODUCTION

The Ministry Council (MC) serves as the primary long- and short-range program planning agency of the Church, striving to ensure that all segments work on a unified mission and that human and material resources are utilized to carry out ministries of the Church in an effective manner. The Ministry Council is accountable to the General Assembly (GA).

Due to the scope of the work related to denominational ministries under the MC, our report has historically been quite lengthy, necessitating the division of the report to multiple GA committees. Since 2017, with the goal of providing crucial information in a concise manner, our report to GA has been significantly condensed. This report focuses on recommendations to the GA. A more detailed annual report, created as a supplement to this Report to the 189th General Assembly, reflects in greater detail the work of the MC and its four Ministry Teams (MT). The supplement is available on our web page *cpcmc.org/mc/ga19-supplement/. We encourage Commissioners and others at GA to visit both the Ministry Council booth and the Ministry Exchange to meet elected members and staff and to share ideas for enhancing ministries.*

1. Ministry Council (MC) Elected Membership and Terms

MC elected members are subject to GA requirements of endorsement by presbytery (clergy) or church (laity), as well as geographical (synodic) and gender representation. It is our belief that God calls people from across the denomination to serve in leadership roles, and that the limited number of Personal Data Forms and related endorsements on file in the Office of the General Assembly does not reflect the abundance of qualified leaders within the Church. The MC respectfully reminds Commissioners of an action of the 186th General Assembly that urged each presbytery ***"to proactively recruit and encourage qualified leaders to prayerfully consider opportunities to serve as elected board members at the denominational level, to include the Ministry Council and all other denominational entities."***

The initial three-year terms of Karen Avery, Carla Bellis, Tsuruko Satoh, and Reverend Mike Wilkinson expire in 2019. All are eligible for an additional term of service; however, Karen Avery and Tsuruko Satoh asked not to be re-nominated due to family and work responsibilities. Both Ms. Avery and Ms. Satoh brought helpful insight and experience to the MC, and their unique perspectives will be sorely missed. The third three-year term of Reverend Troy Green expires in 2019, and he is ineligible for an additional term at this time. Reverend Green has been an active and enthusiastic servant leader on the MC, proactively encouraging new and returning members during their tenure on the MC and has been a strong advocate for MC/ MT staff. The MC and staff deeply appreciate his service and sacrifice over the past nine years. Reverend Lanny Johnson's third three-year term expires in 2020; however, he has recently moved outside the bounds of the synod, and thus cannot continue to serve on the Council. Reverend Johnson's good humor, institutional memory and unflagging, enthusiastic support of the MC and staff will also be greatly missed. The second one-year term of Youth Advisory Member Leighann Morgan concludes with this GA. She is ineligible for a third one-year term. We express appreciation to Ms. Morgan for her dedicated level of engagement in the work of the Church and her two years of service on the MC. Terms of Youth Advisory Members Sydney Holder and Madison Holland conclude with this GA. They are each eligible to serve an additional one-year term. The MC is the only denominational entity with Youth Advisory Members.

2. Ministry Teams plan and implement the program ministries of the Church and are made up of both Staff and Elected Team Members. Ministry Teams report to the MC. MT members are elected by the MC and reflect GA term limits.

Communications Ministry Team (CMT) elected member Reverend Steven Shelton was hired as the new CMT Leader in June 2018, leaving his term unfulfilled, dropping CMT's membership to three after Reverend Jim McGuire's replacement was unable to join the CMT as planned. At its February 2019 meeting, the MC elected Joyce A. McCullough (Manchester CPC, Murfreesboro Presbytery) and Reverend Neal Wilkinson (White Oak Pond CPC, Missouri Presbytery) bringing elected membership up to five. An additional member will be added in 2020 bringing the team back up to a full six elected members.

Discipleship Ministry Team (DMT) elected member Reverend Nancy McSpadden completed two terms and, for health reasons, has chosen not to serve a third term. Reverend Josefina Sanchez also completed two terms and has chosen not to serve a third term as she explores new types of ministry. DMT is grateful for their experience and contributions. At its February 2019 meeting, MC elected Reverend Jesse Thornton to serve a second term; Jonathan Bellis (Orange CPC, Missouri Presbytery) to replace Nancy McSpadden, and Reverend Abby Prevost (Welti CPC, Hope Presbytery) to replace Josefina Sanchez.

Missions Ministry Team (MMT) elected member Reverend Victor Hassell has completed three terms. MMT is thankful for his passion for missions and contributions to the work of the Church. Dominic Lau completed two terms and asked not to be re-elected due to study and work demands. Reverend Cardelia Howell-Diamond was hired as the new Coordinator for Women's Ministry and thus is no longer an elected member. MMT appreciates the energy and enthusiasm they imbued into the work of the MMT. At its February 2019 meeting, the MC elected Dean Reichenbach (Smithville CPC, Murfreesboro Presbytery) and Karen Patten (Faith CPC, West Tennessee Presbytery) to serve on the MMT. Reverend Brittany Meeks and Reverend Chris Warren were re-elected for a third term.

MC re-elected Reverend Duawn Mearns and Reverend Sandra Shepherd to third terms on the **Pastoral Development Ministry Team (PDMT).**

The MC elects MT members in accordance with GA requirements: that individuals have current personal data forms and recommendations from their presbytery (clergy) or pastor (laity) on file with the Stated Clerk prior to GA. A complete list of MT members appears at *cpcmc.org/mc/*.

Staff Team Members are employees of the MC (alphabetical order):
- **CMT:** Publications Manager/Editor Matthew H. Gore; Senior Art Director Sowgand Sheikholeslami; and CMT Leader Reverend Steven Shelton.
- **DMT:** DMT Leader Reverend Elinor S. Brown; Coordinator of Adult Ministry Reverend Chris Fleming (Paducah, Kentucky office); Coordinator of Distribution Cindy Martin; Coordinator of Children and Family Ministry Jodi Hearn Rush (Nashville, Tennessee office); and Coordinator of Youth and Young Adult Ministry Reverend Nathan Wheeler.
- **MMT:** Coordinator for Women's Ministry Reverend Cardelia Howell-Diamond (Huntsville, Alabama office); Cross-Culture Immigrant US Ministry Reverend Johan Daza; Manager, Finance and Administration Jinger Ellis; Director of Congregational Ministries Reverend Kristi Lounsbury (Krum, Texas office); Evangelism & New Church Development Reverend T.J. Malinoski; Director Global Missions Reverend Lynn Thomas (Birmingham, Alabama office); and MMT Leader Reverend Milton Ortiz. Bilingual English/Korean Administrative Assistant Julie Min accepted a position as Korean Language Lecturer at Penn State University, concluding her service in December 2018. Ms. Min provided unique and highly valued gifts to MMT, the MC, and the Church. We extend to her our gratitude and blessings for her time on staff.
- **PDMT:** PDMT Leader Reverend Pam Phillips-Burk.

3. The **Global Ministries Leadership Team (GMLT)** is made up of the four Ministry Team Leaders and Director of Ministries. GMLT works together to apply the MC's vision/mission to the many varied programs and resource materials planned and produced by the MTs, coordinating ministries and a comprehensive budget in a unified, collaborative manner. GMLT meets monthly.

4. **Administration:** Director of Ministries Edith Busbee Old gives executive leadership to the MC in accomplishing duties defined by its Bylaws and supervises the GMLT. The Director of Ministries is under direct employment of and is responsible to the MC. The MC is grateful that the Director and Team Leaders are globally minded without neglecting the stateside church, for their creative and consistent leadership, and for sustaining consistently positive fiscal results.

B. GENERAL INFORMATION

1. **Meetings:** The MC met twice in regular session since the 188th GA. Summaries of MC meetings appear at *cpcmc.org/mc/soa/*.
2. **Future Meeting Dates:** August 15, 2019 (Thursday) – Orientation for newly elected MC/MT members at the Denominational Center, Cordova, Tennessee.

August 16–17, 2019 (Friday and Saturday) – All elected members and staff of the MC and all four MTs meet concurrently at Faith CPC, Bartlett, Tennessee.

February 22–23, 2020 (Saturday and Sunday) – MC Corporation Annual Meeting of the Board of Directors with Team Leaders and the Director of Ministries at the Denominational Center.

3. Elected member accountability and training: Newly elected MC/MT members receive multi-tiered orientation prior to their first meeting. Each year, all elected members sign a Covenant reinforcing their commitment to answering the call to serve God through service to the Church. Elected MC members set individual annual goals and complete annual self-evaluations reflecting on their service. These tools serve as metrics to help guide the MC and its teams. The Covenant may be seen at *cpcmc.org/mc/covenant/*.

4. Human Resources: When a staff position becomes vacant, the MC invests time in a thorough revision of that job description. Input is gathered from elected members, GMLT, and relevant staff. Since the 188th GA, MC has prayerfully considered current and future ministries of all of its MTs. Within the past year, all of its MTs experienced staff changes resulting in the need for MC to painstakingly review and revise job descriptions. Three staff members moved to different MTs and/or new responsibilities within the same team: Matt Gore transitioned from DMT to CMT; Cindy Martin shifted within DMT; Pam Phillips-Burk shifted from MMT to PDMT. The MC affirms these moves as outward examples of their response to Call in using their unique gifts to grow God's Kingdom. Additionally, since the 188th GA, three new staff members came on board: Cardelia Howell-Diamond, Kristi Lounsbury, and Chris Fleming. And though he came on board just days prior to the 188th GA, and was introduced at same, Reverend Steven Shelton was not included in the written MC Report to that GA as it was written in March 2018 prior to his accepting the call to the position of CMT Leader.

5. Unification: The 188th GA encouraged the Unification Task Force (UTF) and MC to establish a viable network of communication so that they may continue to work for a successful unification of the CPC and the CPCA. MC/MT elected members and staff continue to maintain communication with the UTF and CPCA leadership, visit CPCA congregations, and participate in CPCA events. MMT staff member for Evangelism and New Church Development, Reverend T.J. Malinoski, is a dual member of Presbytery of East Tennessee (CPC) and New Hopewell Presbytery (CPCA), serving as a proactive liaison between the CPC and CPCA.

6. The 188th GA assigned a Committee to *"work with the Discipleship Ministry Team (to) develop and to conduct a census/survey of all congregations in regards to particular churches use of the Encounter Publication with the results of that census/survey disseminated through the stated clerks of each presbytery by the 190th General Assembly. The committee members are: Vicky Goodwin, Mission Synod; Lisa Scott, Synod of the Midwest; Grady Prevost, Synod of the Southeast; Ben Lindamood, Tennessee Synod; and Mike Reno, Synod of Great Rivers."* Coordinator of Adult Ministry Reverend Chris Fleming is working with that committee and the results will be disseminated as requested by the 190th GA (2020).

7. The 188th GA requested the Permanent Judiciary and the Unified Committee on Theology and Social Concerns, along with the **MC (for input from a cross-culture/international perspective)**, to work jointly to develop a position statement on issues of human sexuality to be presented to the 189th GA for its consideration. At its August 2018 meeting, the MC heard from three of its MMT staff in regard to input volunteered by CPs outside the US. Following its February 2019 meeting, the MC shared with the joint committee additional information received from pastors in Japan Presbytery. Immediately following both its August and February meetings, the MC relayed summaries of the international perspectives to the Unified Committee on Theology and Social Concerns.

II. MINISTRIES

A. PARAMETERS

The MC created "Parameters to Guide the Work of Our Ministry Teams" as a standard for all work done by MTs. Parameters are on the MC website *cpcmc.org/mc/mt-work-params/*.

B. CMT

CMT continues to explore ways to use technology to support our denomination's connectional nature, and to ensure that we are being the best stewards possible of our resources. In partnership with all MTs,

CMT provides support for website management, audio/ visual services, social networking platforms, and web-based application support, and consultations. In addition to its responsibilities around editing and publishing THE CUMBERLAND PRESBYTERIAN magazine, *The Missionary Messenger* (cooperatively with MMT), the MC Supplemental Report, and the annual Program Planning Calendar, CMT also manages the dissemination of time-sensitive news and information via "News of the Church". Senior Art Director Sowgand Sheikholeslami provides layout and design for numerous projects and programs related to the ministries of the Church, beyond the work of the MC, including artwork for the denomination's Yearbook and GA Minutes.

With the retirement of former CMT Leader Mark Davis, the MC envisioned a broader influence for CMT, adding a full time staff position of Publications Manager/Editor. This division of duties has provided more opportunity for the Team Leader to expand the capacity of the CMT in the realm of church support and technology development. To date, Steven Shelton has coordinated with MMT to develop an online platform for the Missions School and with PDMT to enhance the online capacities of the Leadership Referral Service. As CMT capabilities continue to be cultivated by the expanded team (including this year, the very first live video stream of GA worship and business) they are excited about what new support they may be able to offer in upcoming years.

Publications Manager/Editor Matt Gore has made great strides in returning the magazine to its intended role as the denomination's paper of record, while bringing a rich historical perspective to the publication sharing stories of Cumberland Presbyterians through the centuries. Since Matt began in this capacity in September 2018, subscriptions to THE CUMBERLAND PRESBYTERIAN magazine have increased significantly and we look forward to continued increases in 2019 as word of his journalistic excellence continues to spread.

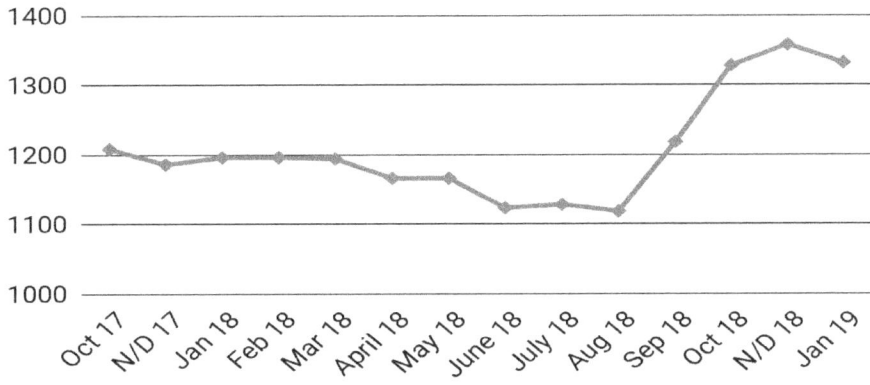

C. DMT

The Cumberland Presbyterian Constitution recognizes that "God has given different gifts to ministers of the word and sacrament and the church recognizes various types of ministry ... not only as pastors of particular churches but as teachers of religion in various kinds of schools, editors of religious publications, chaplains to the military forces and to various types of institutions, missionaries, evangelists, counselors, administrators of church programs and institutions, directors of Christian education in particular churches, and as leaders in other fields of service directly related to the church." *(2.64 Constitution, Confession of Faith)*

DMT continues to uphold its mission statement: The DMT invites and challenges people in all seasons of life to grow in their faith in Jesus Christ by providing training, events, and curriculum to nurture discipleship in the Cumberland Presbyterian Church.

We continue to see that all of our resources include our Core Values to **Inspire**: We strive to empower and equip CPs to think critically and love extravagantly; to maintain **Integrity**: We teach and learn by allowing ourselves to be authentically guided by the Holy Spirit through scripture; and be **Inclusive**: We celebrate the diversity of our churches, cultures, and people that are the body of Christ.

DMT elected members and staff are working together to complete goals set for 2020. These include **Social Media and Marketing** (full-time marketing person, better communication bridge between staff and presbyteries, and videos relating DMT ministries); **Leadership Development** (a safe sanctuary Discipleship Blueprint design that is already completed, another path for ordination, and two grant funding goals for sources for programming); goals for **Age Specific** areas (voting rights for YADs, increased participation at CPYC, 2021 Kaleo, three Children's Fest sites - being done this year - and developing a more robust adult ministry plan); and **Curriculum and Resources** (75% of all CP churches using CP curriculum, attending CP events, and developing core values, beliefs, practices, for all DMT curriculum, resources and events).

D. MMT

MMT serves and equips CPs, congregations and judicatories in pursuing God's mission of redemption and reconciliation. Our *"responsibility is to equip God's people to do his work and build the church, the body of Christ."* (Ephesians 4:12 NLT) Specifically, MMT facilitates those phases of the Church's mission concerned with outreach in terms of evangelism and the establishing of congregations, and other means of Christian witness around the world. MMT's ministry is present in fifteen countries: Australia, Brazil, Cambodia, Colombia, Cuba, Guatemala, Haiti, Hong Kong, Japan, Laos, Mexico, Philippines, South Korea, Spain, and the US. MMT's vision is the development of a fresh identity for the CPC as an evangelism/church planting/missions ***movement***. MMT serves and equips through consultation, expertise, coaching, leadership training, professional development, and ministry opportunities. At present, MMT's focus is in five areas of ministry: Evangelism and New Church Development, Congregational Ministries, Women's Ministry, Cross-Culture Immigrant US Ministry, and Global Ministry. What are our goals and actions?

1. To work towards the practice of evangelism as Cumberland Presbyterians.
    a. Continue to be in conversation with staff and all MTs about the practice of evangelism from various roles and perspectives.
    b. Continue to be in conversation about the practice of evangelism among church leaders, local congregations and all judicatory levels of the church.
2. To promote diverse and innovative methods to plant new churches.
    a. Develop a list of different models of new church developments.
    b. Foster individual and small group conversations about different methods to plant churches.
    c. Continue working with staff to research methods of new church development.
3. To promote various approaches to church development.
    a. Develop a practical process of steps for church assimilation.
    b. Develop a practical process of steps for church consultation.
    c. Consider a new online platform for the Leadership Referral Service (LRS).
4. To engage all women in the CPC in a wide variety of ministry opportunities.
    a. Continue conversation about new and creative possibilities for the Cumberland Presbyterian Women's Ministry Convention.
    b. Continue Young Women's Ministry in partnership with Young Adult Ministry.
    c. Continue developing ministries among cross-culture women.
5. To promote awareness and compassionate involvement in the needs of our communities.
    a. Develop a process to promote awareness and compassionate involvement in the needs of our communities by volunteering, advocating, giving, and working in teams.
    b. Foster individual and small group conversations about the needs in our communities.
6. To promote among all CPs the vision and benefits of having a global church perspective.
    a. Foster individual and small group conversations about the vision and benefits of having a global church.
    b. Develop a process to have more international mission trips.
    c. Continue working with staff to explore ways to be a global church.
7. To increase donors of all types to give strategically to the different offerings and programs.
    a. Continue conversation with staff about learning to market MMT programs and offerings in new ways based on target audiences.
    b. Develop fundraising strategies based on MMT's mission, culture, and the qualities that make MMT unique.

Evangelism and New Church Development

This office provides innovative strategies, guidance, and training that are reaching new people and making disciples of Jesus Christ primarily to, and with, CPs in the US for the transformation of the world. The office of Evangelism and New Church Development also delivers local, on-site support for various judicatories and groups with an emphasis in evangelism. More recently, a new approach to starting worshipping communities called New Exploration Initiatives is addressing a need in the area of church planting. This office intends to capitalize on that need with new projects from planning stages to implementation in early 2019 in Alabama, Florida, Mississippi, and Tennessee. The intention of this office is not only to help those who are starting new churches and forming new communities of faith but also help equip existing congregations in the sharing of the Gospel of Jesus Christ. A priority in the coming year will be to seek out prospective leaders and locations to start new groups.

RECOMMENDATION 1: That the 189th General Assembly request presbyteries to call upon both lay and ordained Cumberland Presbyterians to start new communities of faith in their homes, neighborhoods, towns, cities, and local settings with the encouragement and support of their church session, presbyterial board of missions, presbytery, synod, and MMT for the purpose of extending the Gospel of Jesus Christ.

Women's Ministry

Cumberland Presbyterian Women's Ministry is a thriving community within the CPC. It includes all aspects of ministry that include women. In the CPC that's everything from ordination, sessions, circles, women's fellowships, missions and beyond! Every woman in the CPC is a part of Women's Ministry; some just may not know it yet. The purpose of Women's Ministry in the CPC is to accept the love and joy of Jesus through the ministry of women. We seek to do this as we pray, study God's word, and reach out to others through missions, service, encouragement, and fellowship opportunities. This goal is accomplished on all levels of work from local to denominational.

Women's Ministry Convention is held every year coinciding with GA. We spend time encouraging one another and seeking to engage in biblical study, introduce new outreach, elect officers, and hear from the global missions field. We collect an offering to be divided among different ministries and the Stott-Wallace Missionary Offering Fund. Throughout 2019-2020, Women's Ministry across the denomination will focus on *walking in love* together through worship, prayer, missions, fellowship, retreats, and many other creative endeavors.

Women's Ministry has placed an emphasis on including young women (post high school to 35) in women's ministry activities unique to their needs and interests. We held our annual Young Women's Retreat in January 2019 and look forward to hosting another in February 2020 at Camp Clark Williamson, Humboldt, Tennessee. Young Women's Ministry is now done in partnership with the Young Adult Ministry of DMT.

Beth-El Farmworker

Every year many CP groups plan domestic and international short mission trips. For some of these groups, mission trip opportunities are found outside our denomination. MMT urges and encourages all CPs and mission groups to become familiar with our domestic and abroad mission opportunities. Many of these are constantly receiving mission groups and have an efficient structure to plan team visits throughout the year.

Domestically, Beth-El Farmworker Ministry, founded in 1976 by faithful CPs, serves the farmworker community near Tampa, Florida, through Nuevo Camino (New Path) worshipping community. They provide hunger relief programs, health and wellness programs, and mission and summer programs for churches and short-term mission groups. Beth-El Farmworker Ministry is located in Wimauma, Florida, 45 minutes from Tampa International Airport. Lodging and meals per participant/per day is around $35-40. Several mission trip opportunities are available during the year and all CP churches are welcome. Contact Beth-El Executive Director Reverend Kathleen Dain for more information on mission trip/service opportunities: kathy@beth-el.org, or phone 813-633-1548, extension 223.

RECOMMENDATION 2: That the 189th General Assembly request presbyteries to promote and encourage all congregations to consider Beth-El Farmworker Ministry as a mission field for Cumberland Presbyterian church groups looking for short mission trip opportunities and experiences.

Global Missions

The Stott-Wallace Missionary Offering Fund's monthly contributions over the past three years:

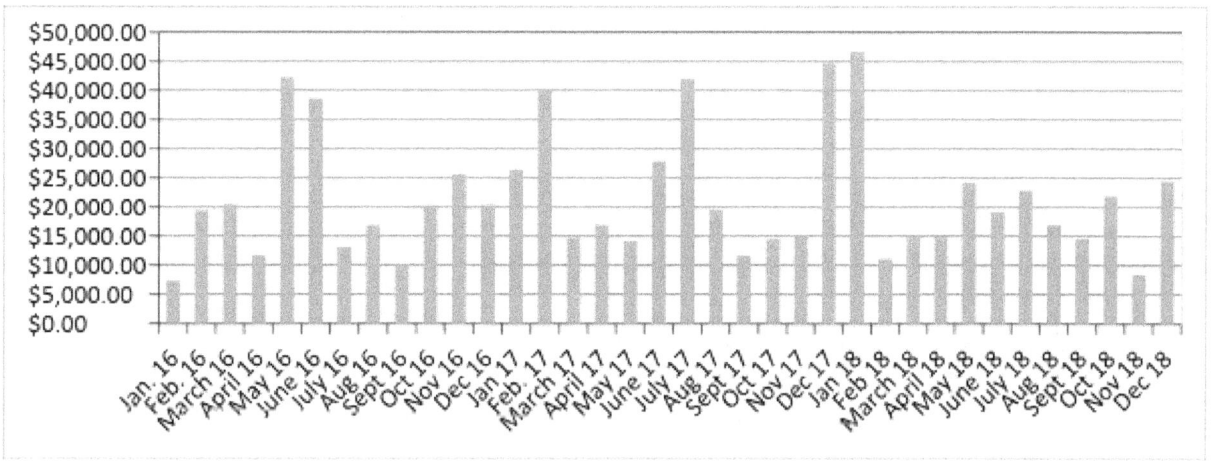

The Stott-Wallace (SW) Missionary Offering Fund is the method the CPC uses to support Cumberland Presbyterian missionaries. Donations are received during the year from churches and individuals, with special focus on Pentecost Sunday (Missions Sunday). In 2018, the SW Missionary Offering Fund produced $240,702 in donations. In 2017, it produced $288,069 and in 2016 a total of $246,832. The SW Missionary Offering Fund is a relatively new concept for CPs. In addition to SW donations, this fund receives a donation from Our United Outreach distributions and a donation from endowments designated for missionary support. To support current CP missionaries the fund needs to generate approximately $350,000 annually.

In 2018, two missionary families resigned and returned home. In late 2018, MMT approved a new missionary family to Brazil and they were deployed in early 2019. It is the goal of the MMT to deploy more new missionaries in 2019; missionary applications are currently being processed. By the end of 2019 we should have 14 missionaries planting CP churches in different places around the world. Pray that God opens doors of prosperity to meet the needs of our missionaries.

RECOMMENDATION 3: That the 189th General Assembly be called to pray during the General Assembly for our missionaries. And that the General Assembly prays that God continues to call churches and individuals to support these missionaries.

Congregational Ministries

Serving as a coach and facilitator to congregations, the Director of Congregational Ministries works with all MC staff to ensure success in the local church. This includes assessing local congregational needs, providing resources to encourage successful ministry and aid in reaching the goals of the congregation. This position is committed to increasing knowledge of opportunities for congregations to engage in through missions, Christian education, youth events, and other activities. Other avenues of support for congregations include: assisting congregations searching for a pastor through the Leadership Referral Service; serving as a resource person for mission opportunities and disaster relief teams; and, promoting events, activities and opportunities through social media. Being a newly expanded position, Congregational Ministries allows for new prospects of growth, outreach, and resources within the denomination, as well as sustainable support of congregations throughout the Cumberland Presbyterian Church.

RECOMMENDATION 4: That the 189th General Assembly request presbyteries to encourage all congregations to engage, promote, support, and participate in opportunities to grow the Kingdom of God in denominational ministries through the following: Explore denominational resources for Small Group Studies, Children and Youth Ministry, and Adult Bible Study; Pray for and support our missionaries through the Stott-Wallace Missionary Offering Fund; Visit and advocate for our Ministry Partners, Beth-El Farmworker Ministry, Project Vida, Coalition of Appalachian Ministries, and National Farm Workers Ministry; Encourage students to attend Bethel University and Memphis Theological Seminary; Support global and local mission opportunities.

E. PDMT

Leadership Referral Service (LRS) is an online application process for churches looking for a pastor and for pastors searching for a call. There are currently 31 CP churches and one CPCA congregation utilizing LRS for their pastor search. All pastors are encouraged to keep an updated Personal Information Form on file with LRS as well as post their resume within the online application. PDMT and MMT's Director of Congregational Ministries work together to provide leadership and support for LRS. The Opportunity List of open churches is posted on the website at *cpcmc.org/pdmt/opplist*. A monthly email is sent to ministers and probationers with an email address (approximately 750) listing churches in an active pastor search. The online application can be accessed at *cpcmc.org/pdmt/lrs*.

Clergy Crisis Fund is available to clergy in crisis and in need of support and care. Circumstances approved for benefits include death, medical bills, counseling, termination (one-time expenditure), and other considerations to be determined. Contact the PDMT Leader for more information.

2019 Pastors Retreats are monthly Sabbath retreats for CP clergy (including their family) free of charge. The 3-day retreats are held at Whitestone Country Inn in Kingston, Tennessee. All meals are included. These retreats are in partnership with the "Whosoever Will Bridge Ministry" at Bethel University and Memphis Theological Seminary. For more information, *cpcmc.org/2019-pastors-retreat*.

Ordination Travel Communion Sets are available to newly ordained CP pastors. PDMT also recognizes probationers as they progress through the ordination process with an appropriate book/resource. Each presbytery Committee on Ministry/Preparation is encouraged to contact PDMT for information on how to request these free gifts.

III. FUNDING

Since the inception of the "new structure" in 2007, the MC/MTs have shared in planning new and ongoing ministries. Each year the collegial environment has grown stronger, enabling the reality of a comprehensive budget. Funding sources include Our United Outreach (OUO), donations, grants, Investment Loan Program (ILP) and endowments (listed within Board of Stewardship section of the preliminary minutes). Endowments are an important part of our funding, though they do not generate usable funds until they reach sufficient size to generate interest payments that can be used. The MC ended fiscal year 2018 $33,000 ahead of budget, in spite of economic downturns and culture shifts that adversely affected other charitable organizations and denominations worldwide. In addition to sound stewardship practices, last year 47% of MC/MT elected members and staff personally donated $14,546 to the ongoing work of the MC and its many ministries. Experience and research show that personal giving by members works in at least three ways:
- It is a public declaration that the member has invested in the MC/MTs.
- It indicates that the member has a commitment to the organization and its mission.
- It encourages other donors to give and impresses institutions that provide grants or other support.

Indeed, many major donors and foundations will not support an organization like the MC unless the board achieves 100% giving (*thebalancesmb.com/how-nonprofit-boards-make-a-difference-2502002*).

As the MC explores additional potential sources of revenue, we hope that first time and long-term donors will feel called to contribute, providing funds for current and future ministry.

IV. MINISTRY COUNCIL CONCLUSION

We are thankful for the sustaining guidance of the Holy Spirit as we work to enhance and implement ministries that draw people to Christ. We encourage 189th GA Commissioners and guests to visit the MC booth and the Ministry Exchange. We encourage you to pick up materials to share with your congregation, groups, and presbytery. MC/MT staff and elected members are eager to listen to your ideas and answer questions.

Not unlike other denominations, ours is an aging denomination. We yearn to see CPs of all generations serving in leadership roles throughout the Church. We yearn for CPs everywhere to commit to sharing actively in the work of the Church, for leaders to rise up from across the globe to further the work of the Church around the world.

The 52 MC/MT elected and advisory members and 17 staff members are committed to serving God through the CPC and ask that the Church remain in prayer for our collaborative work as both staff and elected members proactively serve as conduits of information *to and from* the MC.

Respectfully Submitted,

The Ministry Council of the Cumberland Presbyterian Church
Reverend Mike Wilkinson, President
Reverend Donny Acton, First Vice President
Reverend Kenny Butcher, Second Vice President
Karen Avery, Secretary
Edith B. Old, Director of Ministries/Treasurer

THE REPORT OF THE BOARD OF STEWARDSHIP, FOUNDATION, AND BENEFITS

I. GENERAL INFORMATION

A. BOARD MEETINGS AND ORGANIZATION

The Board of Stewardship, Foundation and Benefits under the direction of its officers, President Randy Davidson, Vice-president Mike St. John, Secretary Debbie Shelton, and Treasurer Robert Heflin, met two times in regular session.

B. BOARD MEMBERS WHOSE TERMS EXPIRE

Members whose terms expire at the 2019 General Assembly are: Ken Byford, Charles (Buddy) Pope, Debbie Shelton and Andrea Smith. Board member Buddy Pope passed away. Debbie Shelton has served for a total of 18 years. Ken Byford and Andrea Smith have agreed to continue to serve. We want to thank them for their service and dedication to the Board of Stewardship, Foundation and Benefits. Please remember the family of Buddy Pope. He is missed.

C. BOARD REPRESENTATIVE TO THE 188TH GENERAL ASSEMBLY

The board's representative to the 188th General Assembly is Gary Tubb.

D. STAFF

Kathryn Gilbert Craig serves as Administrative Assistant, Mark Duck serves as Coordinator of Benefits and Robert Heflin serves as Executive Secretary.

E. 2020 BUDGET

The 2020 line-item budget has been filed with the Office of the General Assembly.

F. 2018 AUDIT

Certified copies of the 2018 audit reports from Fouts and Morgan will be filed with the Office of the General Assembly in compliance with General Regulations E.5. and E.6. The 2018 audit will be printed in the audit section of the 2019 minutes.

II. FINANCIAL FOUNDATION DEVELOPMENT AND MANAGEMENT

A. PURPOSE

One area of work of the board is in financial foundation development and management. The purpose of this program is as follows:
To secure a firm financial undergirding for the ongoing ministry of congregations and the agencies of presbyteries, synods, and the General Assembly as they bear witness to the saving love of God, the grace of our Lord Jesus Christ, and the fellowship and communion of the Holy Spirit.

B. 2018 IN REVIEW

In 2018, both domestic and international markets were volatile. U. S. stocks were up 2.6% as of the end of June 2018. The S&P 500 gained 7.7% in the third quarter. However, the fourth quarter wiped out all the gains and then some, declining 13.5% in the fourth quarter. Developed markets closed the year down 15-20% while emerging markets ended the year down over 14%. Bond markets didn't offer much of a return either, basically ending the year where they started. The slow down in the global economy and the tightening U.S. monetary policy was cause for concern.

The fourth quarter was a reminder of how quickly markets can change direction after long periods of generating above average returns. That is why it is important to be diversified and remain calm during times of market volatility.

The activity in the Cumberland Presbyterian Endowment Fund, Retirement Fund and the Investment Loan Program reflected the volatility of the markets. One example was the performance of the endowment fund. At the end of June 2018, we saw a gain of 3.5% for the first six months but the fund ended 2018 with a loss of 2.5%. The Endowment Fund and the Retirement Fund are diversified portfolios which is an effective strategy during times of market volatility.

We are confident that our investment manager, Gerber/Taylor can continue to help us navigate the turbulent ups and downs of the market. Since October 1981, Gerber/Taylor has done a wonderful job for the Cumberland Presbyterian Church.

C. BOARD OF STEWARDSHIP

The Board of Stewardship ended 2018 with a loss of $133,676 as a result of decreased earnings in the endowment fund and the investment loan program. We are ever mindful of expenses incurred and try to be good stewards of what has been entrusted to the Board. We are grateful for the faithful support from congregations and individuals through their contributions to Our United Outreach.

D. MANAGEMENT OF FUNDS

At the end of 2018 the Endowment Fund portfolio was under the co-management of Gerber/Taylor Management, RREEF America II, Clarion, Tortoise, Headlands Capital and Eagle MLP. The funds of the Retirement Program were co-managed by Gerber/Taylor Management, RREEF America II, Tortoise, Headlands Capital and Eagle MLP.

The church loan portion of the endowment portion of the endowment portfolio and the investments of the Cumberland Presbyterian Church Investment Loan Program, Inc. were under the management of board staff with the help of Stifel Nicholas.

III. ENDOWMENT PROGRAM

Since 1836, the board and its corporate predecessors have sought to be faithful trustees of the funds given into their hands to provide a permanent financial foundation for the work of congregations, presbyteries, synods, and General Assembly agencies. The work of the Endowment Program is the oldest responsibility of the board and fulfills a portion of that task to which all Cumberland Presbyterians are called: "Christian stewardship acknowledges that all of life and creation is a trust from God, to be used for God's glory and service."—*Confession of Faith for Cumberland Presbyterians 6:10.*

A. COMMUNICATION

The Endowment Program report will be distributed to all endowment program participants, general assembly board members, churches, and individual contributors.

Agencies, other participants, and interested parties received quarterly detailed reports on the postings to all their endowments. With the addition of names supplied by the agencies during the year, the number of persons receiving these reports continues to expand. In addition, special reports were made as requested.

B. ASSETS, INVESTMENT MIX, AND PERFORMANCE

1. Assets and Investment Mix

The assets of the Endowment Fund totaled $56,505,941 for 2018 at *market value*. The following table provides a breakdown of the investment mix:

INVESTMENT MIX

Securities & Investments

15.5%	US Equity	$8,757,394
11.6%	Real Assets	$6,553,921
9.5%	Fixed Income	$5,367,435
17.7%	Hedged Equity	$10,000,379
18.1%	Multi-Strategy	$10,226,376
2.3%	Opportunistic	$1,299,484
13.5%	International Equity	$7,627,408
7.8%	Emerging Markets	$4,406,947
4.0%	Private Equity	$2,259,972
0%	Cash	$6,625
100.0%	Total	$56,505,941

2. Performance of the Endowment Fund

The Endowment Fund generated a loss of $1,369,084 in investment earnings during 2018. Net contributions and withdrawals (including income distributions) were a negative $1,324,100.

Since January 2013, we have begun paying out 5% (annualized) to the congregations, presbyteries and agencies. Previously agencies had difficulty in preparing budgets because of the unknown amount they would receive from endowment income. Now, they can better estimate the endowment income they will receive Endowment income paid to congregations, presbyteries and agencies totaled $2,056,976 for 2018.

3. Total Rate of Return for the Endowment Fund

The following table gives the annualized rates of return as contained in the report from Gerber/Taylor Associates for year end 2018:

	One Year Period 01/01/18 12/31/18	Five Year Period 01/01/14 12/31/18	Since Inception 09/30/81 12/31/18
Endowment Fund	-2.5%	4.4%	9.6%

C. ESTABLISHING AN ENDOWMENT AS A LEGACY

The Board of Stewardship, Foundation and Benefits manages 830 endowments established for the benefit of congregations, presbyteries, synods, agencies and other special ministries of the Cumberland Presbyterian denomination. Many of these endowments were established by individuals as a legacy to continue to benefit long after they are no longer with us. Some of the endowments were established by congregations, presbyteries and synods to help further their specific ministries. Some of the endowments were started with very little. Through the years these endowments have grown and the beneficiaries are reaping the gifts of the endowment income and using it in ministry in their local area or worldwide. Please consider establishing an endowment.

List of Endowments

Board of Stewardship

Endowment	Ending Balance 2017	Ending Balance 2018
Grace J. Beasley Memorial	$32,119.92	$30,003.58
Donald Bierhaus Trust	$75,607.78	$70,626.13
C. C. Brock Endowment Fund	$5,241.78	$4,896.40
Lavenia Campbell Cole Annunity Endowment	$71,345.06	$66,644.22
Lavenia Cole Testamentary Trust 25%	$645,522.17	$603,761.61
Lavenia Campbell Cole Trust 20%	$52,994.43	$49,502.72
Lavenia Campbell Cole Finance Endowment	$10,706.47	$10,001.05
Foundation & Finance Trust	$11,991.61	$11,251.33
Freeman Trust	$116,161.63	$108,507.95
Floyd Hensley Trust	$30,034.80	$28,055.88
P. F. Johnson Memorial Endowment	$10,153.58	$9,484.59
Robert H. Jordan Endowment Fund	$7,193.75	$6,719.77
Della Campbell Lowrie 20%	$482,259.31	$450,483.93
J. Richard Magrill, Jr. Endowment	$49,114.37	$46,089.31
Sam B. Miles Endowment	$89,273.52	$83,391.48
M. Dale Orr Endowment	$41,540.12	$38,803.06
William Dana Shriver Fund	$228,576.83	$213,516.29
Maymie Stovall - Frontier Press 25%	$33,240.55	$31,050.37
Evelyn & Gene Walpole Endowment	$31,023.66	$30,421.28
Eugene Warren Endowment Fund	$26,845.38	$25,076.61
Dixie Campbell Zinn Memorial	$16,292.87	$15,219.32
Total	**$2,067,239.59**	**$1,933,506.88**

Ministerial Aid

Endowment	Ending Balance 2017	Ending Balance 2018
Ministerial Aid Endowment	$890,170.65	$842,648.92
Ministerial Aid Surplus Endowment	$36,239.88	$35,536.20
CPWM Endowment for Minister Care	$7,781.26	$7,630.20
Jesse W. Hipsher Endowment	$50,507.19	$49,624.36
Annie Lee Hogue Endowment	$46,945.40	$46,033.88
Herschcl E. Jones Ministers' Trust	$13,763.79	$13,496.53
Kate H., Robert E. & Robert M. King	$185,778.93	$182,171.63
Della Campbell Lowrie Endowment 20%	$1,950,625.27	$1,799,192.21
Special Reserve Retirement Program	$100,512.87	$97,644.46
Sue Stiles Endowment Fund 50%	$114,158.80	$111,942.21
Total	**$3,396,484.04**	**$3,185,920.60**

Ministry Council - Missions Ministry Team

Endowment	Ending Balance 2017	Ending Balance 2018
Missions Ministry Team Budget Reserve Endowment	$1,014,497.67	$848,404.20
Church Loan Fund - General	$1,444,799.26	$1,349,603.63
McKenzie Endowment	$44,592.51	$41,654.40
Advance in Missions Trust Fund	$466,345.85	$435,619.05
Missions & Evangelism Endowment	$121,390.52	$113,392.25
Grace Johnson Beasley Memorial	$39,683.23	$37,068.58
Grace Beasley - Small Rural Church	$53,619.23	$50,086.34
Bennett & Mildred Brown Trust	$61,710.64	$64,078.28
David Brown Endowment	$13,835.37	$13,566.74
CPW Leadership Trust Fund	$104,396.03	$97,545.33
CPWM Bethel College Scholarship	$201,409.24	$197,687.94
Lavenia Campbell Cole Annuity Endowment	$65,942.02	$61,597.18
Lavenia Cole Testamentary Trust (25%)	$676,918.81	$633,089.62
Lavenia Campbell Cole Trust Endowment 20%	$23,401.43	$21,859.52

Ministry Council - Missions Ministry Team (continued)

Endowment	Ending Balance 2017	Ending Balance 2018
Rouine Vodra Coleman Endowment	$1,689.93	$1,657.14
Winnifred M. Dixon Endowment	$61,780.48	$57,709.83
Joseph B. Dungy Endowment	$96,525.99	$90,166.06
Louise & Sam R. Estes Endowment	$15,012.73	$14,024.50
Clifford Gittings Endowment	$7,386.29	$7,242.84
Lelia B. Goodman for Missions	$3,795.95	$3,722.24
P. F. Johnson Memorial End.	$20,319.74	$18,980.92
Finis Ewing & Bessie Keene Memorial	$158,502.14	$148,058.64
Chow King Leong Endowment	$54,518.90	$50,926.71
Mary Katherine Mize Longwell Endowment	$854.37	$837.80
Della Campbell Lowrie Trust 20%	$482,563.41	$450,768.03
Jamie Roy Chaffin Endowment	$2,616.72	$2,565.92
Mark G. Lynch Choctaw Presbytery	$12,740.33	$12,492.92
Clifford W. & Sarah C. McCall NCD	$12,681.21	$12,435.00
Joe E. Matlock Endowment	$55,344.82	$51,698.74
Robert E. Matlock Endowment	$174,030.78	$162,564.17
Robert T. & Dona Milam Endowment	$8,676.82	$8,792.54
Nancy J. Orr Bequest	$5,612.34	$5,503.33
New Church Development Endowment	$103,375.12	$96,563.91
S. Q. Proctor Home Mission Endowment	$12,295.44	$11,485.30
Marguerite D. Richards Rural Church	$26,181.81	$24,456.75
Maymie Stovall - Home Missions 25%	$12,907.40	$12,056.92
Paul & Geneva Richards Memorial	$13,046.62	$12,186.98
William A. & Beverly St. John Endowment	$14,250.42	$13,457.64
Madge Sprague Memorial Endowment	$7,240.18	$7,099.61
Lela Swanson Stricklen NCD	$69,055.10	$64,455.69
Cornelia Swain Endowment	$69,710.11	$66,776.33
Marguerite D. Richards MM Magazine	$10,612.56	$10,406.47
Walkerville CPC Memorial Endowment	$8,679.19	$8,510.65
Brown & Julia Welch Missions Endowment	$33,878.90	$31,646.66
Marvin O. Clement & Clement E. Wilkins Memorial	$1,956.67	$1,918.72
Gina Marie Benzel Ableson Memorial	$13,021.94	$12,769.08
Ashburn-Graf Educational Endowment	$172,770.83	$160,310.65
Maree Blackwell Endowment	$3,176.62	$3,114.95
James A. Brintle II Scholarship	$7,796.68	$7,645.29
Mattie Ree Suddarth Brown Endowment - Missions	$22,218.83	$20,754.89
Gladys H. Bryson Scholarship Fund	$136,401.78	$126,489.63
Davis O. & Gladys H. Bryson Missionary	$90,769.47	$84,788.79
Mary Frances & William Carpenter	$12,235.51	$11,656.36
Mildred Chandler Scholarship Endowment	$169,138.47	$157,018.82
Colombian CPW Elementary Scholarships	$45,314.46	$43,927.31
Colombian University Scholarships	$82,828.09	$72,572.63
Helen Deal Endowment	$55,242.04	$51,602.23
John A. Deaver Mission	$13,136.02	$12,880.96
Chester E. Dickson Endowment	$48,055.39	$44,889.12
Jose & Fanny Fajardo Endowment	$11,118.58	$10,912.74
Foreign Missions Endowment	$365,787.33	$341,686.15
Mrs. G. W. Freeman Bible Woman Trust	$8,264.40	$8,103.96
McAdow and Mae Gam Endowment	$17,390.84	$17,211.11
Samuel King Gam	$30,923.89	$28,890.42
Freda Mitchell Gilbert Endowment (MMT)	$10,325.23	$10,124.74
Bernice Barnett Gonzalez Endowment	$1,803.88	$1,768.85
Gleniel Grounds Endowment	$2,772.18	$2,718.36
Holzer Trust	$101,905.44	$94,557.83
Hong Kong Mission	$43,254.91	$40,404.92
Marvin C. & Ruth M. Kinnard Trust	$19,185.07	$15,683.92

Ministry Council - Missions Ministry Team (continued)

Endowment	Ending Balance 2017	Ending Balance 2018
Warren and Carline Lowe Trust	$3,508.49	$3,440.36
Mamie McAdoo Endowment	$3,447.08	$3,380.15
McClung/Fowler Memorial Endowment	$137,118.12	$126,359.05
Holly Katelyn McClurkin	$868.01	$851.15
Rubye Johnson May Memorial 50%	$9,823.33	$9,632.59
Lucie C. Mayhew Fund for U-P Children	$18,937.16	$17,902.76
Elizabeth A. & James W. Morrow Trust	$25,970.82	$24,259.67
Richard Nicks Memorial Endowment	$65,494.38	$60,772.42
Hamilton & Merion S. Parks Family Trust #2	$31,876.47	$31,257.53
Patron Membership	$872,791.05	$819,601.40
Myra Patton Foreign Mission Endowment	$175,121.01	$165,700.43
Perpetual Membership Fund	$1,081,637.66	$1,013,782.87
Don & Gwen Peterson Endowment Fund	$124,625.70	$116,453.75
Rose Ella Porterfield Scholarship	$24,009.16	$23,542.99
Carl Ramsey Scholarship Fund	$38,789.04	$38,035.85
Marguerite D. Richards Japan	$17,482.87	$16,330.96
Elise Sanders Endowment	$323,067.33	$301,780.88
Scholarship-Universidad Evangelica	$14,004.12	$13,732.22
Buddy & Beverly Stott Endowment	$29,332.35	$27,399.70
Maymie Stovall - Foreign Mission 25%	$12,908.49	$12,057.96
Irvin & Annie Mary Draper Swain	$35,706.71	$34,818.91
Walter Swartz - Jose Fajardo Scholarship Fund	$53,578.00	$49,714.86
William B. & Emma Jo Denson Todd Endow	$8,602.68	$8,435.63
Boyce & Beth Wallace Endowment	$53,674.76	$50,138.27
Robert J. & Marilee B. Watkins	$2,516.81	$2,467.91
Bill & Kathryn Wood	$83,321.56	$81,703.73
Forester World Missions Endowment	$3,808,295.88	$3,557,372.95
Bill & Iona Wyatt Endowment	$13,951.08	$13,031.87
Rev. & Mrs. Tadao Yoshizaki Memorial	$819.69	$803.76
Total	**$14,446,501.97**	**$13,433,668.31**

Ministry Council - Communications Ministry Team

Endowment	Ending Balance 2017	Ending Balance 2018
Masaharu Asayama/CPWM Endowment	$13,100.20	$12,845.87
Ky Curry Publishing Endowment	$46,429.72	$45,528.18
C. Ray Dobbins Endowment	$43,559.47	$42,713.66
Dennis H. Kiefer Endowment	$1,178.85	$1,155.97
Marguerite D. Richards CP Magazine	$23,502.59	$23,046.23
Pat White Endowment	$9,949.21	$9,769.14
Total	**$137,720.04**	**$135,059.05**

Ministry Council - Discipleship Ministry Team

Endowment	Ending Balance 2017	Ending Balance 2018
Paul Allen Endowment for C E	$12,175.52	$11,373.80
Grace Johnson Beasley Mem.	$11,633.47	$10,866.96
Bennett & Mildred Brown for C E	$27,064.76	$25,281.49
Christian Education Mid-Century	$265,670.31	$248,165.67
Christian Education Season Endowment	$198,001.76	$185,137.89
Carl Cook Outdoor Ministry Endowment	$5,181.73	$4,840.32
Lavenia Campbell Cole Annuity End.	$38,246.73	$35,726.72
Jill Davis Carr - Leadership Development	$12,333.38	$11,520.86
Consultant Training Fund	$61,646.57	$57,584.80
C. P. Youth Conference	$175,607.90	$164,985.55
H. Harold Davis Endowment Fund	$176,060.26	$164,459.90
Jack W. Ferguson, Jr. C E Endowment	$11,636.14	$10,869.49
Ira & Rae Galloway for C E	$15,154.71	$14,156.16

Ministry Council - Discipleship Ministry Team (continued)

Endowment	Ending Balance 2017	Ending Balance 2018
Jean Garrett Endowment for C E	$4,399.76	$4,110.02
Louise Adams Heathcock Memorial	$11,689.79	$10,919.56
John Gilbert Horsley - Youth Leaders	$14,217.26	$12,655.61
Donald & Jane Hubbard Endowment for C E	$12,225.91	$11,420.37
Into the Nineties for C E	$293,825.07	$274,465.40
Reverend Gayle J. Keown for C E	$3,808.05	$3,557.14
Earl King Memorial	$11,638.88	$10,872.01
Virginia Malcom Christian Education	$121,474.30	$113,470.55
Wesley & Jackie Mattonen Endowment	$36,685.13	$34,268.00
David & Mary McGregor C E Endowment	$59,122.43	$55,227.07
James D. McGuire Endowment for C E	$17,399.89	$16,254.21
Howell G. & Martha Jo Mims CPYC	$31,034.52	$29,002.00
Morris & Ruth Pepper for C E	$55,325.07	$51,679.77
Bill & Hazel Phalan Endowment	$15,552.88	$14,528.21
Claudette Hamby Pickle C E Endowment	$21,971.94	$20,524.28
Publishing House Endowment 33%	$152,672.99	$142,613.60
Dr. & Mrs. E. K. Reagin Endowment	$60,557.04	$56,566.99
Jodi Hearn Rush Endowment	$12,400.24	$11,592.69
Rev. Rusty Rustenhaven Youth Ministry	$14,516.12	$13,559.67
Give for Good Endowment	$3,005.11	$2,946.76
John W. Speer Endowment for C E	$21,167.80	$19,773.10
Cornelia Swain Endowment for C E	$23,110.70	$23,504.68
Irvin & Annie Mary Swain Endowment	$27,420.78	$27,431.83
Jake Tyler Children's Ministry	$5,492.53	$5,283.56
Frank & Linda Ward Endowment (CE)	$38,561.22	$36,020.81
William Warren Endowment for C E	$12,492.77	$11,669.71
Clark Williamson Memorial	$43,987.20	$41,088.96
Helen Wiman Memorial	$4,886.60	$4,954.64
Young Adult Ministry Endowment	$25,067.05	$23,415.44
Terence R. McCain, Sr. Endowment	$6,599.64	$6,165.10
Total	**$2,172,721.91**	**$2,034,511.35**

Ministry Council - Pastoral Development Team - Ministry Team

Endowment	Ending Balance 2017	Ending Balance 2018
Awards for CP Ministers & Spouses	$27,520.36	$25,707.57
Roosevelt and Ruth Baugh	$5,846.46	$5,732.91
LaRoyce Brown Endowment	$1,821.59	$1,786.27
James & Helen Knight Endowment	$28,369.13	$26,500.39
Ministerial Endowment	$14,929.56	$13,946.09
Ministers Conference	$20,707.74	$19,343.68
Melvin & Naomi Orr Endowment	$23,246.06	$21,714.75
James Lee Ratliff Endowment	$12,392.02	$11,583.46
Norlan & Ellie Scrudder Endowment	$23,585.63	$22,032.03
James & Geneva Searcy Endowment	$35,926.83	$33,560.19
E. G. & Joy Sims Endowment	$25,023.38	$23,375.05
Leonard & Mary Jo Turner Endowment	$15,256.40	$14,251.40
Lyon Walkup Endowment	$17,101.56	$16,503.15
Arturo & Carmen Ortiz Endowment	$16,793.59	$16,467.49
Louisa M. Woosley End. for Sustaining Women in Ministry	$13,693.87	$13,428.00
Total	**$282,214.18**	**$265,932.43**

Office of the General Assembly

Endowment	Ending Balance 2017	Ending Balance 2018
D. W. Fooks Memorial Endowment	$19,838.60	$18,531.49
Publishing House Endowment (33%)	$30,185.47	$28,028.36
Robert & Olene Rush Endowment	$20,230.39	$18,897.44
Trustee Endowment	$390,179.67	$364,471.32
Total	**$460,434.13**	**$429,928.61**

Historical Foundation

Endowment	Ending Balance 2017	Ending Balance 2018
Anne Elizabeth Knight Adams Heritage Fund	$6,719.85	$9,340.19
Rosie Magrill Alexander Trust	$18,247.78	$17,046.05
Paul H. & Ann Middleton Allen Heritage Fund	$7,709.52	$7,201.80
Grace J. Beasley Birthplace Shrine	$61,292.28	$57,255.83
Ethel Beal Benedict Heritage Fund	$5,044.28	$5,086.10
Birthplace Shrine Fund	$205,806.19	$204,959.16
James L. & Louise M. Bridges Heritage Fund	$19,473.62	$18,191.17
Mark and Elinor Swindle Brown Heritage Fund	$7,577.51	$9,829.89
*Sydney & Elinor Brown Heritage Fund	$9,700.17	$9,658.34
Centennial Heritage Endowment	$93,038.75	$86,911.63
Walter Chesnut Endowment	$17,395.56	$16,443.97
Lavenia Campbell Cole Heritage Fund	$73,141.48	$68,324.65
C. P. Church in America Heritage Fund	$15,340.67	$14,330.41
CPW Archival Supplies Endowment	$32,546.11	$30,402.76
Bettye Jean Loggins McCaffrey Ellis Heritage	$2,553.93	$9,955.15
Samuel Russell & Mary Grace Barefoot Estes	$25,292.16	$23,626.56
Family of Faith Endowment	$15,830.72	$14,788.17
Gettis & Delia Snyder Gilbert Heritage Fund	$7,230.91	$6,754.73
James C. & Freda M. Gilbert Heritage Fund	$24,770.78	$23,139.71
James C. & Freda M. Gilbert Trust (HF)	$67,559.27	$63,110.11
Mamie A. Gilbert Trust	$15,622.11	$14,593.30
Henry Evan Harper Endowment CP History	$2,598.38	$2,625.82
Ronald W. & Virginia T. Harper	$5,252.80	$5,023.09
Historical Foundation Trust	$104,820.10	$99,805.21
Donald & Jane Hubbard Heritage Fund	$17,617.35	$16,983.87
Cliff & Jill Hudson Heritage Fund	$6,408.52	$5,986.54
Robert & Kathy Hull Endowment	$17,768.95	$16,599.11
Into the Nineties Endowment	$41,956.89	$39,193.78
Joe Ben Irby Endowment	$8,583.82	$8,275.67
P. F. Johnson Memorial Endowment (HF)	$20,377.79	$19,035.79
Irene A. Kiefer Endowment	$1,935.56	$1,897.95
Mr. & Mrs. Chow King Leong Heritage Fund	$6,036.83	$5,639.29
Dennis L. & Elmira Castleberry Magrill 50%	$25,353.47	$23,683.79
J. Richard Magrill, Jr. Heritage Fund	$11,390.56	$10,735.24
Joe R. & Mary B. Magrill Trust	$181,347.76	$169,404.95
Jimmie Joe McKinley Heritage Fund	$9,052.09	$8,456.05
Edith Louise Mitchell Heritage Fund	$5,070.29	$4,747.65
Lloyd Freeman Mitchell Heritage Fund	$5,070.37	$4,747.76
Snowdy C. & Lillian Walkup Mitchell Heritage	$7,231.02	$6,754.78
Rev. Charles & Paulette Morrow Endowment	$1,504.66	$2,384.25
Virginia Sue Williamson Morrow Heritage	$13,804.87	$12,895.76
Anne E. Swain Odom Heritage Fund	$27,972.61	$27,018.68
Martha Sue Parr Heritage Fund	$36,144.90	$33,764.70
Florence Pennewill Heritage Fund	$5,026.16	$4,695.18
Morris & Ruth Pepper Endowment (HF)	$17,761.75	$16,697.01
Publishing House Endowment 33% (HF)	$85,122.90	$79,702.61
Mable Magrill Rundell Trust	$18,241.46	$17,040.18
Samuel Callaway Rundell Heritage Fund	$12,320.61	$11,509.17

Historical Foundation (continued)

Endowment	Ending Balance 2017	Ending Balance 2018
Paul & Mary Jo Schnorbus Heritage Fund	$8,834.75	$8,252.98
Shiloh CPC Ellis County Texas Endowment	$8,064.76	$7,533.63
Hinkley & Vista Smartt Heritage Fund	$7,870.15	$7,822.43
John W. Sparks Heritage Fund	$104,904.90	$97,996.36
Irvin S. Annie Mary Draper Swain Heritage	$32,863.42	$31,580.16
The Trustee Hertiage Fund	$1,198.90	$5,168.63
F. P. (Jake) Waits Heritage Fund	$12,906.93	$12,056.98
Roy & Mary Seawright Shelton Heritage Fund	$11,410.84	$11,269.00
Gwendolyn McCaffrey McReynolds Hertiage Fund	$11,517.75	$10,761.27
Total	**$1,627,238.52**	**$1,558,695.00**

Our United Outreach

Endowment	Ending Balance 2017	Ending Balance 2018
George F. Battenfield Memorial	$55,091.70	$51,461.86
Daisy Bray Freeman Trust	$59,882.44	$55,936.89
Bertha Feazel Hammons Memorial	$50,901.62	$47,547.84
Kenneth & Myrtle Holsopple Memorial	$251,498.99	$234,928.06
Cliff & Jill Hudson OUO Endowment Fund	$13,091.52	$12,247.17
Knights of Honor Association Trust	$3,548.17	$3,314.40
Lowrie Estate Oil Royalties	$1,864,503.78	$1,789,456.86
Robert L. McReynolds Endowment 50%	$44,666.26	$41,723.27
The Moderators' Endowment for OUO	$40,125.21	$39,589.12
Santa Anna Church Memorial Fund	$22,166.82	$20,706.27
Tithing and Budget Endowment	$396,600.36	$370,468.95
Total	**$2,802,076.87**	**$2,667,380.69**

Cumberland Presbyterian Children's Home

Endowment	Ending Balance 2017	Ending Balance 2018
Merlyn & Joann Kitterman Alexander	$982.91	$910.49
W. A. & Elizabeth Bearden Trust	$11,190.41	$10,365.87
Grace Johnson Beasley Mem	$26,054.59	$24,134.81
Bethlehem CPC, Maury County, TN	$4,258.36	$3,944.60
James L. & Louise Bridges Scholarship	$29,409.00	$27,249.01
J. T. & Dorothy Britt Trust	$7,878.75	$7,298.25
Children's Home Endowment	$227,294.67	$210,546.99
Lavenia Campbell Cole Annuity Endow	$58,204.36	$53,915.62
Lavenia Cole Testamentary Trust - 25%	$471,702.57	$438,283.67
Lavenia Campbell Cole Trust (20%)	$14,331.73	$13,275.72
Mrs. A. L. Colvin Memorial Fund	$1,210.02	$1,186.51
John H. & Eva Cox Trust Fund	$21,814.26	$20,206.91
Steve Currie Trust	$382,922.36	$354,707.31
Daniel Class, Morningside CPC	$22,528.41	$20,868.40
Donnie Curry Davis Memorial	$131,830.31	$122,116.60
Mary Elberta Davis Memorial	$14,066.88	$13,030.39
Fred & Mattie Mae Dwiggins Memorial	$56,481.95	$52,320.13
J. S. Eustis Memorial Trust Fund	$8,917.17	$8,260.14
Winnie & Clester H. Evans, Sr. Trust	$14,887.55	$13,790.60
John M. Friedel Trust	$15,399.74	$14,265.02
Joyce C. Frisby Memorial Endowment	$19,844.59	$18,383.25
Vaughn & Mary Elizabeth Fults Trust	$14,205.17	$13,158.46
Garner-Miller Memorial Trust	$8,763.75	$8,261.03
James C. & Freda M. Gilbert Endowment (CPCH)	$81,773.45	$75,795.86
Henry & Jayne Glaspy Memorial Fund	$5,813.47	$5,385.11
Rev. W. J. Gregory Memorial	$73,069.83	$67,685.79
Glenn Griffin Endowment 33%	$31,150.66	$28,855.37
Rev. & Mrs. Henry M. Guynn Memorial	$3,236.73	$2,998.24

Cumberland Presbyterian Children's Home (continued)

Endowment	Ending Balance 2017	Ending Balance 2018
Chad Evan Harper Memorial Endowment	$13,644.31	$13,619.51
Newsome & Imogene Harvey Endowment	$1,786.74	$1,655.06
Clarence & Lula Herring Endowment	$4,253.15	$3,939.79
Kenneth & Clara M. Holsopple Trust	$37,651.60	$34,877.27
George & Lottie M. Hutchins Trust	$800,754.95	$741,752.49
Norma K. Johnson Memorial Library	$8,036.10	$7,443.95
P. F. Johnson Memorial Endow	$13,340.22	$12,357.28
Robert H. & Genevie Johnson Endowment	$3,894.43	$3,621.32
Mr. & Mrs. Robert L. Johnson	$8,405.63	$7,786.31
Violet Louise Jolly Endowment	$848.71	$786.13
Eulava Joyce Memorial Trust	$7,013.99	$6,497.20
Ruth Cypert & Harlie Kugler Memorial	$14,124.64	$13,083.88
Blanche R. Lake Endowment	$10,179.26	$9,429.20
Wade P. Lane & Maude Dorough Memorial	$6,700.00	$6,206.36
Adolphus M. Latta Memorial Trust	$36,151.16	$33,487.38
Mr. & Mrs. Robert F. Little (CPCH)	$25,526.44	$23,660.73
Charles E. Addie Mae Lloyd Endowment	$15,923.53	$14,750.23
Tony & Ann Martin Endowment	$2,878.51	$2,822.59
Mrs. Lucille (Lucy) Mast Endowment	$2,926.12	$2,869.32
W. B. & Azalee McClurkan, Sr. Memorial	$13,614.00	$12,610.87
William J. McCall Memorial Trust	$7,014.00	$6,497.19
McEwen Church Trust	$5,388.52	$4,991.49
J. C. McKinley Endowment (CPCH)	$13,281.72	$12,303.06
Velma McKinley Trust Fund	$13,281.82	$12,303.13
McKinley & Barnett Families 33%	$600,476.60	$556,936.83
Mary McKnight Memorial Trust	$7,973.97	$7,395.19
Kenneth & Mae Moore Endowment Fund	$4,958.94	$4,593.55
Operational Trust Fund	$104,310.19	$96,621.87
Bert & Pat Owen Endowment for CPCH	$1,103.04	$1,021.78
^Martha Sue Parr Endowment	$1,025.87	$942.89
Mary M. Poole Endowment Fund	$674,583.07	$624,876.71
Jack & Mary Lou Proctor Memorial Trust	$44,977.02	$41,662.86
Mary Acenal Prewitt Trust Fund	$63,583.69	$58,898.49
S. Q. & K. Maurine Proctor Trust	$3,983.72	$3,690.19
Rev. & Mrs. Joe Reed Memorial	$3,289.07	$3,225.23
Marguerite D. Richards Endowment	$17,913.58	$16,593.59
Agnew Durbin Richardson Trust	$21,248.65	$19,682.98
Pat N. & Essie H. Roberts Memorial	$41,474.92	$38,418.82
Frances Benefield Roberts Trust	$1,642.80	$1,521.80
Rev. & Mrs. John A. Russell Memorial	$3,206.85	$2,970.52
John, Ann & Mary Elizabeth Shimer	$10,558.27	$9,780.29
Rev. W. B. & Lydia Snipes Memorial	$22,788.05	$22,345.58
Don M. & Nancy E. Tabor Trust	$24,271.15	$22,483.21
Townsend Trust Fund	$27,069.94	$25,075.33
Hattie E. Wheelis Fund	$13,925.18	$12,899.08
Whitfield Family Endowment	$8,490.01	$7,864.78
Porter & Hattie S. Williamson Memorial	$120,778.01	$111,878.46
Helen and Lewis Wynn Endowment Fund	$12,633.70	$12,388.38
Maxie & Will Young Memorial Endowment	$14,619.78	$13,542.55
Dixie Campbell Zinn Memorial Trust	$4,395.04	$4,071.18
Joe Parr Trust Fund	$55,136.96	$51,074.17
Hamilton & Merion S. Parks Family Trust #3	$13,344.77	$12,416.36
Dr. John P. Austin Endowment	$20,142.27	$18,785.84
Total	**$4,769,748.31**	**$4,424,210.40**

Memphis Theological Seminary

Endowment	Ending Balance 2017	Ending Balance 2018
African-American Studies Chair	$9,907.19	$9,714.82
Emerson A. Alburty Endowment	$6,421.79	$5,291.58
John W. Aldridge Memorial Scholarship	$8,866.99	$7,275.09
Merlyn A. & Joann K. Alexander	$9,683.86	$8,112.56
Alston Family Evangelistic Association	$47,910.90	$45,611.77
Polly Atterbury Aldridge Scholarship	$11,019.35	$9,615.17
Alternate Studies Endowment	$10,946.66	$10,469.35
Virgil R. Anderson Memorial Endowment	$11,094.71	$8,884.16
Baird-Buck Chair of CP Studies	$448,982.21	$434,744.70
Walter & Eula Baker Memorial Fund	$12,510.52	$10,743.29
O. A. Barbee Endowment	$1,879.73	$1,689.97
Richard M. & Martha Carol Barker Scholarship	$10,909.21	$10,697.38
Barnes Seminary Endowment	$65,539.67	$58,392.45
Isaac R. Barnes Scholarship Endowment	$17,347.27	$15,129.65
George B. Bates Trust	$3,757.32	$3,509.77
Grace Johnson Beasley Endowment	$98,186.01	$92,497.63
Joseph E. Bedinger Memorial Library	$5,213.19	$4,869.72
Tarlton M. Belles Fund	$24,902.56	$22,187.06
Marie Blackwell Endowment	$579.33	$475.28
Larry A. Blakeburn Endowment	$2,846.55	$2,659.01
Roy E. Blakeburn Scholarship	$14,156.21	$12,410.40
Dr. Paul F. Blankenship Family Endowed Scholarship	$0.00	$21,857.09
Bowen Chapel Church Trust	$16,762.18	$12,853.98
Bowen Lecture Fund	$23,854.96	$20,637.07
Kyle D. Brantley, M. D. Memorial	$28,796.10	$28,400.70
Wes & Susan Brantley Endowment	$21,749.43	$22,395.63
Brockwell Library Endowment	$12,106.99	$10,303.46
Evelyn Brodeur	$24,725.89	$23,959.25
Brooksville CPC Endowment	$23,411.84	$20,927.30
Beth-Helen-Peggy Brown Endowment	$33,052.19	$32,391.01
Paul B. Brown Endowment - MTS	$20,149.43	$20,094.60
Paul F. & Mattie Suddarth Brown - MTS	$38,792.38	$33,407.64
W. W. Brown Scholarship	$4,775.81	$4,395.26
Finis McAdoo Bruington Board-Designated Endow	$23,411.43	$19,132.28
Davis & Gladys Bryson Education 50%	$30,346.44	$29,718.37
Henry & Alfreda Bunton Scholarship	$27,240.18	$26,432.73
Hal & Gladys Burks Memorial Fund	$7,922.71	$6,391.93
Thomas H. Campbell Library Endowment	$4,949.71	$4,557.70
Thomas H. & Margaret E. Campbell	$32,976.05	$28,919.05
Campbell-Todd Trust	$12,877.82	$10,717.82
Carlock Memorial Trust	$1,295.06	$1,209.73
Cawthon Memorial Fund	$4,300.24	$3,545.47
Mildred Chandler Endowment	$4,776.54	$3,999.77
Rev. Walter & Mrs. Sarah Chesnut Scholarship Endow	$12,808.11	$11,229.40
Gladys Chumbler Endowment	$7,505.27	$6,539.28
Marian Lisenbee Clark Endowment	$5,559.95	$4,420.64
Sallie H. Clay & Alice J. Cooksey	$315,008.72	$320,322.11
Faye E. & Ford F. Claytor Endowment	$8,061.35	$7,249.04
Lavenia Campbell Cole Annuity Endow.	$65,662.32	$60,094.90
Lavenia Campbell Cole Testamentary Trust 25%	$389,855.42	$349,721.91
Lavenia Campbell Cole Trust	$20,730.51	$18,421.74
George E. & Rouine V. Coleman Endowment	$9,372.53	$8,217.64
George E. Coleman Scholarship	$59,650.04	$53,548.57
Willene Cooper Scholarship	$35,979.82	$32,858.93
Hubert & Dortha Covington Memorial	$3,973.70	$3,711.85
James Covington Scholarship	$10,371.53	$8,880.51

Memphis Theological Seminary (continued)

Endowment	Ending Balance 2017	Ending Balance 2018
Thelma Craig Scholarship	$31,581.36	$28,986.13
Cora Hawkins Crutchfield Scholarship Endowment	$50,165.57	$50,954.53
Cumberland Hall Endowment	$5,540.40	$4,138.79
Cumberland Presbyterian Women	$37,567.12	$36,306.78
Sallie Stacy Davenport	$8,149.54	$6,958.82
Mary Elberta Davis Memorial (MTS)	$6,151.93	$5,209.27
Paul & Nancy Dekar/Immersion Studies	$6,233.87	$6,189.46
James W. & Gladys Murray Diamond	$3,350.48	$3,129.74
Margaret M. Dirks	$9,514.91	$9,310.74
Houston Dixon Memorial	$7,584.59	$6,311.76
Winifred M. Dixon Endowment	$34,048.33	$30,204.59
C. Ray Dobbins Endowment (MTS)	$2,132.18	$1,991.67
Jesse R. & Virginia R. Durham Endowment	$909,637.64	$825,707.54
Rev. Dr. Loyce Estes Endowment Fund	$9,358.13	$9,176.40
Expansion & Development Fund	$3,356.72	$3,069.67
Faith CPC, Tulsa, OK - Scholarship	$45,416.04	$40,479.83
Alice Fay Finley	$5,720.13	$5,343.25
H. Glenn Finley Library Fund	$3,028.86	$2,829.29
E. H. & Millie Finley	$2,471.12	$2,308.29
Linda Hester Fooks Memorial	$16,922.63	$13,921.89
James T. Freeman Scholarship Endowment	$0.00	$8,712.94
Jere B. Ford Family Endowment	$13,436.03	$12,715.92
Rev. J. C. & Willie Mae Forester Library	$7,756.05	$8,317.90
Vaughn Fults Endowment	$11,228.24	$10,488.40
Gadsden Area Churches Trust<	$47,505.63	$46,544.41
McAdow Gam Endowment Fund	$33,847.32	$30,716.77
John E. & Anna B. Gardner Endowment	$17,057.76	$14,990.97
Jessie B. & Noella Garner	$1,377.57	$1,286.82
Yoong S. & Anna K. Kim Family President's Fund	$65,356.54	$134,814.26
W. L. & Dot Lacey Gaston Endowment	$12,363.88	$10,767.73
Dale Gentry PAS Scholarship Endowment	$0.00	$7,409.19
Louis E. & Millie Coats Gholson	$184,773.77	$181,127.75
James C. & Freda M. Gilbert Endowment (MTS)	$16,959.25	$16,629.97
James & Martha Gill Sacred Theology	$12,747.19	$10,898.43
David E. Glasgow Endowment	$1,562.03	$1,459.12
James A. & Lenora Greer Endowment	$3,845.58	$3,770.90
Mary Guice Memorial	$15,667.00	$14,881.87
Margaret I. Gunn Memorial	$29,319.28	$28,750.00
Hamilton Chapel Fund	$662,964.76	$650,091.92
Carlton & Margaret Ann Harper Endowment Fund	$12,934.83	$12,683.68
Mrs. George N. Harris Library Memorial	$3,650.43	$3,409.90
Newsome & Imogene Daniel Harvey	$7,936.48	$7,309.75
Bettye & Dick Hendrix Scholarship	$16,172.56	$15,618.86
Henshaw Family Endowment Fund	$5,990.23	$5,124.05
Frank & Margaret Henshaw Endowment 1	$14,510.18	$14,986.13
J. David & Barbara Hester Endowment	$53,681.37	$49,630.97
Rev. E. Samuel Hicks Endowment Fund	$4,806.71	$4,489.99
Dr. Alfred D. Hill Scholarship	$8,851.99	$8,924.40
Cortis E. Hill Library	$3,932.26	$3,673.18
David & Patsy Hilliard	$12,583.28	$12,338.94
Francis A. Hobgood Trust	$32,018.86	$28,440.91
William Clarence Hodge Memorial	$3,520.55	$3,288.56
B. L. & Jewel Looper Holder	$12,314.86	$11,864.61
Lee Hollowell Trust	$14,942.04	$11,940.04
Barbara A. Holmes Lectures	$10,710.35	$10,502.37
Mr. & Mrs. J. S. Holmes Trust	$5,362.43	$5,009.09

Memphis Theological Seminary (continued)

Endowment	Ending Balance 2017	Ending Balance 2018
Kenneth & Myrtle Holsopple Endowment	$32,449.82	$28,690.53
Jack & Gwen Hood Scholarship	$85,618.20	$82,065.21
Rev. John William Howell Memorial	$2,477.84	$2,248.67
Cardelia Howell-Diamond Scholarship	$79,377.89	$77,836.63
Donald & Jane Hubbard Endowment for MTS	$12,253.75	$10,901.59
Bernice A. Humphreys Endowment	$17,933.17	$14,865.80
Charles E. & Helen Humphreys Endowment	$11,540.82	$9,593.93
Gerald S. & Louise Felts Hunter	$2,978.10	$2,781.84
George & Lottie M. Hutchins 33%	$228,100.50	$208,937.28
Mattie Hutchison Seminary Fund	$1,776.66	$1,659.61
Eugenia Turner Ingram Endowment	$3,372.10	$3,084.03
Lillian Johnston Ingram Library	$6,108.62	$5,640.25
Tom & Barbara Ingram Student Asst.	$52,086.50	$51,075.14
Virginia Howell Ingram Endowment Fund	$95,382.12	$93,530.08
Rev. W. T. Ingram, Sr. & Family Scholarship	$106,189.49	$97,184.63
William T. & Virginia H. Ingram Lectures	$133,424.81	$126,504.76
Joe Ben Irby Trust	$4,397.10	$4,107.39
Joe Ben & Julia Irby Endowment Fund	$91,032.71	$81,262.88
Virginia Irwin Memorial Endowment	$5,165.52	$4,117.99
Johns Lectures	$18,317.21	$17,961.53
P. F. Johnson Memorial	$52,548.16	$46,870.59
Robert A. & Jo S. Johnson (MTS)	$69,515.92	$66,236.75
Roby M. Johnston Endowment	$88,269.79	$80,567.92
Joiner Ministerial Scholarship	$6,421.36	$5,998.27
V. A. Jones Library Memorial	$4,321.10	$4,036.35
Kiningham-Kuehn Endowment	$11,347.85	$9,591.41
Franklin W. Latta Memorial Scholarship	$15,673.97	$13,566.61
Ruth Fumbanks Latta Endowment	$15,756.72	$13,709.73
Randal (Randy) Leslie Endowment Fund	$17,838.95	$16,780.65
C. S. Lewis & His Friends Lecture	$33,552.36	$32,924.88
Library Reserve - Seminary Development	$2,659.72	$2,418.55
Mr. & Mrs. Robert F. Little (MTS)	$31,132.87	$28,012.41
James & Louella Lively Family Endowment	$8,855.53	$8,272.03
Inez Lovelace Endowment	$38,833.85	$38,041.02
Virgil L. & Della M. Lowrie Lectures	$123,386.23	$120,893.33
Della Campbell Lowrie Endowment 20% (MTS)	$351,018.75	$307,508.59
Dennis L. & Elmira C. Magrill 50%	$30,652.43	$26,747.04
Rev. George Malone / Rev. Edmong Weir	$96,520.24	$94,607.25
W. A. Johnson Family Endowment	$16,765.75	$14,739.42
Dessa Jane Manuel Scholarship 50%	$42,157.34	$38,198.47
Marshall (Texas) CPW Endowment	$11,277.04	$10,549.93
Dr. & Mrs. Arleigh G. Matlock Scholarship	$35,502.63	$31,014.09
Charles R. Matlock Library Endowment	$5,424.88	$5,067.92
Walter L. Mayo Endowment Fund	$6,116.51	$5,713.52
Mr. & Mrs. David M. McAnulty Memorial	$14,477.33	$13,523.40
Doris McCall Memorial Endowment	$14,148.05	$12,346.22
James W. & Mary H. McCulloch Memorial	$15,937.52	$14,394.19
Margaret McCulloch Scholarship	$9,788.86	$8,625.57
F. Dwight & Bernice K. McDonald	$174,684.44	$160,988.87
McGuinness-Wood Endowment	$21,869.58	$18,544.52
Jack B. McKamey Endowment Fund	$5,897.88	$4,670.33
^Velma McKinley Memorial Endowment	$4,829.52	$4,511.27
McKinley & Barnett Families 33% (MTS)	$256,456.17	$227,234.94
Wesley McKinney Memorial Endowment	$14,197.89	$13,902.76
Maude McLin Memorial Endowment	$4,552.59	$4,252.61
Robert W. McReynolds Memorial	$5,745.59	$4,593.96

Memphis Theological Seminary (continued)

Endowment	Ending Balance 2017	Ending Balance 2018
Mr. & Mrs. W. J. McReynolds Trust	$6,297.62	$5,882.69
John E. Meeks Family Endowment Fund	$29,689.36	$31,603.29
Memphis Methodist Conference Fund	$35,800.49	$35,105.36
Ed Mikel Doctoral Scholarship Memorial	$10,798.96	$10,116.50
Sam B. & Naurine W. Miles Endowment	$5,123.10	$4,785.56
Sam B. Miles Board Designated Endowment	$50,421.49	$47,324.46
Mary Elliott Miller Endowment	$10,096.22	$9,659.73
Rev. & Mrs. W. E. Miller Scholarship	$5,995.74	$5,534.80
Robert Lynn & Elizabeth P. Mills	$9,068.64	$7,999.73
Ministerial Scholarship Endowment 40%	$10,575.13	$8,674.24
Missouri-Arkansas CO-OP PCUSA	$5,162.65	$5,062.36
John L. Mize Scholarship	$9,169.45	$8,027.97
Clinton & Eva B. Moore Endowment	$36,246.94	$35,523.74
Frank C. Moore Endowment Fund	$12,885.27	$12,615.68
The Hillman & Lorene Moore Endowment Fund	$0.00	$24,434.31
Mary E. Morefield Memorial 40%	$5,471.61	$5,111.06
Hubert W. Morrow Endowment PAS	$40,635.91	$36,026.97
Virginia Sue Williamson Morrow MT	$37,303.09	$34,649.40
Ruby Page Morton Endowment	$12,270.63	$11,166.18
William Taylor Morton Endowment	$12,917.99	$11,863.50
John & Gail Moss Endowment	$7,796.58	$7,384.53
Dr. Arthur Murrell Memorial Scholarship	$4,779.97	$4,399.13
Walter & Anna Murrie Endowment	$6,649.74	$6,211.60
Willard & Bettie Murrie Endowment	$11,628.63	$15,421.49
Gladys Teter Nichols	$103,075.03	$91,437.15
North Central Texas Presbytery Scholarship	$5,478.43	$5,117.44
Northside Presby. Church, Cleveland, TN Seminary Ed.	$113,510.95	$103,921.10
Northside Presby. Church, Cleveland, TN PAS End.	$56,755.52	$55,653.54
William H. & Nola A. Oliver Scholarship	$5,895.16	$5,440.84
Bert & Pat Owen - Shepherd's Rest	$119,263.45	$116,947.65
Palestine CPC Endowment at MTS	$3,962.62	$3,691.59
Walter G. (Pete) Palmer Endowment (PAS)	$281,701.13	$259,623.02
Paskell & Bernice Parker Endowment	$4,648.14	$4,341.89
Parr Scholarship Endowment	$52,328.28	$46,584.55
Hughston R & Lorraine Peyton Endowment	$7,600.62	$7,316.70
Rev. G. F. Phelps Memorial Scholarship	$16,163.23	$11,176.33
John W. Piper Endowment Fund	$25,205.10	$21,592.66
Platte-Lexington Seminary	$22,186.47	$19,653.18
Gertie Allen and Martha Jean Faith Endowment	$7,475.96	$6,988.95
Bernice A. Humphreys Scholarship Endowment	$159,725.16	$156,623.79
Bettie Press Library Fund	$4,915.58	$4,591.66
S. Q. Proctor Ministerial Scholarship	$8,690.22	$7,985.84
Klahr & Iris Raney Endowment Fund	$19,743.67	$16,425.22
Eugene & Agnes Richardson Endowment	$7,986.53	$6,385.65
Evelyn B. Crick Richmond Endowment	$61,537.47	$59,506.79
Roy Roberts Memorial Endowment	$1,720.80	$1,607.38
Mrs. W. H. Rochelle Endowment Fund	$10,358.60	$8,733.23
Hudson & Robbie C. Roseberry	$92,824.57	$90,076.91
W. L. & Mary K. Rolman Scholarship	$17,257.20	$15,114.79
William & Dolores Rustenhaven Endowment	$5,673.19	$5,299.40
Beverly St. John/Theology & Arts	$10,010.83	$10,308.78
Saint Timothy CPC	$3,591.76	$3,355.09
Herschel A. & Iris L. Schultz	$135,643.13	$119,633.94
Clara Scott Family Chair - Part I	$358,525.14	$301,571.05
Clara Scott Family Chair - Part II	$222,206.58	$207,539.91
George W. Scott Endowment Fund	$7,256.66	$6,880.04

Memphis Theological Seminary (continued)

Endowment	Ending Balance 2017	Ending Balance 2018
W. H. Scott Family Endowment	$11,373.67	$10,558.34
Marie C. Scrudder Memorial	$4,553.83	$4,253.81
Seminary Commitment Campaign	$3,326.97	$2,975.98
Seminary Development Fund Endowment	$843.09	$787.55
Seminary Scholarship Fund	$9,427.78	$8,203.34
Ed Shannon Endowment	$9,858.37	$9,174.91
E. Thach & Jerry Shauf Endowment	$16,615.48	$15,049.26
Robert E. Shelton Scholarship	$4,680.83	$4,589.92
Robert M. Shelton Scholarship	$3,588.88	$3,352.44
Ruby Burris Shelton Endowment	$5,308.21	$4,958.45
Dick & Virginia Singellton Endowment	$14,326.61	$12,439.72
Esther Smith & Search Parish Endowment	$2,238.63	$2,091.10
Odus H. Smith Memorial Endowment	$5,039.94	$4,707.88
Katherine Hinds Smythe Endowment	$6,767.34	$6,635.97
W. B. Snipes Memorial Scholarship	$14,822.89	$4,378.52
Truman Barrett Snowden Memorial	$5,870.60	$5,036.08
Dorothea Snyder Endowment	$5,846.65	$5,260.46
L. D. & Dathel Jones Stacey Endowment	$677.04	$632.44
Henry L. Starks Scholarship	$220,011.08	$214,529.19
Anne Stavely Endowmet Fund	$2,429.76	$2,269.69
Eva Jane Stewart Trust 50%	$57,131.05	$52,120.17
J.W. Stiles Lectures	$42,983.91	$42,149.24
Rev. Elizabeth Stone Mem. Schol.	$2,168.25	$2,101.03
Lela Stricklen Endowment	$31,047.05	$24,892.49
Maymie Stovall Memorial Trust 25%	$12,310.21	$10,556.19
Roy Stucker Scholarship Fund 50%	$45,129.92	$44,214.81
Charles Studdard Memorial	$19,039.46	$16,710.33
Emma Elizabeth Suddarth Memorial	$7,138.31	$6,667.96
Robert H. & Lois Went Taylor Endowment	$12,294.47	$10,475.66
Thomas V. Taylor Seminary Student	$6,392.77	$5,905.64
Verdys E. Taylor Trust	$2,410.82	$2,251.78
A. J. Terry Scholarship	$2,294.96	$2,143.75
Theological Seminary General Endowment	$5,259.92	$1,472.89
Virgil H. & Irene R. Todd - OT EXCL	$88,557.78	$86,838.26
Tri-Mu Bible Class Scholarship	$72,672.41	$70,146.62
R L Truax, M L Truax, R L Truax, Jr Award for Academic Ach	$9,579.94	$9,393.95
Carl Walker Endowment	$8,574.74	$7,001.21
Mr. & Mrs. Carl Forbis Ward Memorial	$5,657.68	$5,284.87
Tom V. Warnick Memorial	$54,632.01	$54,776.70
Geneverette Warr Endowment	$5,985.19	$4,817.79
Warren, MI, First CPC Endowment	$8,996.67	$8,821.95
Rev. David & Leota Watson Scholarship Endowment	$6,146.07	$5,961.43
The Rev. Harlon & Mary Edith Watson Endowment	$59,971.98	$60,510.79
Virgil T. & Sue B. Weeks	$7,870.12	$7,351.53
Lynn Westbrook Memorial Endowment	$9,438.83	$8,279.60
Mae Westbrook Memorial Endowment Fund	$4,489.46	$4,193.65
The Weston Endowment	$15,205.63	$13,260.82
J. W. Wilder Scholarship	$205,849.71	$189,387.37
Alline Williams Endowment	$9,200.75	$7,651.65
Wayne Wiman Scholarship	$31,666.94	$27,642.44
Davis/Winston Scholarship for National Baptist Students	$4,713.26	$4,621.73
Lamar & Ellen Wilson Memorial Scholarship	$17,806.78	$14,045.48
Women's Issues in Ministry Endowment	$6,613.17	$6,484.76
Louisa Woosley Endowment Fund	$90,380.21	$89,407.57

Memphis Theological Seminary (continued)

Endowment	Ending Balance 2017	Ending Balance 2018
Rev. Charles W. Hall Endowment for Pastoral Excellence	$24,566.88	$24,489.16
Dr. Thomas D. Campbell Endowment	$11,447.02	$10,279.48
Rev. Matthew Miller Endowment	$2,446.48	$2,398.97
Total	**$11,258,591.87**	**$10,608,594.56**

Miscellaneous

Endowment	Ending Balance 2017	Ending Balance 2018
Lavenia Cole Test. Trust Temp.	$10,428.22	$49,357.28
CP Retirement & Health Maintenance (Sue Galey)	$16,827.53	$15,937.18
Lillie M. Dickerson Memorial Fund	$79,114.49	$74,739.84
Verna Fillius Green Charities Endowment	$9,038.34	$7,106.89
Hodgeville Cemetery Association	$16,614.97	$16,292.38
Jamie Aros Endowment Fund	$106,785.86	$104,712.40
Laddie Lollar Scholarship	$21,873.85	$16,642.37
McKinley & Barnett Families Temp.	$2,949.82	$12,183.22
Matching Gift Endowment Fund	$59.34	$58.22
Terrell D. and Jacqueline C. Maynard Endowment	$21,557.53	$21,138.94
Ethel Phillips Endowment	$66,793.58	$67,494.99
Thomas P. & Barbara J. Semmens Scholarship	$2,040.77	$2,001.15
Stobbe Mathematics Scholarship	$55,464.57	$54,387.66
Maymie Stovall Trust	$309,489.75	$295,335.94
Mary Ann Walton Trust	$2,463,065.36	$2,305,762.64
Parr Estate/Mission Synod Ministerial Aid	$166,227.54	$162,999.90
Total	**$3,348,331.52**	**$3,206,151.00**

Bethel University

Endowment	Ending Balance 2017	Ending Balance 2018
J. E. Ash Memorial	$8,261.55	$7,717.20
Daisy J. Barger & Lena J. Davis	$20,951.89	$19,571.38
Grace Johnson Beasley (Memorial)	$18,445.56	$17,230.22
Herman Osteen Beasley Memorial	$45,527.88	$42,528.07
Bethel CPC, Columbia Presbytery	$2,095.32	$1,957.29
Boyett Trust	$36,854.14	$34,425.85
Rev. & Mrs. C. L. Bruington Library	$12,312.34	$11,501.13
Davis O. & Gladys Bryson Educ. 50%	$45,930.79	$42,904.46
Lavenia Campbell Cole Annuity End	$82,744.53	$77,292.63
Lavenia Campbell Cole Trust - 20%	$20,145.52	$18,818.14
Cumberland Presbytery Scholarship	$13,517.31	$12,626.66
J. Claud & Mary L. Dickinson Fund	$8,311.74	$7,764.09
Mary L. Claud Dickinson Educ.	$472,453.97	$441,324.71
Rev. & Mrs. Walter E. Dillow Memorial	$26,153.73	$24,430.52
Winifred M. Dixson Endowment	$52,509.12	$49,049.36
Jack & Ewie Freeman Trust	$21,517.23	$20,099.48
Vaughn & Mary E. Fults Min. Scholarship	$41,598.71	$38,857.85
Samuel K. Gam & Mamie S. Gam Endowment	$26,687.05	$24,932.66
Greensburg CPC Memorial Scholarship	$8,418.99	$7,864.29
Glenn Griffin Endowment - 33%	$40,328.34	$37,671.17
Fenner Heathcock Memorial Fund	$86,317.75	$80,630.39
Roy Hickman & Ruth Hughes Hickman	$45,262.85	$42,280.56
Francis A. Hobgood Trust 25%	$35,441.63	$33,106.44
George & Lottie M. Hutchins (Trust)	$290,534.05	$271,391.21
Dr. P. F. Johnson Memorial Endowment	$64,241.44	$60,008.66
Joiner Ministerial Scholarship (Bethel)	$6,961.46	$6,502.79
Rev. E. R. & Forest Ladd Memorial	$2,733.74	$2,553.61
Robert F. & Jane L. Little (BC)	$30,830.89	$28,804.59

Bethel University

Endowment	Ending Balance 2017	Ending Balance 2018
Della Campbell Lowerie 20%	$415,304.63	$387,940.83
Dessa Jane Manuel Scholarship 50% (Bethel)	$194,138.77	$181,347.28
Albert & Belle McDonald Trus	$521,400.53	$487,046.22
Cliff McElroy Memorial Trust	$24,496.75	$24,021.09
Nyta Miller Scholarship	$7,770.50	$7,080.11
Nell Miller Scholarship	$3,476.27	$3,247.27
Ministerial Scholarship Endowment 60%	$136,672.38	$127,667.23
Bert & Pat Owen Endowment for Bethel	$2,318.94	$2,166.13
Max & Ethel Mize Parker Scholarship	$22,543.27	$21,057.95
S. Q. Proctor Ministerial Scholarship	$13,393.42	$12,510.96
Agnes D. Richardson Endowment Fund	$10,604.23	$9,905.64
Pauline Rucker Memorial	$4,763.79	$4,449.95
Rev. & Mrs. J. Howard Scott Memorial	$11,629.97	$10,863.69
Esther M. Smith Trust	$7,882.87	$7,363.48
Martha S. & W. Horace Snipes Scholarship	$2,666.65	$2,491.11
Eva Jane Stewart Trust - 50%	$66,370.24	$61,997.20
Roy Stucker Scholarship 50%	$56,089.43	$52,393.78
Richard Swain Memorial Scholarship	$25,746.39	$24,049.98
Weigel Bible Class	$11,099.72	$10,368.38
Total	**$3,105,458.27**	**$2,901,813.69**

Cumberland Presbyterian Church in America

Endowment	Ending Balance 2017	Ending Balance 2018
CP Church in America Min. Education	$730.62	$716.46
CP Church in America World Mission	$923.13	$905.21
National Missionary Society of the CPCA	$0.00	$28,545.52
Total	**$1,653.75**	**$30,167.19**

Congregations

Endowment	Ending Balance 2017	Ending Balance 2018
Kate Maxwell Allen Trust	$6,557.30	$6,125.20
Robert & Jane Long Endowment	$0.00	$94,303.96
Grace Bright Circle Missions	$11,918.64	$11,490.10
Brunswick Cumberland Presbyterian Church Trust	$15,745.62	$14,945.70
Jane and Ed Chapman Endowment	$2,722.21	$888.88
Chinese Mission of San Francisco	$29,547.28	$27,600.45
Christ (FL) Tom W. Kelley Ed Fund	$33,095.45	$31,084.14
Christ (FL) Mary Beth Swindle Scholarship	$99,274.96	$91,945.24
Calico Rock CPC - Christian Service Center End	$6,470.51	$6,344.85
The Mary Cloud Fund	$45,952.40	$42,924.59
Lavenia Campbell Cole Endowment	$233,440.44	$203,026.51
Dyersburg - Charles F. Moore C/T	$62,516.54	$61,302.65
Dyersburg - Jenny Edwards Endowment	$37,415.06	$36,688.56
1st Presbyterian Church of Alabaster - Gillis Endow	$12,582.32	$12,338.03
1st Presbyterian Church of Alabaster - Kent Endow	$9,420.50	$9,237.61
Fairfield C P Church Trust	$60,596.82	$56,052.97
Frankie Floyd Fund for Education	$16,036.57	$15,725.17
Faith-Hopewell CPC Ministries Endowment	$1,195.04	$1,171.86
Germantown - Christian Education Ministry	$32,997.74	$28,949.81
Germantown - Outreach Ministry	$7,991.45	$7,836.24
Germantown - Worship Ministry	$2,550.06	$2,500.57
Germantown - Eugene/Rosa Mae Warren	$15,072.26	$14,779.60
Germantown - William Pickle Member Care	$6,968.95	$6,895.23
Basil & Gertrude Green Scholarship Fund	$69,510.10	$63,567.37
Glenn Griffin Endowment 33% (Congregational)	$47,832.83	$44,681.22
Francis A. Hobgood Trust 50%	$71,735.83	$67,009.25

Congregations

Endowment	Ending Balance 2017	Ending Balance 2018
Hohenwald CPC (Congregational)	$366,191.73	$342,063.89
Hopewell Cumberland Presbyterian Church Endow	$597.56	$731.96
Albert M. & Delia Jackson Memorial	$5,263.83	$4,917.40
Albert S. Johnston Trust	$64,071.34	$59,849.76
Orn/Laughlin Trust	$7,074.98	$6,608.87
Lawrenceburg CPC - Jack & Marjorie Anderson End	$152,089.90	$143,936.25
Lawrenceburg CPC - Mason/Jennings	$102,707.31	$95,940.09
Della Campbell Lowrie Trust	$86,764.74	$47,427.83
Lucado Endowment	$778,918.12	$719,203.45
Manchester CPC - Christian Education Endowment	$15,466.46	$15,662.02
Marshall (MO) David Guthrie Youth	$7,476.48	$7,331.36
Marshall (MO) 50 Year Church Member Rec	$8,762.10	$6,217.93
CPC of Marshall (TX) Endowment	$134,758.20	$63,007.20
Marshall (TX) Ewing Chapel Cemetery	$74,683.07	$73,569.19
McKenzie CPC - Beasley Endowment	$77,499.52	$72,393.20
McKenzie CPC - Julia Patterson Irby	$13,942.51	$13,023.88
Medina CPC Trust	$3,107.15	$3,046.82
Louise Moffitt Trust Fund	$316,406.89	$295,559.33
Mount Moriah Cemetery Fund (W. TN Presbytery)	$365,352.68	$350,167.40
New Salem Cemetery Fund	$115,584.50	$111,424.67
Oliver's Chapel Cemetery Trust	$117,938.57	$115,648.57
Trimble CPC - Horace J. Coffer Memorial Trust	$5,889.82	$5,501.73
Trimble CPC - Howard Glasgow Memorial Trust	$5,889.77	$5,501.76
Trimble CPC - Bob & Chris Page Family Trust	$3,674.81	$3,432.67
Carolyn Smythe Parks Memorial Trust	$173,916.83	$162,457.73
E. E. Parks Memorial Trust	$4,508.76	$4,211.66
Hamilton & Merion S. Parks Family	$56,882.26	$53,313.53
Rev. Hamilton Parks Memorial Trust	$12,949.93	$12,101.56
W. H. Parks Memorial Trust	$7,154.55	$6,683.16
Franklin Pierce Memorial Trust	$10,308.48	$9,629.23
William W. & Lou W. Pierce Memorial	$2,050.20	$1,914.74
Prigmore Endowment	$85,119.15	$83,466.40
J. Dixie Johnson Primm Endowment	$2,048.29	$2,008.54
Red Bank CPC Endowment	$36,035.91	$35,393.77
Robinson Cemetery Endowment	$42,594.42	$41,767.37
Saint Timothy CPC Trust	$2,185.03	$1,083.01
Short Creek CPC Memorial Fund	$23,730.64	$24,250.68
Swan Cumberland Presbyterian Church	$17,091.47	$16,759.62
Inman & Mildred Swain Memorial	$69,301.90	$64,735.70
Thomas D. & Mary Jo (Adams) Vaughan	$581,979.86	$543,634.10
Thomas & Mary Jo Vaughan Outreach	$58,538.48	$54,681.45
West Union Cemetery - Old Committee	$63,396.37	$57,371.91
Rev. Jonathan Clark Endowment	$814.10	$1,559.58
Calico Rock CPC - Mildred B. Curless Danielson	$2,097.80	$2,057.06
Calico Rock CPC - Every Member Endowment	$11,418.69	$11,969.98
Calico Rock CPC-J. W. & Frances Fountain Endow	$1,031.49	$1,207.33
Calico Rock CPC -Dixie Jennings Gray Endowment	$8,897.76	$8,725.00
Calico Rock CPC - Ernie Horton Gray Endowment	$8,421.96	$8,258.41
Calico Rock CPC-Fayetta Hall Endowment	$1,822.96	$1,787.59
Calico Rock CPC - Willis Newton Hankins End.	$866.18	$849.33
Calico Rock CPC - Joann Smith Hudson Endowment	$2,322.05	$2,277.00
Calico Rock CPC - Zelda Killian Endowment	$1,709.29	$1,676.08
Calico Rock CPC - James & Ariel Utt-Landrus End	$8,636.97	$8,469.25
Calico Rock CPC- John & Ernette "Ernie" Parker	$1,933.39	$1,895.88
Calico Rock CPC - Ray & Velma Perryman End	$9,392.25	$9,209.86
Calico Rock CPC - Beatric Virginia Pino End	$757.67	$742.96

Congregations (continued)

Endowment	Ending Balance 2017	Ending Balance 2018
Calico Rock CPC - Pietro "Pete" Pino Endowment	$5,967.27	$5,851.40
Calico Rock CPC - Muriel Thompson Ryan End	$1,720.34	$1,686.93
Calico Rock CPC - Sean Vann Endowment	$4,198.65	$3,925.33
Calico Rock CPC - Wayland - Seay Endowment	$16,154.57	$15,840.89
Calico Rock CPC - Wayne & Gaye Wood End	$12,958.84	$12,707.23
Calico Rock CPC - Trimble House Maintenance Endow	$7,285.06	$7,143.62
Calico Rock CPC - Pete & Betty Riggins	$2,317.26	$2,272.25
Calico Rock-Dr. Thomas D. & Linda Coleman Campbell	$0.00	$2,915.37
Total	**$5,129,776.00**	**$4,810,075.48**

Congregations

Endowment	Ending Balance 2017	Ending Balance 2018
Arkansas Presbytery - Camp Peniel	$27,843.66	$26,009.60
Arkansas Presbytery - Higher Education	$67,557.89	$63,298.55
Rev. Leo E. Smith Min. Memorial Scholarship	$14,314.69	$14,346.55
Daisy Bell Belcher Estate	$36,971.39	$36,253.53
Cauca Valley Presbytery - Hogar Samaria	$145,493.11	$144,573.33
Columbia Presbytery Endowment	$376,405.58	$360,549.55
Crystal Springs Camp - Fred Ramsey	$36,582.26	$35,871.90
East Tennessee - Philip Norris Jones	$11,792.83	$11,563.88
William J. Eldredge Trust Fund	$12,394.85	$11,578.20
Ephraim McLean Sr. Memorial Fund	$64,457.21	$63,205.63
Missouri Presbytery - Education Fund	$48,379.57	$47,440.17
Missouri Presbytery - Church Development & Revitalization	$29,325.26	$28,755.86
Missouri Presbytery - Missions Growth	$28,432.82	$27,880.73
Oklahoma/Kansas/Nebraska Mission	$1,517,006.70	$1,453,754.99
Red River Presbytery - Camp	$53,143.80	$52,111.88
Red River Presbytery Christian Ed. General	$10,024.03	$9,829.39
Tennessee Georgia Presbytery Capital	$32,829.75	$33,159.04
Tennessee Georgia Presbytery Candidate Education	$27,941.55	$28,293.83
Trinity Presbytery - Trinity Investment Fund	$927,979.10	$926,528.04
Trinity Presbytery - Trinity Church Development Fund	$147,969.33	$162,066.56
W. Tennessee Presbytery - Grace Beasley Fund	$127,753.33	$125,272.71
W. Tennessee Presbytery - Camp Clark Williamson	$21,316.91	$20,903.02
Covenant Presbytery - Russ Milton Scholarship End	$15,304.92	$15,196.77
Cumberland Presbytery -Missions - McInteer End	$67,458.92	$63,014.17
Cumberland Presbytery - Missions - Millwood	$5,736.98	$5,358.94
Cumberland Presbytery -Missions - Ray A. Morris	$2,108.00	$1,969.12
Cumberland Presbytery - Missions - NCD	$147,881.17	$138,489.53
Cumberland Presby Missions - Reid's Chapel End	$48,486.01	$45,291.32
Cumberland Presbytery - Missions-Royal Oak End	$46,381.98	$43,325.24
Cumberland Presby - Scholarships - Freeman End	$141,241.86	$131,935.66
Cumber Pres Scholarships - E. L. Freeman Farms	$198,576.23	$185,492.30
Cumberland Presby - Scholarships - Howard End	$52,702.18	$49,229.71
Cumberland Presby - Min. Educ - Bremen CPC 25%	$54,723.46	$51,117.84
Cumberland Presby - Cont. Educ - Hampton End	$126,485.53	$118,151.58
Cumberland Presbytery - Cont. Edu - KY Synod	$5,256.82	$4,910.45
Cumberland Presby - Gen. Prog - Bremen CPC 75%	$164,170.25	$153,353.30
Cumberland Presby - General Program - KY Synod	$10,540.49	$9,846.01
Cumberland Presby -Gen Prog - Eugene A. Leslie	$3,068.08	$2,865.92
Cumberland Presby - Gen Prog - Wilcoxson End.	$4,216.20	$3,938.38
Cumberland Presby Christian Ed - Camp Koinonia	$34,392.60	$32,126.52
Cumberland Presby - Christian Ed - Cecil Huff	$4,468.55	$4,174.13
Cumberland Presby - Christian Ed - Sam Macy	$1,552.92	$1,450.63
Cumberland Presby Higher Ed - Joseph H. Butler	$1,961.46	$1,832.20
Cumberland Presby - Higher Ed - Sharon Church	$28,523.20	$26,643.88
Cumberland Presbytery -Robert L. McReynolds 50%	$44,882.22	$41,924.98
Total	**$4,976,035.65**	**$4,814,885.54**

D. ENDOWMENT PROGRAM LOANS

Historical Review

Through investing up to 40% of the assets of the Endowment Program in the witness of the Church, the message of good news concerning Christ is strengthened both in the United States and overseas. A survey of old files in the Historical Foundation and in the vault of the Board of Stewardship reveals the important role played by this aspect of the investment policy. Over the past sixty-five years from 1944 to 2009, 841 loans were made to congregations, presbyteries, and synods. From 2010 through 2018 an additional 17 loans have been made. Through these loans, $42,714,405 has been provided in financing for expansion of facilities and extension of witness.

A look at the different periods during which loans have been made provides a picture of growing endowments (and of post-World War II inflation!).

Period	Loans	Total Loaned	Average
1944-49	35	$145,755	$4,164
1950-59	171	$1,360,441	$7,955
1960-69	208	$3,056,891	$14,697
1970-79	166	$3,609,084	$21,741
1980-89	101	$4,349,120	$43,061
1990-99	102	$14,440,837	$141,577
2000-09	58	$10,571,723	$182,271
2010-18	17	$5,180,554	$304,738

While looking at the table, it should be noted that the Cumberland Presbyterian Church Investment Loan Program began January 1, 2001. Since its creation most of the larger loans are made through the Investment Loan Program. At the end of the year the Endowment Loan Balance was $1,720,549.

Down through the years, donors to endowments have found satisfaction in the knowledge that the prudent investment of their gifts strengthened not only the work of particular churches, institutions, and causes which they designated to receive the income but also the broader witness of the Church.

E. OTHER CHURCH LOANS

In addition to loans from the Investment Loan Program and the Endowment Program there is another source available to the board for loans to churches.

1. Small Church Loan Fund

This fund, formerly known as the Revolving Church Loan Fund, was created through an endowment established by Lavenia Cole and gifts to the "Into the Nineties" Capital Gifts Campaign. All interest earned by the loans is added to the fund to increase the amount available for loans. There were five loans from the Small Church Loan Program at the end of 2018 totaling $112,353.

The rate of interest for the Small Church Loans made during 2018 was based on the loan rate established by the Cumberland Presbyterian Church Investment Loan Program at the beginning of each quarter. These loans are generally small loans of $70,000 or less and most are amortized over five years.

IV. CUMBERLAND PRESBYTERIAN CHURCH INVESTMENT LOAN PROGRAM, INC.

In 1976, the board began a program to provide an opportunity for flexible investment of current temporary cash assets of congregations and agencies of the church. The primary purpose of the program is to provide income to participants as a foundation for ministry. On January 1, 2001, the assets of the original program, Cash Funds Management, were transferred to the new Cumberland Presbyterian Church Investment Loan Program, Inc.

For the year ending 2018, the assets for the Investment Loan Program were $26,115,421 compared to $25,608,257 in 2017. There were 324 individual, congregation and agency accounts. At year end, deposits on account totaled $17,461,773. The total loans were $6,753,862 at year end.

For 2018, the corporation complied with the regulatory requirements in the states of Tennessee and Kentucky and was able to offer investment opportunities to individual Cumberland Presbyterians in the states of Tennessee, Kentucky, Texas, Missouri and New Mexico.

The board of directors is composed of the following: Mike St. John, president; Jim Shannon, vice-president and Debbie Shelton, secretary, and Gary Tubb. Robert Heflin serves as Treasurer and Executive Secretary. During the past year, the board met twice in regular session.

In order to simplify administration and focus on the strengths of the Investment Loan Program, the board took action to limit the offering of notes and depository accounts to "ready access accounts." All note holders (individuals) and depository account holders (churches and church agencies) with funds invested in these "on demand" accounts participated in the $618,348 which the program paid in interest. For 2017 the interest rate paid to account holders was 2.75%. The interest rate paid to account holders can fluctuate from one quarter to the next. In recent years there has been renewed interest for congregations to open new accounts because the interest paid is higher than current CD rates.

The table below provides a breakdown of the investment mix.

INVESTMENT LOAN PROGRAM
Securities & Investments

20.6%	Cash Equivalents	$3,645,211
9.9%	Preferred Stocks	$2,422,966
0.9%	Mutual Funds	$1,392,861
68.6%	Taxable Fixed Income	$10,000,735
100.0%		$17,461,773

At the end of 2018 there were 20 loans to congregations made through the Investment Loan Program. The loan balance was $6,753,862. Every accountholder is investing in the future ministry of the Cumberland Presbyterian Church as well as receiving interest on their investment.

V. EMPLOYEE BENEFITS ADMINISTRATION AND RESEARCH

A. PURPOSE

The second of two broad areas of the work of the board is in employee benefits administration and research. The purpose of this program is as follows:

To support the lay and ordained employees of the church as they venture to be faithful under the call of Christ and the Church to the daily demands of providing leadership to congregations and Church agencies whom are the incarnation of the Body of Christ, the family of God at work in the world.

B. VISION

The board has a vision of uniform benefits for all Cumberland Presbyterian clergy, including group health insurance, group long-term disability coverage, and participation in the General Assembly's retirement plan. Ministers would then know what to expect when they are called to another church. No longer would some ministers have to do without what is considered in the secular world to be basic employee benefits. No longer would ministers and their families have to settle for being relegated to second class status. The reality is, as several General Assemblies have recognized, that this is possible if we work together in much the same manner that we send out missionaries and do a lot of other ministry. Good employee benefit plans are in place and they would be healthier and stronger if used and supported by all employees of the Cumberland Presbyterian Church.

VI. RETIREMENT PROGRAM

Since 1952, the board has provided a retirement program open to all church employees of the Cumberland Presbyterian Church. The program gives opportunity for churches and their employees to provide a source of retirement income based on voluntary contributions. In 1987, a new Cumberland Presbyterian Retirement Plan No. 2 was established as a qualified 403(b) defined contribution plan and in 1990 the General Assembly amended the plan to include the churches and employees of the Second Cumberland Presbyterian Church, now known as the Cumberland Presbyterian Church in America.

A. PLAN AMENDMENTS

As new needs arise or deficiencies in the original plan document for Cumberland Presbyterian Retirement Plan No. 2 become apparent, the General Assembly has the authority under Article IX Section 9.01 of the Plan to amend the same. In 2012 a revised plan document was approved by the General Assembly. Recently the IRS has adopted a pre-approved program for 403(b) plans, thus in 2018 the plan was restated to take advantage of the new regulations. At this time we are also able to make updates to the plan. The only update made, was the ability to contribute up to the IRS deferral limit each year. In 2019, this amount is $19,000 and may change in the coming years with no need to amend the plan.

B. YEAR END REPORT

On December 31, 2018, there were 306 active participants in the Retirement Plan. There were 18 receiving direct monthly payments as a result of their elections. In addition to these participants, there were 10 persons who were receiving annuity payments purchased through the Plan and for whom the Plan issues 1099-R's.

During 2018, $1,332,792 was dispersed to or for participants, a decrease of 18.7% over 2017s $1,638,563. Contributions totaled $704,541 and were down 11.8 % over 2017s $799,189. Realized and unrealized loss on investments totaled $694,389 compared to 2017 gain of $2,736,328. The rate of return credited to the accounts for the year was -3.1% compared to 12.5% for 2017. (Comparative annual rates of return for: previous three years +5.3%, previous five years +4.1%, and from the beginning of professional management in March 1982, +9.1%.)

Effective January 1, 2011, Gerber/Taylor Management was retained to manage our stock portfolio. We have continued our relationship with Met West, a bond manager, and RREEF, a private real estate investment trust manager. Matt Robbins and Stacy Miller of Gerber/Taylor continue to be very helpful with keeping the board updated on market conditions and investment strategies.

VII. MINISTERIAL AID PROGRAM

A. MINISTERIAL AID

1. Full Benefit Recipients

As of March 2019, there are 5 Cumberland Presbyterian Church recipients of the full benefit of $546 (adjusted for inflation yearly) per month (increased from $300 on July 1, 2010), and 3 that receive partial benefits due to them having more income than the threshold established. The monthly total of these payments is $3,622; annually, $43,464 is paid. Beginning May 1, 2015, the method of distributing funds to overseas presbyteries was revised with the help of the Missions ministry team. Ministerial aid will now be offered in overseas presbyteries on an individual basis. Presently there are 7 recipients in Cauca Valley Presbytery and 5 recipients in Andes Presbytery that are receiving aid in the amount of $300 a month, for a total of $3,600 a month or $43,200 annually.

In October 2005, the board decided to distribute 75% of the previous year's surplus to the state side recipients. The Board of Stewardship has approved a cap of a maximum of $4,000 in lieu of large distributions that may have a negative effect on other benefits received, such as SSI, or state assistance.

2. Basic Requirements. The new basic requirements and amount for stateside recipients for the Ministerial Aid program were approved at the General Assembly of the Cumberland Presbyterian Church in June 2010. The poverty levels have been updated to the latest available figures. They are as follows:

Full Benefit of $546 a month for State Side Recipients

1. Minimum age is full retirement age set forth by the Social Security Administration.
2. Minimum years of service to the church - 15.
3. Can qualify for aid if a participant in the Cumberland Presbyterian Retirement Plan if income is below poverty level as established by the US Census Bureau.
4. Physical and/or mental disability (doctor's statement required) at any age, however, a minimum of ten years of service is required if less than 60 years of age.
5. Individuals' income cannot exceed federal poverty guidelines set forth for the year by the US Census Bureau. Poverty level is $12,490 a year or $1,040.83 a month for 2019.
6. Couples income cannot exceed federal poverty guidelines set forth for the year by the US Census Bureau. Poverty level is $16,910 a year or $1,409.17 a month for 2019.
(The GA Board of Stewardship is authorized to look at each case in light of unusual financial hardship; thus, application may be made even if income levels exceed the ceiling.)
7. Presbytery obtains information and approves (approval can be given by the committee or board charged by presbytery with this responsibility); certification of approval is sent to the General Assembly Board of Stewardship.
8. Surviving spouse is eligible if above items 2, 3 and 4 have been met.

**Note: Recipient is responsible to verify if receiving Ministerial Aid would affect his or her SSI, Social Security or other benefits.

Cumberland Presbyterian Church applicants must submit to the Board a listing of assets and liabilities, so the net worth can be determined. The board urges presbyteries to maintain contact with persons under the Ministerial Aid Program who live within their bounds. Should there be serious unmet needs, the presbytery is urged to contact the board so that it may determine how the Ministerial Aid program can be of assistance in meeting those needs.

3. Cumberland Presbyterian Church in America. The CPCA currently has 3 participants who receive monthly payments. On June 1, 2015, the aid amount increased from $109 a month to $510 a month and the CPCA contributes 50% of the yearly aid and the CP Ministerial Aid Endowments 50%. The current amount received monthly per participant is $546. The CPCA normally pays its share in June or July following their General Assembly.

4. Ministers in Overseas Presbyteries. Since May 1, 2015, with the help of the Missions Ministry Team, Aid is available to those in overseas presbyteries who qualify on an individual basis. The Cumberland Presbyterian Church is present in 13 different countries and each country presents its unique legislation of how they manage pension plans according to laws and standards for salaries. The Mission Ministry Team will be the liaison between the Board of Stewardship and the Presbyteries outside of the United States aiding the Board in identifying the needs overseas and interpreting pension laws and standards for salaries. At present, aid is being sent to the Cauca Valley Presbytery and Andes Presbytery in Colombia, South America.

B. SPECIAL FINANCIAL NEEDS AID

At the Spring 2014 Board of Stewardship meeting, the Board approved the use of funds from the Ministerial Aid Cash Fund ILP to be used in special situations where illness has caused a financial hardship for those that are not eligible for Ministerial Aid. At present there are eight individuals who have received payments.

VIII. INSURANCE PROGRAMS

The insurance programs of the board have been assigned by the General Assembly beginning in the middle of the previous century. Dental and Vision Insurance is the newest, begun in December 2008. Property and casualty insurance is the oldest, begun in 1951. While all of the insurance programs are important, group life and health insurance, begun in 1961, touches many lives in a personal way and often at times of deep anxiety. In all, about 179 men, women, and children depend on this program to meet their health care needs.

A. PROPERTY & CASUALTY INSURANCE

The Board of Stewardship, Foundation and Benefits secures property and casualty insurance coverage against accidental loss for the General Assembly Corporation, Board of Stewardship, Discipleship Ministry Team, Missions Ministry Team, Ministry Council, Communications Ministry Team, Pastoral Development Ministry Team, Memphis Theological Seminary, and Historical Foundation.

Our broker is Lipscomb & Pitts of Memphis, Tennessee. For 2019, Travelers Insurance carries our Property & Casualty policy and $2,500,000 in earth quake coverage, Mt. Hawley Insurance Company provides an additional $16,120,473 in earthquake coverage. Philadelphia carries our Directors & Officers coverage and Hanover carries our General Liability, Professional Liability, Crime, Automobile, and Umbrella policies. Beginning October 23, 2014, Workers Compensation coverage has been with Bridgefield Casualty.

B. GROUP LONG TERM DISABILITY INSURANCE

The presbyteries of Arkansas, Columbia, Covenant, Cumberland, del Cristo, East Tennessee, Missouri, Murfreesboro, Nashville, North Central, Red River, Robert Donnell, Trinity, West Tennessee and The Center have now established non-contributory long term disability programs insured currently through Cigna. This leaves only four stateside presbyteries (Choctaw, Hope, Grace and Tennessee Georgia) without a program. The quarterly rate applied to participant's salaries is .45 per $100 of salary.

There are three primary reasons for ministers to want the coverage and for presbyteries to want to provide the protection. The group rate is significantly lower than individual policy rates and does not require a large cash outlay to cover all full-time ministers in a presbytery; housing allowance and/or the fair rental value of a manse is included in the definition of salary for ministers; and, there is no medical qualification requirement in order to enroll. These advantages over individual policies make this coverage very attractive, especially to those who have previously purchased their own policies. In addition, a provision was negotiated with Cigna by the Board's consultant, whereby ministers, upon leaving a participating presbytery to serve in a non-participating presbytery, may continue the coverage if he or she so desires. The new employing church is then billed for the quarterly premium. There are now 10 ministers and two employees who are receiving or have received benefits from this insurance program. There are 167 participants as of January 1, 2019.

C. GROUP TRAVEL ACCIDENT INSURANCE

This policy provides twenty-four hour coverage on "named employees" for accidental death, dismemberment, or loss of sight while on business travel. The maximum benefit is $50,000 and there is also a $1,000 medical benefit. The annual premium is $900. We renew this policy every 3 years. Thirty-one named positions are covered under this policy.

D. GROUP HEALTH & LIFE INSURANCE

The board has used a fully-insured, managed care approach to provide group health insurance for Cumberland Presbyterian clergy and lay employees since March 1, 1999. Blue Cross / Blue Shield of Tennessee is our insurance carrier in 2019. In 2016, the group plan was split into 4 separate community rated groups which provided more competitive rates. For 2019, the plans premiums were flat after an increase in the deductible amounts. Lipscomb & Pitts, a Memphis based insurance company, is our insurance broker, and Craig Wright, our agent.

1. Premiums.
Efforts to maintain affordable premiums and comprehensive coverage are the biggest challenges we face. Premiums for 2018 are listed below and reflect the assistance from the Premium Stabilization Reserve. The goal for 2019 is to utilize approximately $140,633 from the Premiums Stabilization Reserve to help reduce the premiums participants pay for health insurance. In 2018 we utilized $154,583.96 from the Premium Stabilization Reserve.

Health Insurance Premiums for 2019		
	Option 1	Option 2
Employee Only	$700	$564
Employee & Spouse	$1,385	$1,111
Employee & Child(ren)	$1,280	$1,027
Family	$1,977	$1,586

The Health Plans are on a calendar year as far as deductible and pricing is concerned. It is our objective with the new community rated plans to have the renewal pricing by no later than October 1, so presbyteries and agencies can have the figures for their fall meetings and better plan their budgets for the coming year. Periodically we seek bids from other carriers in an effort to keep premiums competitive. When this is done, we may not have the new premium information by October 1.

Open enrollment period is the month of December. It is during this time that an employee can enroll or change their health insurance coverage unless there are special circumstances.

2. Participation.

As of February 1, 2019, 109 employees and 70 dependents for a total of 179 people depend on the Cumberland Presbyterian Church Health Insurance Program. A breakdown of family units by size at February 1, 2019 is listed below.

FAMILY UNITS BY SIZE

	Number of Units	Total
Emp. Only	75	75
Spouse Only	0	0
E & 1	0	0
E & 2	5	15
E & 3	0	0
E & S	14	28
Families of 3	5	15
Families of 4	5	20
Families of 5	4	20
Families of 6	1	6
Families of 7	0	0
Total	109	179

The following table shows the enrollment figures from January 2018 to December 2018. As one can see the numbers fluctuate from month to month.

	MONTHLY GROUP INSURANCE ENROLLMENT		
	EMPLOYEE COVERAGE	DEPENDENT COVERAGE	TOTAL
January	76	43	119
February	76	44	120
March	76	44	120
April	76	43	119
May	75	43	118
June	74	42	116
July	75	42	117
August	73	39	112
September	73	37	110
October	73	37	110
November	75	37	112
December	76	36	112

3. Premium Stabilization Reserve (Formerly Emergency Reserve)

The Premium Stabilization Reserve is invested in the Endowment Program Fund account which had a balance of $1,791,320 as of December 31, 2018. The Emergency Health Insurance Reserve was established in compliance with the 1992 General Assembly directive to be used in "emergency" situations to match presbyterial emergency fund disbursements. The 1998 General Assembly approved the Board's recommendation to allow the Board to use the Emergency Reserve to maintain the stability of the group health and life insurance plan. This allows these funds to be used for purposes outside of the original scope of the reserve. In 2018, the Board of Stewardship used $154,584 to help offset some of the cost of the health insurance premiums and have estimated that approximately $140,633 will be used in 2019 to help in reducing premiums for the health insurance participants.

4. Dental and Vision Insurance

On December 1, 2008, we began offering Dental and Vision insurance, on a voluntary basis, for anyone working at least 30 hours or more for any Cumberland Presbyterian Church, its agencies, boards, and institutions. Peter Whitely is the agent of record. At present there are 71 participating employees.

5. Jessie W. Hipsher Health Insurance Endowment

The Jesse W. Hipsher Health Insurance Endowment was created as the first step in the board's goal to raise $10,000,000 in endowments for the support of the Cumberland Presbyterian Health and Life Insurance Program. The endowment was established on March 6, 2004. At its establishment $11,450 had been raised. The balance of the endowment as of December 31, 2018 was $46,624.

6. Health Education / E-Mail Newsletter

To further educate participants in matters concerning healthcare, participants receive a monthly e-newsletter entitled, *TopHealth,* published by Oakstone Publishing. The monthly e-newsletter is full of health related tips that can be easily implemented by readers. The two page newsletter can be read within a matter of minutes. Also initiated in 2008 is the E-Mail newsletter that is designed as an information tool to help the participants of the Health and Retirement programs stay on top of happenings within the Board of Stewardship.

7. Wellness Program

Blue Cross offers a Preventive Health Guide and the Blue 365 discount program for a range of item from fitness, healthy eating, personal care and wellness and even information on financial health. Also offered are the Nurse chat 24/7/365 and Physician Now where you can speak to a physician on call.

Respectfully submitted,
Gary Tubb, Board Member
Robert Heflin, Executive Secretary

THE REPORT OF THE HISTORICAL FOUNDATION

I. GENERAL INFORMATION

A. OFFICERS OF THE BOARD

The officers of the board are as follows: Pat Ward, president; Rev. Mary Kathryn Kirkpatrick, vice-president; and Michael Fare, secretary. Susan Knight Gore is the director and treasurer of the Historical Library and Archives.

B. BOARD REPRESENTATIVES TO THE CPC & CPCA GENERAL ASSEMBLIES

The board's representative to the 189th General Assembly of the Cumberland Presbyterian Church and the 144th General Assembly of the Cumberland Presbyterian Church in America is Pat Ward. The alternate is Jackie Cooper.

C. MEMBERSHIP AND MEETINGS OF THE BOARD

The board is currently composed of the following members: from the Cumberland Presbyterian Church in America—Jackie Cooper, Dorothy Hayden, Rev. Joe Howard III, Willie Lynk, and Pat Ward, from the Cumberland Presbyterian Church—Michael Fare, Robin McCaskey Hughes, Rev. Mary Kathryn Kirkpatrick, Ashley Lindsey, Lisa Oliver, and Kelly Shanton.
The Board of Trustees met, September 15, 2018, and February 22, 2019.

D. MEMBERS WHOSE TERMS EXPIRE

The first terms of Robin Hughes and Ashley Lindsey expire with the 2019 meeting of the Cumberland Presbyterian General Assembly, and they are eligible for reelection. The third term of Mary Kathryn Kirkpatrick expires with the 2019 meeting of the Cumberland Presbyterian General Assembly, and she is not eligible for reelection.
The first term of Willie Lynk expires with the 2019 meeting of the Cumberland Presbyterian Church in America General Assembly, and he is eligible for reelection.

E. STAFF

Susan Knight Gore serves as the Archivist of the Historical Foundation. Missy Rose is the archival assistant for the Foundation.

II. ASSEMBLY REPORTING

As a matter of official structure, relative to the CPC, there is a Board of Trustees composed of members from both the CPC and CPCA, and relative to the CPCA, there is a committee composed of members from the CPCA.

III. PROGRAMS AND ACTIVITIES

A. HISTORY INTERPRETATION AND PROMOTIONAL ACTIVITIES

1. The 1810/1874 Circle
In order to enlist the financial support of interested members of our churches in the work of the Foundation, the 1810/1874 Circle was created. Membership is based on a financial contribution of $25 or more per year. Income through such gifts enables the Foundation to meet expenditures and is vital to the continued work of the Foundation.
We appreciate the support given to the Foundation by all members of the 1810/1874 Circle and encourage other members of the Cumberland Presbyterian Church and the Cumberland Presbyterian Church in America to join this donor group.

2. Patrons

Persons who contribute $100 or more to one of the endowments of the Historical Foundation become patron members and receive a certificate. Patron memberships may also be given in honor or in memory of an individual.

3. Heritage Churches

Congregations contributing a minimum of $1,000 to an endowment of the Historical Foundation become Heritage Churches and receive a framed certificate. There are six categories of recognition and churches can move from one level to another.

Heritage Church $1,000 - $4,999
Silver Heritage Church $5,000 to $9,999
Golden Heritage Church $10,000 to $24,999
Platinum Heritage Church $25,000 to $49,999
Diamond Heritage Church $50,000 to $99,000
Jubilee Heritage Church $100,000 and up

4. Presbyterial Heritage Committees/Presbyterial Historians

To promote interest in the work of the Foundation and to nurture work in history on the presbyterial level, the Historical Foundation seeks to work cooperatively with the Presbyterial Heritage Committees/Presbyterial Historians of both general assemblies. The brochure, *Suggestions for Heritage Committees and Presbyterial Historians,* is available from the Foundation. The board expresses its appreciation to the presbyteries that have Heritage Committees/Presbyterial Historians.

5. Denomination Day Offering

The 2019 Denomination Day Offering was designated to fund the conversion of fragile and deteriorating analogue media to digital formats in order that it might better be preserved.

The Foundation expresses appreciation to congregations and others groups who received special offerings for the work of the Historical Foundation on Denomination Day. This special offering provides an opportunity for congregations to directly contribute to the support of the Historical Foundation as well as the Foundation supplying educational materials to each congregation.

B. PUBLICATIONS

1. Promotional Materials

The Historical Foundation provides promotional materials describing its purpose and work, the various means of financially supporting this work, and listings of available publications and prints for sale through the Foundation. These materials are available on the Foundation's website.

2. Publication Series

The Foundation has a number of titles and prints available for purchase. Income from the sale of these items goes into the Historical Foundation Trust, a permanent endowment supporting the Foundation's work. Titles available are:

1883 Confession of Faith.
1895 Cumberland Cook Book.
Cumberland Presbyterianism and Arminianism Compared/Contrasted on Selected Doctrines by Joe Ben Irby.
Faith Once Delivered; Some Indispensable Doctrines of the Christian Faith by Joe Ben Irby.
Family of Faith: Cumberland Presbyterians in Harrison County [Texas], 1848-1998 by Rose Mary Magrill.
God So Loved by Roy Hall.
History of East Side Cumberland Presbyterian Church, Memphis, Tennessee, Memphis Tennessee: 1926-1986, by the Historical Committee.
History of the Cumberland Presbyterian Church by B. W. McDonnold.
Jerusalem Cumberland Presbyterian Church: A Documentary and Pictorial History by Anne Elizabeth Swain Odom.
Legacy of Grace: Louisiana and Texas Cumberland Presbyterian People & Places of Trinity Presbytery by Rose Mary Magrill.
Life and Thought of Finis Ewing by Joe Ben Irby.

Life and Thought of Milton Bird by Joe Ben Irby.
Life and Thought of Reuben Burrow by Joe Ben Irby.
Life and Thought of Robert Verrell Foster by Joe Ben Irby.
Life and Thought of Stanford Guthrie Burney by Joe Ben Irby.
Life and Times of Finis Ewing by F. R. Cossitt.
Soundings by Morris Pepper.
Theological Snippets by Joe Ben Irby.
This They Believed by Joe Ben Irby.
What Cumberland Presbyterians Believe by E. K. Reagin.
Women Shall Preach: Celebrating 125 Yeas of Ordained Women in Ministry in the Cumberland Presbyterian Church.
Prints of the *Samuel McAdow Home* and the *First Meeting of Cumberland Presbytery*.
These items are available for sale from Cumberland Presbyterian Resources.

3. Denomination Day Resources

All the Past is but the Beginning of Beginning (Denomination Day resource) is available on the Foundation's web site under the Resources section: http://www.cumberland.org/hfcpc/resource/
It includes eight dramas intended to present the birth of the Cumberland Presbyterian Church and the Cumberland Presbyterian Church in America. A hard copy may be requested from the Foundation office.

4. Online Promotion

Recognizing the increasing value of emerging social media, the Historical Foundation employs a Facebook group, "Historical Foundation of the CPC & CPCA," to engage an expanding audience of Cumberland Presbyterians in denominational history and heritage. By showcasing collection acquisitions, the Foundation expands the knowledge of those materials sought for preservation as well as the nature of archival development. The Foundation also employs a Facebook Page. The Facebook Page is somewhat more informal and is ideal for announcements.

C. HISTORICAL FOUNDATION AWARDS

1. Award in Cumberland Presbyterian History

The Foundation encourages the writing and publication of papers on all aspects of the history of the Cumberland Presbyterian Church in America and the Cumberland Presbyterian Church. One means of promoting such writing is the Historical Foundation Award in Cumberland Presbyterian History. A $300 prize is awarded to the author entering the best paper on any CPC or CPCA history subject which meets in form and content the requirements set by the Board of Trustees and judged by the board appointed awards committee. All manuscripts submitted to the competition become property of the Foundation and are added to the Historical Library and Archives.

The contest follows the calendar year, and entries for the 2019 competition are encouraged. All entries will be accepted through December 2019 for this year's contest. Any entries received following the deadline of December 31st will be automatically entered in the 2020 competition.

Guidelines and entry forms for submitting manuscripts to the competition are available from the Foundation office as well as on the internet, http://www.cumberland.org/hfcpc/Awards.htm. The Historical Foundation appreciates the participation of past and future CPCA and CP historians in this program.

2. Awards of Recognition

Awards of recognition are certificates given to organizations or individuals in recognition of historic events or contributions to the preservation of our heritage as Cumberland Presbyterians. Appropriate applications for the award are: particular churches celebrating anniversaries of their organization; any judicatory or agency celebrating publication of a written history; celebrations of history or historic event in a creative or unusual manner; individuals who have provided continued service for 50 years or more as members of a local congregation or presbytery; individuals who have served for 40 years or more in a continuing leadership role (including pastors) within a local church. Individuals, churches, or presbyterial heritage committees may make application for the issuing of an award by contacting the Foundation office. Application forms are supplied by the Foundation office as well as the internet, http://www.cumberland.org/hfcpc/Awards.htm.

D. RELATIONSHIPS

Presbyterian Historical Society of the Southwest

The Presbyterian Historical Society of the Southwest is an agency of The Synod of the Sun, Presbyterian Church (USA) and Cumberland Presbyterian Churches in Arkansas, Louisiana, Oklahoma and Texas. Members of the Cumberland Presbyterian Church who serve on the board of this organization are Reverend Norlan Scrudder, Reverend Perryn Rice, and Doctor Rose Mary Magrill.

IV. HISTORICAL LIBRARY AND ARCHIVES

A. RESEARCH SERVICE

The Foundation's main research commitment is to the agencies, local congregations, and members of the Cumberland Presbyterian Churches. Since the Historical Library and Archives of the Historical Foundation serves as the official repository for the Cumberland Presbyterian General Assemblies, this is our focus. Although the separation of research into two types designated by their mode of access has been rapid and dramatic, both the traditional and "cyber" mode contribute to and enhance the other.

1. Traditional/Physical Access

Hands on access to primary source material remains the vital heart of historic and theological research. Rather than being diminished by increased electronic resources, traditional research has broadened due to heightened awareness of primary sources in an expanding information age. The Foundation receives research requests by personal visitors, mail, e-mail, and telephone. As time permits, requests are researched. Responses are sent to the requestor, as well as pertinent information on ministers, congregations, presbyteries and synods being placed on our website for future researchers.

2. Electronic Access

The Foundation's website continues to expand in order to provide greater access to the materials in the Historical Library and Archives. As well as being a research tool, the internet provides an invaluable and inexpensive means of promotion for the physical collections of the Historical Library and Archives, the activities of the Historical Foundation, and for the greater community of faith called Cumberland Presbyterians. Information at the site includes: general information about the Foundation, entire texts of important historical documents, historical information on particular congregations, ministers, presbyteries, and synods. Beginning in 2018, the Foundation added a YouTube Channel for historic films documenting the faith-life of Cumberland Presbyterians. The gateway URL to the Foundation's website is http://www.cumberland.org/hfcpc/. The YouTube Channel can be accessed directly at https://www.youtube.com/channel/UCTk4Wnc8b1T96d0L8Vkt4lg or through the gateway URL.

B. ACQUISITIONS

The Historical Library and Archives regularly receives items published by the two denominations, *Minutes of the General Assembly of the Cumberland Presbyterian Church, Preliminary Minutes of the General Assembly of the Cumberland Presbyterian Church, Yearbook of the General Assembly of the Cumberland Presbyterian Church, The Cumberland Presbyterian, Missionary Messenger, Minutes of the General Assembly of the Cumberland Presbyterian Church in America, Preliminary Minutes of the General Assembly of the Cumberland Presbyterian Church in America,* and *The Cumberland Flag.* Synods and presbyteries deposit four copies of their printed minutes in the Historical Library and Archives. In addition, books, pamphlets, theses, dissertations, records and publications of general assembly, boards, agencies, institutions, and task forces; records and publications of synods and presbyteries, session records and other materials of particular churches, biographical material of Cumberland Presbyterian and Cumberland Presbyterian Church in America ministers, photographs, audiovisual materials, and museum items were among the accessions received. The 2018 Accession List closed with 124 accession groups.

Some of the highlights added to the collection in 2018 include:

Audiovisual Items

Reverend Joel Rice preaching at the 120th General Assembly of the Cumberland Presbyterian Church in America. Wednesday Morning Worship, June 8, 1994. DVD.

Hendersonville Cumberland Presbyterian Church. Hendersonville, Tennessee. Sermons on DVD. June 26, 2016-March 5, 2017.

Books

Acts of the General Assemblies of the Presbyterian Church in the U.S.A. and the Cumberland Presbyterian Church in the Matter of the Reunion and Union of the Respective Churches: 1903-1906. Philadelphia, Pennsylvania: Office of the Stated Clerk, 1909.

Buchanan, Candice L. *A Waynesburg College Family: The Legacy of Alfred Brashear & Margaret Kerr (Bell) Miller.* Pittsburgh, Pennsylvania: by the author, 2015.

DeBoer, Clara Merritt. *His Trust is Marching On: African Americans Who Taught the Freedmen for the American Missionary Association 1861-1877.* New York: Garland Publishing, 1995.

Robinson, John L. *The Possibilities of Salvation a Common Heritage.* First Anniversary Sermon Delivered by Rev. John L. Robinson, Pastor of the Cumberland Presbyterian Church, Henderson, Ky., Sunday, June 8th, A. D. 1890. Henderson Journal Steam Print.

Spence, Tom, and Elmo Guthrie. *The History of the Burns Flat Cumberland Presbyterian Church*, 2018.

Tasty Dishes from Here and There. Compiled by the Maggie Connor Guild. First Cumberland Presbyterian Church, Daingerfield, Texas, 1954.

West, Marvin. *Thank You, Lord for Beaver Creek Cumberland Presbyterian Church.* Powell, Tennessee: 1 Source Printing and Graphics, 2017.

White Oak Pond Cumberland Presbyterian Church. Lebanon, Missouri. *150th Celebration.* August 12, 2018.

Periodicals

Colored Cumberland Presbyterian Church In the United States of America and Liberia, Africa. *Minutes of the Seventy-Ninth General Assembly*. June 11-15, 1953.

Cumberland Presbyterian Banner. Volume IV, Number 39 (July 31, 1908). Tullahoma, Tennessee. T. A. Havron, Editor and Publisher.

Cumberland Flag. Volume 51, Number 11 (November 1982).

Intermediate-Senior Quarterly. Volume 25, No. 4 (October, November, December, 1933). Rev. W. H. McLeskey, Editor.

Second Cumberland Presbyterian Church. *Souvenir Book.* 113th General Assembly. June 15-20, 1987. Louisville, Kentucky.

Institutions

By-Laws of Bethel College, M'Lemoresville, Carroll County, Tenn. Adopted by the Board of Trustees, at Their Annual Meeting, Held August A. D. 1850. Trenton, Tennessee: Printed at the Star Spangled Banner Office, 1850.

Catalogue of Cumberland University, Lebanon, Tennessee. 1885. Lebanon, Tennessee: Printed at the Register Book and Job Office, 1885.

Laws of Cumberland College, at Princeton, Kentucky: Revised and Amended by the Board of Directors, August 1, 1841. Princeton, Kentucky: Printed by M. Rodgers, 1841.

Museum Items

Bowling Green Cumberland Presbyterian Church. Bowling Green, Kentucky. Pulpit from the old church that was downtown.

Hope Presbyterian Church. Valrico, Florida. Stained glass window made by Sidney and Lita Swindle. Removed from the church when it closed.

Margaret Hank Memorial Cumberland Presbyterian Church. Paducah, McCracken County, Kentucky. Communion Set.

Tennessee Synodical CPW. Cumberland Presbyterian Church. Quilt. Has names of local church CPW members. Women of Faith. Carolyn Mahew Jackson gathered signatures while serving in leadership positions in the late 70s and early 80s. She completed this quilt top shortly before her death in July of 2016. Quilted by Clarksville Cumberland Presbyterian Mission Quilters in 2016.

Rev. Joel Rice. Pulpit Robe.

Other Congregational Records

Austin, First Cumberland Presbyterian Church. Austin, Texas. Women's Organization. Various names and records. Ladies Aid Society 1915-1922, 1925-1941, Missionary Society 1935-1964, 1941-1942; 1943-1945, 1945-1951; Mamie Brown Auxiliary 1961-1976; Janie Thomas Auxiliary 1923-1955, 1967, 1983, 1986-1989; Senior Missionary Auxiliary 1951; Mattie Turner Missionary Auxiliary 1952-1955; Mora Griffith Circle 1969-2004; Cumberland Presbyterian Women 1976-1983, 1983-1991; Ruth and Naomi Auxiliary 1975-1985.

Canaan Cumberland Presbyterian Church. Madison County, Alabama. Court Document. *This is to certify that David Maxwell, Wm. Gray Jr. And Daniel P. Friend are appointed Commissioners of the*

Canaan Congregation of the Cumberland Presbyterian Church. Madison County, Alabama and are hereby autherised [sic] to transact any and all business pertaining to sd. Congregation assigned by session on behalf of sd. Congregation. Finis E. Harris, George Davis, Wm. Gray Jr., Daniel B. Friend. This 18 of March 1833.

Mount Vernon Cumberland Presbyterian Church. Hawesville, Hancock County, Kentucky. Deeds. August 5, 1870 and August 25, 1884.

Nashville, First Cumberland Presbyterian Church. Nashville, Tennessee. *Annual Report of the Session of the First Cumberland Presbyterian Church of Nashville, to the Congregation, for 1869.* Nashville, Tennessee, 1870.

Photographs

General Assembly. Cumberland Presbyterian Church. Photograph. Panoramic. Bowling Green, Kentucky. May 15, 1913.

Grace Cumberland Presbyterian Church. Lincoln Park, Michigan. Photograph. 8 x 10, B & W. Tenth Anniversary, April 24, 1949.

Rev. Samuel Coleman Lockett 1853-1922. Photograph. 10 ½ x 14. B & W.

Mt. Sterling Cumberland Presbyterian Church in America. Sturgis, Kentucky. Photographs. Color, 8x10.

N.A.C.P.Y.F. Cumberland Presbyterian Church. Photograph. 35th N.A.C.P.Y.F. July 14-21, 1958, Ovoca, Tennessee.

Postcards

Arkansas Cumberland College. Clarksville, Arkansas. In 1920 the name was changed to The College of the Ozarks. In 1987 the school achieved full university status and was renamed The University of the Ozarks. Postcard. Lithograph, divided back, about 1905.

Bethel College. McKenzie, Tennessee. Postcard. Lithograph, divided back, about 1903.

Union City Cumberland Presbyterian Church. Union City, Tennessee. Postcard. Divided back, lithograph, about 1910.

Willamette Presbytery. Presbyterian Church (U.S.A). Postcard. Group photo, divided back, real photo, 1913.

Presbyterial Records

Gadsden Presbytery. Cumberland Presbyterian Church. Minutes. October 29, 1932-June 29, 1939; March 13-14, 1941-March 15-16, 1951; September 13, 1951-March 14, 1957; September 12, 1957-October 24, 1963; March 5, 1964-October 19, 1967. Original manuscript books.

Princeton Presbytery. Cumberland Presbyterian Church. Minutes. April 3, 1906-October 3, 1922; April 3, 1923-October 8, 1940; April 8, 1941-October 9, 1956.

Talladega Presbytery. Cumberland Presbyterian Church. Minutes. November14, 1929-February 18, 1932 and May 29, 1932-July 21, 1932.

Sermons

Reverend Morris Grethel Clark 1921-2008. Sermons.
Reverend Dr. James David Hester 1931-2014. Sermons.
Reverend Dr. Robert McElroy Shelton 1934-2018. Sermons.

Session Records

Austin, First Cumberland Presbyterian Church. Austin, Travis County, Texas. Session Records. February 28, 1846-June 13, 1852; January 1859-October 15, 1869; December 12, 1869-November 3, 1883; June 29, 1884-May 15, 1898; June 6, 1898-November 15, 1904; December 2, 1906-December 3, 1918; December 9, 1904-November 14, 1905; November 1906-July 1909; January 7, 1919-December 6, 1921; January 10, 1922-November 5, 1931; January 12, 1932-December 15, 1940; March 18, 1949-April 11, 1963; May 14, 1963-January 12, 1964; January 12, 1964-December 20, 1981; January 17, 1982-December 17, 1989; January 28, 1990-December 20, 1994; January 17, 1995-December 27, 1998; January 26, 1999-December 16, 2002; July 25, 2000-December 10, 2000; February 25, 2002-December 16, 2002; January 26, 2003; January 23, 2006-December 18, 2006; January 22, 2007-December 17, 2007; January 28, 2008-December 22, 2008.

Bethel Cumberland Presbyterian Church. Atoka, Tipton County, Tennessee. Session Records. April 18, 1932-March 26, 1962; June 27, 1962-February 12, 1978; November 12, 1978-August 23, 1981; April 12, 1988-July 24, 1994; August 10, 1994-November 12, 1997.

Blackford Cumberland Presbyterian Church. Blackford, Webster county, Kentucky. Session Records. December 22, 1904-August 29, 1924; May 31, 1925-April 5, 1942; September 4, 1949-September 6, 1959.

Brandon Cumberland Presbyterian Church. Valrico, Hillsborough County, Florida. Name changed to Hope Presbyterian Church, Valrico, Florida. Session Records. December 6, 1988-November 16, 1995.

Brooksville Cumberland Presbyterian Church. Noxubee County, Mississippi. Session Records. December 1, 1884-November 29, 1925.

Christ Cumberland Presbyterian Church. Tampa, Florida. Session Records. September 8, 2002-December 2015.

Forrest Avenue Cumberland Presbyterian Church. Gadsden, Etowah County, Alabama. Session Records. January 9, 1956-March 4, 1959; October 6, 1958-December 20, 1964; January 6, 1965-December 14, 1970; January 11, 1971-December 12, 1977; January 8, 1978-December 19, 1983; January 16, 1984-August 21, 1989; September 18, 1989-December 18, 1995; January 15, 1996-November 15, 2000; January 24, 2001-October 22, 2014.

Hope Presbyterian Church. Valrico, Hillsborough County, Florida. Session Records. October 14, 1999-October 9, 2006; November 13, 2006-December 20, 2016; January 24, 2017-May 15, 2018.

Margaret Hank Memorial Cumberland Presbyterian Church. Paducah, McCracken County, Kentucky. Session Records. October 9, 1944-March 5, 1951; April 1, 1951-April 11, 1955; May 6, 1955-April 1, 1956; November 27, 1955-December 2, 1968; January 6, 1969-December 17, 1979; January 21, 1980-December 21, 1987; January 3, 1988-August 27, 1995; September 24, 1995-June 27, 2001; July 25, 2001-June 23, 2005; July 27, 2005-August 1, 2007; and also 1928-1963 on microfilm.

Mount Hermon Cumberland Presbyterian Church. Cookeville, Tennessee. Session Records. May 25, 1889-March 25, 1906; June 1907-April 1952; 1960-July 25, 1964; July 9, 1978-October 29, 2008.

Park Avenue Cumberland Presbyterian Church. Paducah, McCracken County, Kentucky. Session Records. January 8, 1928-December 6, 1935.

Park Avenue Cumberland Presbyterian Church. Paducah, McCracken County, Kentucky. Name changed to Margaret Hank Memorial Cumberland Presbyterian Church by Mayfield Presbytery April 5, 1938. Margaret Hank Memorial Cumberland Presbyterian Church. Paducah, McCracken County, Kentucky. Session Records. January 3, 1936-September 24, 1944.

Pilgrim's Rest Cumberland Presbyterian Church. McKenzie, Carroll County, Tennessee. Session Records. April 11, 1954-April 10, 1977; February 12, 1978-September 25, 2005.

Salem Cumberland Presbyterian Church. Greensburg, Green County, Kentucky. Session Records. January 22, 1887-March 12, 1918; March 9, 1919-October 3, 1965.

Union Grove Cumberland Presbyterian Church. Repton, Crittenden county, Kentucky. Session Records. December 1948-January 26, 1964; April 26, 1964-October 8, 1972.

Walnut Grove Cumberland Presbyterian Church. Burlison, Tipton County, Tennessee. Session Records. August 25. 1932-May 6, 1962.

Whitney Cumberland Presbyterian Church. Whitney, Hill County, Texas. Session Records. February 16, 1908-September 1940; April 13, 1941-February 17, 1980; March 9, 1980-June 27, 2015.

Woodlawn Cumberland Presbyterian Church. Steens, Lowndes County, Mississippi. Session Records. June 8, 1890-September 14, 1905; April 11, 1915-May 12, 1935; July 15, 1950-Nov. 11, 1962; January 1, 1963-February 20, 1972; December 9, 1973-January 27, 1991.

Synodical Records

Kentucky Synod. Cumberland Presbyterian Church. Minutes. October 28-30, 1896; October 27-29, 1897. Printed minutes.

Illinois Synodical Camp. Illinois Synod. Cumberland Presbyterian Church. "Pop-Off." Camp Newsletter. August 7-12, 1934. Dixon Springs, Illinois.

In all judicatories, from the session of the congregation through presbytery, synod, and the General Assemblies of both the Cumberland Presbyterian Church and the Cumberland Presbyterian Church in America, minutes form the legal record of the judicatory. Without these records there is often nothing to document persons joining the church, ordination as elder and clergy, disciplinary actions, etc. It is important to be aware that legally original minutes are always the property of the judicatory for which they are created. Should that judicatory cease to exist, the next higher judicatory becomes custodian responsible for securing and preserving the records of the extinct body. It can be difficult to convince persons that records kept by their relative are not family property but the General Assemblies of both denominations have ruled the only legal repository for the records of extinct judicatories is the Historical Foundation.

RECOMMENDATION 1: That the General Assembly instruct presbyteries to obtain the session records of a congregation at the time the church is closed and then deposit them in the Historical Foundation.

V. BIRTHPLACE SHRINE

The Birthplace Shrine located at Montgomery Bell State Park near Dickson, Tennessee was dedicated June 18, 1960. This site consists of the Memorial Chapel and a replica of the Reverend Samuel McAdow's log house. Since 1994, the Foundation has been responsible for the preservation and promotion of the Birthplace Shrine. Four endowments provide funds for maintenance and repairs: the Grace Johnson Beasley Birthplace Shrine Fund, the Birthplace Shrine Fund, the Henry Evan Harper Endowment for Cumberland Presbyterian History, and the P.F. Johnson Memorial Endowment. Gifts to these endowments provide for the continued preservation of the Birthplace Shrine. Interested donors are encouraged to contact the Foundation office. Another means of support are the fees collected from couples who use the chapel for their wedding ceremony. These funds are added to the Birthplace Shrine Fund and earnings are used for maintenance and special projects. The Board encourages individuals and groups to visit the Birthplace Shrine as an act of remembering our heritage and envisioning our future as Cumberland Presbyterians.

Recognizing the recognition and visibility that the Birthplace Shrine provides for the Cumberland Presbyterian denominations, the Foundation both sponsors and regularly participates in three activities at the Birthplace: Denomination Day, Easter Sunrise Service, and Christmas at the Bell. Both the Denomination Day and Christmas at the Bell events are costume re-enactments which interactively interpret denominational history for both Cumberland Presbyterians and other park visitors.

Groups and individuals are encouraged to contact the Foundation to set up work days and special projects. The Foundation thanks the Heritage Committee of Nashville Presbytery and the Charlotte Cumberland Presbyterian Church for their continuing volunteer upkeep of the property.

VII. FINANCIAL CONCERNS AND 2020 BUDGET

A. BUDGETS

The 2020 line-item budget of the Historical Foundation has been filed with the CPC General Assembly Office.

B. ENDOWMENTS

Anne Elizabeth Knight Adams Heritage Fund
Rosie Magrill Alexander Trust
Paul H. and Ann M. Allen Heritage Fund
Grace Johnson Beasley Birthplace Shrine Fund
Ethel Beal Benedict Heritage Fund
Birthplace Shrine Fund
James L. and Louise M. Bridges Heritage Fund
Mark and Elinor Swindle Brown Heritage Fund
Sydney and Elinor Brown Heritage Fund
Centennial Heritage Endowment
Walter Chesnut Heritage Fund
Lavenia Campbell Cole Heritage Fund
Cumberland Presbyterian Church in America Heritage Fund
Cumberland Presbyterian Women Archival Supplies Endowment
Bettye Jean Loggins McCaffrey Ellis Heritage Fund
Samuel Russell & Mary Grace (Barefoot) Estes Endowment
Family of Faith Endowment
Gettis and Delia Snyder Gilbert Heritage Fund
James C. and Freda M. Gilbert Heritage Fund
James C. and Freda M. Gilbert Trust
Mamie A. Gilbert Trust
Henry Evan Harper Endowment for Cumberland Presbyterian History
Ronald Wilson and Virginia Tosh Harper Endowment
Historical Foundation Trust
Donald and Jane Hubbard Heritage Fund
Cliff and Jill Hudson Heritage Fund

Robert and Kathy Hull Endowment
Into the Nineties Endowment
Joe Ben Irby Heritage Fund
P. F. Johnson Memorial Endowment
Irene A. Kiefer Endowment
Chow King Leong Endowment
Dennis Lawrence & Elmira Castleberry Magrill Trust
J. Richard Magrill Heritage Fund
Joe Richard and Mary Belle Magrill Trust
Gwendolyn McCaffrey McReynolds Heritage Fund
Jimmie Joe McKinley Heritage Fund
Edith Louise Mitchell Heritage Fund
Lloyd Freeman Mitchell Heritage Fund
Snowdy Clifton and Lillian Walkup Mitchell Heritage Fund
Rev. Charles and Paulette Morrow Endowment
Virginia Sue Williamson Morrow Heritage Fund
Anne Elizabeth Swain Odom Heritage Fund
Martha Sue Parr Heritage Fund
Florence Pennewill Heritage Fund
Morris and Ruth Pepper Endowment
Publishing House Endowment
Mable Magrill Rundell Trust
Samuel Callaway Rundell Heritage Fund
Paul and Mary Jo Schnorbus Heritage Fund
Roy and Mary Seawright Shelton Heritage Fund
Shiloh CPC Ellis County Texas Endowment
Hinkley and Vista Smartt Heritage Fund
John William Sparks Heritage Fund
Irvin Scott and Annie Mary Draper Swain Heritage Fund
F. P. Waits Historical Trust

Respectfully submitted,
Pat Ward, President
Susan Knight Gore, Archivist

THE REPORT OF THE BOARD OF TRUSTEES OF MEMPHIS THEOLOGICAL SEMINARY

Introduction

Memphis Theological Seminary is the only seminary of the Cumberland Presbyterian Church. Our history is traced back through the Cumberland Presbyterian Theological Seminary in McKenzie to the organization of the graduate School of Theology at Cumberland University and the Theological Department at Bethel College, both of which began in 1852. Those two schools of theology continued the legacy begun in the work of founder Reverend Finis Ewing, who educated candidates for the ministry in his home, and many other ministers, who trained young candidates in homes, churches, and on the trail. For one hundred sixty-six years, Cumberland Presbyterians have been providing formal theological education for the church's ministers. For two hundred years, the Cumberland Presbyterian Church has valued the importance of an educated ministry.

With the denomination's decision to move its seminary to Memphis in 1964, Memphis Theological Seminary of the Cumberland Presbyterian Church began to serve a larger and more diverse student body. Though students from other denominations were admitted during the McKenzie years, the move to a major metropolitan area opened the opportunity to attract more students from more denominations. Today, Memphis Theological Seminary has one of the most diverse student populations, in terms of denomination and race, of any seminary in the United States. This theological and denominational diversity provides a rich environment for educating pastors, chaplains, Christian educators, and other leaders for the church of Jesus Christ. The sign on our campus that faces Union Avenue reads: "Memphis Theological Seminary: an Ecumenical Mission of the Cumberland Presbyterian Church." Every Cumberland Presbyterian can be proud of the mission our seminary fulfills of educating our own church leaders, and leaders from more than 25 other denominations.

We, the trustees and administration of Memphis Theological Seminary, are privileged to be a part of this legacy, born out of and guided by the ecumenical and evangelical spirit of the Cumberland Presbyterian Church. We look forward to what God has in store for our ministry in the future. With gratitude for God's grace, guidance and provision in the past year, we make the following report to the 188th General Assembly of the Cumberland Presbyterian Church, meeting June 9-14, 2019, in Huntsville, Alabama.

I. BOARD OF TRUSTEES

A. OFFICERS
The following officers were elected by the Board to serve during the past year:

- **2018 Vice-Moderator to Moderator** - Reverend Nancy Cole (United Methodist, North Alabama Conference) Reverend Cole assumed the Board chair following the resignation of the Reverend Jennifer Newell (Cumberland Presbyterian, Chattanooga, Tennessee) and was elected Moderator in May 2018.

- **2018 Vice-Moderator** - Reverend Anne Hames (Cumberland Presbyterian, McKenzie Tennessee) served as Vice-Moderator of the Board, through May 2018, until the election of Nancy Cole as Moderator and Reverend Jimmy Mosby (who came on the MTS Board in June 2017) as Vice Moderator in May 2018.

- **2018-19 Secretary** - Mrs. Sondra Roddy (Cumberland Presbyterian, Lexington, Kentucky)

- **2018-19 Treasurer** - Mrs. Cassandra Price-Perry (VP of Operations/CFO, MTS)

- **2019 Vice-Moderator** - Reverend Jimmy Mosby (United Methodist Minister, Arkansas Conference) served as Vice-Moderator of the Board from May of 2018 - Feb. 2019.

- **2019 Moderator** - Reverend Nancy Cole (United Methodist, North Alabama Conference) resigned from the Board January 7, 2019.

- **2019 Moderator** - Reverend Jimmy Mosby (United Methodist, Arkansas Conference) was elected to the office of Moderator in February 2019, following the resignation of Reverend Nancy Cole in January 2019.

- **2019 Vice-Moderator -** Reverend Kip Rush (Cumberland Presbyterian, Nashville, Tennessee) was elected Vice- Moderator following the election of Reverend Jimmy Mosby to Moderator of the Board at the February 2019 Board meeting.

B. BOARD REPESENTATIVE
The Board's representative(s) to the 2019 General Assembly will be elected in the May 2019 meeting.

C. MEETINGS
The Board met twice since the 2018 General Assembly: October 11, 2018 and February 8, 2019. The Board is scheduled to meet on May 10, 2019. By rule of the General Assembly, thirteen of the twenty-four members are representatives of the Cumberland Presbyterian Church. The remaining trustees are ecumenical partners, currently United Methodist, Baptist and Presbyterian Church (USA) representatives.

D. EXPIRATION OF TERMS
The trustees who are eligiblet o succeed themselves and have agreed to serve another three year term on the MTS Board are:
- Ms. Jane Folk (Presbyterian (USA), Memphis, Tennessee) eligible for 2 more terms.
- Reverend Larry Hilliard (United Methodist, Gulfport, Mississippi) eligible for 2 more terms.
- Reverend Deborah Smith (United Methodist, Cordova, Tennessee) eligible for 2 more terms

The three resignations from Board service listed below have been communicated to the Office of the General Assembly and the NominatingCommittee:
- Reverend Nancy Cole (United Methodist, Leeds, Alabama) eligible to serve for another term **resigned from the MTS Board of Trustees**.
- Ms. Molly Williams (Cumberland Presbyterian, Dyer, Tennessee) eligible to serve another term **declined to be re-elected the MTS Board of Trustees**.
- Reverend RickKirchoff (United Methodist, Memphis, Tennessee) eligible to serve another term **declined to be re-elected the MTS Board of Trustees**.

The trustees completing their terms on the Board this year who are ineligible for re-election are:
- Mr. Michael Allen (Cumberland Presbyterian, Alabaster, Alabama)
- Mrs. Diane Dickson (Cumberland Presbyterian, Houston, Texas)
- Reverend Inetta Rogers, (Baptist, Memphis, Tennessee)

We are grateful to God for all who have served in this important role on behalf of MTS and the Cumberland Presbyterian Church. Each has served faithfully and contributed greatly to the life of the seminary.

Following the resignations after the 2018 General Assembly of trustees Reverend Linda Howell (Cumberland Presbyterian, Keller, Texas) and Reverend Susan Parker (Cumberland Presbyterian, Rogersville, Alabama), and in keeping with the General Assembly requirement that a majority of the twenty-four member Board represent the Cumberland Presbyterian Church, the following Cumberland Presbyterian trustees were elected by the CP Corporate Board to serve the unexpired terms of Howell and Parker.

Reverend Gloria Villa Diaz, (Cumberland Presbyterian, Houston, Texas)
Reverend Wes Johnson, (Cumberland Presbyterian, Atlanta, Georgia)

E. UPDATE ONLEADERSHIP
In July 2018 the Board accepted the resignation of President Reverend Jay Earheart-Brown after thirteen years of servant leadership. On August 1 Reverend Susan Parker accepted the call to be the Interim President. Susan was serving on the Board in her fifth year of service. Her background is in higher education as a Vice President of Advancement at Athens State University. She also served in two statewide elected offices in Alabama: State Auditor 1998-2002 and Public Service Commissioner 2006-2010. Susan completed the Program of Alternate Studies in 2014 and in April 2014 was ordained as a Cumberland Presbyterian minister at Rogersville Cumberland Presbyterian Church in Rogersville, Alabama. She served various CP churches as Interim and Stated Supply from 2014-2018. She still serves as Moderator and preaches once per month at two CP churches in Lauderdale County, Alabama.

At the October board meeting, Susan stated, "It is a tremendous honor to be selected to fill this important role at a critical time of change at the Seminary. The board, faculty, staff, students and alumni have made me feel welcome and appreciated. One of my favorite things about serving at MTS is the mission of the institution expressed on the sign at the entrance that reads, 'Memphis Theological Seminary an ecumenical mission of the Cumberland Presbyterian Church'. I realize that it is likely the founders had no idea just how diverse and ecumenical the seminary would become; now serving over twenty different denominations. I believe it is testament to the love of God by CP's to be so welcoming to all of God's children.

F. PRIORITIES

The Board has reviewed and adopted the Strategic Plan but is still in the process of revising and enhancing this plan and the measurements of success. Four major priorities of the plan are:

1. Strengthen our integration of Scholarship, Piety and Justice in our administrative and educational support units and Board Governance as well as our degree programs. When we had our site visits from ATS and SACS-COC last year we were made aware that our strategic planning, ourcurriculum, and our administrative work did not flow from and draw upon our mission statement in a consistent manner. Our Quality Enhancement Plan for SACS-COC is dedicated to developing greater awareness and integration of scholarship, piety, and justice among our students. But we need to do similar work across the institution to make sure not only students, but also faculty, staff, and Board members are formed in and share the mission of the institution. Further, we need to draw upon that mission to shape how we live out our mission statement in every dimension of our institutional life, so that the integration of scholarship, piety, and justice is a shared goal for the work of the institution.

2. Ensure financial sustainability. We have relied heavily upon tuition and annual fund raising for our financial operation as an institution. SACS COC saw a number of issues related to our financial situation and placed MTS on "warning" status. We need a more secure basis for the operations of the seminary so that we are not as dependent upon tuition and the annual fund to have a balanced budget. Endowment dollars for scholarships, faculty chairs, and other programs are necessary for the financial sustainability of the Seminary. Such financial sustainability is a basic need for the Seminary to carry out its mission.

3. Create partnerships with other institutions and organizations to expand our academic offerings for both traditional and on-line delivery. In response to enrollment challenges and the shifting needs of both churches and the larger society for theological education, MTS sees the need to expand beyond its traditional academic programs to develop new ways for those to be delivered and to develop new programs that address church and societal needs. Our location in Memphis, Tennessee is an asset we need to build upon. We can partner with other educational institutions, large churches, as well as hospitals and non-profits associated with a faith community. We recognize numerous opportunities to collaborate with different kinds of institutions to broaden our scope as we meet the needs for theological education that is responsive to these various settings. We also recognize the need to continue to expand and develop our on-line offerings so that we can be flexible in addressing people from a variety of settings.

4. Create a culture of assessment that relates to strategic planning. Prior to our recent reaccreditation we recognized we had not created a robust and viable program of assessment of our academic programs. We began that work prior to the reaccreditation visits, but both SACS-COC and ATS saw our need to fine tune those efforts and continue to integrate them into overall academic and institutional planning. At the same time, assessment of every aspect of our shared work at MTS in relation to strategic planning for the whole institution was flagged as a weakness by the accrediting organizations, and our strategic planning has been very inadequate. To create a culture of assessment, the lessons learned from academic assessment need to be integrated with the whole institution so that a clear plan for and process of assessment can be carried out in the whole seminary and that assessment can lead to date based (rather than anecdotal based identification of strengths and weaknesses to be addressed by the strategic plan.

G. ACCREDITATION ISSUES

American Theological Schools (ATS) and Southern Association of Colleges and Schools Commission on Colleges (SACS-COC) Accreditation Status.

In March 2018, both accrediting agencies had reviews with on-site visits to the campus. The ATS accreditation was renewed for seven years but the institution was given a notation concerning student learning outcomes. In February 2019, that notation was removed due to the fact that MTS had satisfied the issues regarding outcomes.

At its meeting in December 2018, the SACS-COC Board of Trustees voted to place MTS under the sanction of "warning" for twelve months. This is the lowest level of sanction. The seminary is and will remain accredited. The lack of reaffirmation without sanctions is due to several areas of deficiency. The primary and most challenging issue is a balanced budget. All the areas of concern are being addressed and documentation will be submitted to SACS-COC in September. Their Board will make a decision in December 2019 regarding the status. The Seminary can have the "warning" removed, stay on "warning" for another year or have the "warning" changed to"probation." MTS looks forward to working with the SACS-COC team to continue to address and correct these deficiencies and remove the warning.

H. UPDATE ON THE HAMILTON CHAPEL/FINANCIALSTATUS

During the past several years, the student body at MTS has become more and more diverse in a number of ways. One of the changes that has taken place is the diversity in class offerings. Currently, students attend classes in the morning, afternoon, evenings, on-line/hybrid and off campus. Because of these changes, there is no longer the need for a large facility where all students would gather at the same time. Therefore, the seminary began to consider other options for the chapel.

Due to the changing needs of the student population and the urgent need for a balanced budget because of the SACS-COC warning, in February 2019 the Board voted to explore the possibility of asking Mrs. Barbara Hamilton if her remaining gift for a stand alone chapel could be utilized in a different manner.

When consulted regarding her gift, Mrs. Hamilton said her concern was that the seminary needed a nice chapel versatile enough to meet the needs but did not necessarily feel there was a need for a large stand-alone chapel. Therefore, we made the decision to utilize the $1.6M gift that remained for the construction of a new chapel as follows: (1) major renovation of the existing chapel, (2) the endowment of a Methodist House of Studies Chair and (3) the remaining to be used to balance the annual budget. These funds should allow the seminary to have a balanced budget for several years, if the continuing fundraising is successful.

I. FUTURE FUNDING

While the Hamilton gift will enable the seminary to have a balanced budget, it does not mean that the other regular funding is not necessary. The seminary has been operating under a deficit budget for many years. The SACS-COC warning is a call to arms. There must be a balanced budget with three years. Thankfully, this can be done but not without continued and growing support from the Cumberland Presbyterian family and others.

Donors site many reasons for contributing to MTS. But most donors are focused on the importance of training men and women to lead congregations in a diverse, changing and challenging time. Never has the church or the world needed more good leaders to seek the Kingdom of God on earth.

So please give. Please ask your congregation, friends and other members of other denominations to contribute. It is a new day at MTS and we need your support.

RECOMMENDATION 1: That the General Assembly encourage Presbyteries to share the mission, vision and passion of MTS to train and sustain men and women for the Christian ministry and ask members to support the seminary with their financial resources and prayers.

II. ADMINISTRATION

A. PRESIDENT

Reverend Susan Parker, Ph.D. was selected by the Board to be interim president beginning August 2018. Susan was ordained as a Cumberland Presbyterian minister in April 2014 after completing the Program of Alternate Studies. Prior to being named interim president, Susan was serving stated supply and interim calls at CP and Presbyterian USA churches. She spent several years in statewide elected office in the state of Alabama and twenty-five years in higher education. Susan holds a Ph.D. from the University of Alabama, a Masters from UAB, Bachelors from Athens College and an Associates from Calhoun Community College.

A. VICE PRESIDENT OF ACADEMIC AFFAIRS/DEAN

Dr. Pete Gathje became the Vice President of Academic Affairs/Dean in February 2017. Pete served previously as Professor of Ethics at MTS and Associate Dean of Curriculum and Instruction. He is a lay Roman Catholic and is deeply committed to the mission of Memphis Theological Seminary, having taught on our faculty for the past ten years.

B. VICE PRESIDENT OFOPERATIONS/CFO

Ms. Cassandra Price-Perry began work with MTS in August 2010 as Vice President of Operations and Chief Financial Officer. She is a Certified Public Accountant with over 20 years of experience in business and accounting. Cassandra is an active laywoman in her Roman Catholic Church in Southaven, MS. She has received high praise from our auditors and our Board for her work over the past almost seven years.

III. INSTRUCTION

A. DEGREE PROGRAMS

Memphis Theological Seminary offers four degree programs and three certificate programs, including the certificate offered through the Program of Alternate Studies. The Master of Divinity is the basic degree program for persons preparing for ordained ministry in many denominations. It continues to be our largest degree program, with over 70% of students enrolled. The M.Div. requires 84 semester hours and takes three years of full-time study to complete.

The Doctor of Ministry degree is a professional degree designed for pastors and other ministers who have at least three years of full-time work in ministry after their M.Div. and who want to engage in further theological reflection on the practice of ministry. The D.Min. is designed around five two-week residencies, in January and July, and the implementation of and report on a major project in ministry. It usually takes 3-5 years tocomplete.

A third program is the Master of Arts in Youth Ministry (MAYM). Through our partnership with the Center for Youth Ministry Training in Brentwood, Tennessee, and the new certificate program in youth ministry through the Cumberland Presbyterian Church, we have over thirty students enrolled in this degree program. MTS currently has, we believe, the largest master's program in yonth ministry in the UnitedStates.

In the spring of 2016, we were approved by our accrediting bodies (The Southern Association of Colleges and Schools, and the Association of Theological Schools in the United States and Canada) to offer a new degree, the Master of Arts in Christian Ministry (MACM). This degree program began in the fall of 2016 with concentrations offered in Christian Education, Urban Ministry, and Social Justice Ministry. The MACM is a 42 hour degree for persons interested in pursuing specialized ministries. We plan to offer additional concentrations in the future (possibly rural ministry, counseling,etc.)

At Commencement in May of 2018, Memphis Theological Seminary awarded the Master of Arts in Youth Ministry degree to twelve graduates. Three persons were awarded the Master of Arts (Religion) degree. Three persons received the Master of Arts in Christian Ministry degree. Thirty-eight persons were awarded the Master of Divinity degree, and fourteen were awarded the Doctor of Ministry degree.

Cumberland Presbyterian Master of Divinity graduates were: Jamie Adams. Paul Earheart-Brown and William Arnold. Cumberland Presbyterian Doctor of Ministry were: Jin Koo Kang, Myeong R. Ree, and Cory D. Williams

B. CERTIFICATE PROGRAMS

In addition to the four degree programs, MTS offers the following certificates: Program of Alternate Studies of the Cumberland Presbyterian Church, Drug and Alcohol Addiction Counseling Graduate Certificate, James Netters Certificate in Ministry and Certificate in Wesleyan Studies.

C. FACULTY

For the current academic year, Memphis Theological Seminary has thirteen full-time teaching faculty, four administrative faculty members who teach part-time, and one Louisville fellow. In addition, the seminary curriculum is greatly enhanced by the work often to fifteen adjunct professors, most of whom are active in pastoral or other ministries.

Members of the MTS faculty continue to publish books and articles both for the academy and the church. Many faculty members preach in area churches on a regular basis, deliver lectures for local churches and judicatories, deliver papers at academic conferences, and write articles for a wide range of readers.

Under the leadership of VP/Dean Gathje, the faculty implemented our new M.Div. online hybrid program. Twenty-two students are enrolled as a cohort and will be able to complete their entire degree by coming to campus four times per semester for a two day intensive period and doing their on-line classwork.

D. ENROLLMENT

Total enrollment in Memphis Theological Seminary for the fall term of 2018 was 257, including all degree and certificate programs. We continued to see a drop in enrollment in our largest degree program, the Master of Divinity. Declining enrollments led again to painful budget adjustments during the year, including the elimination of several part-time and full-time positions. Our largest number of students comes from the United Methodist Church, with 23.6% of total enrollment. Cumberland Presbyterians are the second largest denomination represented in the student body with about 13.3% of all students.

The Bridge Program. In 2018 an anonymous donor created the Whosoever Will Bridge Program. This program will enable any student who completes his/her degree at Bethel University and the M.Div at MTS and then is called to serve full-time at a CP church to receive a stipend of $12,000 per year. We continue to work to recruit Cumberland Presbyterian students as we believe this program will help encourage more students to pursue their call and utilize both Bethel and MTS as the route of preparation. We are thankful for the gift that made this possible.

RECOMMENDATION 2: That the Presbyteries inform all congregations of the Whosoever Will Bridge program and provide probationers with the necessary information so they will be aware of this program.

E. PROGRAM OF ALTERNATE STUDIES (written by Dr. Michael Qualls, Director)

Memphis Theological Seminary has administered theProgram of Alternate Studies as an alternative route to ordained ministry in the Cumberland Presbyterian Churchs since its inception in 1984. In addition to the basics of preparing ministers of word and sacrament in a myriad of circumstances we are becoming a reliable resource for foundational education of *lay persons* interested/involved in congregational leadership in the Cumberland Presbyterian Church.

• A reduced rate tuition of $200 allows those not seeking ordination to take any of our online or face-to-face courses.

• A targeted lay-leader weekend conference will again be a feature of our SES in2019. We ask the General Assembly to help us promote these opportunities through the presbyteries.

SES 2019

The heart of the program is a fifteen-day period in the summer. At that event students come together for community, fellowship, worship and intensive classroom experience. Students may take up to 9 courses of the 27 or so that are taught during three five-day blocks. The 2019 Summer Extension School will be held on the Campus of Bethel University July 13-27. Graduation will be July 13th at 11:00 am in Odom Hall with Reverend David Lancaster as our commencement speaker. We anticipate 5 graduates.

ONLINE and WEEKEND CLASSES

In the "off season" we have offered eleven courses on-site in various locales or online in both synchronous (live interactive) and asynchronous format. Three were in conjunction with MMT at a Latino Conference at El Camino Church in the Miami area. This enables students nearing graduation to complete requirements and others to move more quickly along than their limited availability during the summer school would allow.

PARTNERS IN EDUCATIONAL MINISTRY

Once again we will have the MTS MDiv. students in a joint class with the PAS students. The joint class this year occurs in the first block, Educational Ministry in the Smaller Church featuring Dr. Cannichael Crutchfield as professor.

We are also collaborating to help current Cumberland Presbyterian MDiv. students complete the Cumberland Presbyterian specific courses for credit by including the PAS courses as part of the course requirements. This is a viable model given the overlapping interests.

We have now opened a pathway for PAS courses to be considered, on a case by case basis, for partial transfer credit (up to 17 hours possible) for anyone who wishes to pursue the MDiv. degree at MTS. PAS graduates are encouraged to contact the MTS Registrar for evaluation. The PAS office can assist with getting transcripts.

PARTNERS IN MISSION

We continue to work with MMT and Cross Cultural Ministry Program Director to assist with assimilation of immigrant pastors/churches and to assist the global outreach of the Cumberland Presbyterian church. These non-typical circumstances often call for additional flexibility and often are not in a position to financially sustain the costs of the resources. We are grateful for the support of OUO and mission-minded partners to enable this important ministry. We anticipate a large group in the first official graduating class of PAS-Colombia in 2020.

STANDARDIZING SYLLABI

In response to the request of the 188th General Assembly the PAS Advisory Council approved a format for course syllabi. We have communicated this to all instructors and requested updatedcopies of their course syllabus. We also reflect appreciation for the flexibility inherent in a diverse faculty and continue to affirm the many ways of learning/teaching reflected in an alternative educational environment.

RECOGNITION

The strength of the Program of Alternate Studies rests in its dedicated, capable and empathetic teachers. Throughout the existence of the program it has been privileged to access the best and the brightest the denomination has to offer, from credentialed educators and theologians to acknowledged ministry professionals. We gratefully express appreciation to Reverend Clinton Buck who began teaching in the very first summer school (1984) and Reverend David Lancaster who began soon thereafter (1986). These faithful servants, and many others, have returned year after year to joyfully pour themselves into the lives of women and men who seek to gain insight and wisdom to fulfill the Lord's calling.

IN MEMORIUM

Sadly, we seldom get to acknowledge the sacrificial service of our mentors adequately. Please help us express appreciation, to a true hero of the Program of Alternate Studies, the first Director, Dr. William "Bill" Rustenhaven Jr. Dr. Rustenhaven referred to the summer extension schools each July as "Mt. Bethel", an allusion to the campus which hosted them and also to the Biblical experience of Jacob who discovered afresh the presence of God on his sojourn.

Rustenhaven took great delight in the relationships with students, traveling and visiting extensively in their homes. He served as pastor to them as well as mentor. He spent endless hours in informal conversation with students who joined him as he would pull away to "burn incense," a euphemism he often employed to describe smoking his pipe. He is remembered by students as a consummate instructor, both tender and tenacious.

I warmly associate myself with the concluding remarks in Dr. Rustenhaven's report to the PAS Advisory Council at the end of his first year as director. *The position I hold is one of great responsibility and is an awesome challenge. At times I am overwhelmed. Yet I feel strongly in the worth of this program of educational preparation for ministry. My prayer is for strength, wisdom and humility to see if we can make a difference for the building of the Kingdom in and through our responsibility as participants in that Kingdom. Please remember me in your prayers and concern.*

Respectfully,
Michael Qualls, Director PAS

IV. FACILITIES

A. FACILITIES IMPROVEMENTS

As described earlier in the report, the existing chapel will be renovated and extensively remodeled using the Hamilton gift. Part of the usage of the Hamilton gift will also be used to renovate the entrances to and from the Chapel. Therefore, the entrance to the rear of Founders Hall is being renovated to make this part of the entrance to the Chapel more attractive. Also, the flooring outside the Chapel and surrounding areas will be replaced.

In addition, funds and volunteers are being sought to repair the damage to the student housing and rental properties of the seminary. A generous donor has agreed to pay for the materials and we are currently seeking volunteer mission teams or individuals to do repairs, painting and pressure washing to preserve these properties.

We have also applied for funds from the CPW General Assembly offering to do much needed repairs to Cumberland Hall.

B. DEBT ON PROPERTY
The debt on property as of 12/31/18 was $2.5M.

C. SAFETY
The Office of Safety of MTS continues to explore ways to enhance the safety of our students in the context of our urban campus. Through the use of lighting, security officers, secure locks, and well articulated safety plans, the seminary seeks to provide a safe environment for students and visitors to our campus.

During the past seven years, MTS has contracted with a local security company to provide regular patrols around our neighborhood. This additional safety measure has been well received by our students and by our neighbors. We continue to seek ways to provide a safe environment for our campus community.

V. ADVANCEMENT AND FINANCE

A. BUDGET
Our Board of Trustees will approve a budget for the 2019-2020 academic year at its May meeting. Copies of that budget will be provided at the meeting of General Assembly.

Like seminaries across the country, we continue to face budget challenges from declining enrollments. The Board of Trustees has become more involved with the budgeting process to insure funds are spent as wisely as possible. Renewed efforts toward transparency and involvement of the board have been undertaken.

B. SCHOLARSHIPS AND GRANTS
We continue to cultivate relationships with foundations whose mission closely aligns with ours. The following grants for scholarships and other projects have been received in recent years:

1. The Eli Lilly Endowment, Inc. - Center for Faith and Imagination
In December 2017, MTS was notified that it had been selected to receive a grant of $1 million dollars from the Lilly Endowment, Inc., for use over five years to fund a Center for Faith and Imagination at Memphis Theological Seminary. Working with partners including the Methodist Healthcare Clergy Coaching Network, the Center for Transfonning Communities, the Cumberland Presbyterian Pastoral Ministry Development Team, and the Memphis Annual Conference of the UMC, the work of the Center will focus on supporting and sustaining clergy in their first five years of ministry post seminary. The new Center at MTS will provide services to our graduates to help them develop networks of support, encouragement, and spiritual depth to help them understand and survive the challenges of pastoral ministry in ourtime.

2. The Kemmons Wilson Family Foundation
The Kemmons Wilson family, founders of the Holiday Inn hotel chain and noted philanthropists in Memphis, has renewed funding of the Wilson Scholarships at $15,000 for this year.

3. The H.W. Durham Foundation
In 2018 the Memphis-based H.W. Durham Foundation renewed its gift of $5,000 to provide 5 $1,000 scholarships for students who are 55+ years of age. These Durham Scholars will represent much of our student body who are second-career students.

C. ENDOWMENTS

One of the most exciting things this year has been the establishment of the Baird-Buck CP House of Studies. bSeveral years ago, the Baird and Buck families established an endowment designed to one day reach the $1.2M required for an endowed chair. Much progress has been made. The families continue to contribute and Dr. Clinton Buck continues to seek funding. This year the families approved for the seminary to begin to spend a portion of the endowment annual earnings ($20,000) to fund the CP House of Studies. This intermediate step allows us to connect students more intentionally with their CP heritage and to create emphases on historical events of interest to the CP church. Dr. Michael Qualls, the Director of the Program of Alternate Studies, is leading the efforts to engage all CP students, prospective students, faculty, staff and alumni in worship, fellowship, and lecture activities. We are grateful for these activities and all are enjoying the renewed emphasis on all things CP.

Currently we have 289 endowments. These endowments are varied both in amount and purpose. Scholarships, ofcourse, makeup the largest group. But endowments are set aside for the general fund, lectures, the library, music and other good purposes. The seminary welcomes endowments and has recently set $5,000 as a minimum for establishing a new endowment.

D. ESTATE GIFTS

We continue to have conversations with friends and donors about the importance of remembering MTS (and their local churches, and other ministries they care deeply about) in their estate plans. Almost daily we receive gifts in memory of someone. We are grateful for these ways to honor the individual and help the seminary at the sametime.

In September 2018 we were blessed to receive a gift of $133,196 from the Burnita Hudgins Charitable Trust. This generous gift was to fund the Sallie Clay and Alice Coooksey Endowment and for the general fund.

We are deeply grateful for the generosity that faithful Cumberland Presbyterians and others exhibit in remembering MTS, and other denominational ministries, in their estate planning. The MTS Advancement Staff and President are available to present programs on Planned Giving to churches, groups of churches, or presbyteries to encourage our members to remember their local churches and-denominational ministries that are important to them in their wills and other planned giving vehicles.

E. SEMINARY/PAS SUNDAY

We have many churches in our denomination, and in other denominations we serve who recognize Seminary Sunday in their local churches. This provides time for education of members about the work of MTS and the Program of Alternate Studies and provides an opportunity for members to make a special one-time gift to support the work of the seminary. Please contact the seminary for more information on how you can recognize Seminary Sunday in your local church, and to request a speaker for theoccasion.

RECOMMENDATION 3: That the third Sunday in August, (August 18, 2019)be included in the General Assembly Calendar as Seminary/PAS Sunday, and that Presbyteries encourage all churches to share information about MTS and PAS and receive a special offering on that day, or on a more convenient day of the session's choosing.

F. ANNUAL FUND

Memphis Theological Seminary could not operate without the faithful contributions of its alumni and friends. Annual Fund contributions help us keep the cost of tuition down, so hopefully students do not leave seminary with a large burden of debt to have to pay during their early years inministry. Raising $1M year after year for the Annual Fund is a daunting task.

The Whosoever Will Bridge program can help ease the burden on Cumberland Presbyterian graduates by giving them a stipend of $12,000 per year for five years. This is a tremendous blessing for MTS and these students.

MTS friends and alumnia reencouraged to consider joining the"1852 Society," a group of persons who pledge to give at least $18.52 per month to help support the work of the seminary. Information on the "1852 Society" is available at the MTS display table during the week of General Assembly, and can be accessed through our website: MemphisSeminary.edu.

In some respects, the income we receive from OUO puts us in a better position than many theological seminaries, whose income from denominational sources has declined significantly over the past twenty years. Our income from OUO has remained relatively steady over that time period. However, as a percentage of our total income, OUO has fallen from almost 20% to about 3% of our operating budget. We are grateful for the commitment of Cumberland Presbyterians to the ministry of MTS, and all our common ministries, expressed so tangibly through giving to Our United Outreach.

At the same time, we do not expect income from denominational contributions to increase significantly in the future. This means that we are required to put more time and energy into fund raising than ever before. We are grateful for the many alumni who have made a commitment to help raise funds through their own contributions, asking for their churches to contribute and also putting MTS in their will.

G. AUDIT REPORT

The auditing firm of Cannon, Wright, Blount, PLLC. has audited the books of Memphis Theological Seminary for the 2017-2018 fiscal year. The audit was unqualified. Copies of that report have been filed with the office of the Stated Clerk.

Respectfully submitted,
Jimmy Mosby, Moderator of the Board of Trustees
Susan Parker, Interim President
Memphis Theological Seminary Board of Trustees

THE REPORT OF THE
OUR UNITED OUTREACH COMMITTEE

The 2009 General Assembly established a denominational Our United Outreach Committee to be made up of 12 voting representatives, one from each Synod and the rest from the church programs and institutions. Executives from the church programs and institutions participate on the Committee as advisory members. This Committee meets annually unless there is a needed called meeting.

A goal of the Our United Outreach Committee is to encourage ALL churches to contribute to Our United Outreach. Approximately 25 percent of the churches do not give anything with a high percentage of other churches not giving at the 10 percent level. This past year, 2019, the budgeted goal for Our United Outreach was $2,600,000 – 97.74% giving was achieved. The Committee seeks to involve ALL churches with Our United Outreach giving and at a greater level of participation.

I. OUR UNITED OUTREACH FUNDS ALLOCATION

The Our United Outreach Committee met March 1, 2019, to allocate the Our United Outreach funds for the 2020 year. The Our United Outreach allocation basis for 2020 is $2,600,000.

A line item of $35,000 for Unification Task Force and $92,044 for the OUO Development Office, including the Director, Regional Representatives, and all expenses thereto, have been approved as guaranteed amounts and are deducted from the goal amount prior to allocation purposes.

RECOMMENDATION 1: That General Assembly adopt the following Our United Outreach allocations for 2020:

The allocation is to be as follows:	$2,600,000.00		
Development Coordinator Office and OUO Committee		92,044.00	
Unification Task Force		35,000.00	
Sub-total	127,044.00		
(Amount to be allocated)	2,472,956.00		
Ministry Council	$ 1,236,478.00		50%
Bethel University	123,648.00		5%
Children's Home	74,189.00		3%
Stewardship	148,377.00		6%
General Assembly Office	197,836.00		8%
Memphis Theological Seminary/ Program of Alternate Studies	173,107.00		7%
Historical Foundation	74,189.00		3%
Shared Services	395,672.00		16%
Contingency	12,365.00		.5%
(Next four items total 1.5%)			
Comm. on Chaplains	14,356.00		.581%
Judiciary Committee	13,539.00		.548%
Theology/Social Concerns	5,045.00		.204%
Nominating Committee	4,155.00		.168%
	2,472,956.00		
Our United Outreach Goal	$2,600,000.00		

From the agencies listed above, all should be self-explanatory except maybe Shared Services. Maintenance, utilities, mowing, trash pick-up, pest extermination, and custodial are all examples of Shared Services for agencies sharing the Cumberland Presbyterian Center.

II. OUR UNITED OUTREACH COMMITTEE REQUESTS

Our committee believes that many across our denomination may not fully understand the ministry of OUO in supporting, and making possible the entire ministry of the Cumberland Presbyterian Church. We feel there is much work to do in educating individuals, congregations, and churches how their support of OUO makes a difference in the life of our church. We are searching for new ways to share the message, and promote the ministries that OUO makes possible in our denomination.

RECOMMENDATION 2: **The OUO Committee request that General Assembly challenge churches to invite an OUO Representative or member of the OUO Committee to speak in their congregations.**

Respectfully submitted,
Reverend Bruce Hamilton, Chairperson
Mikel Davis, Vice-Chairperson
Robin Wills, Secretary
and the Our United Outreach Committee

THE REPORT OF THE COMMISSION ON MILITARY CHAPLAINS AND PERSONNEL

The General Assembly Commission on Military Chaplains and Personnel is made up of three members, each serving terms of three years on the Commission. Those people are Reverend Cassandra Thomas (2019), Reverend Charles McCaskey (2020), and Reverend Tony Janner (2021). They can serve up to 9 years (3 three year terms). (Note: Reverend Thomas will rotate off the council after her second term ends this year due to family reasons and another minister will be appointed to serve on the commission by the GA). These three members, along with the Stated Clerk, Reverend Michael Sharpe, are also members of the Presbyterian Council for Chaplains and Military Personnel (PCCMP), also doing business as Presbyterian Federal Chaplaincies and Presbyterians Caring for Chaplains and Military Personnel. The office is located at 4125 Nebraska Avenue NW, Washington DC. The Council represents the following member denominations: Cumberland Presbyterian Church, Cumberland Presbyterian Church in America, Korean Presbyterian Church Abroad, and Presbyterian Church (U.S.A) in all matters relative to member chaplains who serve in all branches of the United States (U.S.) Armed Forces, United States Department of Veterans Affairs, United States Federal Bureau of Prisons, and United States Civil Air Patrol. The Council ministers in appropriate ways to the families of Chaplains and to U.S. military personnel, veterans and their families of the member denominations. The Council also approves Seminary students of the member denominations for participation in the U.S. Chaplain Candidacy programs of the military services.

I. SUPPORT OF THE PCCMP

Financial support for the Presbyterian Council for Chaplains and Military Personnel (PCCMP) is received from the four member denominations and individuals, church judicatories and individual churches. The constant decrease of financial support is an issue that the PCCMP is constantly dealing with. The Cumberland Presbyterian Church has a budget line in the denominational budget to support the PCCMP. The Cumberland Presbyterian Church and the individual churches have traditionally received an offering on U.S. Memorial Day Sunday with those offerings being given directly to the PCCMP for its budget. However, other special days may be considered to receive this special offering in the individual churches – the Sunday nearest U.S. Veterans day, "Four Chaplain's Sunday" (the first Sunday in February), the Sunday nearest the 4th of July or some other Sunday as a witness to support the men and women who have or are serving in the U.S. military, the Federal Bureau of Prisons, the Veterans Affairs and the Civil Air Patrol. These offerings should be sent to the General Assembly Stated Clerk and are forwarded to the PCCMP for the outreach, mission, and maintenance of the PCCMP.

RECOMMENDATION 1: That each Cumberland Presbyterian Church provide an opportunity for their congregations to receive an offering on the last Sunday of May, or another special day, to support our ministry through the PCCMP.

The PCCMP provides ecclesiastical endorsement for chaplains of the United States Armed Forces from the four member denominations who are serving on active duty or serving the Reserves/National Guard. The PCCMP also endorses Ministers of Word and Sacrament who serve as chaplains in the U.S. Federal Bureau of Prisons and the Civil Air Patrol. The PCCMP also provides special training to chaplains and pastoral support to chaplains and their families who are endorsed for those positions from the four member denominations. The PCCMP provides an influential voice for the member denominations to the U.S. National Council on Ministry to the Armed Forces in matters relating to the ministry and welfare of the endorsed chaplains. The PCCMP also promotes a closer communications between chaplains and their denominational bodies.

RECOMMENDATION 2: That individual congregations of the Cumberland Presbyterian Church and Cumberland Presbyerian Church in America determine and designate special days through the year to hold up the chaplains and their families in the service to which they have been endorsed.

II. MEETINGS, DIRECTOR, AND CPC/CPCA MEMBERS NOTES

The PCCMP, and the representatives of the member denominations normally meets at least once a year. This past year, the annual meeting was hosted by the Korean Presbyterian Church Abroad in Toronto, Canada. All three CPC members were able to attend and participate in the decision making of the council. PCCMP Chair, Reverend Cassandra Thomas (CPC) and Director Lyman Smith led the council through several days of decision-making and strategic planning.

The 2019 Annual Meeting will be hosted at the denominational headquarters of the Cumberland Presbyterian Church in Cordova, Tennessee, October 1-2, 2019.

The PCCMP held its 2018 Chaplains Credentialing Training and Family Retreat, August 5-10, 2018 in Montreat, North Carolina. On the last night, the preacher was Chaplain Zachary Nash, USAF Active Duty (CPC) with worship and communion support from Chaplain Candidate Garrett Burns (CPC), Reverend Sandy Thomas (CPC), Chaplain David Lockhart, US Army Active Duty (CPCA), and an US Army active duty chaplain (KPCA).

Due to the stationing of chaplains and their families around the world with time zone challenges, East Coast and West Coast training opportunities are planned to reach as many chaplains and their families as possible for reformed tradition renewal, Presbyterian updates, and self-care resources in 2019.

Director Lyman Smith is providing excellent leadership and endorsement abilities to chaplains and chaplain candidates. His impeccable work with federal agencies, chaplain organizations, denominational leaders, and council members stabilized the council and its influence in multiple spheres. He is to be commended for his excellent service to our denomination on the behalf of chaplains and their families and our presbyteries and congregations.

Reverend Cassandra (Sandy) Thomas (CPC) concludes her second year as chair of the council as she rotates off the council at the 2019 Annual PCCMP Meeting. She humbly thanks the GA for allowing her to serve these past six years on the council. Reverend Tony Janner is on the council's Communication Team and Reverend Charles McCaskey is on the council's Pastoral Care Team. They provide keen insights and recommendations to the director and council.

The following is an approximate list of CPC and CPCA Chaplains (by categories) within the PCCMP as of March 4, 2019:

CPCA: 1 Military Active Duty
CPC: 4 Military Active Duty
3 Military Reserves with 1 Pending for the Reserves
2 Chaplain Candidates
7 Veteran Affairs (VA) with 2 Pending for the VA
13 *Retired *(Includes the 3 CPC members on the PCCMP)

Chaplain names and addresses are included in the Yearbook of the Cumberland Presbyterian Church. Information concerning the process of becoming a chaplain may be obtained by visiting the PCCMP website: www.pccmp.org.

Submitted:
Members of the Cumberland Presbyterian Commission on Chaplains and Personnel
Reverend Cassandra (Sandy) Thomas
Reverend Tony Janner
Reverend Charles McCaskey

THE REPORT OF THE PERMANENT JUDICIARY COMMITTEE

The Judiciary Committee met March 7, 2019 in Huntsville, Alabama. Present were Pam Brown, Annetta Camp, Harry Chapman, Geoff Knight, Rachel Moses, Andy McClung, Jan Overton, Jim Ratliff, and Bill Tally. Also present were Mike Sharpe, stated clerk, and Jaime Jordan, legal counsel.

I. INQUIRY

An inquiry to the committee asked if a person is eligible to serve simultaneously on the Board of Directors for both Bethel University and Memphis Theological Seminary. It is the committee's opinion that due to the limitations defined in General Assembly Bylaws 10.01.01, 10.01.02, 10.02.06, 10.02.07, a person may not serve simultaneously on the Board of Directors for both Bethel University and Memphis Theological Seminary.

II. COMMUNICATION

The committee received and discussed "Arkansas Petition to 2019 Joint Meeting of the General Assembly". It is the committee's opinion that the Arkansas Petition to 2019 Joint Meeting of the General Assembly deals with the subject of the Cumberland Presbyterian Church's position on human sexuality and, therefore, presents substantially the same question which was referred by the 2018 General Assembly to the Permanent Judicial Committee, Unified Committee on Social Concerns, and the Ministry Council. Because the petition presents the same question as one which remains within the control of the assembly, the committee advises the stated clerk that it would not be in order for the Arkansas petition to be considered by the General Assembly in its 2019 meeting. This opinion is based on Robert's Rules of Order, Newly Revised, section 10, page 112.

III. REVIEW OF SYNOD MINUTES

The following synod minutes from 2018 were reviewed. The committee appreciates the work and ministries of our synods, and notes the following mistakes in the minutes:

Mission Synod
- A "secretary" was elected. Our Rules of Order call for a "stated clerk".

Tennessee Synod
- The minutes record that the Executive Council report was considered seriatim, but it appears the report was actually divided. These are different actions (see Rules of Order 8.34 e and f).
- No closing prayer is indicated.
- The minutes record that Bedford County being part of Columbia Presbytery was "announced." It is unclear if this was informational or a ruling.
- Copies of the incorporation papers should be included in the minutes.
- The minutes indicate an appeal was dealt with. The appeal and written response should be included in the minutes.
- Nominations were treated as recommendations. This is improper. See Rules of Order 11.0.

Synod of the Midwest
- No concerns

Synod of the Southeast
- No concerns

Synod of Great Rivers
- No concerns

IV. REVIEW OF MISSIONS MINSTRY TEAM FUNCTIONING AS A PRESBYTERY

This committee fulfills the role of a synod in providing oversight and review of the Missions Ministry Team as MMT functions as a presbytery in certain circumstances (GA Bylaw 11.05.06). The committee reviewed the 2018 minutes and found the following concerns:
- The minutes do not indicate that meetings were opened or closed with prayer.
- The minutes do not indicate that a quorum was present.
- The minutes state that a candidate was received but will be asked the constitutional questions for candidacy at a later time. This violates Constitution 6.15 in that the receiving body must hear the person's affirmative answers to the constitutional questions for candidacy before formal reception.

V. GENERAL ASSEMBLY REPRESENTATIVES

Geoff Knight was elected to serve as this committee's representative to the 189th General Assembly. Andy McClung was elected as the alternate.

VI. JOINT COMMITTEE ON AMENDMENTS

Pam Brown and Jan Overton were elected as representatives to serve on the Joint Committee on Amendments.

VII. ORGANIZATION OF THE COMMITTEE

Annetta camp is chairperson, Geoff Knight is vice-chair, and Jan Overton is secretary.

Respectfully submitted,
The Judiciary Committee

THE REPORT OF THE NOMINATING COMMITTEE

The Nominating Committee consists of a minister and a lay person from each synod, preferably from different presbyteries. Members may serve a three year term, but cannot succeed themselves. Cumberland Presbyterian members of any board or committee can be re-elected to the same board after a two year absence. Ecumenical representatives may be re-elected to the same board after a one year absence. With the exception of the Nominating Committee any person elected to serve on a denominational entity may serve three consecutive terms. Filling an unexpired term counts as one term, thus members of any entity do not always serve nine years before completing eligibility on a board/agency.

The members of the various Ministry Teams are no longer elected by the General Assembly, but are to be appointed by the Ministry Council.

The Committee submits the following list of nominees:

I. THE BOARD OF DIRECTORS OF THE GENERAL ASSEMBLY CORPORATION

(Members whose terms expire in 2022)

(3) REV. BOBBY COLEMAN, 107 E Henson, Springdale, AR 72764, Salem Congregation, Arkansas Presbytery, Great Rivers Synod, to succeed himself for a three-year term

(1) REV. RICKEY PAGE, 736 Rodney Drive, Nashville, TN 37205, West Nashville Congregation, Nashville Presbytery, Tennessee Synod, for a three-year term

II. MINISTRY COUNCIL

(Members whose terms expire in 2022)

(2) MS. CARLA BELLIS, 19264 Law 2170, Aurora, MO 65605, Orange Congregation, Missouri Presbytery, Synod of Great Rivers, to succeed herself for a three-year term.

(1) MS. DEBBIE HAYES, 69 Cactus Drive, Benton, KY 42025, Unity Congregation, Covenant Presbytery, Synod of the Midwest, for a three-year term.

(1) MR. TED SHIRAI, 25 Minami Kibogaoka, Asahi-ku, Yokohama, Kanagawa, JAPAN, Japan Presbytery, Mission Synod, for a three-year term.

(1) REV. TIM SMITH, 214 Jeffery Drive, Fayetteville, TN 3733, Fayetteville Congregation, Columbia Presbytery, Tennessee Synod, for a three-year term.

(2)REV. MIKE WILKINSON, 6900 Nubbin Ridge Drive, Knoxville, TN 37919, Knoxville Congregation, Presbytery of East Tennessee, Southeast Synod, to succeed himself for a three-year term.

(Members whose terms expire in 2020)

(1) REV. MICHAEL CLARK, 2353 Blue Springs Road, Dechard, TN 37324, Winchester 1st Congregation, Murfreesboro Presbytery, Tennessee Synod, to fill an unexpired one-year term.

YOUTH ADVISORY MEMBERS
(shall be between the ages of 15 and 17 years of age, elected for a one year term and is eligible for an additional one term)

(2)MS. SYDNEY HOLDER, 6589 County Road 747, Cullman, AL 35055, Welti Congregation, Hope Presbytery, Synod of the Southeast, for a one-year term.

(2)MS. MADISON HOLLAND, 565 County Road 17, Scottsboro, AL 35768, Scottsboro Congregation, Robert Donnell Presbytery, Synod of the Southeast, for a one-year term.

(1) MS. LACEY YOUNG, 1211 Michael Drive, Alabaster, AL 35007, First Church Alabaster Congregation Robert Donnell Presbytery, Southeast Synod, for a one-year term.

III. TRUSTEES OF HISTORICAL FOUNDATION

(Members whose terms expire in 2022)

(2) MS. ROBIN MCCASKEY-HUGHES, 1205 Olde Bridge Road, Edmond, OK 73034, Stonegate Congregation, Red River Presbytery, Mission Synod, to succeed herself for a three-year term
(2) MS. ASHLEY LINDSEY, 2090 Claypool Boyce Road, Alvaton, KY 42122, Bowling Green Congregation, Cumberland Presbytery, Synod of Midwest, to succeed herself for a three-year term.
(1) MS. MARTHA JO MIMS, 3011 Wolfe Road, Columbus, MS 39705, Mt Zion Congregation, Grace Presbytery, Southeast Synod, for a three-year term

IV. TRUSTEES OF MEMPHIS THEOLOGICAL SEMINARY OF THE CUMBERLAND PRESBYTERIAN CHURCH

(Members whose terms expire in 2022)

(1) MR. GREG ALLEN, 1138 Balbade Drive, Nashville, TN 37215, Brenthaven Congregation, Nashville Presbytery, Tennessee Synod, for a three-year term
(1) REV. JILL CARR, PO Box 1547, Lebanon, MO 65536, White Oak Pond Congregation, Missouri Presbytery, Synod of Great Rivers, for a three-year term
(2) *MS. JANE ASHLEY FOLK, 4405 Dunwick Lane, Fort Worth, TX 76109, to succeed herself for a three-year term
(2) *MR. LARRY HILLIARD, 206 E Bankhead Street, New Albany, MS 38652, to succeed himself for a three-year term
(1) MRS. CHERYL LESLIE, 3374 Walnut Grove Road, Memphis, TN 38111, Germantown Congregation, West Tennessee Presbytery, Synod of Great Rivers for a three-year term
(1) *MS. LISANNE MARSHALL, 325 Meadow Grove Lane, Memphis, TN 38120, for a three-year term
(1) *REV. DR. KEITH NORMAN, 2835 Broad Avenue, Memphis, TN 38112, for a three-year term
(2) *DR. DEBORAH SMITH, 584 E McLemore Avenue, Memphis, TN 38106, to succeed herself for a three-year term

(Members whose terms expire in 2020)

(1) *MS. ANNA ROBBINS, 2714 Lombard Avenue, Memphis, TN 38111, to fill an unexpired one-year term

V. STEWARDSHIP, FOUNDATION AND BENEFITS

(Members whose terms expire in 2022)

(2) REV. KEN BYFORD, 23746 Highway 9 N, Piedmont, AL 36272, Piedmont Congregation, Grace Presbytery, Southeast Synod, to succeed himself for a three-year term
(2) MS. ANDREA SMITH, 1715 Water Cure Road, Winchester, TN 37398, Winchester Congregation, Murfreesboro Presbytery, Tennessee Synod, to succeed herself for a three-year term.
(1) MRS. MARY JO RAY, 16 Nottingham Lane, Columbus, MS 39705, Mt Zion Congregation, Grace Presbytery, Southeast Synod, for a three-year term
(1) MR. OWEN SMITH, 119 Pine Island Drive, Marshall, TX 75672, Marshall Congregation, Trinity Presbytery, Mission Synod

GENERAL ASSEMBLY COMMISSIONS:

VI. MILITARY CHAPLAINS AND PERSONNEL

(Members whose terms expire in 2022)

(1) REV. SHELIA O'MARA, PO Box 170, Gadsden, TN 38337, Presbytery del Cristo, Mission Synod, for a three-year term.

GENERAL ASSEMBLY COMMITTEES

VII. JUDICIARY

(Members whose terms expire in 2022)

(2) REV. JAN OVERTON, 3320 Pipeline Road, Birmingham, AL 35243, Crestline Congregation, Grace Presbytery, Southeast Synod, to succeed herself for a three-year term.
(2) MS. RACHEL MOSES, 1138 Blaine Avenue, Cookeville, TN 38501, First Church Cookeville Congregation, Murfreesboro Presbytery, Tennessee Synod, to succeed herself for a three-year term
(1) REV. DR. ROGER REID, 637 Colburn Drive, Lewisburg, TN 37091, First Church Lewisburg Congregation Columbia Presbytery, Tennessee Synod, for a three-year term.

VIII. NOMINATING

(Members whose terms expire in 2022)

(1) MS. ALLISON CARR, PO Box 1547, Lebanon, MO 65536, White Oak Pond Congregation, Missouri Presbytery, Synod of Great Rivers, for a three-year term
(1) MS. DIANN PHELPS, 4743 Happy Hollow Road, Hawesville, KY 42348, Dukes Congregation, Cumberland Presbytery, Synod of Midwest, for a three-year term
(1) REV. MICAIAH TANCK, 902 Tipperary Drive, Scottsboro, AL 35768, Scottsboro Congregation, Robert Donnell Presbytery, Southeast Synod, for a three-year term
(1) REV. BRENT WILLS, 4607 E Richmond Shop, Lebanon, TN 37090, Jerusalem Congregation, Murfreesboro Presbytery, Tennessee Synod, for a three-year term

IX. OUR UNITED OUTREACH COMMITTEE

(Members whose terms expire in 2022)

(2) REV. BRUCE HAMILTON, 1037 Binns Drive, Monticello, AR 71655, Rose Hill Congregation, Arkansas Presbytery, Synod of Great Rivers, to succeed himself for a three-year term
(Members whose terms expire in 2020)

YOUTH ADVISORY MEMBERS
(shall be between the ages of 15 and 17 years of age, elected for a one year term
and is eligible for an additional one term)

(1) MS. SIERRA ALEXANDER, 1014 Wren Street, Dyersburg, TN 38024, Dyersburg Congregation, West Tennessee Presbytery, Synod of Great Rivers, for a one-year term
(1) MS. KAILEY SUNDSTROM, 309 Bryson Lane, Clarksville, TN 37043, Clarksville Congregation, Nashville Presbytery, Tennessee Synod, for a one-year term
(1) MR. NATE WOOD, 17246 Highway K, Aurora, MO 65605, Orange Congregation, Missouri Presbytery, Synod of Great Rivers, for a one-year term

X. UNIFIED COMMITTEE ON THEOLOGY AND SOCIAL CONCERNS

(Members whose terms expire in 2022)

(1) REV. VIRGINIA ESPINOZA, PO Box 132, Boswell, OK 74727, Pigeon Roost Congregation, Choctaw Presbytery, Mission Synod, for a three-year term
(1) REV. TERRA SISCO, 811 W Cheyenne Street, Marlow, OK 73055, Marlow Congregation, Red River Presbytery, Mission Synod, for a three-year term
(1) REV. JO WARREN, 811 Wall Street, Morrilton, AR 72110, Trinity Congregation, Arkansas Presbytery, Synod of Great Rivers, for a three-year term

*Ecumenical Representative   +Cumberland Presbyterian Church in America

THE REPORT OF THE PLACE OF MEETING COMMITTEE

The Place of Meeting Committee consists of the Moderator, a representative of the Cumberland Presbyterian Women's Ministry, and the Stated Clerk who serves as the chairperson. The representative of the Cumberland Presbyterian Women's Ministry is the Convention Coordinator.

The 165th General Assembly, "authorized the committee to select meeting places up to five years in the future and that preference be given that keeps, insofar as possible, the General Assembly and the Convention of Cumberland Presbyterian Women's Ministry, and guest rooms in one facility. It is recognized that these places are hard to find and may cost some additional monies. The place of meeting committee will use its best judgment." The 173rd General Assembly approved exploring the use of college campuses and very large conference centers in addition to hotels/convention centers. When the Office of the General Assembly receives an invitation from a congregation or a presbytery, the Stated Clerk makes a site visit. If adequate facilities are discovered, a follow up visit is made by the Stated Clerk, the Assistant to the Stated Clerk, and the Convention Coordinator of the Cumberland Presbyterian Women's Ministry.

Commissioners, delegates to Conventions, and visitors are encouraged to stay at the General Assembly/Convention hotel, to assure meeting the contracted room block. Hotel contracts also include a commitment on food and beverages, thus it is important for boards/agencies to continue to sponsor special meal functions. The luncheons/dinners provide opportunities for the sponsoring agencies/boards to keep the church informed about their respective programs, thus enhancing support.

I. INFORMATION ABOUT FUTURE GENERAL ASSEMBLIES

Continued discussions with the leadership of the Cumberland Presbyterian Church in America regarding joint meetings of the General Assemblies in 2020 and 2021 may impact future meeting locations.

It is helpful to continue scheduling a few years in advance of the meeting to assure that adequate hotel/convention space is available and to negotiate a good rate. If a congregation or a presbytery is interested in hosting the General Assembly/Convention, the Office of the General Assembly will provide information on hosting responsibilities. Hosting the General Assembly/Convention is a service to the Church, allowing the Church to celebrate the good ministries occurring within a particular presbytery, and provides persons within a presbytery the opportunity to participate more fully in the annual meeting.

In the event that no invitation is received in a particular year or a situation arises requiring a change of venue for a particular year, the Corporate Board will be responsible for selecting a place of meeting.

The Office of the General Assembly has received an invitation from West Tennessee Presbytery to host a future meeting of the General Assembly.

II. SCHEDULE OF MEETINGS BY PRESBYTERIES

The following schedule shows the annual meetings and the year that the General Assembly last met in the bounds of a particular presbytery.

Presbytery	Year	Presbytery	Year
Choctaw & Red River	2018	Columbia	2005
Grace	2017	East Tennessee	2003
Nashville	2016	Covenant	2002
Cauca Valley & Andes	2015	del Cristo	2001
Tennessee-Georgia	2014	Cumberland	2000
Murfreesboro	2013	North Central	1980
Hope & Robert Donnell	2012	Trinity	1969
Missouri	2011		
Nashville	2010		
West Tennessee	2009		
Japan	2008		
Arkansas	2007		

Respectfully submitted,
Michael G. Sharpe
Jo Ann Shugert
Jay Earheart-Brown

THE REPORT OF THE UNIFIED COMMITTEE ON THEOLOGY AND SOCIAL CONCERNS

I. MEETING AND OFFICERS

The Unified Committee on Theology and Social Concerns (UCTSC) met in Nashville, Tennessee on November 2-3, 2018 and in Huntsville, Alabama, March 8-9, 2019. The following officers were elected during the fall meeting: Reverend Edmund Cox (CPCA) and Reverend Mitch Boulton (CPC) Co-Chairs; and Reverend Nancy Fuqua (CPCA), Secretary.

II. EXPIRATION OF TERMS

The Committee notes that the terms of service for Reverend Byron Forester, Elder Joy Wallace expire in 2019. Reverend John Smith resigned from the committee to join the Presbyterian Church (USA).

III. GENERAL ASSEMBLY REPRESENTATIVE

The Committee elected Reverend Edmund Cox (CPCA) to serve as the representative to the meeting of the CPC/CPCA General Assembles in Huntsville, Alabama. Reverend Lisa Scott (CPC) was elected as the alternate.

IV. GENERAL ASSEMBLY REFERRAL

The 188th CPC General Assembly referred to the UCTSC to work jointly with the Permanent Judiciary Committee and Ministry Council to develop a position statement on the issues of human sexuality and to present the statement to the 189th General Assembly. The UCTSC received many study papers on the subject and are grateful to those who submitted papers. Due to the complexity, various opinions and cultural differences on human sexuality, the UCTSC has not been able to finalize a statement in time for this year's General Assembly

RECOMMENDATION 1: The UCTSC requests more time to consider other pertinent information from various perspectives in order to set forth a loving, Biblical and theological sound response.

The UCTSC will continue it's work on the referral, by seeking to hear voices from within the church that would like to speak to this issue. Anyone who would like to speak to the UCTSC, is invited to contact either Co-Chairs or the Secretary of the committee. Contact information can be found on the UCTSC website (www.cumberland.org/uctsc).

V. STUDY PAPERS

The Committee is currently reviewing the following study papers. 1. "A Theological Statement on Inclusion of the LGBTQIA Community in the Cumberland Presbyterian Church." 2. "Human Sexuality in the Bible". 3. "Homosexuality Activity and Marriage in the Cumberland Presbyterian Church". 4. "Authority of Jesus". The Committee expects to complete its review of these papers prior to the meetings of the 190th General Assemblies.

VI. WORKS IN PROGRESS

The UCTSC has developed guidelines for a theological/social concerns panel made up of representatives of the CPC/CPCA to address emerging issues in a timelier way. Panel responses would not have the official sanction of the CPC or CPCA but would provide useful reflections for persons in our two churches. The Committee expects to launch the panel during 2019. Communications announcing the panel and its work will be distributed to both churches.

Respectfully Submitted,
Unified Committee on Theology and Social Concerns

THE REPORT OF THE UNIFICATION TASK FORCE

I. MEETING AND OFFICERS

The Unification Task Force of the Cumberland Presbyterian Church in America (CPCA) and the Cumberland Presbyterian Church (CPC) since the last meeting of the General Assemblies: November 1-2, 2018 and March 21-22, 2019 in Nashville, Tennessee. Officers elected are: Elton Hall and Steve Mosley - co-chairs; and Craig White and Jay Earheart-Brown - secretaries. Other members of the UTF from the CPCA are: Leon Cole, Arthur Heywood, Lynne Herring, William Robinson, and Mitchell Walker. Other members from the CPC are: Perryn Rice, Robert Rush, Gloria Villa-Diaz, Joy Warren, and Mike Sharpe.

Steve Mosley and Perryn Rice were elected to serve as representatives of the UTF to the meetings of the General Assemblies in Huntsville, Alabama.

II. WORK OF THE TASK FORCE

Members of the UTF have traveled widely in our two churches, and spoken to many different gatherings of Cumberland Presbyterians, answering questions and providing educational sessions about the Plan of Union. We have also written articles for the church magazines, and worked to advocate for Unification at every opportunity. Members of our Task Force have covenanted to pray for unity between our churches at noon each day, and we continue to seek God's will for our churches.

We have consulted with the attorneys for our two churches and continue to seek the best way to bring about the proposed unification - the way that will be least disruptive, most cost effective, and honoring to the traditions of both denominations.

III. PLAN OF UNION

Our latest revisions have been completed during this year with advice from counsel, and taking into account continued input from across our churches. Believing that the time is right for our two churches to decide if the time is right to move ahead, we offer the Plan of Union with the prayer that it will receive favor from commissioners to the General Assemblies of the CPCA and the CPC.

PROPOSED PLAN OF UNION
A Brief Overview

The 2014 General Assemblies, in concurrent session at Chattanooga, Tennessee, approved for study a Proposed Plan of Union. That plan has been distributed widely across both denominations, and has generated a great deal of discussion and feedback. For almost four years the plan has been studied. We are grateful for all the responses the Task Force has received, both positive and negative. The Task Force has carefully studied the responses, from the table discussions at Chattanooga, to the surveys distributed at Presbytery meetings and on-line, to individual letters received by the GA offices and by members of the Task Force. On the basis of all the responses to the proposed plan, and several meetings attended by members of the Task Force, we voted in our November meeting not to ask for a formal vote on the plan at the 2016 meetings of the General Assembly, which would have been the earliest possible date for such a vote.

We, instead, spent significant time revising the Proposed Plan of Union, and presented it to the concurrent meetings of the two General Assemblies in 2016, with the recommendation that the revised plan be approved for study in the two churches. At the 2017 General Assemblies, meeting concurrently near Tampa, Florida, we proposed that 2017-2019 both churches devote two years to relationship building and continued study of the Plan of Union. We then suggested that the plan be put to a vote at the concurrent General Assemblies meeting in Huntsville, Alabama in June of 2019. If approved by both Assemblies, the Plan of Union would be sent to the Presbyteries of both churches for approval of the Plan between the 2019 and 2020 Assemblies. If approved by a majority of Presbyteries of both churches, the 2020 Assemblies would meet to finalize their business, adjourn sine die, and organize the new Assembly of the United Church in 2021.

While we do not know what the outcome of such a vote at next year's assemblies will be, we on the Task Force are convinced that the time is right for both churches to decide if we are ready to move forward with our union or not. If now is not the time, then we do not need to continue the work of the Task Force at the present, but put our energies into our cooperating when and where we can as brothers and sisters in Christ. It is our sincere desire as members of the Task Force to see this union happen, and we have been deeply enriched by our work together on this project for the past six years. But ultimately it is the churches who must decide this matter.

We urge the commissioners to the 2018 General Assemblies to read the Plan carefully and make any proposed amendments the Assemblies would like to see incorporated into the plan this year, so that the Task Force will have time to incorporate those changes before next year's vote. Of course, the 2019 Assemblies will have the opportunity to amend the Plan before approving it, but amendments made next year will have to be dealt with in a well-structured manner in order to receive consideration by both Assemblies.

During the April meeting (2018), we decided to write, with consultation from our attorneys, draft Bylaws, Standing Rules, and Constitutional Amendments that will be circulated to both churches prior to the vote in 2019, so that there are as few details left hanging as possible. We hope to have those documents ready for distribution prior to the 2019 General Assembly meetings, so that commissioners and others will have ample time to study them prior to the vote.

With thanksgiving to God for the relationships we have developed as we have worked together for the past six years, and in hopes that all Cumberland Presbyterians may one day live and work together in one church, the UTF submits the following Proposed Plan of Union.

Proposed Plan for Union of the Cumberland Presbyterian Church and the Cumberland Presbyterian Church in America

"There is one, holy, universal, apostolic church. She is the body of Christ, who is her Head and Lord" (*Confession of Faith* 5.01). "The church is one because her head and Lord is one, Jesus Christ. Her oneness under her Lord is manifested in the one ministry of word and sacrament, not in any uniformity of covenantal expression, organization, or system of doctrine" (5.02). "The church, as the covenant community of believers who are redeemed, includes all people in all ages, past, present, and future, who respond in faith to God's covenant of grace, and all who are unable to respond, for reasons known to God, but who are saved by his grace" (5.06). It is on this belief that the Unification Task Force recommends the union of the Cumberland Presbyterian Church in America (CPCA) and the Cumberland Presbyterian Church (CPC). We are one in Christ by the grace of God and the power of the Holy Spirit! We believe that becoming one will strengthen our witness as Christian believers in the world, and that together we will be able to accomplish more for the glory of God. United together in Christ by faith, we are united to one another in love. In this communion we share the grace of Christ with one another, bear one another's burdens, and reach out to all other persons (*Confession of Faith* 5.10).

1.00 Mission Statement for the New Church
The Cumberland Presbyterian Church United affirms the great commission of Christ: "Go, therefore, and make disciples of all nations, baptizing them in the name of the Father, and of the Son, and of the Holy Spirit, and teaching them to obey everything that I have commanded you. And remember I am with you until the end of the age" (Matthew 28:19-20). We celebrate our oneness in faith. As disciples, we seek through worship, global witness, and service to be the hands and feet of Christ and to live out the love of Jesus Christ to the glory of God.

2.00 The *Confession of Faith and Government*
The Cumberland Presbyterian Church United will use the *Confession of Faith and Government* of the Cumberland Presbyterian Church and the Cumberland Presbyterian Church in America, approved by both General Assemblies of the former denominations in 1984 as its system of faith and government.

2.01 The Cumberland Presbyterian Church United will use the *Catechism for Cumberland Presbyterians* (2008) for instruction in the faith and will include it in an updated edition of the *Confession of Faith and Government of the Cumberland Presbyterian Church United*.

2.02 The CP *Digest* (CPC) and Summaries of Actions (for both denominations) will continue to serve as resource tools. A new *Digest* will begin with the formation of the Cumberland Presbyterian Church United.

3.00 The Presbyteries and Synods
3.01 In an effort to make union something more than just an idea on paper, and to engage the grassroots in creating the new church, we recommend a restructure of the synod boundaries to create eight synods for the

new church, with the following presbyteries in each –

Synod A*	Synod B*	Synod C	Synod D
Brazos River	Angelina	Covenant	Cleveland, Ohio
Del Cristo	Arkansas	Missouri	Cumberland
Red River	East Texas	New Hopewell	North Central
Hong Kong	Trinity	Purchase	Ohio Valley
Japan	Andes	West Tennessee	
Choctaw	Cauca Valley		
	Emaus		

Synod E	Synod F	Synod G	Synod H
Columbia	East Tennessee	Florence	Birmingham
Elk River	Hiawassee	Hope	Grace
Murfreesboro	Tennessee-Georgia	Huntsville	South Alabama
Nashville	East Coast Korean	Robert Donnell	Tuscaloosa
		Tennessee Valley	

For relationship building during the first six years, all synods will be encouraged to hold an annual general meeting (*Constitution* 8.2) as opposed to a delegated meeting. Synods may petition General Assembly at any point for a change in boundaries.

NOTE: There are dreams for organizing a third presbytery in Asia. As soon as it is practical to do so, whether before or after union, two additional synods could be constituted. Synod I would include Andes, Cauca Valley, Emaus and any other presbyteries organized in Latin America. Synod J would include Hong Kong, Japan, and any other presbyteries organized in Asia.

3.02 Presbyteries will remain as they are constituted at the time of union. During the first six years of the new church's life, synods will be encouraged to study the most beneficial presbyterial boundaries within their jurisdiction to fulfill of the mission of the church. Presbyteries may petition their synod at any time for a change in boundaries.

4.00 Commissioners and Youth Advisory Delegates to the General Assembly
4.01 Commissioners to General Assembly - Each Presbytery will be entitled to send 2 minister commissioners and 2 elder commissioners to the General Assembly.

NOTE: If presbytery boundaries remain as currently constituted at the time of unification, this will allow for a total possible membership in the General Assembly of 152 commissioners. Of these potential commissioners, 60 would come from former presbyteries of the CPCA, and 92 would come from the former CPC.

4.02 Youth Advisory Delegates - Each presbytery will be entitled to send up to two Youth Advisory delegates to the General Assembly.

5.00 Moderator and Vice Moderator of General Assembly
5.01 The moderator/vice moderator will be elected each year during the first six years with the two offices alternating between persons from the two former denominations.

5.02 The moderator and vice moderator of the Cumberland Presbyterian Church United will reflect its diverse nature, to include international representatives. The church expects the moderator and vice moderator to travel within the denomination, sharing and gathering information among its local churches. Expenses and particular duties will be detailed in the Bylaws of the Cumberland Presbyterian Church United.

6.00 Stated Clerk and Associate Stated Clerk of the General Assembly

6.01 The new church shall employ a Stated Clerk and an Associate Stated Clerk. Both positions will be full-time jobs. During the first six years of the Cumberland Presbyterian Church United, the Stated Clerk will serve six years and the Associate Stated Clerk will serve four years, after which each would be elected for a four-year period. One position will be filled by a former CPCA and the other position filled by a former CPC during their first terms. The subsequent election of each position will allow for continuity during transitions. Particular duties and responsibilities of the Stated Clerk and Associate Stated Clerk will be detailed in the Bylaws of the Cumberland Presbyterian Church United.

7.00 Boards and Agencies of the General Assembly

7.01 Each church has programs in various stages of planning and implementation that are the result of commitment to ministry through the church. Insofar as possible, these plans and programs will be continued without interruption for a period of three years. The Cumberland Presbyterian Church has covenantal relationships with the Cumberland Presbyterian Children's Home in Denton, Texas and Bethel University in McKenzie, Tennessee. These covenantal relationships will remain in effect as they exist at the time of Unification, to be renewed every four years. The Cumberland Presbyterian Church United will continue ecumenical partnerships, such as with the World Communion of Reformed Churches

7.02 Institutional Boards

The General Assembly shall have the following institutional boards: Trustees of Memphis Theological Seminary to include the Program of Alternate Studies and School of Continuing Education Committee, and Trustees of the Historical Foundation. Representation on each Board of Trustees will remain as they are constituted at the time of union.

7.03 Administrative Boards

The General Assembly shall have the following administrative Boards: The Board of Stewardship, Foundation and Benefits and The Board of Directors of the General Assembly Corporation. During the transition period, each of these boards will have equal number of members from each of the former denominations.

7.04 Commission

The General Assembly shall have the following commission: Chaplains and Military Personnel. Representation on the commission will be merged as they are constituted at the time of union until natural rotation occurs.

7.05 Standing Committees

The General Assembly shall have the following standing committees: Theology and Social Concerns, Judiciary, Our United Outreach, Nominating, and Multi-Cultural Ministry.

Committee representation on the Theology and Social Concerns Committee will remain as constituted at the time of union until natural rotations occurs.

Judiciary and Nominating committees in both denominations will each be merged at the time of union.

Committee representation for Our United Outreach will be expanded to include two elected representatives from each new synod (one voting representative from each of the former denominations until natural rotation occurs).

The Committee on Multi-Cultural Ministry is a new committee that will reflect the diversity of the Cumberland Presbyterian Church United. This committee will be comprised of eight (8) elected persons that will reflect the celebrative understanding of humanity in the areas of culture, language, heritage, and experience in the Cumberland Presbyterian Church United. Believing that all have been created in God's image, this committee works to answer the question of our sameness in God's image lived out in diverse ways.

7.06 Program Board

The Cumberland Presbyterian Church United will have a Mission and Ministry Program Board to provide coordination and oversight for those ministries formally planned and implemented by the two former denominations. After the three-year period, the new programming and denominational structure will consist of the following ministry teams and auxiliaries:

- Christian Education & Nurture (Youth Convention & National Sunday School Convention,

Discipleship Ministry Team)
- Missions (Evangelism, Missionary Auxiliary, Women's Ministry, Missions Ministry Team)
- Clergy Care & Development (Pastoral Development Ministry Team)
- Communications (Cumberland Flag, Cumberland Presbyterian Magazine, Missionary Messenger, Ministry Council website, Communications Ministry Team)

Composition of each ministry team will include equal number of persons from each of the former denominations in the new church at the time of union. Composition of the new Missions and Ministry Program Board will include one staff person (serving as an advisory member) and one elected member from each ministry team, along with one elected member representing each of the synods. The elected members will be equally representative of the two former denominations for the first six years. A Ministry Coordinator would provide executive leadership for the Mission and Ministry Program Board.

8. Denominational Staff & Personnel
The current breakdown of the number of denominational staff by the employing entities housed at each Denominational Center is as follows:
Cumberland Presbyterian Church in America Center in Huntsville, AL
General Assembly Office – 2.
Cumberland Presbyterian Church Center in Memphis, TN
General Assembly Office – 2, Board of Stewardship – 3, Central Accounting – 1,
Historical Foundation – 2, Ministry Council – 17 (5 of which have distant office locations).

8.01 The new organizational structure will discontinue the positions of Administrative Director (CPCA) and the Director of Ministries (CPC) and will create the positions of Associate Stated Clerk and Mission and Ministry Program Coordinator. The Stated Clerk and Associate Stated Clerk will be elected during the General Assembly of 2021. The Mission and Ministry Program Coordinator will be employed by the Mission and Ministry Program Board.

8.02 Staffing for the Cumberland Presbyterian Church United will reflect the diversity of the new church. As new staff positions become available, equal opportunity employment practices will prevail.

8.03 Denominational Offices –During the first six years, steps are to be taken to assure that regional sites be located in a minimum of three and a maximum of five locations. Thus, neither the Center in Huntsville nor the Center in Memphis will be designated as "the denominational center." By placing regional sites in a variety of locations this will assure that all areas of the church will be served equally. These regional sites can make use of offices in existing churches, or in homes of regional staff persons. Possible regional locations could be Memphis, Huntsville, Louisville, Texas, South America, Asia, etc.

8.04 Global Staff - There will be endorsed missionaries, mission liaisons, and partner missionaries in the new church. The new church will continue to support current and future missionaries and global work. Current missionaries include – Patrick and Jessica Wilkerson (Colombia, South America), Beth Wallace missionary emeritus (Colombia, South America), Fhanor and Socorro Pejendino (Guatemala), Daniel & Kay Jang (Philippines), Kenneth & Delight Hopson (Uganda), Josue and Sara Guerrero (Brazil), Wilson and Diana Lopez (Spain), David and Sarah Lee (Cambodia), Missionaries in undisclosed countries (2), CP missionaries supported by their presbyteries – Iwao Satoh, Mission liaisons working in Haiti and Brazil. Undisclosed (yet to be announced) missionary couple to be deployed to Guatemala.

9.00 Stewardship and Finance
9.01 Legal control of assets of both churches will be transferred to the Cumberland Presbyterian Church United through appropriate legal transaction. The intent of all designated gifts and endowments will be honored.

9.02 The Cumberland Presbyterian Church United will develop an approach to the financing of the programs of the church that reflects the stewardship understanding of the new constituency. Such a unitary approach will be developed as soon as possible after formation and no later than the end of the first six years.

10.00 Recognition of Ordination
All ordinations, both clergy and lay (elders and deacons), of both denominations will be recognized by

the Cumberland Presbyterian Church United. All future ordinations will be governed by the conditions specified in the Constitution. Persons who are recognized by their respective presbyteries as candidates and licentiates at the time the new church is formed will fulfill the requirements as specified by presbytery at the time they became probationers.

11.00 The Name of the New Denomination
The name of the denomination shall be the Cumberland Presbyterian Church United.

12.00 The Logo of the New Church
A new logo will be fashioned by the new church.

III. REVISED TIMELINE FOR THE PLAN OF UNION

· **2019** – Meeting concurrently in Huntsville, Alabama, the two assemblies vote on approving the Plan of Union, Draft Bylaws and Draft Constitutional Amendments, pending approval of a majority of presbyteries of the two churches. Any Constitutional amendments are sent to the Joint Committee on Amendments for review and preparation of final wording. Both Judiciary committees and Joint Committee on Amendments will be reviewing draft documents at their March meeting.

· **2019-2020** – If approved by a majority of both assemblies, the Plan is sent to the Presbyteries of both churches for approval (Much like a Constitutional Amendment is circulated to Presbyteries for ratification).

· **2020** – The two Assemblies, meeting concurrently, announce the vote of their Presbyteries, and if approved by a majority of both, vote on final approval of Bylaws and Standing Rules for the General Assembly of the new church (2/3 vote of approval necessary). Constitutional amendments reviewed and prepared by the Joint Committee on Amendments are approved (3/4 vote of approval necessary to refer amendments to Presbyteries for approval, and 3/4 of presbyteries, voting by simple majority, needed to approve amendments). If both assemblies approve Bylaws, the two assemblies vote to adjourn sine die, and will meet in 2021 to organize the new Assembly of the united Church. The Unification Task Force is dismissed, and an Implementation Task Force is elected to guide the transition for the first few years to the new denomination.

• **2021** – The new Cumberland Presbyterian Church United is officially organized.

RECOMMENDATION 1: That this Proposed Plan for Union be adopted by the General Assemblies of the CPCA and the CPC; and that upon such approval, it be forwarded to the presbyteries of the CPCA and the CPC for ratification during the 2019-2020 year. Presbyteries will be instructed to submit a report of their vote to their respective General Assembly clerks in time to be announced by the 2020 General Assemblies.

IV. UNITY SUNDAY

Both denominations have added unity Sunday to our calendars for the fourth Sunday in June. We encourage presbyteries to encourage their churches to observe this day as a time to give thanks to God for the unity we have in Christ, and to pray for greater unity among all Cumberland Presbyterians.

Members of this Task Force are deeply grateful for the trust placed in us, and the opportunity afforded us to work on this task over the past several years. Our lives have been enriched by new and deepened relationships, and our knowledge of and appreciation for our two denominations has been increased immeasurably.

Respectfully submitted,
Unification Task Force
Elton Hall and Steve Mosley, co-chairs

THE REPORT OF BOARD OF TRUSTEES OF BETHEL UNIVERSITY

The 2018-2019 Bethel University school year has been a very busy year for our University. Our Fall 2018 total enrollment was 4,850 students. 1,315 of these students attend classes on our McKenzie campus. Another 168 attend in our Health Sciences College in the Physician Assistant Program, Nursing Program and the Athletic Training Program. The remainder 3,367 students attend either our adult programs or our dual enrollment programs in local Tennessee High Schools.

In the calendar year of 2018, we submitted our 10 year Reaffirmation Plan to Southern Association of Colleges and Universities Commission on Colleges (SACSCOC). It was a University wide effect. In December 2018, at the annual SACSCOC meeting, we found that we were reaffirmed and reaccredited for another 10 years. We will have to send a financial monitoring report this October, 2019, to SACSCOC for our only follow-up. Our next 10 year reaffirmation plan for SACSCOC will be 2028.

Our Board of Trustees has announced that our long awaited Chapel should be completed during the 2020-2021 academic school year. As we write this report, our architects are finalizing the plans for our current site, adjacent to our Vera Low Center for Student Enrichment. Initial plans have the chapel seating over 1,200 at worship.

During this current academic year, Bethel has seen many awards/honors for our students. Our Bass Fishing Team was crowned National Champions for 2018 and The Bass Fishing Team of the year (the first time ever a school has received both awards). Our sport programs have also been awarded The Gold Medal for Champions of Character. That is the highest award a school can be given and is not based on wins and losses, but is based on a team's GPA, Character and Service. Both basketball teams went to the National Tournament and our football team finished the regular season 10-0.

Our students have traveled on medical and humanitarian trips to Belize, Cuba, Columbia, and Thailand this year. Our Global Studies Department is growing fast and new trips are being planned. If you are interested in joining our group on a trip contact freemans@bethelu.edu.

In March of 2019, we finally won in our lawsuit with The Tennessee State Board of Education over our ability to propose students for teacher licensure. You may recall in July of 2016, The State of Tennessee Department of Education said we could no longer recommend students for teacher licensure. We had 7 court appearances and prevailed in every one. There are now no more appeals available to The State of Tennessee. The decision by The State of Tennessee, in July of 2016, has financially been very harmful to Bethel University. We are hopeful The State of Tennessee will make some financial amends.

Finally, we are excited to partner with The Memphis Theological Seminary and a donor in the "Whosoever Will Ministry Bridge" program. Students from Bethel University who go on to attend the Memphis Theological Seminary can be eligible for a $1,000.00 tax free stipend for 60 months. It is the most innovative idea to grow The Cumberland Presbyterian Church we have ever seen.

Please pray for Bethel University. Please donate to Bethel University. Please visit Bethel University. Bethel Forevermore!

Dr. Walter Butler, President
Bethel University

THE REPORT OF THE BOARD OF TRUSTEES OF THE CUMBERLAND PRESBYTERIAN CHILDREN'S HOME

Introduction

Because of the life-giving grace through Jesus Christ, we at Cumberland Presbyterian Children's Home serve God by serving others. We accept individuals as they are and help them through their journey. We build relationships with those we serve through strength-based love and support. We want our children and families to be empowered as we strive to achieve excellence through our mission work. Our mission statement is:

In response to Christ's love and example
we serve children and families by providing healing and hope.

Our ministry has continually focused on serving children and families for over 115 years.

I. OUR GOAL

Our goal is for children to be protected and live free from abuse and neglect while healing from the devastating impacts of past trauma. We do this in our Children's Residential Program by providing both emergency shelter and long term residential care to youth in foster care, so they flourish in a safe place. In addition to housing, we provide therapeutic services such as weekly individual and group counseling, case management, life skills training and other supportive services. The Family Residential Program provides transitional housing, case management, counseling, parent education and other supportive services to single parent families who are experiencing crisis. The goal of the Family Residential Program is to help families find a new beginning and work toward independence and healing. Our goal is to engage our community by having a thriving volunteer program and welcoming environment for all who support us in our undertaking by building relationships with our community partners and individuals who wish to make a difference in the lives of children and families. We serve to bring ourselves and others closer to God.

II. OUR VALUES

Our values are based on the greatest commandments. Love the Lord your God with all your heart and with all your soul and with all your mind and with all your strength: this is the first commandment. The second is this: Love your neighbor as yourself. There is no commandment greater than these. Mark 12:30-31.

All we are and all we do at the Children's Home is an act of love for our neighbors. Our neighbors who are so in need. The Child Welfare Information Gateway reported 437,465 children in foster care across the country. Within Texas Region 3, where the Children's Home is located, there are 3,681 children in foster care, but only 214 homes for these children. National statistics indicate that children in foster care are nine time more likely to commit a crime, 25 time likely to get pregnant as a teenager and there is a 30% chance they will continue the cycle of abuse against their own children.

The Children's Home provides hope and healing for vulnerable children and families as an act of love for God and our neighbors. We use our guiding principles of faith, acceptance, care, and excellence in all we do at the Children's Home.

III. OUR BOARD OF TRUSTEES AND GOVERNANCE

Cumberland Presbyterian Children's Home is a non-profit and tax exempt under IRS Code section 501(c)(3). Our board currently has 15 trustees (up to 18 total) and they meet twice per year in February and September. Ten of those seats must be filled by members of the Cumberland Presbyterian Church or the Cumberland Presbyterian Church of America.

IV. OUR CURRENT BOARD OF TRUSTEES

Chair: Mr. Charles Harris; Vice Chair: Mr. Brian Martin; Secretary: Mrs. Guin Tyus; Board at Large Members: Mr. Pete Carter; Mr. Brian Cartwright; Mr. Richard Dean; Mrs. Carolyn Harmon; Ms.

Patricia Long; Mr. Cameron Marone; Reverend Joyce Merritt; Mr. Knight Miller; Reverend Dr. Perryn Rice; Mr. Sam Suddarth; Mr. Jay Thomas; and Mr. Matthew Whitten.

V. FINANCIALS

Cumberland Presbyterian Children's Home depends on denominational support, OUO, donations, grants, planned-giving, investments, fee for service revenue, and endowments to operate. Relationships with our donors are essential to growing and expanding our relationships to others who wish to be involved with our mission. We need your support. We need monetary donations, gifts in kind, and benefit from annual and legacy giving. Our goal is to provide the best care and the best environment for our children and families. The following is the breakdown in revenue received in these key categories. Based on our annual audit, in 2017 the Children's Home received the following in donations and revenue for our home.

- 25% in individual contributions and grants
- 23% in Texas Department of Family & Protective Services reimbursement revenue
- 2% in other program fees
- 2% in denomination support
- 3% in income on long term investments
- 13% on unrealized gains on investments
- 1% on oil and gas royalties
- 16% on rental revenue

In 2019, the Children's Home is working hard to decrease costs and ensure we are being good stewards of the donations and support we have received throughout our history. Continued giving allows us to fulfill our mission and build our endowments. The Children's Home legacy continues to flourish. Cumberland spends approximately 83% of all revenue on our children and families. The small reminder is spent on administrative and fundraising costs.

VI. OUR PROGRAMS

A. CHILDREN'S RESIDENTIAL PROGRAM

The Children's Home has two cottages dedicated to long term residential care and one emergency shelter cottage that provide housing and services for children in foster care who have been removed from their homes as a result of abuse or neglect.

Cole Cottage: A long term care cottage that serves 8 children, boys and girls, ages 11-17 with a basic or moderate level of care. In addition to residential housing, we provide case management, weekly counseling with on-site therapists, life skills training, mentoring, culturally competent activities, spiritual development, access to individualized therapeutic activities and access to medical, dental and behavioral health. The average length of stay in Cole Cottage is approximately one year.

Heard Cottage: A long term care cottage that serves 10 girls ages 11-17 with a specialized level of care. Children who need specialized level of care have severe problems in one or more areas of functioning, including: unpredictable, non-violent, anti-social acts, physical aggression, withdrawal and isolation, self-injurious actions, primary diagnosis of substance abuse or dependency, developmental delays or intellectual disabilities, medical or habilitative needs that require assistance. Beyond long term residential care, the Children's Home treatment team and chaplain provide case management, weekly individual and group counseling with on-site therapist, life skills training, mentoring, culturally competent activities, spiritual development, access to individualized therapeutic activities and access to medical and dental care. The average length of stay for the Specialized Cottage is anticipated to be six months.

Currie Long Cottage: A emergency shelter for foster care youth ages 5-17. We serve 8 children with an average length of stay of approximately 90 days. The Children's Home treatment team and chaplain provide case management, weekly counseling with on-site therapists, life skills training, culturally competent activities, spiritual development, and access to medical and dental care.

B. FAMILY RESIDENTIAL PROGRAM

This program serves single parent families in crisis by providing transitional housing, case management, family counseling, financial coaching through United Way and education assistance through a local community college. Our program helps them work toward self-sufficiency and independence. We have four duplexes on campus that serve eight families and up to 36 children between them. Eligibility for the Family Residential Program requires participants be at or below 80% of the HUD income limits for their family size, have full custody of at least one child, be employed or in school full time, have a reliable transportation, must pass a criminal background check and drug test and must be willing to fully participate in weekly case management, counseling and parenting classes. The average length of stay for single parent families is one year.

VII. OUR SUCCESSES

In 2018, we served approximately 68 children in our Children's Residential Program and 12 single parent families in our Family Residential Program. We provided 472 counseling sessions to children in our residential program and 274 counseling session to families in our program. We also have a growing volunteer base filled with individuals from churches, business organizations, educational institutes, and our community who wish to become involved in our ministry.

It's important to understand both our quantitative impact and the number of children and families we serve, but also the qualitative impact. We would like to share a recent success story from both our Children's Residential Program and our Family Residential Program.

Children's Residential Program Success: Isabella (her name has been changed) came to Cumberland in our emergency shelter at the age of 14 and worked her way into our long term care program. Prior to coming to Denton, all of her siblings had been adopted, but Isabella had spent 4,272 days in foster care, been in 20 different placements and attended 12 different schools. While here she was further devastated by two failed adoptions. But being with us for an extended period of time helped Isabella learn better ways to deal with her feelings, she began to trust others and was able to positively interact with others. While living at the Children's Home, one of her teachers at Denton High School decided to foster Isabella. Her teacher and new foster mother sent us an update last month. She said: "I saw in the classroom that she had a heart of gold and learned that she wanted nothing more than to share her heart with a family. We're proud to announce that we finalized her adoption yesterday!!! Isabella thought we were at the courthouse for family pictures. When we announced to her that this was actually her adoption day...I wish you could have seen her reaction! She couldn't believe it at first and then proceeded to double over and cry many tears of joy! Thank you for your support along the way!"

Family Residential Program Success: Maritza (her name has been changed) lived at the Children's Home for about a year. She recently told us, "My daughters and I experienced emotional abuse and physical trauma before moving to Cumberland's Family Residential Program. My husband leaving us and losing my home was devastating for me, but even more so for my daughters. After that, my daughter was also diagnosed with Leukemia. Cumberland helped us by providing low-cost housing and case management to help sort through all the difficult circumstances. We were also able to see a counselor to help us work through some emotional issues. The Journey's class helped me learn to be a better parent and helped me learn to manage my finances and really just helped me to be a better person in general. It has really been a blessing to be here at Cumberland. The support and love that we have received has helped me begin to trust in God again. Knowing there is a place like Cumberland to help my family is what I needed to show my daughters that there is a God. Thank you for your support."

VIII. OUR STAFF

Our staff is passionate about the work they do. We work each day to carry out the mission that God has called us to do. We invite everyone to come and visit. Come and join us in our work so that we can make a difference in the lives of others together. We want to continue to share the news about the amazing work we do at Cumberland Presbyterian Children's Home. We are thankful for our staff, our board, our donors, our supporters, and our friends. Please keep the Children's Home close in your prayers.

Respectfully submitted,
Courtney Banatoski
President/CEO

THE REPORT OF THE
JOINT COMMITTEE ON AMENDMENTS

The Joint Committee on Amendments met March 7. 2019, in Huntsville, Alabama. Representing the CPCA were Willie Cowan and Vanessa Midgett. Representing the CPC were Geoff Knight and Jan Overton. Also present were Craig White (Stated Clerk, CPCA), Mike Sharpe (Stated clerk, CPC), Jaime Jordan (legal counsel, CPC), and Andy McClung (secretary).

I. REFERRALS

The committee reviewed the proposed constitutional amendments referred to us by the 188th General Assembly, slightly adjusted the wording of the proposed amendment to 7.06 to make it more compatible with CPCA structure, and approved these proposed amendments as ready to be placed before the 189th General Assembly.

RECOMMENDATION 1: That the Preamble to the Constitution be amended by inserting the following paragraph between the first and second existing paragraphs: "Cumberland Presbyterian congregations are found around the world. While the mission of the church is the same everywhere, the forms and structures of the Constitution and Rules of Discipline do not always fit seamlessly with the cultures, traditions, and legal systems of some countries. In countries other than the United States the provisions of the Constitution and Rules of Discipline should be applied so far as possible, but the Constitution and Rules of Discipline are, at heart, documents which exist to promote spiritual objectives. If there are instances in which the letter of the Constitution and/or Rules of Discipline cannot be applied without compromising the mission of the church and the spiritual objectives identified in the Confession of Faith, it is the spirit of the law, rather than the letter, which must prevail."

That Constitution 3.03 be amended to read: "The authority of each level of church government is limited by the stated provisions of the Constitution. Although each judicatory exercises exclusive original jurisdiction over all the matters specifically belonging to it, the lower judicatories are subject to the review and appellate authority of the next higher judicatory."

That Constitution 3.35 be amended to read: "A particular church shall not sell, convey, lease, pledge, mortgage, or encumber its real property used for purposes of worship, nurture, or ministry without the written permission of the presbytery in which the particular church is located, transmitted through the session of the particular church. In granting its permission, the presbytery does not become a party to the church's agreement, nor a guarantor of any indebtedness."

That Constitution 7.06, which refers to the relationships of pastor, assistant/ associate pastor, stated supply, and interim pastor, be amended to read "A person shall enter into one of these relationships with a particular church only with the approval of the presbytery in the bounds of which the particular church is located. The church session shall bear responsibility for the selection of the person, and the presbytery's approval shall relate to the person's ministerial credentials, commitment to the theology and government of the Cumberland Presbyterian Church/Cumberland Presbyterian Church in America, and standing in his or her current presbytery, if any. The presbytery may authorize its board of missions or equivalent body to act on its behalf in examining the call and to give tentative approval to a relationship between a particular church and a minister, licentiate, or candidate, subject to formal approval at a meeting of the presbytery."

That Constitution 8.5(f) be amended to read "In general, to order with respect to the presbyteries, sessions, and churches under its care according to the government of the church, whatever pertains to their spiritual welfare and the edification of the church."

That Constitution 9.4 (d) be amended to read "Institute and review the work of denominational entities."

That Constitution 9.4(g) be amended to read "Take care that the lower judicatories observe the government of the church and exercise its review and appellate authority to redress what they may have done contrary to order."

That Constitution 9.4(m) be amended to read "Keep watch over the affairs of the whole church."

II. UNIFICATION

The committee reviewed potential constitutional amendments to Constitution 9.2, 10.5, 11.1, 11.2, 11.3, 3.32a & b which will be necessary if unification of the CPC and CPCA occurs, noting that the two Assemblies will need to specify when the changes take effect.

Respectfully submitted,
The Joint Committee on Amendments

THE REPORT OF THE GENERAL ASSEMBLY EVALUATION COMMITTEE
Relative to Memphis Theological Seminary and the Historical Foundation

To the 189th Meeting of General Assembly on June 9-14, 2019 in Huntsville, Alabama.

I. MEMPHIS THEOLOGICAL SEMINARY

A. GENERAL ASSEMBLY DIRECTIVE

1. The 188th General Assembly charged the Evaluation Committee with the responsibility of assessment of the Memphis Theological Seminary with respect to:
- Make-up of the Board of Trustees of the Memphis Theological Seminary;
- Short and long term goals of the Board of Trustees;
- Board's fiduciary responsibilities and the governance of the Seminary;
- Financial solvency and stability of the Seminary;
- Recruitment and hiring procedures of the faculty and staff of the Seminary;
- Recommendations to the General Assembly related to the Board of Trustees;
- Curriculum and theology taught at the Memphis Theological Seminary as it relates to the practices and beliefs of the Cumberland Presbyterian Church as set forth in the Confession of Faith;
- Make-up (theological/diversity) of the faculty (full-time and adjunct) and staff of the Seminary;
- Practical preparation and skill set training provided by the Seminary to equip and prepare seminary students to become and succeed as ministers of the Cumberland Presbyterian Church;
- Statistical review of the placement of recent graduates of the Seminary in churches within the Cumberland Presbyterian Church;
- Relationship between the Seminary and the Presbyteries of the Cumberland Presbyterian Church;
- Recommendations to the General Assembly for improvement of the faculty, staff, curriculum and programs provided by the Seminary based upon the above assessment.
- Other relevant area of inquiry as determined by the Evaluation Committee.

2. The Evaluation Committee met with the interim President, Dr. Susan Parker, and a member of the committee attended a meeting of the Board of Trustees of Memphis Theological Seminary. This preliminary report addresses the following items referred by General Assembly.

B. THE MISSION OF MEMPHIS THEOLOGICAL SEMINARY
1. Clarification of the purpose of MTS.
  a. Is it primarily an ecumenical mission of the Cumberland Presbyterian Church with a secondary purpose of educating Cumberland Presbyterians for ministry?
  b. Is the primary purpose to educate Cumberland Presbyterians for ministry in an ecumenical setting?
  c. Does it serve a dual purpose of being the primary means of educating Cumberland Presbyterians for ministry as part of an ecumenical mission of the denomination?

2. Do we affirm a need for an ecumenical graduate school?
(see Appendix 1 for the Amended and Restated Charter of MTS, the Mission Statement, Vision Statement, and Values Statement)

RECOMMENDATION 1: That we affirm our need for an ecumenical seminary.

C. PRESIDENTIAL SEARCH
1. It is critical that the next president of MTS have experience in and enthusiasm for fundraising and strategic planning (see Appendix section I.A. for Presidential Search information and the concerns of ATS and SACS/COC).
2. While we acknowledge the need to hire the most qualified person for the position of president, regardless of denominational affiliation, we stress the importance of having a strong Cumberland Presbyterian presence in the administration and on the faculty.

RECOMMENDATION 2: That General Assembly encourage Memphis Theological Seminary to strengthen the Cumberland Presbyterian presence in leadership and teaching at the seminary.

D. THE INTERIM PRESIDENT
1. Dr. Susan Parker has been Interim President since August 2018. She is an ordained Cumberland Presbyterian minister and former board member of MTS. She received her Ph.D. in higher education administration from the University of Alabama.
2. She is doing an excellent job leading MTS during this interim period, but she stressed her desire for it to be a temporary position.

RECOMMENDATION 3: That we express our appreciation to Dr. Parker for her leadership at Memphis Theological Seminary during this critical interim period (see Appendix section III for additional information on Dr. Parker).

E. THE BOARD OF TRUSTEES
1. The size of the Board inhibits communication and participation (see Appendix section IV for Board of Trustees information).

RECOMMENDATION 4: That the Board of Trustees of Memphis Theological Seminary reduce the number of trustees from 24 to 14 by 2024 and that after any given trustee election the majority of members must be Cumberland Presbyterian.

Notes: 1) This would require a change in the General Assembly Bylaws.
2) A suggested formal to decrease membership would be to reduce each elected class size by two beginning in 2020 and each subsequent class through 2024.

2. We need to identify and recruit individuals with expertise in fundraising and finances for the Board of Trustees.

RECOMMENDATION 5: That the Board of Trustees and Memphis Theological Seminary leadership actively identify and recruit individuals with the skill set in fundraising and fiscal responsibility to serve on the Board of Trustees so that the denominational Nominating Committee can recommend candidates from pool of individuals with those skills to serve on the MTS Board.

3. We need to ensure proper leadership training including the development of a Strategic Plan and the ability to execute said plan. A review and analysis of the MTS Accreditation Report by an outside Accreditation Compliance Officer and examiner for SACS recommends hiring a SACS Consultant to help guide MTS with the remediation of the issues presented in the Accreditation Reports.

RECOMMENDATION 6: That the Board of Trustees and Memphis Theological Seminary leadership seek to employ a SACS consultant to help develop a strategic plan and move towards compliance in other areas mentioned in the SACS report to MTS.

F. ACADEMIC ASSESSMENT
1. **ATS and SACS/COC:** There was no concern and no recommendations regarding the academic program from the accrediting agencies. The faculty and the academic content of the institution were considered to be strengths of MTS. They made the following comments:
   a. "The evaluation committee commends MTS for its student body that is richly diverse in race, ethnicity, gender, and ecclesial families… The school's commitment to racial, ethnic, gender, and denominational diversity is one of its unique strengths."
   b. "The faculty has a diverse makeup in terms of gender, race, and denominational affiliation. This diversity is mirrored in the school's administration as well. The school's diversity lends itself to a rich tapestry of life experiences, viewpoints and cultural practices, which is beneficial to the students' development."

2. Curriculum and Theology: The research shows that the curriculum and theology taught at MTS relates well to the practices and beliefs of the Cumberland Presbyterian Church.

3. Practical Preparation and Placement: Over the past three years MTS has had a student placement rate of 83.5%. The national average is 77%.

4. Placement of Cumberland Presbyterian Graduates: 60% are serving as pastors, 30% state that they do not have a call, and 10% are serving in other denominationally related positions, such as chaplains.

G. FINANCIAL ASSESSMENT
1. The financial position of Memphis Theological Seminary must be strengthened.
a. The Seminary has had significant operational deficits for the last three years:
2015-16 ($431,318)   2016-17 ($1,232,317)   2017-18 ($510,122)
b. The Seminary has taken major steps to bring expenses down while bolstering revenue. The budget projections for fiscal years 2019-2021 reflect a zero-dollar loss for each respective year. This projected move to greater financial stability hinges on increased enrollment (tuition) and contributions, as well as more intentional day-to-day fiscal management.

2. However, the Seminary has a one-million-dollar line of credit with First Tennessee Bank and has utilized $700,000. Furthermore, as of December 31, 2018 the Seminary has over $2.5 million-dollar outstanding note payable due to the People's Bank of Mississippi in 2025. Property (Hillard-Cumberland, Founder's-Brown Shannon) has been mortgaged to guarantee the note payable. Monthly interest payments are being met. These obligations are considerable in the light that the Seminary has no Development Department.

3. In the last three years from fifteen percent to thirty-two percent of operating revenue came from a single individual which leaves the Seminary vulnerable if this individual decides not to continue or becomes incapable of continuing the donations.

H. ASSESSMENT OF THE RELATIONSHIP BETWEEN THE SEMINARY AND THE PRESBYTERIES
1. A survey was circulated to assess the relationship between MTS and our Presbyteries (see Appendix 2). Only six (6) presbyteries responded.
2. Of those responding, 66.6% believe that it is necessary to have a denominational seminary, 83.3% preferred the Program of Alternate Studies (PAS) to MTS, and PAS had a slightly higher satisfaction rating than MTS.
3. The low number of presbyteries that responded to the survey limits our ability to adequately assess the relationship between MTS and our presbyteries. We feel that the survey should be circulated again in an attempt to give us a better assessment.
4. Since 83.3% of those responding indicated that they preferred PAS to MTS, should the PAS program be evaluated? It is a certificate program and not a degree program. Is it adequately preparing people for ministry?

RECOMMENDATION 7: That the Evaluation Committee continue to:
• **Assess the relationship between Memphis Theological Seminary and the Presbyteries of the Cumberland Presbyterian Church.**
• **Monitor the financial solvency and stability of Memphis Theological Seminary in light of the concerns of both accrediting agencies. MTS has until April 2, 2020 to show that their financial resources are adequate for long-term stability.**
• **Assess the short and long-term goals of Memphis Theological Seminary. MTS has until November 1, 2019 to develop a coherent and comprehensive institutional strategic plan.**
• **Montior progress made by MTS towards compliance with findings addressed in the ATS and SACs Report.**

II. HISTORICAL FOUNDATION

A. GENERAL ASSEMBLY DIRECTIVE
1. The 188th General Assembly charged the Evaluation Committee with the responsibility of assessment of the Historical Foundation with respect to:
- The stated mission of the Historical Foundation
- Progress towards continuance of their stated mission
- Procedures, tool and equipment used and/or needed by the Historical Foundation to continue their stated mission
- Recommendations to the General Assembly related to the Historical Foundation
- Other relevant area of inquiry as determined by the Evaluation Committee.

2. The Evaluation Committee met with the director, Susan Gore, and a member of the committee attended a meeting of the Board of Trustees of the Historical Foundation. This report addresses the issues referred by General Assembly.

B. MISSION OF THE HISTORICAL FOUNDATION
1. The Charter states "the corporation was formed to collect and preserve the materials of, and to promote the knowledge of the history of, the churches, institutions, and people of the Cumberland Presbyterian denominations; and to establish and maintain a library, archives, and museum for the acquisition and care of such material and records."

2. Great effort is exhibited in collecting materials related to the history of the Cumberland Presbyterian Church. This effort accounts for the majority of the director's time. There is a professional archivist who works part time. This archivist aids those who are doing research at the Archives as well as responding to request for information. The Director and part time archivist work to digitize as much materials as time allows. Preservation of materials is a critical issue, as the facility is not designed as such. Water infiltration continues to be an issue. Most materials are stored in boxes not designed for archival preservation.

3. The promotion of the history of the church increasingly relies on electronic/internet means. The Historical Foundation has more data online than any other denominational entity, and has more "hits" than all other denominational sites combined.

4. Materials for and promotion of Denominational Day remain the primary means of print promotion. The Historical Foundation provides events regularly at the Birthplace Shrine within Montgomery Bell State Park. Many of these events regularly attract members of the general public as well as Cumberland Presbyterians. Displays at the General Assemblies of the CP and CPCA also provide information relative to the work and purpose of the foundation.

5. The Historical Foundation's ability to "establish and maintain a library, archives, and museum for the acquisition and care of materials and records" is a distinct challenge. Limited personnel, space, and materials challenge the ability to meet this function of the charter. If "acquisition and care of materials and records" are critical to the denomination, then General Assembly in conjunction with the Board of Trustees of the Historical Foundation must take steps to insure the viability of this aspect of the Charter.

C. PROGRESS TOWARDS CONTINUANCE OF THEIR STATED MISSION
1. Evaluation and observation by the committee revealed how committed the Director is to the mission of the Historical Foundation. However, the purposes as outlined in the charter are more than one person can do. The "acquisition and care of materials and records" can't be done adequately by volunteers. As a result, priority is given to the acquisition of materials.

2. Adequate funding is not available to meet stated purposes of the charter. Endowments have recently reached a level to begin providing funding. Donations to the foundation are limited in amount and individuals.

3. Concerns raised need to be addressed by General Assembly and the Trustees of the Historical Foundation. This need is heightened by the likelihood the director will be retiring in the near future.

D. PROCEDURES, TOOLS AND EQUIPMENT USED TO CONTINUE THEIR STATED MISSION

1. Materials contained in the collection are in varied formats. Computers able to access storage devices such as floppy disk of all sizes, microfiche, and print require possession and maintenance of outdated equipment. Many of these in possession of the Historical Foundation have been donated as cast off from other agencies. Malfunction in any of these devices will inhibit future work in the Archives.

2. The link to the Historical Foundation provided through cumberland.org provides a list of needs of the Archives.

E. FINANCIAL ASSESSMENT

1. For the year ending December 31, 2016 the net assets were $1,780,508 with a net change of $29,246. (page 186) from the 187th meeting of the General Assembly.

2. For the year ending December 31, 2017, the net assets were $1,907,840 with a net change of $127,332 (page 155) from the 186th meeting of the General Assembly. In 2017, investments gained $163,485.13.

3. For the year ending December 31, 2018, the net assets total $1,838,250.66 with a net change (loss) of $69,585.00. The loss for the year is primarily the result of loss on endowments during the 4th quarter as result of down turn in stock market. In 2018, investments lost $45,240.68.

4. For the year ending December 31, 2018, the income was $193,818.07 with 37% coming from Our United Outreach (OUO); 37% from contributions; and the remainder from investments and endowment. Expenses were $263,503.07 with salary and benefits accounting for roughly 40% of the budget. The financial reversals from investment incomes in 2017 and 2018 highlight the need for more strategic planning in terms of budgeting and development and/or increased funding from OUO.

RECOMMENDATION 7: That General Assembly recommend that the Board of Trustees of the Historical Foundation review and/or revise the charter in light of the issues raised in this evaluation.

RECOMMENDATION 8: That the Board of Trustees of the Historical Foundation develop a long-range strategy to fulfill the requirements outlined in the Charter and include a transition strategy for replacing the Director and part time archivist.

RECOMMENDATION 9: That the Board of Trustees of the Historical Foundation engage in leadership training. (It might be possible to partner with MTS who will be providing this training for its board.)

RECOMMENDATION 10: That the Board of Trustees of the Historical Foundation develop a job description for the director and part time archivist.

RECOMMENDATION 11: That General Assembly revise funding strategies enabling the Historical Foundation to fulfill the requirements of the charter.

Respectfully submitted,
Kevin Henson, Chair
Larry Blakeburn
Bobby Coleman
Charles McCaskey
Rickey Page
Lisa Scott
Judi Truitt

APPENDIX 1

I. THE MISSION OF MEMPHIS THEOLOGICAL SEMINARY

A. The Amended and Restated Charter of MTS states: "The Corporation is organized exclusively for the following purposes: to maintain and operate a theological seminary or graduate school for the instruction, education, training and preparation of persons called of God to the ministry, mission work, Christian education work or other service in the Church, and especially in the Cumberland Presbyterian Church..." (Section I B, page 1, Recommendation 1)

B. MTS Mission Statement: "To educate and sustain men and women for ordained and lay Christian ministry in the church and the world through shaping and inspiring lives devoted to scholarship, piety and justice." (Section I, page 1)

C. Under Our Values, MTS states: "The identity of Memphis Theological Seminary has been shaped by the tradition of the Cumberland Presbyterian Church, its location in Memphis, a partnership with the broader Christian community, a commitment to dialogue with people of other faiths, and participation in the community of higher education." (Section I, page 1)

D. The Vision Statement: "Memphis Theological Seminary pursues its mission so that Christian leaders and the churches they serve can effectively proclaim and embody God's mission of redemption, justice, and peace in service to the new creation in Jesus Christ." (Section I, page 1)

II. PRESIDENTIAL SEARCH

A. "Memphis Theological Seminary is searching for its eighth president. We are seeking a President who has experience in and enthusiasm for fundraising and strategic planning, who is an effective communicator, demonstrates collaborative leadership skills, and values and embodies the MTS mission." (Section II A, page 1)

B. It is critical that the next president have expertise in fundraising and strategic planning. MTS is accredited by the Association of Theological Schools in the United States and Canada (ATS), and regionally by the Commission on Colleges of the Southern Association of Colleges and Schools (SACS/COC). MTS has until November 1, 2019 to address their concern about comprehensive strategic planning: "regarding the development of a coherent and comprehensive institutional strategic plan that focuses the school's core mission on key priorities linked to specific strategies for how these major challenges will be addressed..." April 2, 2020 is the deadline to address their concern about the financial stability of MTS: "The institution's financial resources are not adequate for long-term institutional viability and there is no credible plan to address this issue in a timely and effective manner." (Section II A, page 1)

C. MTS has sustained losses from operations in unrestricted funds in four of the last five fiscal years. Over this same period, tuition revenue has decreased due to decline in student enrollment. MTS has eliminated 22 positions in the last three years, many of which were part time, and now has 40 employees on the payroll. The seminary also eliminated the vice president of advancement position and all those employed in that area. They were not raising enough money to pay their salaries. (Section II A, page 1)

D. MTS was placed on "warning" by SACS. While "warning" is not what any institution is seeking, it is certainly better than being placed on "probation". The implication of warning is basically, "You are not meeting the standards, but we think you can." The implication of probation is, "You are not meeting the standards and we are not sure you can." (Section II A., page 1)

E. It is critical for MTS to hire the most qualified person for the position of president, regardless of denominational affiliation; however, the seminary needs a strong Cumberland Presbyterian presence in the administration and on the faculty. The Interim President is Cumberland Presbyterian but the Academic Dean is not. We have one faculty member who is Cumberland Presbyterian. (Section II B, page 1, Recommendation 2)

III. THE INTERIM PRESIDENT (Section III A&B, Recommendation 3)

A. Dr. Susan Parker, Ph.D. has been Interim President since August 2018. She is an ordained Cumberland Presbyterian minister and former board member of MTS. She received her doctorate in higher education administration from the University of Alabama in Tuscaloosa. She is the first female president in MTS history. She worked in higher education for twenty-five years at Calhoun Community College and Athens State University.

B. Dr. Parker is doing an excellent job leading MTS and cultivating a culture of transparency in the aftermath of layoffs and budget cuts. She has experience in strategic planning and fundraising, which is critical if the seminary is going to survive and thrive. She does not plan on being in this position for more than two years.

IV. THE BOARD OF TRUSTEES (Section IV, Page 1, Recommendations 4 & 5)

A. The General Assembly of the Cumberland Presbyterian Church elects all members of the school's governing board, the board of trustees. The trustees are, in turn, responsible to the General Assembly. According to the bylaws of the General Assembly, there is to be a total of twenty-four trustees, divided in three classes of eight. The term of service is three years. Members may be reelected to two subsequent, back-to-back, three-year terms. At least eleven of the twenty-four positions are to be held by ecumenical partners of MTS. The board of trustees convenes formally three times per year and understands that its role is one of strategic oversight and policy-making rather than attending to the day-to-day operations of the school, which it delegates to the President and administrative team. The board recognizes the difference between governing the school and managing it. The board's primary responsibility is to focus on the school's long-term viability and strategic vision.

B. The size of the board inhibits communication and participation. In an attempt to facilitate engagement and maximize the effectiveness of the Board of Trustees, we are recommending a reduction in the number of board members.

C. The composition of the Board of Trustees is also a concern. MTS received a grant to help with Board development through a program called "Wise Stewards," which includes a consultant. This will be a wise use of time by the Board, but it would also be helpful to identify and recruit individuals with expertise in fundraising and finances.

MEMORIALS

I. MEMORIAL FROM MISSOURI PRESBYTERY REGARDING THE PROGRAM OF ALTERNATE STUDIES

WHEREAS the Cumberland Presbyterian Denomination was formed out of the Revival of 1800 resulting in the rapid creation of many churches on the frontier of western territories;

WEREAS the newly created denomination leadership felt the urgent need to provide ministerial leadership required exceptions be made to educational requirements for ordination;

WHEREAS through the history of the denomination, there have been various routes of alternative education leading to ordination that did not require a traditional seminary educational degree;

WHEREAS those alternative education paths have produced ministers that were effective in spreading the gospel of Jesus Christ and serving the needs of the Church;

WHEREAS many called to the ordained ministry have been, and will continue to be bi-vocational pastors needing to maintain full-time employment outside the pulpit;

WHEREAS current educational theories have identified that adult learners respond to a variety of learning styles;

WHEREAS the current Program of Alternate Studies (PAS) is a certificate, non-degree awarding program requiring 35 courses;

WHEREAS the program length has made it difficult for some who attend PAS in response to their call to ministry to maintain their current employment;

WHEREAS many students in PAS are currently ministering to churches; and

WHEREAS it is the goal of PAS to provide an alternative educational pathway to ministry for the preparation of ministers in the Cumberland tradition,

THEREFORE BE IT RESOLVED, that alternative methods of education and assessment of learning should continue and be reviewed so that those called to ministry can be prepared in an alternative to seminary attendance;

THEREFORE BE IT RESOLVED, that instructors should use a variety of teaching and evaluation of learning methods that are compatible with alternative types of preparation for ministry;

THEREFORE BE IT RESOLVED, that PAS should explore granting credit for relevant pastoral experiences as they do for educational experience, including but not limited to creative expression and application of ministerial principles, alternate measures of assessment, independent study, and assessment of applied ministry activities on-site or through distance learning; and

THEREFORE BE IT RESOLVED, that it is encouraged that the directors of PAS evaluate the number of courses, consider combining courses and streamlining the curriculum, continue to offer weekend and on-line courses, and create a multi-year schedule of courses to afford ample opportunity for planning a satisfactory completion of the program.

I certify that this is a true copy of a memorial adopted by Missouri Presbytery on March 16, 2019.
Signed Larry Nottingham, Stated Clerk, Missouri Presbytery

II. MEMORIAL FROM MISSOURI PRESBYTERY REGARDING THE REQUIREMENTS FOR RECOGNITION OF ORDINATION

WHEREAS there are ministers from another ecclesiastical body that desire to have their ordination recognized and become ministers in the Cumberland Presbyterian Church;

WHEREAS the constitution of the Cumberland Presbyterian Church (CP) currently states the following:

6.40 Recognition of Ordination

6.41 A minister of another ecclesiastical body who desires to become a minister in the Cumberland Presbyterian Church/Cumberland Presbyterian Church in America shall appear before the committee on the ministry of the presbytery in which he or she wishes to be received. The committee on the ministry shall investigate the following:

   a. Whether the minister has proper credentials from his or her ecclesiastical body;
   b. Whether the minister has a degree from a college and graduate school of theology;

c. Whether the minister has a knowledge of the history, theology, and government of the Cumberland Presbyterian Church/Cumberland Presbyterian Church in America;
d. Whether the minister seems fit for service as a minister in the Cumberland Presbyterian Church/Cumberland Presbyterian Church in America.

6.42 The committee on the ministry, if satisfied in each of the areas described in Section 6.41 may recommend to presbytery that the minister be received as an ordained minister in the Cumberland Presbyterian Church/Cumberland Presbyterian Church in America, upon giving affirmative answer to the questions put to licentiates at their ordination. Such procedure shall not exclude the opportunity for presbytery to examine the minister.

WHEREAS currently the Committee on the Ministry (COM) in Missouri Presbytery has been told that they are not to recommend recognition of the ordination until the minister of another ecclesiastical body has taken classes through the Program of Alternate Studies of CP History, CP Polity, Cumberland Presbyterian Theology I and Cumberland Presbyterian Theology II;

WHEREAS the COM has also been told that the minister must take two (2) of these courses on site at the Program of Alternate Studies (PAS) summer session;

WHEREAS the ministers already have a degree from a college and graduate school of theology and completing four classes at PAS would take a substantial period of time as well as at current fees cost the individual or the presbytery at least $1,480 in class fees, $163 in room and board plus travel expenses;

WHEREAS some of those wanting their ordination recognized are nearing or at retirement age;

WHEREAS there are CP churches that want the services of these ministers and want these ministers to provide all the sacraments granted ordained CP ministers;

WHEREAS there are opportunities other than PAS for a minister to experience CP culture and develop friendships throughout the denomination such as attendance at presbytery meetings, presbyterial retreats and denominational retreats or conferences;

THEREFORE BE IT RESOLVED, that the presbyterial COM should be allowed to individualize the program needed for each minister of another ecclesiastical body who is seeking to have their ordination recognized. This would be determined after a review of previous education, interview of the person and review of the individual circumstances leading to wanting the ordination recognized;

THEREFORE BE IT RESOLVED, that if formal coursework is needed, PAS should develop a course of study (not 4 courses) specifically for the minister seeking this recognition of ordination. This course of study should be offered as independent study, online study, weekend class, or at PAS summer session;

THEREFORE BE IT RESOLVED, that the presbyterial COM should make the minister, seeking to have their ordination recognized, aware of the various opportunities to experience CP culture and encourage attendance at PAS but that would not be a requirement for the ordination being recognized.

I certify that this is a true copy of a memorial adopted by Missouri Presbytery on March 16, 2019.
Signed Larry Nottingham, Stated Clerk, Missouri Presbytery

III. MEMORIAL FROM PRESBYTERY DEL CRISTO REGARDING A DENOMINATIONAL DAY OF PRAYER AND FASTING

189th General Assembly of the Cumberland Presbyterian Church,

Believing that God, in creating persons, gives us the capacity and freedom to respond to God's mighty act of reconciling love accomplished in Jesus and that we are responsible for our choices and actions toward God, one another and the world;

Confessing that we rebel against God, reject our dependence, abuse the gift of freedom, willfully sin, both individually and collectively, and stand in need of God's redemption;

Rejoicing that God acts to heal the brokenness and alienation caused by our sin to restore us through the reconciliation of Jesus Christ and the outpouring the Holy Spirit calling every person toward repentance and faith;

Responding to God's acts of saving grace and forgiveness of sin, we make honest confession of sin against God, our brothers and sisters, and all of creation, amending the past so far as in our power through our choices, actions, and prayer;

Recalling that the renewal of believers is solely of God's grace, that when we trust in the Lord Jesus, we are recreated, born again, renewed in spirit, and made new persons in Christ who are empowered by the illuminating influence of the Holy Spirit to love and glorify God and to love and serve our neighbor;

Reminding all Cumberland Presbyterians that prayer is inseparable from the Christian life and to be a Christian is to pray and to join others in prayer and that we pray not primarily to receive from God but as an expression of our creaturehood and our dependence upon God as our Creator;

Guided by the primary purposes of prayer being to enter the presence of God, to experience anew God's judgement, grace, and power, to praise God and to invite God into our world and into our lives;

Declaring that the Cumberland Presbyterian Church, being nurtured and sustained by worship, by the proclamation and study of the word, and by the celebration of the sacraments, is commissioned to witness to all persons who have not received Christ as Lord and Savior;

Calls upon the 189th General Assembly of the Cumberland Presbyterian Church who is meeting concurrently with the 144th General Assembly of the Cumberland Presbyterian Church in America and;

Requests that a denominational day of Prayer and Fasting be set and observed by all members of the Cumberland Presbyterian Church at every level and in every nation to renew and revitalize us to bear witness to God's mighty act of reconciling love accomplished in Jesus Christ by which the sins of the world are forgiven.

Submitted by: Karen Avery, Presbytery del Cristo on March 15, 2019

IV. MEMORIAL FROM NASHVILLE PRESBYTERY REGARDING SACRAMENT OF BAPTISM

WHEREAS the *Confession of Faith, Section 5.18*, states that the Sacrament of Baptism "*symbolizes the baptism of the Holy Spirit and is the external sign of the covenant which marks membership in the community of faith*", and

WHEREAS the *Confession of Faith, Section 5.21*, states that "*in administering the sacrament the pouring or sprinkling of water on the person by the minister fittingly symbolizes the baptism of the Holy Spirit*", and

WHEREAS the General Assembly in 1968 granted a Memorial which allowed a minister to "perform the sacrament of baptism with the mode best suited to the specific situation" (Digest, page 18, 2.63d "interpretative"), and

WHEREAS the resulting practice of baptism over the years by Cumberland Presbyterian ministers is now so varied so as to have lost seemingly its connection to baptism as defined in the *Confession of Faith*, and has opened the door for practices not affirmed in the *Confession* such as "infant dedications" and repeating the sacrament (despite Section 5.19 of the Confession) under the guise of "believer's baptism",

THEREFORE BE IT RESOLVED that Nashville Presbytery memorializes the General Assembly to refer this Memorial to the General Assembly's Permanent Committee on the Judiciary to report back to the next General Assembly and to provide guidance and direction, particularly to presbyteries, on how to maintain and affirm the Confession of Faith in relation to the Sacrament of Baptism in actual practice.

Respectfully Submitted, Reverend Fred E. Polacek

GENERAL ASSEMBLY AGENCIES

I. OFFICE OF THE GENERAL ASSEMBLY

A. GENERAL ASSEMBLY OFFICE

	Revised 2019	Proposed 2020
INCOME		
Our United Outreach	$197,836	$197,836
Endowments/Interest	20,000	20,000
Interest on Cash Funds Management	2,500	2,500
Sales of yearbook/digest	2,000	2,000
TOTAL INCOME	**$222,336**	**$222,336**
EXPENSE		
ECUMENICAL RELATIONS		
World Communion of Reformed Churches	$ 6,000	$ 6,000
CANAAC	2,000	2,000
Ecumenical Travel	1,000	1,000
Sub-Total	$ 9,000	$ 9,000
LIAISON WITH CHURCH		
General Assembly Meeting	$ 10,000	$ 10,000
Preliminary Minutes	5,000	5,000
GA Minutes/Mailing	500	500
Yearbook/Mailing	2,500	2,500
Travel/Moderator	8,500	8,500
Travel/Stated Clerk & Staff	8,500	8,500
Sub-Total	$ 35,000	$ 35,000
OFFICE		
Computer Supplies	$ 2,000	$ 2,000
Equipment/Supplies	2,500	2,500
Postage	2,000	2,000
Sub-Total	$ 6,500	$ 6,500
PERSONNEL		
Salaries/Housing	$139,420	$139,420
FICA (Asst to Stated Clerk)	4,300	4,300
Retirement	6,800	6,800
Health Insurance	30,000	30,000
Disability Insurance/Worker's Compensation	800	800
Sub-Total	$181,320	$181,320
STATED CLERK'S CONFERENCE/BOARD EXPENSE		
Legal Fees / Clerk's Conference	$ 1,963	$ 1,963
Corporate Board Expense	2,000	2,000
Sub-Total	$ 3,963	$ 3,963
TOTAL EXPENSE	**$235,783**	**$235,783**
From Reserves	$ 13,447	$ 13,447

B. GENERAL ASSEMBLY COMMISSIONS AND COMMITTEES

INCOME		
Contingency	$ 12,365	$ 12,365
Nominating Committee	2,770	2,770
Commission on Chaplains	9,570	9,570
Judiciary Committee	9,026	9,026
Theology and Social Concerns Committee	3,363	3,363
Our United Outreach Committee	92,044	92,044
TOTAL INCOME	**$129,138**	**$129,138**

	Revised 2019	Proposed 2020
EXPENSE		
Contingency	$ 12,365	$ 12,365
Nominating Committee	2,770	2,770
Commission on Chaplains	9,570	9,570
Judiciary Committee	9,026	9,026
Theology and Social Concerns Committee	3,363	3,363
Our United Outreach Committee	92,044	92,044
TOTAL EXPENSE	**$129,138**	**$129,138**

II. MINISTRY COUNCIL

	Revised 2019	Proposed 2020
INCOME		
Endowments	$ 15,000	$ 15,000
Grants	$ 0	$ 0
ILP Transfers		
MMT Budget Reserve Fund	514,008	521,376
MMT New Church Development	108,160	108,160
DMT Contingency Fund	51,362	54,562
DMT Faith in 3D	1,030	1,030
DMT Faith Out Loud	609	609
DMT Revolving Publication Fund	7,500	7,500
DMT Young Adult Ministry	361	361
CMT The Cumberland Presbyterian	996	996
Contributions/Gifts		
DMT - General	1,250	1,250
MC - General	2,900	2,900
Our United Outreach		
OUO Income	1,116,634	1,159,724
In lieu of Our United Outreach	6,720	6,720
Adult Ministry	500	5,000
Birthplace Shrine Chaplaincy	3,750	3,750
Children's Fest	9,900	9,900
Clergy Crisis	6,000	6,000
CP Magazine Subscriptions	30,000	30,000
Cumberland Presbyterians Resources	69,360	66,320
CPWM		
Convention	8,000	8,000
Convention Offering	250	250
General	3,000	3,000
Sales Merchandise	700	700
Girls and Young Women Council	8,000	8,000
CPYC	98,165	112,750
Discipleship Blueprints	2,400	2,400
Encounter	105,640	108,680

THE CUMBERLAND PRESBYTERIAN CHURCH

	Revised 2019	Proposed 2020
Kaleo	$ 13,500	$ 3,500
Leader Development	5,492	5,492
Missionary Setup	15,000	15,000
Missionary Support	256,088	352,348
New Church Development (NCD) Subsidies	157,194	157,194
New Exploration Iniative - NCD	71,650	71.650
NPI: Children's CP Curriculum	500	1,000
Presbyterian Youth Triennium	5,000	5,000
Program Planning Calendar - Sales	920	920
Stir	1,500	1,500
The Symposium	6,000	6,000
Third Age Ministry	500	500
Young Adult Ministry	8,000	8,000
Youth Evangelism Conference	2,350	2,350
Youth Ministry Planning Council	648	0
Youth Workers Retreat	4,500	4,500
TOTAL INCOME	**$2,720,537**	**$2,213,818**

EXPENSES
Ministry Council Administration Salaries

Salaries	$ 838,040	$ 838,040
Clergy Housing Allowance	180,196	180,196
Health Insurance	139,200	145,920
Retirement	54,192	54,192
FICA	35,894	35,894
Tax Sheltered Annuity	10,266	10,266
Insurance/Disability	4,366	4,366

Ministry Council Administration General Expenses

Annual Credit Card Fees	$ 3,678	$ 4,678
Computer Equipment	0	6,500
Computer Software (Wufoo, Adobe, BaseCamp)	10,175	12,550
Educational Publications for Distribution	3,000	3,000
Employee Events	2,500	2,500
Employee Recognition	3,550	3,550
Government Fees (annual reports)	40	40
Legal	2,000	2,000
MC Supplemental Report	5,000	4,000
P & C Insurance	16,263	15,150

	Revised 2019	Proposed 2020
Staff Resource Materials	1,997	1,997
Subscriptions/Membership	2,246	2,246
Telephone/Internet	2,892	4,092
Temporary Help	14,400	14,400
MC/Elected Team Member Recognition	1,040	1,040
Office Supplies	12,000	12,000
Postage	1,800	1,800
Professional Development	0	1,200
Adult Ministry	500	5,000
Beth-El Farmworker	$ 40,500	$ 40,500
Birthplace Shrine Chaplaincy: Chaplain's Stipend	3,750	3,750
Children's Fest	9,900	9,900
Clergy Crisis Support: Distribution	6,000	6,000
Coalition of Applachian Ministry	12,700	12,700
CP Magazine	54,033	54,033
Cumberland Presbyterian Resources	69,940	71,868
CPWM		
General	9,100	9,100
Sales Merchandise	2,000	2,000
Convention	12,200	12,200
CPYC	98,165	112,750
Cross-Culture Immigrant Leadership Training	4,000	4,000
Discipleship Blueprints	2,400	2,400
Ecumenical Stewardship Center	4,500	4,500
Encounter	36,812	36,812
Family Ministry	550	550
General Assembly	36,550	36,550
General Consultants	22,400	52,400
Kaleo	13,500	3,500
Leadership Referral Services	2,100	2,100
Leader Development	5,492	5,492
Ministers		
Encouragement & Recognition	3,818	3,818
Retreat	1,000	1,000

	Revised 2019	Proposed 2020
Missionary Messenger	59,480	59,480
Missionary Setup	15,000	15,000
Missionary Support	256,088	352,348
National Farm Worker	4,300	4,300
New Church Development (NCD) Subsidies	157,194	157,194
New Exploration Initiative	71,650	71,650
New Program Iniatives		
Children's Curriculum	1,000	1,000
CPWM Girls and Young Women Council	8,000	8,000
PREP Staff Expenses	400	0
Presbyterian Youth Triennium	5,000	5,000
Presbyteries/Councils	195,120	195,120
Program Planning Calendar	5,150	5,150
Project Vida	8,500	8,500
Stir	5,000	5,000
Support Ministries	1,000	1,000
The Symposium	16,000	16,000
Travel (includes elected member travel)	80,060	88,510
Web Development/Maintenance	2,000	2,000
Young Adult Ministry	14,300	14,750
Youth Evangelism Conference	7,350	5,000
Youth Ministry Planning Council - UBCD	6,000	5,000
Youth Workers Retreat	4,500	4,500
TOTAL EXPENSES	**$2,720,537**	**$ 2,879,042**
Surplus/(Deficit)	$ 0	$ 0

III. BOARD OF STEWARDSHIP

INCOME
  Contributions

Contributions/Gifts	$ 3,000	$ 3,000
ILP Contributions	2,000	2,000
Endowment Contributions	20,000	20,000
Total Contributions	**25,000**	**25,000**
Our United Outreach	135,000	135,000
Investment Earnings		
Endowment Earnings	96,000	96,000
ILP Earnings	8,000	8,000
Endowment WF Income	19,400	19,400
Total Investment Earnings	**123,400**	**123,400**

	Revised 2019	Proposed 2020
Realized Gain/Loss - Endowment	10,000	10,000
Unrealized Gain/Loss - Endowment	116,000	116,000
Total Investment Gains/Losses	**126,000**	**126,000**
Service Fees		
Management Fees - Acct Coordinator	1,600	1,600
Management Fees	61,000	61,000
Total Service Fees	**62,600**	**62,600**
TOTAL INCOME	**$472,000**	**$ 472,000**

EXPENSE

	Revised 2019	Proposed 2020
Salaries		
Salaries	$205,783	$ 207,751
Housing Allowance	21,000	21,000
Total Salaries	**226,783**	**228,751**
Benefits		
Health Insurance	70,500	70,500
Retirement	11,339	11,438
FICA	10,117	10,202
Insurance/Disability	1,000	1,000
Total Benefits	**92,956**	**93,140**
Events		
Conference/Events	500	500
Tax Guide for Ministers	4,100	4,500
Total Events	**4,600**	**5,000**
Board Expense		
Board/Agency Travel	15,000	13,000
Board/Agency Recognition	$ 600	$ 200
Total Board Expense	**15,600**	**13,200**
Resource Purchases		
Subscriptions	600	100
Total Resources Purchases	**600**	**100**
Contracted Services		
Legal	500	500
Audit	2,100	2,100
Temporary Help	1,000	1,000
Total Contracted Services	**3,600**	**3,600**
Insurance		
Insurance/Liability	4,200	4,200
	4,200	**4,200**
Professional Development		
Subscriptions & Membership	100	449
Total Professional Development	**100**	**449**
Payment/Subsidies		
ESC Stewardship Expense	3,500	3,500
ILP Withdrawal	2,500	2,500
Endowment Distribution	102,000	102,000
Total Payments/Subsidies	**108,000**	**108,000**
Equipment		
Office Equipment	800	800
Computer Equipment	2,000	2,000
Computer Maintenance	150	150
Computer Software	$ 500	$ 500
Total Equipment	**3,450**	**3,450**
Supplies		
Computer Supplies	500	500
Office Supplies	3,000	3,000
Total Supplies	**3,500**	**3,500**

	Revised 2019	Proposed 2020
Postage/Shipping		
Postage	1,486	1,486
Shipping	325	325
Total Postage/Shipping	**1,811**	**1,811**
Employee Recognition		
Employee Recognition	1,200	1,200
Total Employee Recognition	**1,200**	**1,200**
Travel		
Staff Travel	4,500	4,500
Total Travel	**4,500**	**4,500**
Miscellaneous		
Miscellaneous	1,000	1,000
Total Miscellaneous	**1,000**	**1,000**
Organization		
Organizational Expense	100	100
Total Organization	**100**	**100**
TOTAL EXPENSE	**$472,000**	**$ 472,000**

IV. HISTORICAL FOUNDATION

	Revised 2019	Proposed 2020
INCOME		
Our United Outreach	$ 73,000	$ 70,000
Endowments	75,000	72,000
Gifts	23,800	63,000
TOTAL INCOME	**$ 171,800**	**$ 205,000**
EXPENSE		
Salaries	$ 97,128	$ 86,000
FICA / Retirement	14,764	15,160
Insurance	10,034	10,000
Board Travel	7,000	12,000
Legal Fees	200	500
Continuing Education	2,000	500
Subscriptions/Memberships	2,000	4,000
Archival Equipment	2,000	4,000
Computer Supplies	500	500
Office Supplies	2,000	2,000
Postage	125	240
Acquisitions	5,649	20,000
Birthplace Shrine	5,000	13,500
Employee Recognition	600	600
Staff Travel	6,000	12,000
Denomination Day Project	5,000	10,000
Purchases for Resale	800	1,000
Temp Help	5,000	6,000
Property Insurance/Liability Insurance	4,000	4.000
Advertising/Promotion	2,000	3,000
TOTAL EXPENSE	**$ 171,800**	**$ 205,000**

	Revised 2019	Proposed 2020

V. MEMPHIS THEOLOGICAL SEMINARY

	Revised 2019	Proposed 2020
REVENUE		
Student Tuition Fees	$2,023,950	$ 1,950,725
Investment	303,431	315,000
Endowment Draw	200,000	200,000
Gifts and Grants	1,000,000	1,000,000
Other Revenues	102,009	255,863
TOTAL REVENUES	**$3,629,390**	**$ 3,721,588**
EXPENSES		
Business Office	$ 332,733	$ 304,508
Dean's Office	116,412	109,933
Chapel	1,900	1,900
Educational Development Committee	15,000	10,000
Advancement Office	335,951	178,741
Doctor of Ministry	61,550	65,630
Facilities	497,531	492,032
Faculty	815,646	653,704
Financial Aid	52,659	51,078
Information Technology	190,779	183,040
Library	238,664	193,913
President's Office	261,823	250,589
Admissions	110,881	121,634
Registrar & Institutional Research	99,125	104,280
Housing	120,695	119,115
Student Services	0	76,802
Student Government	2,700	2,145
Scholarships	347,483	334,638
Program of Alternate Studies	123,364	130,475
Formation For Ministry	89,556	90,172
Summer Classes	34,800	0
January Classes	8,000	0
Certificate & Continuing Education	15,950	0
Methodist House of Studies	24,432	0
Depreciation	197,752	207,259
TOTAL EXPENSES	**$4,134,033**	**$3,721,588**
Increase (decrease) in net assets	(504,643)	(0)

VI. SHARED SERVICES

	Revised 2019	Proposed 2020
REVENUE		
Our United Outreach	$ 346,967	345,375
TOTAL REVENUES	**$ 346,967**	**$ 345,375**
EXPENSES		
Salaries	$ 53,332	$ 54,665
Health Insurance	31,659	19,200
Retirement	2,667	2,733
FICA	4,080	4,182
Accounting Coordinator	1,600	1,600
Audit	22,500	22,500
Payroll Service	7,400	8,500
Bank Charges	14,000	14,000
Technology System Consultants - EMS	18,000	18,000
Software Maintenance Agreement - Blackbaud	17,000	18,500
Building & Maintenance	45,845	45,845
Pest Control	840	900
Lawn & Ground Maintenance	18,500	18,500
Lawn Treatment	1,500	1,500
Utilities - Building 1	24,650	25,000
Utilities - Building 2	17,000	19,000
Janitorial Service	8,100	8,100
Security System Monitoring	1,200	1,200
Trash Collection	2,500	2,800
Telephone/Internet	10,000	11,000
Heating & AC Maintenance Agreement	12,000	12,000
Insurance/Liability	11,844	12,000
Office Equipment Maintenance	14,000	16,500
Computer Maintenance	500	500
Computer Software	2,500	2,500
Office Supplies	2,000	2,400
Postage	750	750
Employee Events	1,000	1,000
TOTAL EXPENSE	$ 346,967	$ 345,375
Surplus/Deficit	$ 0	$ 0

FOR INFORMATION ONLY

(Because this petition presents the same question as one which remains within the control of the assembly (a referral from the 188th General Assembly re: Human Sexuality), the General Assembly Permanent Committee on Judiciary advised the clerk that it would not be in order for the Arkansas Petition to be considered by the General Assembly in its 2019 meeting - see page 99, Section II. Communication, of the Preliminary Minutes).

Arkansas Petition to 2019 Joint Meeting of the General Assembly

WHEREAS the Confession of Faith for Cumberland Presbyterian Church and Cumberland Presbyterian Church in America states in Section 6.17:

> 6.17 Marriage is between a man and a woman for the mutual benefit of each, their children, and society. While marriage is subject to the appropriate civil law, it is primarily a covenant relationship under God. As such, it symbolizes the relationship of Jesus Christ and the church, and is that human relationship in which love and trust are best known.

WHEREAS the Constitution of the Cumberland Presbyterian Church and the Cumberland Presbyterians Church in America states the following in Sections 2.61 and 2.73:

> 2.61 The office of minister of word and sacrament is unique in the life of the church as to responsibility and usefulness. God calls persons and sets them apart for this ministry. The persons who fill this office should be sound in the faith, exemplary in conduct, and competent to perform the duties of the ministry. Persons who become ministers of the word and sacrament are due such respect as belongs to their office, but are not by virtue of their office more holy or righteous than other Christians. They share in the same vocation that belongs to all Christians to be witnesses to the gospel in word and deed. They differ from other Christians only with regard to the office to which they are called, which is their station in life.

> 2.73 Persons who fill the office of elder may be male or female, young or old. Elders share in the same vocation that belongs to all Christians to be witnesses to the gospel, but the vocation of this office places an additional responsibility of leadership upon them. They should exemplify the gospel by their good character, sound faith, wisdom, maturity of judgment, discretion, conversation, knowledge of the doctrine and government of the church, and competency to perform the duties of the office.

WHEREAS the Constitution has within in it the means by which the Presbyteries can decide the direction of doctrine and polity for the Cumberland Presbyterian Church and the Cumberland Presbyterian Church in America. These means are stated clearly in Section 11.0 "Amendments" of the Constitution of the Cumberland Presbyterian Church and the Cumberland Presbyterian Church in America. Section 11.1 through 11.4 are as follows:

> 11.1 Amendments to the Confession of Faith, Catechism, Constitution, Rules of Discipline, Directory for Worship, and Rules of Order may be proposed to the General Assembly of the Cumberland Presbyterian Church or the General Assembly of the Cumberland Presbyterian Church in America. If received favorably by either General Assembly, all proposed amendments shall be referred to a Joint Committee on Amendments composed of the five members of the Permanent Committee on Judiciary of each General Assembly for preparation for the two assemblies for action.

> 11.2 When a proposed amendment to the Confession of Faith, Catechism, Constitution, or Rules of Discipline is presented by the Joint Committee on Amendments to the General Assembly of each church, on recommendation of each assembly the amendment may be transmitted to its presbyteries by three-fourths vote of the members thereof voting thereon, provided there is present and voting not less than 75% of the full membership of the assembly based on the complete representation of all its presbyteries.

11.3 An amendment to the Confession of Faith, Catechism, or Rules of Discipline shall have been adopted when, on its transmission by both assemblies to their presbyteries, a three-fourths majority of the presbyteries of each General Assembly shall have approved it and such approval is declared by each General Assembly to have been given. The vote of a presbytery shall be by simple majority.

11.4 An amendment to the Constitution shall have been adopted:
a. For both churches, when a three-fourths majority of the presbyteries of each General Assembly shall have approved it and such approval is declared by each General Assembly to have been given; each presbytery voting by simply majority, and,
b. For either church when a three-fourths majority of its presbyteries shall have approved it and such approval is declared by its General Assembly to have been given; each presbytery voting by simple majority. In such instances the amendment shall be identified as applicable to the Constitution of the church adopting it, and the original section to which the amendment was applied shall remain a part of the Constitution of the church rejecting it.
c. Presbyteries shall act upon an amendment referred by the General Assembly within the first year of the referral and report their vote no later than the next meeting of the General Assembly after the amendment was transmitted to the presbyteries.

THEREFORE, Arkansas Presbytery petitions the 2019 General Assembly of the Cumberland Presbyterian Church meeting concurrently with the Cumberland Presbyterian Church of America to place the following amendments to the Constitution before Presbyteries of the Cumberland Presbyterian Church and Cumberland Presbyterian Church in America as directed by Section 11.1 and 11.2 of the Constitution.

The Amendment to be placed before the Presbyteries of the Cumberland Presbyterian Church and Cumberland Presbyterian Church in American is that the following paragraphs be added to the Constitution as 4.2 and 7.02 and the numbering of the sections 4.0 "Sessions" and 7.0 "Relations Between Ministers, Licentiates, or Candidates and Churches" be renumbered to include their insertion.

4.2 When a person is in a sexual relationship that is outside the boundaries of marriage as described in the Confession of Faith 6.17, with no desire to abstain, then such a situation makes that person ineligible to serve as an elder on the session of a church.

7.02 When a person is in a sexual relationship that is outside the boundaries of marriage as described in the Confession of Faith 6.17, with no desire to abstain, then such a situation makes that person ineligible to serve a church in any of the relationships stated in 7.01.

If amended Section 4.0 "Sessions" will appear as follows in the Constitution:

4.0 SESSION
4.1 The session of a particular church consists of the minister in charge and elders elected by the congregation. There must be a minimum of two elders, but the actual number shall be detennined by the congregation in accordance with such rules as it may establish.

4.2 When a person is in a sexual relationship that is outside the boundaries of marriage as described in the Confession of Faith 6.17, with no desire to abstain, then such a situation makes that person ineligible to serve as an elder on the session of a church.

4.3 In a church which has no pastor, or in the absence of the minister in charge or of the moderator appointed by presbytery, the session may meet and transact any business.

4.4 The session may be convened when two or more of its members so request. The minister in charge may convene the session at any time during or immediately following a regular service of worship and at other times by giving proper notice to session members.

4.5 A majority of the session constitutes a quorum unless the congregation has set a quorum otherwise; but any two elders, in conjunction with the minister may receive members and grant letters of dismission.

4.6 The session is charged with pastoral oversight of the particular church and has the responsibility to:
a. Call a pastor(also an associate/assistant pastor) subject to the approval of presbytery;
(Form for issuing a call to a pastor or associate/assistant pastor, see Constitution, Appendix 4 .)
b. Receive members into the church;
c. Resolve questions of doctrine and discipline in the congregation;
d. Admonish or suspend members found guilty in a disciplinary hearing, subject to appeal to presbytery;
e. Urge upon parents the importance of presenting their children for baptism;
f. Grant letters of dismission, which when given for parents shall always include the names of their baptized children;
g. Ordain and install elders and deacons when elected and require these officers to devote themselves to their responsibilities;
h. Examine the proceedings and supervise the work of the deacons;
i. Establish and give oversight to church schools, Bible classes, fellowship and other organizations within the church, with special attention being given to nurture of the children;
j. Encourage the stewardship of church members, order and supervise collections for Godly purposes, and in general, oversee the finances of the church;
k. Assemble the congregation and provide for worship when there is no minister;
l. Initiate and coordinate the best measures for promoting and extending the work of the church;
m. Elect representatives to the higher church judicatories, and require on their return a report of their diligence and the decisions of the judicatory;
n. Observe and carry out the injunctions of the higher judicatories.

4.7 The session may designate two elders, either of whom, when authorized by the presbytery, may administer the sacrament of the Lord's Supper to the congregation.

4.8 The members of the session, excluding the minister, are the trustees of the church. They shall hold title to the property of the church and shall execute all transactions required by civil law. If it seems desirable the session may elect a smaller number of persons to serve as trustees. In this instance the trustees may act only as specifically authorized by the session. The tenure of office of such trustees may be for an indefinite period or for definite terms on a rotation basis.

4.9 Each session shall keep an accurate record of its proceedings which must be submitted to presbytery, at least annually, for review. Each session shall also keep a record of congregational meetings, of marriages, of baptisms, of additions, and of the death and dismission of church members.

If amended Section 7.0 "Relations Between Ministers, Licentiates, or Candidates and Churches" will appear as follows in the Constitution:

7.00 RELATIONS BETWEEN MINISTERS, LICENTIATES, OR CANDIDATES AND CHURCHES
7.01 A person may be called to a particular church to one of four relationships: pastor, associate/assistant pastor, stated supply, or interim pastor.

7.02 When a person is in a sexual relationship that is outside the boundaries of marriage as described in the Confession of Faith 6.17, with no desire to abstain, then such a situation makes that person ineligible to serve a church in any of the relationships stated in 7.01.

7.03 The office of pastor is to be held only by an ordained minister, whom the particular church has called for an indefinite time and to whom the presbytery has entrusted the spiritual care of the church, including the office of moderator of the session.

7.04 The office of associate/assistant pastor is to be held only by an ordained minister whom the particular church has called for a definite or indefinite time to fulfill various pastoral functions as outlined by the church issuing the call, and approved by the presbytery. In the absence of the pastor, the associate pastor may, with the approval of the pastor and session, serve as moderator of the session or of a congregational meeting.

7.05 The office of stated supply may be held by an ordained minister, a licentiate, or a candidate, whom the particular church has called for an indefinite time, or, in the case of an interim supply, for a definite time, for less than full time work. An ordained minister serving as stated supply may fulfill all duties and functions pertaining to the spiritual care of the church, including moderating the session. A licentiate or a candidate serving as stated supply may fulfill the duties and functions except moderating the session, administering the sacraments, and solemnizing marriages.

7.06 The office of interim pastor is to be held by an ordained minister who is invited by the session of a church without an installed pastor. An interim pastor may preach the word, administer the sacraments, and fulfill pastoral duties for a specified period of time not to exceed twelve months, while the church is seeking a pastor. An interim pastor may not be called to be the next installed pastor or associate/assistant pastor of a church served as interim pastor.

7.07 A person shall enter into one of these relationships with a particular church only with the approval of the presbytery in the bounds of which the particular church is located. The church session shall bear responsibility for the selection of the person, and the presbytery's approval shall relate to the person's ministerial credentials, commitment to the theology and government of the Cumberland Presbyterian Church/Cumberland Presbyterian Church in America, and standing in his or her current presbytery, if any. The presbytery may authorize its board of missions to act on its behalf in examining the call and to give tentative approval to a relationship between a particular church and a minister, licentiate, or candidate, subject to formal approval at a meeting of the presbytery.

7.08 The relationship between a minister, licentiate, or candidate and a particular church may be dissolved only by presbytery, acting on the request of both parties, or on the request of one party if sufficient reasons are presented, or when, in the opinion of the presbytery, the well-being of the particular church demands it.

Note: After 7.08 the numbering went to 7.10, thus no renumbering was necessary.

The
Proceedings
of the

ONE HUNDRED EIGHTY-NINTH
GENERAL ASSEMBLY

of the

CUMBERLAND PRESBYTERIAN CHURCH

session held in

HUNTSVILLE, ALABAMA

June 9 - 14, 2019

At Huntsville, Alabama and within the facilities of the Von Braun Convention Center, there the ninth day of June in the year of our Lord, two thousand nineteen, at the appointed hour of seven thirty o'clock in the evening, Minister and Elder Commissioners from the various presbyteries, youth advisory delegates and visitors assembled for Concurrent meetings of the General Assemblies of the Cumberland Presbyterian Church and the Cumberland Presbyterian Church in America.

FIRST DAY – SUNDAY – JUNE 9, 2019

OPENING WORSHIP

At Huntsville, Alabama and within the North Hall of the Von Braun Convention Center, the one hundred eighty-ninth General Assembly of the Cumberland Presbyterian Church, the one hundred forty-fourth General Assembly of the Cumberland Presbyterian Church in America, the Convention of Cumberland Presbyterian Women's Ministry, and visitors gathered for worship at 7:30 p.m. Participants in the service were Ms. Yvonne Frierson, National Missionary Society President (CPCA); Elder Lewis Leon Cole, Jr., Cleveland-Ohio Presbytery, Moderator (CPCA); Ms. Cathy Littlefield, Women's Ministry Convention President (CPC); and Reverend Jay Earheart-Brown, West Tennessee Presbytery, Moderator (CPC). The Music Director was Elder Victor Garth, Mt. Zion (CPCA). Special Music was offered by the Host Choir. The Pianist was Mr. Michael Knotts, Madkins Chapel (CPCA). An offering of $2,652.61 was taken and will be shared between the Clergy Crisis Fund (CPC) and the North Alabama Sickle Cell Foundation (CPCA).

Reverend Stan Wood, New Hopewell Presbytery (CPCA) presented the sermon, "Walk In Love," taken from the scripture passage Ephesians 5:1-2. The Sacrament of Holy Communion was led by co-celebrants Reverend Joy Warren, Murfreesboro Presbytery (CPC) and Reverend Mitchell Walker, Sr., Huntsville Presbytery (CPCA). Serving communion from the Cumberland Presbyterian Church in America: Reverend Theoldis Acklin, (Huntsville Presbytery); Reverend Kay Ward Creer, (East Texas Presbytery); Reverend Nancy Fuqua, (Florence Presbytery); Elder John W. Humphrey, (Huntsville Presbytery); Reverend Robert Jefferson (Huntsville Presbytery); Elder Deborah Smith, (Huntsville Presbytery); Elder Brenda Sutherlin, (Tennessee Valley Presbytery), and Elder Thomas Ward (Huntsville Presbytery). Serving communion from the Cumberland Presbyterian Church: Elder Sally Sain, (Columbia Presbytery); Elder Lina Maria Velasquez, (Emaus Presbytery); Elder IP Shun-Tak Andy, (Hong Kong Presbytery); Reverend Tiffany McClung, (West Tennessee Presbytery); Elder Debbie Shanks, (North Central Presbytery); Reverend Alfonzo Marquez, (Presbytery of East Tennessee); Reverend Wilfrido Quinones, (Cauca Valley Presbytery), and Reverend Virginia Espinoza (Choctaw Presbytery).

SECOND DAY – MONDAY – JUNE 18, 2018

The day began with orientation for Commissioners and YAD's at 8:00 a.m. led by Stated Clerk Michael Sharpe. Following the orientation, the YAD's were dismissed with Nathan Wheeler, Director of Youth and Young Adult Ministry. The Chairs and Co-Chairs of the GA Committees met with Engrossing Clerk Vernon Sansom for further orientation.

A joint opening devotion was held at 10:30 a.m. in North Hall 2 & 3. Participants in the devotion were: Liturgists Reverend Mitchell Walker, Sr., Huntsville Presbytery (CPCA) and Reverend Joy Warren, Murfreesboro Presbytery (CPC); Pianist Mr. Michael Knotts, Madkins Chapel (CPCA); and Music Director Elder Victor Garth, Mt. Zion (CPCA).

The Unification Task Force presented a very informative and uplifting presentation on the upcoming vote on unification that is before both General Assemblies this week. We heard greetings from both host pastors, Reverend Chris Warren led in the singing of "They Will Know We are Christians by Our Love." Reverend Cardelia Howell-Diamond gave a reflection on Ephesians 5:1-2.

The Unification Task Force presentation answered three questions: Why union?, What Is the plan?, and How do we unify?

Reverend Jay Earheart-Brown (CPC) and Elder Leon Cole, Jr. (CPCA) answered the question "Why Union?" We need each other. Our children are calling us to be one and we need to be an example to the nation. 3. We are more alike than different.

Reverend Gloria Diaz (CPC) answered the question, "What is the Plan?" She discussed the Plan of Union that has been published.

Reverend Steve Mosley (CPC) and Reverend Perryn Rice (CPCA, CPC) answered the question, "How do we unify?" By simple majority on the General Assembly level to send to presbyteries. Each presbytery passes by simple majority. If passed by a simple majority of the presbyteries, the General Assemblies vote on final approval of Bylaws and Standing Rules (2/3 vote of approval necessary) for the General Assembly of the new church. Constitutional amendments will be reviewed and approved by 3/4 vote and 3/4 of the presbyteries by simple majority vote. If both assemblies approve the Bylaws, the two assemblies vote to adjourn sine die, and the Cumberland Presbyterian Church United will be organized in 2021.

THE ASSEMBLY IS CONSTITUTED

The Moderator, the Reverend Earheart-Brown, called the assembly to order at 2:00 p.m. with forty-seven (47) ministers, forty-four (44) elders for a total of 91 Commissioners and 25 Youth Advisory Delegates present. The constituting prayer was offered by Reverend Mark Hester, Presbytery of East Tennessee.

ADOPTION OF THE AGENDA

The Moderator thanked the Commissioners for their service to the 189th General Assembly before asking for a motion that the agenda, as found in the Preliminary Minutes, be adopted. On Motion, the agenda was adopted.

REPORT OF THE CREDENTIALS COMMITTEE

Reverend Virginia Espinoza, Choctaw Presbytery, presented the Report of the Credentials Committee. There were forty-six (46) ministers, forty-three (43) elders, for a total of eighty-nine (89) commissioners and twenty-one (21) youth advisory delegates registered as of 2 p.m. On motion, the report of the Credentials Committee was received, marked Appendix "A" and filed.

ELECTION OF THE MODERATOR

Moderator Earheart-Brown declared the floor open for nominations for the Office of Moderator of the 189th General Assembly of the Cumberland Presbyterian Church. Reverend Shelia C. O'Mara, Presbytery del Cristo, and Reverend Michael Clark, Murfreesboro Presbytery, were nominated. After asking for further nominations and there being none, the Moderator declared nominations closed and moved to hear from those speaking on behalf of the nominees.

Reverend Perryn Rice was given permission to address the body on motion to speak on behalf of Reverend Clark by consent.

Reverend Nancy J. Fuqua, (CPCA), was given permission to speak on behalf of Reverend O'Mara.

The Moderator called both nominees to the podium to share with the body their qualifications and visions for holding the office of Moderator. Following the hearing of both nominees, the Moderator called for commissioners to cast their votes. The ballots were collected by the credentials committee who met with the Stated Clerk to count the ballots.

While the ballots were being counted, the Moderator introduced the Ministry Council Team Leaders. Reverend Milton Ortiz, Missions Ministry Team Leader, introduced Reverend Cardelia Howell-Diamond as the new Director of Women's Ministry and Reverend Kristi Lounsbury as the new Director of Congregational Ministry; Reverend Elinor Brown introduced Cindy Martin who has been moved to the position of Resources Distribution Manager, and the new Coordinator of Adult Ministry, Reverend Chris Fleming; Reverend Steven Shelton, Communications Ministry Team Leader, introduced Matt Gore as the new Editor of the Cumberland Presbyterian Magazine.

The Moderator introduced the new Director of the Cumberland Presbyterian Children's Home, Courtney Banatoski, and the Interim President of Memphis Theological Seminary, Dr. Susan Parker.

The Moderator shared the following prayer concerns with the body: Reverend Tom Spence (Red River Presbytery) who had a light stroke, and the family of Jacob Kennemer who passed away suddenly. Jacob was the grandson of Reverend Richard and Marsha Hughes and the nephew of Reverend Darren Kennemer.

Reverend Virginia Espinoza, Credentials Committee chair, announced that by a vote of 57 to 31, Reverend Shelia O'Mara was elected Moderator of the 189th General Assembly of the Cumberland Presbyterian Church. Reverend Nate Matthews escorted Moderator O'Mara to the podium. Former Moderator Jay Earheart-Brown presented Moderator Shelia O'Mara the Moderator's Cross and gavel.

Moderator O'Mara appointed Reverend Geoff Knight, (Trinity Presbytery) as Parliamentarian.

ELECTION OF THE VICE-MODERATOR

Moderator O'Mara opened the floor for nominations for Vice-Moderator of the 189th General Assembly. Reverend Michael Clark, Murfreesboro Presbytery, was nominated to be Vice-Moderator of the 189th General Assembly of the Cumberland Presbyterian Church. There being no other nominations, the Moderator declared Reverend Michael Clark to be Vice-Moderator of the 189th General Assembly of the Cumberland Presbyterian Church.

PRESENTATION BY THE STATED CLERK

The Stated Clerk, Reverend Michael Sharpe, invited retiring Moderator Jay Earheart-Brown to the podium. The Stated Clerk thanked Moderator Earheart-Brown for his service to the 188th General Assembly. The Stated Clerk presented the former Moderator with replicas of the moderator's cross and gavel used in the 188th General Assembly of the Cumberland Presbyterian Church.

COMMUNICATIONS

Reverend Jimmy Peyton, Hope Presbytery, made the motion that the Arkansas Petition be accepted as a communication for consideration. The Parliamentarian, Reverend Geoff Knight explained that the communication could not be considered when the same issue is under referral until such time as the referral has been brought back to the General Assembly and dealt with. The Motion was ruled out of order by the Moderator. The ruling of the Moderator was appealed by motion and seconded. The appeal failed and the ruling stands.

The Stated Clerk reported that there were no communications.

CORRECTIONS

The Engrossing Clerk, Reverend Vernon Sansom, called the attention of the body to changes to the Preliminary Minutes: On page 5, Reverend Joy Warren and Elder Pete Miller, Murfreesboro Presbytery, should be deleted as the presbytery is only eligible to have 3 elder and 3 minister commissioners (the Credentials Committee wrote their report with this change in mind). On page 83 in the Preliminary Minutes, Section VII should read "Financial Concerns and 2020 Budget" instead of 2019.

INTRODUCTIONS

The Stated Clerk introduced the Board/Agency Representatives:

Bethel University	Robert Truitt
Commission on Chaplains	Cassandra Thomas
Children's Home	Courtney Banatoski
GA Evaluation Committee	Rickey Page
Historical Foundation	Pat Ward
Judiciary	Geoffery Knight
Memphis Theological Seminary	Vanessa Midgett
Ministry Council	Charelle Webb
Our United Outreach	Bruce Hamilton
Stewardship	Gary Tubb
Theology and Social Concerns	Edmund Cox (CPCA)
	Mitch Boulton (CPC)
Unification Task Force	Perryn Rice (CPCA)
	Steve Mosley (CPC)

COMMISSIONER RESOLUTIONS

A resolution was presented by Cauca Valley Presbytery concerning ordinations and marriage. The Moderator ruled that the resolution was out of order because it could not be considered when the same issue is under referral until such time as the referral has been brought back to the General Assembly and dealt with.

A Motion was made that any further papers brought before this body be forwarded to the United Committees on Theology and Social Concerns for their consideration. Motion was seconded. After some discussion, the question was called for and seconded. Motion carried.

It was noted that all resolutions pertaining to the issue of sexuality that were brought to the body for consideration will be distributed to commissioners and the Theology and Social Concerns Committee for information only and to let the sending presbyteries voices be heard.

The Stated Clerk reminded the body that the Bookstore, concessions and displays are in the East Hall #3.

The Moderator asked for prayers during the week for herself as she serves as Moderator.

RECESS

A Recess was announced by the Moderator following prayer at 3:47 p.m. until Thursday at 9:30 a.m.

The Committees met at 3:30 p.m. and 7:30 p.m.

EVENING PROGRAM

There was a joint moderator and women's ministry reception at the Cumberland Presbyterian Church in America Center and Church Street Cumberland Presbyterian Church in America. All in attendance enjoyed fellowship and hors d'oeuves while greeting Moderators of the Cumberland Presbyterian Church in America and Cumberland Presbyterian Church as well as honoring the Officers of the Women's Ministry.

THIRD DAY – TUESDAY – JUNE 11, 2019

The General Assembly began the day with a Joint Fun Run & Walk at 7:00 a.m. at Big Springs International Park. The day was devoted to committee work from 9:30 a.m. until 5:00 p.m. and an evening session at 7:00 p.m. The attendance for the day: forty-five (45) Minister Commissioners, forty-five (45) Elder Commissioners for a total of ninety (90) Commissioners and twenty-five (25) Youth Advisory Delegates.

EVENING PROGRAM

At 8:30 p.m., commissioners and visitors participated in a Joint Reception honoring Women in Ministry in South Hall, Ballroom 1. Attendees enjoyed fellowship, refreshments, and wonderful door prizes. It was noted that 16 years ago at the first reception honoring Women in Ministry there were just enough participants to sit around one table. Sixteen years later, the event was so well attended that there was a full room filled with CP's showing their support for Women in Ministry.

THIRD DAY – WEDNESDAY – JUNE 12, 2019

The General Assembly and visitors began the day with a joint devotional at 8:30 a.m. led by the National Missionary Society (CPCA). Leading the service were Sister A.M. Phillips, Texas Synod (CPCA), Sister Rita Godwin, Tennessee Synod (CPCA), Sister Annie Harris, HPMS President, Alabama Synod (CPCA), Sister Yvonne Frierson, CPCA NMS, President, Alabama Synod (CPCA), and Elder Leon Cole, CPCA Moderator. The devotional, "Walk in Love," based on Ephesians 5:1-2, was offered by Sister Venessa Edmonds, Hills Chapel Cumberland Presbyterian Church in America, Alabama Synod.

The Committees used the remainder of the day in meetings, preparing and reviewing reports and collecting signatures. Attendance for the day: forty-five (45) minister commissioners, forty-three (43) elder commissioners for a total of eighty-eight (88) and twenty-four (24) youth advisory delegates.

The evening program was presented at 7:00 p.m. by the Discipleship Ministry Team. The program, Soul Shop gave training on suicidal desperation among adolescents and also, how to help prevent suicide among adolescents.

FOURTH DAY – THURSDAY – JUNE 13, 2019

At 8:30 a.m., the General Assembly and visitors began the day with joyful singing and a devotional based on I John 4:16, "What's Love Got To Do With It?," led by Youth Advisory Delegate, Olivia Pruitt, Missouri Presbytery. The opening prayer was offered by Reverend Joy Warren, Murfreesboro Presbytery (CPC). The Closing Prayer was offered by Reverend Mitchell Walker, Sr., Huntsville Presbytery (CPCA).

At 9:00 a.m., Reverend Milton Ortiz, Missions Ministry Team Leader, led a commissioning service for the Lopez family, Reverend Wilson and Reverend Diana Lopez and their daughters, Marcel and Valery, as they prepare to begin their missionary work in Spain. The service began with the singing of "How Great Thou Art" in Spanish. Reverend Lynn Thomas, Director of Global Cross-Cultural Missions, gave a brief devotion from Acts about the spreading of the Gospel after being sent from the church in Antioch.

Reverend Wilson Lopez addressed the body asking for prayers as they start their ministry to Spain. The Moderator and Vice-Moderator laid hands on the Lopez family as they were commissioned through prayer in English and in Spanish for their mission to Spain. Lynn Thomas blessed the Lopez family and pronounced a benediction.

CALL TO ORDER

The Moderator, Reverend Shelia O'Mara, called the assembly to order at 9:36 a.m. There were forty-seven (47) ministers, forty-two (42) elders for a total of eighty-nine (89) commissioners and twenty-two (22) youth advisory delegates present. The opening prayer was shared by the Moderator.

GREETINGS AND PRESENTATION

The body was greeted by Elder Leon Cole, Retiring Moderator of the Cumberland Presbyterian Church in America. He reported that this concurrent meeting of the General Assemblies of the Cumberland Presbyterian Church and the Cumberland Presbyterian Church in America felt more like one single meeting rather than two separate meetings. He also announced that the Cumberland Presbyterian Church in America General Assembly voted to go forward with the unification plan. He urged that we continue to have fellowship between the two denominations regardless of the results of the presbytery votes. Elder Cole offered a prayer for our General Assembly meeting.

ANNOUNCEMENTS

The Stated Clerk, Michael Sharpe, shared some "housekeeping" details.
* Reminder to invite the youth advisory delegates to vote prior to the commissioner vote.
* Instructed commissioners and youth advisory delegates wishing to address the Assembly to approach the microphone, introduce themselves by name and the presbytery they represent.
* To please write out any motions and give a copy to the Engrossing Clerk before returning to their seat.
* As committee reports are presented, committee members will come forward and be seated in the front rows of chairs
* The Stated Clerk explained how the indicator cards convey responses toward content of speech and to indicate the mood of the General Assembly.
* Each commissioner received a copy of the Ten Essential Rules of Order to assist with following Robert's Rules of Order.

Moderator O'Mara reported that a prayer will be offered before each report is presented.

THE REPORT OF THE COMMITTEE ON THEOLOGY AND SOCIAL CONCERNS/ UNIFICATION TASKFORCE

The Moderator offered a prayer for this report and the Committee who presented it.

Reverend Linda Snelling, Red River Presbytery, introduced the readers of The Report of the Committee on Theology and Social Concerns/Unification Task Force: Youth Advisory Delegates Kenzie Cornelius, Hope Presbytery, and Grace Holland, West Tennessee Presbytery.

Following the reading of the report, a motion was made by Reverend Edurado Montoya, North Central Presbytery, to receive the report and adopt the recommendations. Motion Seconded.

A motion to divide the question was made and seconded resulting in each recommendation being dealt with separately.

After discussion of Recommendation 1, the Youth Advisory Delegates were polled, and the majority of the Youth Advisory Delegates were in favor of this recommendation. By vote of the Commissioners, Recommendation 1 passed.

After discussion of Recommendation 2, the question was called for and seconded. Motion passed. The Youth Advisory Delegates were polled, and the majority were in favor of this recommendation. By vote of the Commissioners, Recommendation 2 passed.

Recommendation 3 – a motion to amend the recommendation by changing the word "ratification" to "approved" was made and the motion seconded. After further discussion, the Youth Advisory Delegates were polled, and they are in favor of the amendment. By vote of the Commissioners, the motion to amend carried.

After further debate on Recommendation 3 as amended, the question was called for and seconded. Motion to call for the question passed. The Youth Advisory Delegates were polled as being in favor of Recommendation 3 as amended. By vote of the Commissioners, Recommendation 3 as amended passed.

By vote of the Commissioners, The Report of the Committee on Theology and Social Concerns/ Unification Task Force was concurred in and the Recommendations, as amended, were adopted.

Reverend Jay Earheart-Brown, West Tennessee Presbytery, asked that the body give thanks for those who worked hard for many years on this issue and who are no longer with us: Beverly St. John, Marion Sweet, Margaret McKee and James Knight.

The report was marked "B" and filed.

RECESS

The Moderator announced a 15-minute Recess.

BUSINESS CONTINUED

The Moderator called the meeting back to order at 10:55.

The Moderator introduced the incoming Moderator of the Cumberland Presbyterian Church in America, Reverend Theodis Acklin and invited him to address the body. Moderator Acklin reported that he looks forward to our two denominations working together toward unification.

A Motion was made and seconded to seat Reverend Theodus Acklin as an advisory member. Motion passed.

ANNOUNCEMENTS

The Moderator granted an excuse for Elder Sally Sain, Columbia Presbytery, at 10 a.m. to attend a family funeral.

The Moderator reported that a letter that was distributed before the meeting of the General Assembly began does not express the views of all of the Youth Advisory Delegates and should not have been distributed.

THE REPORT OF THE NOMINATING COMMITTEE

The Moderator offered a prayer for the work of the Nominating Committee as well as those being nominated and the report that has been sent to this body.

The Report of the Nominating Committee was presented by Reverend Derek Jacks, Grace Presbytery. Reverend Jacks made a motion to place the names in the Report of the Nominating Committee as printed in the Preliminary Minutes into nomination. Motion seconded. The moderator opened the floor for further nomination. There being no further nominations, the nominations were closed. By vote of the Commissioners, the Report was concurred in and those nominated were elected to the named positions.

REPORT OF THE COMMITTEE ON MINISTRY COUNCIL

Moderator offered a prayer for the Ministry Council and Ministry Council Committee as well as the report that is before the body.

The Report of the Committee on Ministry Council was presented by Reverend Mark Hester, Presbytery of East Tennessee. The report was read by Youth Advisory Delegate Hannah Davis, Arkansas Presbytery.

Reverend Hester made the motion that the report be concurred in and the recommendations be adopted. Motion seconded. (A document is included with the report on the situation in Hong Kong.)

The youth were polled, and they were in favor of this report. By vote of the Commissioners, the Report of the Committee on Ministry Council was concurred in and the recommendations adopted. The report was marked "C" and filed.

Reverend Lynn Thomas, Director of Global Cross-Cultural Ministries, shared with the body the situation in Hong Kong and the protests that were happening currently. Reverend Thomas invited the Commissioners from Hong Kong to the podium and led the body in prayer for all in Hong Kong affected by the unrest, especially our churches and members in Hong Kong.

THE REPORT OF THE COMMITTEE ON JUDICIARY

The Moderator prayed for the Committee on Judiciary.

The Report of the Committee on Judiciary was presented by Reverend Tammy Greene, Presbytery of East Tennessee. The report was read by Youth Advisory Delegates Noah Jenkins, North Central Presbytery; Robert Rush, Red River Presbytery; Will Suiter, West Tennessee Presbytery; and Brandon Smith, Presbytery of East Tennessee Presbytery.

A motion was made by Reverend Greene that the report be concurred in and its recommendations be adopted.

A Motion was made that the question be divided. Motion seconded. The recommendations were considered separately.

RECESS

Moderator placed the report of the Committee on Judiciary on the table and declared a recess until 2 p.m.

BUSINESS CONTINUES

The Moderator called the meeting back to order at 2:05 p.m.

INTRODUCTION OF CPWM CONVENTION PRESIDENT

The Moderator introduced Mrs. Judy Truitt, president of the CPWM Convention. She reported that there were about 100 in attendance at the Convention. Mrs. Truitt reported that the CPWM was in good shape and the program for the week was a very good one.

THE REPORT OF THE COMMITTEE ON JUDICIARY (continued)

The Moderator took the Report of the Committee on Judiciary Report off the table for continued consideration. The Chair of the Judicatory Committee clarified the amendments in the report and was available for questions. The Youth Advisory Delegates were polled, and they were in favor of Recommendation 1. On Vote of the Commissioners, Recommendation 1 was adopted.

The Youth Advisory Delegates were polled, and they were in favor of Recommendation 2. On vote of the Commissioners, Recommendation 2 was adopted.

A Motion was made to amend the report to include Recommendation 3, "That the Unified Committee on Theology and Social Concerns be instructed to propose a report for the 190th General Assembly on how the Cumberland Presbyterian Church and Cumberland Presbyterian Church in America can better teach, practice and hold ministers and sessions accountable for following our theology of baptism."

The Youth Advisory Delegates were polled, and they were in favor of Recommendation 3. On Vote of the Commissioners, Recommendation 3 was adopted

By vote of the Commissioners, The Report on Judicatory, as amended, was concurred in and the recommendations adopted.

The report was marked "D" and filed.

THE REPORT OF THE COMMITTEE ON CHAPLAINS/HISTORICAL FOUNDATION

Moderator O'Mara called Vice-Moderator Michael Clark to take the Podium.

The Vice Moderator offered a prayer before receiving the report.

The Report of the Committee on Chaplains/Historical Foundation was presented by Reverend Lisa Cook, Nashville Presbytery. The report was read by Isaac Ebry, Cumberland Presbytery.

A motion was made by Reverend Cook to concur in the Report of the Committee on Chaplains/Historical Foundation and adopt the recommendations with noted editorial changes. Motion Seconded.

The Youth Advisory Delegates were polled and approved the report. By vote, The Report of the Committee on Chaplains/Historical Foundation was concurred in and the recommendations, as edited, adopted.

The report was marked "E" and filed.

THE REPORT OF THE COMMITTEE ON STEWARDSHIP/ELECTED OFFICERS

The Vice-Moderator offered a prayer for the Report and all who are touched by it.

The Report of the Committee Stewardship/Elected Officers was presented by Reverend Mary Catherine Kirkpatrick. The report was read by Mr. Randy Gannon, Nashville Presbytery; Reverend Alan Mink, Red River Presbytery; Reverend Chris Darlin, Cumberland Presbytery; Sarah Davis, YAD, Arkansas Presbytery; Reverend Brian Tanck, Robert Donnell Presbytery; Nyah Anderson, YAD, Robert Donnell Presbytery; and Olivia Pruitt, YAD, Missouri Presbytery,

A Motion was made to amend the Report with the date of Ash Wednesday as a day of prayer and fasting. The Youth Advisory Delegates were polled as being in favor of the amendment. By vote of the Commissioners, the motion to amend passed.

A Motion made to make an editorial change on the Report of the Moderator on "d" to add "and agencies." The Youth Advisory Delegates were polled as in favor of the editorial change. By vote of the Commissioners, the editorial change passed.

A motion was made by Elder Randall Hooper, Covenant Presbytery, and seconded, to amend Recommendation 9 by placing "All GA Agencies" before "include" passed.

The Motion that the report, as amended, be concurred in and the recommendations adopted carried.

The Report was marked "F" and filed.

Reverend Jay Earheart-Brown offered a prayer for the memory of Former Vice Moderator Reverend Buddy Pope.

The Vice-Moderator took a moment of personal privilege to thank the Youth Advisory Delegates for their service. The Vice-Moderator stated that the Youth Advisory Delegates are not the future of the church, they are the church.

MODERATOR RETURNED TO THE PODIUM

The Vice-Moderator turned the podium back to Moderator O'Mara.

THE REPORT OF THE COMMITTEE ON CHILDREN'S HOME/HIGHER EDUCATION

The Moderator offered a prayer for the Cumberland Presbyterian Children's Home and our institutions of Higher Education.

The Report of the Committee on Children's Home/Higher Education was presented by Reverend Jimmy Peyton, Hope Presbytery. The Youth Advisory Delegates who read the report were Victoria Hassell, Covenant Presbytery; Daniel Fowler, Grace Presbytery; Anna Wood, Presbytery of East Tennessee; and Colten Lash, North Central Presbytery.

A motion was made by Reverend Peyton that the report be concurred in and the recommendations adopted. The motion was seconded.

The Moderator asked that Recommendation 10 be considered separately. A motion was made to amend Recommendation 10 to read: (after 6 directors) " at least 1/2 of the directors be members of the Cumberland Presbyterian Church or Cumberland Presbyterian Church in America. It is understood that this reduction in the number of trustees will be accomplished over a period of three years." Motion seconded.

A motion was made to amend the amendment to strike "1/2" and replace with "50% + 1."

By vote of the Commissioners, the amendment to the amendment carried.

By vote of the Commissioners, the amended amendment to Recommendation 10 carried.

By vote, the amended Recommendation 10 carried by the required 2/3rds majority vote.

The vote on the remaining Recommendations 1-9, 11-18 carried.

By vote, The Report of the Committee on Children's Home/Higher Education was concurred in and the recommendations, as amended, adopted. (The Youth Advisory Delegates were polled before each vote and polled in favor)

The report was marked "G" and filed.

Reverend Michael Qualls offered a prayer of thanksgiving for the life and memory of Reverend William "Bill" Rustenhaven, the first Director of the Program of Alternate Studies, pastor, teacher, and mentor for many.

RESOLUTION OF GRATITUDE

A Resolution of Gratitude was presented by Reverend Steve Delashmit, Cumberland Presbytery, which reads:

The 189th General Assembly of the Cumberland Presbyterian Church wishes to express its thanks and gratitude to God for the opportunity to assembly and to serve our Lord and Savior, Jesus Christ in the power of the Holy Spirit through the ministries and work of the Cumberland Presbyterian Church.

The body of this 189th General Assembly, meeting in Huntsville, Alabama, wishes to thank Robert-Donnell Presbytery (Cumberland Presbyterian Church) and Huntsville Presbytery (Cumberland Presbyterian Church in America) for their hard work and warm hospitality in hosting this assembly; to pastor hosts, the Reverend Cardelia Howell-Diamond and the Reverend Terrence Haley, and to all local Cumberland Presbyterian churches and Cumberland Presbyterian Church in America churches who helped organize and plan this assembly. Now go and continue to "Walk in Love" as dearly loved children of God.

The body wishes to thank Moderator, the Reverend Shelia O'Mara, for her leadership and guidance during deliberations and Vice-Moderator, the Reverend Doctor Michael Clark. Our prayers go with you both as you represent our church through this coming year. Now go and continue to "Walk in Love" as dearly loved children of God.

The body wishes to thank retiring Moderator, the Reverend Doctor Jay Earheart-Brown, for his wonderful leadership throughout this past year. Now go and continue to "Walk in Love" as a dearly loved child of God.

The body wishes to thank our Co-Worship Directors, Reverend Joy Warren (CPC) and Reverend Mitchell Walker (CPCA), for the worship services we have been able to participate in. We praise the Spirit for Vanessa Edmonds and the Reverend Doctor Stan Wood (CPCA) and Youth Advisory Delegate, Olivia Pruitt (CPC) who shared the Good News of the Gospel of Jesus Christ through preaching and our host choir under the direction of Elder Victor Garth (CPCA). Now go and continue to "Walk in Love" as dearly loved children of God.

The body wishes to thank the staff of the General Assembly Office: Reverend Mike Sharpe, Stated Clerk; Reverend Vernon Sansom, Engrossing Clerk; and Mrs. Elizabeth Vaughn, Assistant to the Stated Clerk; for their tireless leadership and support. Now go and continue to "Walk in Love" as dearly loved children of God.

The body also gives thanks for each committee chairperson and for each commissioner and youth advisory delegate who has participated in the deliberations of the Assembly. Now go and continue to "Walk in Love" as dearly loved children of God.

The body wishes to celebrate and give thanks to Reverend Wilson and Reverend Diane Lopez, Cauca Valley Presbytery, who were commissioned as missionaries to Spain. May they go and continue to "Walk in Love" as dearly loved children of God.

The body wishes to thank the Joint Unification Task Force for its diligence and hard work "for such a time as this." Now go and continue to "Walk in Love" as dearly loved children of God.

Finally, brothers and sisters let us thank God for His Word, the Word written, the Word spoken and the Word made flesh. Now let us go, "Walk in Love", follow God's example, as dearly loved children and walk in the way of love, just as Christ loved us and gave himself up for us as a fragrant offering and sacrifice to God. (Ephesians 5:1-2 NIV)

A Motion was made and seconded to adopt the Resolution of Gratitude. Motion Carried.

Reverend Alfonzo Marquez asked the body to recognize and pray for the Casa de Oracion House of Prayer and Pastor Reverend Neil and Lidia Agular, Decatur, Alabama,

READING OF THE MINUTES

The minutes for Wednesday and Thursday were read by the Engrossing Clerk, Vernon Sansom. On motion, the minutes were approved as read.

RECESS

The Moderator announced a short recess to prepare for Closing Worship.

CLOSING WORSHIP

The Closing Worship began with the Invocation and Call to Worship by Reverend Mitchel Walker, Sr. (CPCA). Reverend Chris Warren, Murfreesboro Presbytery led the music with Mrs. Frances Dawson, Robert Donnell Presbytery, serving as pianist.

The Memorial Rolls of Elders for Cumberland Presbyterian Church and Cumberland Presbyterian Church in America and Ministers of the Cumberland Presbyterian Church were read by the Reverends Walker and Warren. Reverend Walker offered a prayer of thanksgiving for those named.

The Homily "Walk In Love" was offered by Reverend Joy Warren. The Closing Prayer was offered by Reverend Mitchell Walker, Sr.

ADJOURNMENT

A motion was made to adjourn the meeting of the 189th General Assembly of the Cumberland Presbyterian Church to meet June 7-12, 2019 at in Louisville, KY. Motion passed at 3:23 p.m.

The closing prayer was offered by Moderator O'Mara.

AUDITED FINANCIAL STATEMENTS OF

THE AGENCIES OF
THE CUMBERLAND PRESBYTERIAN
CHURCH CENTER

DECEMBER 31, 2018

THE AGENCIES OF
THE CUMBERLAND PRESBYTERIAN CHURCH CENTER

TABLE OF CONTENTS
DECEMBER 31, 2018

	PAGE
Independent Auditor's Report	1
Combined Statement of Financial Position	2
Combined Statement of Activity	3
Combined Statement of Functional Expenses	4
Combined Statement of Cash Flows	5
Notes to Financial Statements	6 - 23
Supplementary Information	
Statement of Financial Position Information	
Our United Outreach	24
General Assembly Corporation	25
Ministry Council	26
Shared Services	27
Historical Foundation	28
Board of Stewardship, Foundation, and Benefits	29
Small Church Loan Program	30
Insurance Program	31
Ministerial Aid	32
Investment Loan Program	33
Retirement Fund	34
Endowment Program	35
Statement of Activity Information	
Our United Outreach	36
General Assembly Corporation	37
Ministry Council	38
Shared Services	39
Historical Foundation	40
Board of Stewardship, Foundation, and Benefits	41
Small Church Loan Program	42
Insurance Program	43
Ministerial Aid	44
Investment Loan Program	45
Retirement Fund	46
Schedule of Change in Endowments Held in Trust	47

THE AGENCIES OF
THE CUMBERLAND PRESBYTERIAN CHURCH CENTER

TABLE OF CONTENTS - Continued
DECEMBER 31, 2018

Statement of Functional Activities Information	
Our United Outreach	48
General Assembly Corporation	49
Ministry Council	50
Shared Services	51
Historical Foundation	52
Board of Stewardship, Foundation, and Benefits	53
Small Church Loan Program	54
Insurance Program	55
Ministerial Aid	56
Investment Loan Program	57
Retirement Fund	58

To the General Assembly Corporation
The Agencies of The Cumberland Presbyterian Church Center
Memphis, Tennessee

INDEPENDENT AUDITOR'S REPORT

We have audited the accompanying combined financial statements of The Agencies of The Cumberland Presbyterian Church Center, which comprise the combined statement of financial position as of December 31, 2018, and the related combined statements of activities, functional expenses and cash flows for the year then ended, and the related notes to the combined financial statements.

Management's Responsibility for the Financial Statements

Management is responsible for the preparation and fair presentation of these financial statements in accordance with accounting principles generally accepted in the United States of America; this includes the design, implementation, and maintenance of internal control relevant to the preparation and fair presentation of financial statements that are free from material misstatement, whether due to fraud or error.

Auditor's Responsibility

Our responsibility is to express an opinion on these combined financial statements based on our audit. We conducted our audit in accordance with auditing standards generally accepted in the United States of America. Those standards require that we plan and perform the audit to obtain reasonable assurance about whether the financial statements are free from material misstatement.

An audit involves performing procedures to obtain audit evidence about the amounts and disclosures in the combined financial statements. The procedures selected depend on the auditor's judgment, including the assessment of the risks of material misstatement of the combined financial statements, whether due to fraud or error. In making those risk assessments, the auditor considers internal control relevant to the entity's preparation and fair presentation of the combined financial statements in order to design audit procedures that are appropriate in the circumstances, but not for the purpose of expressing an opinion on the effectiveness of the entity's internal control. Accordingly, we express no such opinion. An audit also includes evaluating the appropriateness of accounting policies used and the reasonableness of significant accounting estimates made by management, as well as evaluating the overall presentation of the combined financial statements.

We believe that the audit evidence we have obtained is sufficient and appropriate to provide a basis for our audit opinion.

Opinion

In our opinion, the combined financial statements referred to above present fairly, in all material respects, the financial position of The Agencies of The Cumberland Presbyterian Church Center as of December 31, 2018, and the changes in their net assets and their cash flows for the year then ended in accordance with accounting principles generally accepted in the United States of America.

Adoption of New Accounting Standard

As discussed in Note A, Management has adopted ASU 2016-14, Not-for-Profit Entities, an accounting standard recently issued by the Financial Accounting Standards Board which supersedes accounting standards that currently exist under generally accepted accounting procedures for the presentation of not-for-profit financial statements. This ASU, required for years beginning after December 15, 2017, prescribes a new financial reporting model which includes several changes to the presentation of financial statements, primarily the change from presenting three classes of net assets (unrestricted, temporarily restricted, and permanently restricted) to two classes (with donor restrictions and without donor restrictions) as well as the changes within each of the categories. Investment return is to be presented net of external investment expenses. The ASU also prescribes enhanced disclosures regarding the liquidity of resources to be used to meet the cash needs of the organization within the next year.

Report on Supplementary Information

Our audit was conducted for the purpose of forming an opinion on the financial statements as a whole. The additional information as noted in the Table of Contents is presented for purposes of additional analysis and is not a required part of the financial statements. Such information is the responsibility of management and was derived from and relates directly to the underlying accounting and other records used to prepare the financial statements. The information has been subjected to the auditing procedures applied in the audit of the financial statements and certain additional procedures, including comparing and reconciling such information directly to the underlying accounting and other records used to prepare the financial statements or to the financial statements themselves, and other additional procedures in accordance with auditing standards generally accepted in the United States of America. In our opinion, the information is fairly stated in all material respects in relation to the financial statements as a whole.

Fouts & Morgan
FOUTS & MORGAN
Certified Public Accountants

Memphis, Tennessee
June 18, 2019

THE AGENCIES OF
THE CUMBERLAND PRESBYTERIAN CHURCH CENTER

COMBINED STATEMENT OF FINANCIAL POSITION
DECEMBER 31, 2018

ASSETS

Cash		$ 550,416
Due from other agencies, boards, and divisions		4,668,731
Accounts receivable		5,789
Interest and dividends receivable, net of allowance for uncollectible interest		138,005
Securities and investments		
Cash equivalents	$ 5,426,699	
Mortgage backed securities	16,656,607	
Equity mutual funds	1,251,562	
Real estate investment trusts	5,521,099	
Private investment entities	72,284,707	
Real estate	90,573	101,231,247
Other assets		52,080
Loans receivable, net of allowance for loan losses		7,359,182
Buildings and land		2,760,412
Furniture and equipment		156,745
Less: Accumulated depreciation		(874,929)
Total Assets		$ 116,047,678

LIABILITIES AND NET ASSETS

Liabilities:		
Accounts payable		$ 11,842
Unearned subscriptions		8,215
Due to other agencies, boards, and divisions		4,943,534
Funds held in trust for others		33,286
Endowments held in trust for external agencies		30,855,238
Endowments held in trust for internal agencies		27,435,527
Notes payable to individual investors		3,309,926
Depository accounts held for church organizations		15,845,276
Less: Net endowment held in trust for internal agencies		(27,435,527)
Total liabilities		55,007,317
Net Assets:		
Without donor restrictions		
Undesignated	$ 6,303,119	
Designated	12,370,846	
Invested in buildings, land, and equipment	2,042,228	
Net assets without donor restrictions		20,716,193
With donor restrictions		
Perpetual in nature	12,353,405	
Purpose restrictions	4,039,964	
Net assets with donor restrictions		16,393,369
Net assets available for retirement benefits		23,930,799
Total net assets		61,040,361
Total Liabilities and Net Assets		$ 116,047,678

See accompanying notes.

THE AGENCIES OF
THE CUMBERLAND PRESBYTERIAN CHURCH CENTER

COMBINED STATEMENT OF ACTIVITY
FOR THE YEAR ENDED DECEMBER 31, 2018

	Without Donor Restrictions	With Donor Restrictions	Net Assets Available for Benefits	Totals
Revenues, gains, and other support:				
Contributions and gifts	$ 4,768,669	$ 985,325	$ -	$ 5,753,994
Insurance program premium revenue	1,531,846	-	-	1,531,846
Endowment earnings	(166,987)	107,082	-	(59,905)
Interest and dividend income	408,585	52,053	75,054	535,692
Management service fees	56,278	-	(17,443)	38,835
Registration fees	2,687	-	-	2,687
Sales and subscription income	166,028	-	-	166,028
Net realized and unrealized gain on investments	(934,533)	(663,104)	(694,389)	(2,292,026)
Other income	40,264	-	-	40,264
Participant retirement plan contributions	-	-	704,541	704,541
Net assets released from restrictions	1,353,151	(1,353,151)	-	-
Total revenues, gains, and other support	7,225,988	(871,795)	67,763	6,421,956
Provision for loan losses	(100,000)	-	-	(100,000)
Net revenues, gains, and other support - after provision for loan losses	7,125,988	(871,795)	67,763	6,321,956
Expenses:				
Our United Outreach	516,960	-	-	516,960
General Assembly Corporation	430,654	-	-	430,654
Ministry Council	4,590,046	-	-	4,590,046
Shared Services	437,030	-	-	437,030
Historical Foundation	187,758	-	-	187,758
Board of Stewardship, Foundation and Benefits	359,487	-	-	359,487
Small Church Loan Program	44,654	-	-	44,654
Insurance Program	1,717,380	-	-	1,717,380
Ministerial Aid	258,088	-	-	258,088
Investment Loan Program	84,132	-	-	84,132
Retirement Fund	-	-	1,326,833	1,326,833
Total expenses	8,626,189	-	1,326,833	9,953,022
Change in net assets	(1,500,201)	(871,795)	(1,259,070)	(3,631,066)
Net assets at beginning of year, as restated	22,216,394	17,265,164	25,189,869	64,671,427
Net assets at end of year	$ 20,716,193	$ 16,393,369	$ 23,930,799	$ 61,040,361

See accompanying notes.

THE AGENCIES OF
THE CUMBERLAND PRESBYTERIAN CHURCH CENTER

COMBINED STATEMENT OF FUNCTIONAL EXPENSES
FOR THE YEAR ENDED DECEMBER 31, 2018

	Program Services	Management and General	Fundraising	Total
Audit fees	$ -	$ 29,305	$ -	$ 29,305
Archival acquisitions	41,294	-	-	41,294
Archival equipment	2,858	-	-	2,858
Bank fees	-	12,310	-	12,310
Birthplace shrine	9,338	-	-	9,338
Computer	14,293	2,666	-	16,959
Conferences and events	146,415	-	-	146,415
Consulting fees	6,800	44,348	-	51,148
Contract labor	33,898	4,041	-	37,939
Depreciation	-	65,289	-	65,289
Distribution to other agencies, boards, and divisions of The Cumberland Presbyterian Church	439,702	27,676	92,044	559,422
Dues and subscriptions	8,046	-	-	8,046
Employee benefits	-	254,537	-	254,537
Equipment maintenance	3,807	22,120	-	25,927
Financial assistance payments	257,155	-	-	257,155
Grants made	2,844,781	-	-	2,844,781
Health insurance premiums	1,686,372	-	-	1,686,372
Insurance	27,533	11,379	-	38,912
Legal fees	584	5,419	-	6,003
Miscellaneous	27,103	93,668	-	120,771
Missionary support	253,742	-	-	253,742
Occupancy expenses	-	85,685	-	85,685
Office	3,525	2,878	-	6,403
Payroll taxes	-	55,718	-	55,718
Postage and shipping	38,670	957	-	39,627
Printing and publications	114,938	-	-	114,938
Program management fees	55,000	-	-	55,000
Property tax	2,192	1,005	-	3,197
Purchases for resale	30,358	-	-	30,358
Retirement for Center employees	-	68,427	-	68,427
Retirement plan participant withdrawals	1,322,792	-	-	1,322,792
Salaries	-	1,414,078	-	1,414,078
Stewardship fees	3,540	-	-	3,540
Supplies	21,957	1,723	-	23,680
Telephone	2,493	10,542	-	13,035
Travel	248,021	-	-	248,021
Total Functional Expenses	$ 7,647,207	$ 2,213,771	$ 92,044	$ 9,953,022

See accompanying notes.

THE AGENCIES OF
THE CUMBERLAND PRESBYTERIAN CHURCH CENTER

COMBINED STATEMENT OF CASH FLOWS
FOR THE YEAR ENDED DECEMBER 31, 2018

Cash flows from operating activities	
Cash received from:	
Contributions and gifts	$ 5,594,536
Insurance program premium revenue	1,531,846
Interest from loans	327,383
Interest and dividends from investments	191,784
Retirement plan participant contributions	704,541
Miscellaneous income	249,160
Cash paid for:	
Employee wages and benefits	(1,830,699)
Ministries, programs and grants	(3,355,678)
Health insurance premiums	(1,686,372)
Retirement plan participant withdrawals	(1,322,792)
Management and general expenses	(1,134,629)
Other agencies	(412,030)
Net cash used in operating activities	(1,142,950)
Cash flows from investing activities	
Proceeds from sale of investments:	
Endowment Program	6,477,015
Retirement Fund	4,601,197
Investment Loan Program	11,675,682
Purchases of investments:	
Endowment Program	(4,831,971)
Retirement Fund	(4,200,927)
Investment Loan Program	(13,344,009)
Purchase of assets for perpetual endowments	(159,458)
Loan principal payments received	724,848
Net cash provided by investing activities	942,377
Cash flows from financing activities	
Contributions to perpetual endowments	159,458
Net decrease in cash	(41,115)
Cash at the beginning of the year	591,531
Cash at the end of the year	$ 550,416

See accompanying notes.

THE AGENCIES OF
THE CUMBERLAND PRESBYTERIAN CHURCH CENTER

NOTES TO COMBINED FINANCIAL STATEMENTS
DECEMBER 31, 2018

Note A - Nature of Activities and Significant Accounting Policies

Nature of Activities - By the covenant of Abraham and his descendants according to faith, God has established the church in the world through His Son Jesus Christ. This household of faith, the universal church, consists of all those persons in every nation and every age who confess Jesus Christ as Lord and Savior and who respond to His call for discipleship. The church in the world never exists for herself alone, but to glorify God and work for reconciliation through Christ. Christ claims the church and gives her the Word and Sacraments in order to bring God's grace and judgment to persons.

The General Assembly is the highest judicatory of this church and represents in one body all the particular churches thereof. It bears the title of the General Assembly of the Cumberland Presbyterian Church and constitutes the bond of union, peace, correspondence, and mutual confidence among all its churches and judicatories. The Agencies of The Cumberland Presbyterian Church Center (the "Center") have been established by the General Assembly, and in 2000 it caused the Cumberland Presbyterian Church General Assembly Corporation to be formed. The Agencies consist of the following entities:

Cumberland Presbyterian Church General Assembly Corporation
Ministry Council of the Cumberland Presbyterian Church, Inc.
Board of Stewardship, Foundation, and Benefits of the Cumberland Presbyterian Church, Inc.
The Cumberland Presbyterian Church Investment Loan Program, Inc. (a subsidiary corporation of the Board of Stewardship, Foundation, and Benefits of the Cumberland Presbyterian Church, Inc.)
Historical Foundation of the Cumberland Presbyterian Church and the Cumberland Presbyterian Church in America
Cumberland Presbyterian Retirement Plan Number Two

Change in Accounting Policy - The Financial Accounting Standards Board recently issued Accounting Standard Update (ASU) 2016-14, *Not-for-Profit Entities*. This ASU, required for years beginning after December 15, 2017, prescribes a new financial reporting model which includes several changes to the presentation of financial statements, primarily the change from presenting three classes of net assets (unrestricted, temporarily restricted, and permanently restricted) to two classes (with donor restrictions and without donor restrictions) as well as the changes within each of the categories. Investment return is to be presented net of external investment expenses. The ASU also prescribes enhanced disclosures regarding the liquidity of resources to be used to meet the cash needs of the organization within the next year and additional information regarding net assets with donor restrictions and net assets designated by the General Assembly Corporation. The Center has adopted this ASU effective January 1, 2018, which will be applied on a prospective basis.

Management has also elected to present the Statement of Cash Flows on the direct method, a presentation which is also acceptable under existing generally accepted accounting principles.

Contributions - Contributions received are recorded as without restrictions or with restrictions depending on the existence of any donor restrictions.

NOTES CONTINUED

Note A - **Nature of Activities and Significant Accounting Policies** - Continued

Net Assets - Net assets, revenues and support, gains, and losses are classified based on the existence or absence of donor-imposed restrictions. Accordingly, net assets and changes therein are classified and reported as follows:

Net Assets Without Donor Restrictions - Net assets available for use in general operations and not subject to donor restrictions. This category also includes amounts which the General Assembly Corporation has designated and set aside for certain ministries, programs, and other purposes.

Net Assets With Donor Restrictions - Net assets subject to donor-imposed restrictions. Some donor-imposed restrictions are temporary in nature, such as those that will be met by the passage of time or other purposes specified by the donor. Other donor-imposed restrictions are perpetual in nature, where the donor stipulates that resources be maintained in perpetuity. Donor-imposed restrictions are released when a restriction expires, that is, when the stipulated time has elapsed, when the stipulated purpose for which the resource was restricted has been fulfilled, or both.

Net Assets Available for Retirement Benefits - Net assets held in trust for beneficiaries of the Cumberland Presbyterian Church Retirement Plan.

Donated Equipment and Services - Donated equipment is reflected as contributions in the accompanying financial statements at their estimated values at the date of receipt. No equipment was donated to the Center during the year ended December 31, 2018. No amounts have been reflected in the statements for donated services because they did not meet the criteria for recognition under FASB ASC 958-605-25.

Use of Estimates - The preparation of financial statements in conformity with generally accepted accounting principles requires management to make estimates and assumptions that affect the reported amounts of assets and liabilities and disclosure of contingent assets and liabilities at the date of the financial statements and the reported amounts of revenues and expenses during the reporting period. Actual results could differ from these estimates.

The Cumberland Presbyterian Church Investment Loan Program, Inc.'s notes receivable consist of loans made to congregations, governing bodies, church organizations, and other qualifying related entities. The ability of each borrower to repay its loan generally depends upon the contributions received from its members. The number of members of each congregation and its revenue is likely to fluctuate.

The Program must rely on the borrower's or guarantor's continued financial viability for repayment of loans. If a borrower or guarantor experiences a decrease in contributions or revenues, payments on that loan may be adversely affected. Even though the loans are collateralized by real estate, realization of the appraised value upon default is not assured and is dependent upon the local economic conditions of the borrower. Therefore, the determination of the adequacy of the allowance for notes receivable losses is based on estimates that are particularly susceptible to significant changes in the economic environment and market conditions for the geographic areas where the borrowers are located.

While management uses available information to recognize losses on notes receivable, further reductions in the carrying amounts of notes receivable may be necessary based on changes in the economic conditions for the geographic area of the borrowers. It is therefore reasonably possible that the estimated losses on notes receivable may change materially in the near term. However, the amount of the change that is reasonably possible cannot be estimated.

NOTES CONTINUED

Note A - **Summary of Significant Accounting Policies** - Continued

Promises to Give - Unconditional promises to give are recognized as revenue or gains in the period received and as assets or decreases of liabilities depending on the form of the benefits received. Conditional promises to give are recognized when the conditions on which they depend are substantially met. The Center has no promises to give at December 31, 2018.

Depreciation - The Center capitalizes the cost of real estate and improvements and computer equipment and software. Purchases of other equipment are not capitalized, but expensed when purchased; therefore, no depreciation expense has been recorded for these items. The difference between the cost of equipment expensed and depreciation expense that would be recorded is immaterial. In 2008, the Center purchased land and two incomplete office buildings. The cost of these plus the construction costs necessary to complete the new Center are being depreciated over an estimated useful life of 39 years. The computer equipment owned by the Center was assigned an estimated useful life of four years and is now fully depreciated.

Property and Equipment - Property and equipment is recorded at historical cost. Donated property and equipment is recorded at fair market value at the date of donation. Such donations are reported as unrestricted support unless the donor has restricted the donated asset to a specific purpose. Assets donated with explicit restrictions regarding their use and contributions of cash that must be used to acquire property and equipment are reported as restricted support. Absent donor stipulations regarding how long those donated assets must be maintained, the Center reports expirations of donor restrictions when the donated or acquired assets are placed in service as instructed by the donor. The Center reclassifies these amounts from net assets with restrictions to net assets without restrictions at that time.

Securities and Investments - Investments are stated at fair value. Investments in private investment entities are valued based on the Center's proportional share of the net asset valuations reported by the general partners of the underlying entities. The reported values of all other investments (with the exception of notes receivable) are measured by quoted prices in active markets. Realized and unrealized gains and losses are reflected in the statement of activities. (See Note L)

The Center's investments include various types of securities in various companies within various markets. Investment securities are exposed to several risks, such as interest rate, market and credit risks. Due to the risks associated with certain investment securities, it is at least reasonably possible that changes in the values of investment securities will occur in the near term and those changes could materially affect the amounts reported in the Center's combined financial statements.

Fair Value Measurements - Fair value under accounting principles generally accepted in the United States of America is defined as the price that would be received to sell an asset or paid to transfer a liability in an orderly transaction between market participants at the measurement date. Generally accepted accounting principles establishes a three-tier fair value hierarchy that prioritizes the inputs used to measure fair value. These tiers include: Level 1, defined as observable inputs such as quoted prices available in active markets for identical assets or liabilities; Level 2, defined as pricing inputs other than quoted prices in active markets that are either directly or indirectly observable; and Level 3, defined as unobservable inputs about which little or no market data exists, therefore requiring an entity to develop its own assessment about the assumptions the market participants would use in pricing an asset or liability.

NOTES CONTINUED

Note A - Summary of Significant Accounting Policies - Continued

Income Tax Status - The Center is a not-for-profit organization exempt from federal income taxes under Internal Revenue Code (IRC) Section 501(c)(3); thus, no provision for federal income taxes has been made. The Center has a defined contribution retirement plan which is qualified under Internal Revenue Code Section 403(b); thus, no provision for income taxes has been included in the Plan's financial statements.

Cash and Cash Equivalents - For purposes of the statement of cash flows, all highly liquid investments with a maturity of three months or less are considered to be cash equivalents. However, cash and cash equivalents reported as securities and investments by the Endowment Program, Investment Loan Program and Retirement Fund are considered investments for purposes of the statement of cash flows.

Loans Receivable and Allowance for Losses - Loans receivable are stated at unpaid principal balances, less the allowance for notes receivable losses. Inter-agency loans are shown as due to/from other agencies, boards, and divisions.

The allowance for loans receivable is maintained at a level which, in management's judgment, is adequate to absorb credit losses inherent in the loans receivable portfolio. The amount of the allowance is based on management's evaluation of the collectibility of the portfolio, including the nature of the portfolio, credit concentrations, trends in historical loss experience, economic conditions, and other risks inherent in the portfolio. Although management uses available information to recognize losses on notes receivable, because of uncertainties associated with the various local economic conditions of the borrowers and collateral values, it is reasonably possible that a material change could occur in the allowance for notes receivable in the near term. However, the amount of the change that is reasonably possible cannot be estimated. When considered necessary, the allowance is increased by a charge to expense and reduced by actual charge-offs, net of recoveries.

Note B - Retirement Plan

General - The Cumberland Presbyterian Church Retirement Plan Number Two is available to certain employees of the Church and its agencies. All agencies, boards, and divisions match each employee's contribution up to five percent of the employee's salary. The total retirement contribution expense for The Agencies of The Cumberland Presbyterian Church Center for 2018 was $68,427.

The Plan obtained its latest determination letter on January 31, 1972, in which the Internal Revenue Service stated that the Plan, as then designed, was in compliance with the applicable requirements of the Internal Revenue Code. The Plan has been amended since receiving the determination letter. However, the Plan administrator and the Plan's tax counsel believe that the plan is currently designed and being operated in compliance with the applicable requirements of the Internal Revenue Code. The Plan is a "church plan" and is, therefore, not subject to ERISA.

Eligibility - Employees who are 18 years of age are immediately eligible to participate in the plan.

Vesting - Participants are immediately 100% vested in their accounts.

NOTES CONTINUED

Note B - Retirement Plan - Continued

Investments - The Plan's investments are held by a bank-administered trust fund. The trust is the funding vehicle for the Plan, and all contributions are made to the trust. The cost and market value of the Plan's investments at December 31, 2018, are as follows:

	Cost	Market Value
Total	$ 16,827,176	$ 23,930,799

Note C - Endowment Program

The Endowment Program includes assets of The Agencies of The Cumberland Presbyterian Church Center and the assets of other agencies, boards, and divisions. The Program includes the Agencies' donor-restricted endowments and funds designated by the General Assembly Corporation as endowments. Funds representing amounts held in trust for external agencies affiliated with the Cumberland Presbyterian Church are reported as liabilities on the statement of financial position. Income from donor-restricted endowments is restricted for specific purposes, with the exception of the amounts available for general use. Neither donor-restricted endowment funds nor amounts held in trust are available for general expenditure.

The Program's investments, other than notes receivable, real estate, and certificates of deposit, are held by a bank-administered trust fund. The cost and market value of the Program's investments held in trust at December 31, 2018, are as follows:

	Cost	Market Value
Total	$ 40,166,802	$ 56,848,388

The Center has interpreted the Uniform Prudent Management of Institutional Funds Act ("UPMIFA") as requiring a portion of a donor-restricted endowment be classified as net assets with restrictions that are perpetual in nature. The amount of the endowment that must be retained in perpetuity is in accordance with explicit donor stipulations as outlined in their respective trust agreements. Accumulation of net investment earnings are reported as net assets with restrictions that are subject to purpose or time restrictions or as net assets without restrictions, depending on further stipulation made by the donor in the trust agreement.

The primary objective of these endowments is to provide a balance between capital appreciation, preservation of capital, and current income. This is a long-term goal designed to maximize returns without undue risk. The Board of Stewardship has set distribution rates with certain beneficiaries of the Endowment Program.

Unless otherwise stated in the donor agreement, the Board of Stewardship shall select the investment portfolio where the endowments will be invested as described in the Investment Policy of the Center. The Investment Policy of the Center outlines the asset allocations, permissible investments, and objectives of the portfolios.

NOTES CONTINUED

Note C - Endowment Program - Continued

Endowment net asset composition by category as of December 31, 2018:

	Without Donor Restrictions	With Donor Restrictions	Total
Available for general use	$ 620,411	$ -	$ 620,411
Board-designated endowment funds	12,370,846	-	12,370,846
Donor-restricted endowment funds Original donor-restricted gift amount and amounts required to be maintained in perpetuity by donor	-	11,876,203	11,876,203
Accumulated investment gains	-	2,568,067	2,568,067
	$ 12,991,257	$ 14,444,270	$ 27,435,527

Changes in endowment net assets for the year ended December 31, 2018:

	Without Donor Restrictions	With Donor Restrictions	Total
Endowment net assets, beginning of year	$ 13,985,425	$ 15,353,463	$ 29,338,888
Investment return, net	(497,817)	(546,070)	(1,043,887)
Contributions	598,648	11,804	610,452
Appropriation of endowment assets pursuant to spending policy	-	(374,927)	(374,927)
Distribution from board-designated endowment pursuant to policy	(1,094,999)	-	(1,094,999)
Endowment net assets, end of year	$ 12,991,257	$ 14,444,270	$ 27,435,527

NOTES CONTINUED

Note C - **Endowment Program** - Continued

Endowment assets with donor restrictions are subject to appropriation and expenditure for the following specified purposes:

Endowments:		
Subject to appropriation and expenditure for specified purpose when a specified event occurs:		
General work of Board of Stewardship	$	1,903,534
Aid for clergy		2,995,485
Missions		4,479,133
Communications		92,345
Christian education		1,004,120
Clergy support		219,215
General Assembly operations		18,897
Promote Church heritage		1,434,630
Available for general use for all programs		2,296,911
	$	14,444,270

The General Assembly Corporation has designated a portion of the funds maintained by the Endowment program for specific uses as of December 31, 2018. These amounts are included in net assets without donor restrictions and are designated for the following purposes:

Health insurance	$	1,840,954
Retirement fund		97,644
General work of Board of Stewardship		72,687
Aid for clergy		43,166
Church loans		1,349,604
Church development		161,829
Leadership development		97,545
Missions		7,263,279
Christian education		887,778
Clergy support		33,290
General Assembly operations		383,003
Promote Church heritage		44,362
Other programs		95,705
	$	12,370,846

NOTES CONTINUED

Note D - Net Assets with Donor Restrictions

Certain agencies have received funds which have been restricted by the donors for specific purposes, which are in addition to net assets maintained within the Endowment Program. These funds are monitored by the Ministry Council and Historical Foundation to ensure they are expended in accordance with the donor restrictions. The specific purposes are as follows:

	Perpetual in Nature	Purpose Restrictions
Church loans	$ 477,202	$ -
Missions	-	919,603
Christian education	-	304,385
Clergy support	-	50,301
Communications	-	15,477
Church heritage	-	182,130
	477,202	1,471,896
Donor-restricted endowments	11,876,203	2,568,068
Net assets with donor restrictions	$ 12,353,405	$ 4,039,964

Note E - Investment Loan Program

Nature of Activities - On March 19, 1999, the State of Tennessee approved the charter for the Cumberland Presbyterian Church Investment Loan Program, Inc., a subsidiary corporation of the Board of Stewardship, Foundation and Benefits of the Cumberland Presbyterian Church, Inc. The Program is designed to allow participants to help provide the loans needed to finance the growth of Cumberland Presbyterian congregations in the 21st century.

1. It provides building loans secured by first mortgages to congregations, presbyteries, and church agencies.
2. It allows congregations, presbyteries, church agencies, and individual members of the Cumberland Presbyterian Church to invest their funds in interest-bearing accounts from which withdrawals can be made "on demand", replacing the function of the Cash Funds Management Program.
3. All participants have the opportunity to invest funds for specific terms (such as three years or five years) in order to receive a higher rate of interest. A prospectus outlines the added investment options offered.

Securities and Investments - The cost and market values of Investment Loan Program investments at December 31, 2018, are as follows:

	Cost	Market Value
Total	$ 21,204,866	$ 20,369,700

NOTES CONTINUED

Note E - Investment Loan Program - Continued

Notes Payable to Individual Investors - Notes payable to individual investors are made through a general offering in the states of Kentucky, New Mexico, Tennessee, and Texas to eligible individual investors and must be purchased in minimum face amounts of $500. All notes payable to individual investors shown in these financial statements are Adjustable Rate Ready Access Notes. Adjustable Rate Ready Access Notes are payable on demand and pay an adjustable interest rate that may be adjusted each month. Additions of principal may be made to Adjustable Rate Ready Access Notes at any time. Withdrawals from Adjustable Rate Ready Access Notes may be made at any time and are payable upon written request of the investor; however, the Program reserves the right to require the investor to provide up to thirty (30) days written notice of any intended withdrawal before such withdrawal is made. Both additions to and withdrawals from Adjustable Rate Ready Access Notes must be made in minimum amounts of $250. The Program may review certain factors, such as investment gap analysis, loan demand, cash flow needs, and the current policy of the Federal Reserve, before establishing each month's rate of interest.

The notes are non-negotiable and may be assigned only upon the Program's written consent. The notes are unsecured and of equal priority with all other current indebtedness of the Program.

Depository Accounts Held for Church Organizations - The Cumberland Presbyterian Church Investment Loan Program, Inc. accepts depository accounts in which church organizations may place funds with the Program, in minimum amounts of $500. All depository accounts shown in these financial statements are Adjustable Rate Ready Access accounts. Like the Program's notes, depository accounts are general obligations of the Program, are unsecured and not insured, and are of equal priority with all other current indebtedness of the Program, including notes. The interest rate on the depository accounts is adjusted pursuant to the policies of the Cumberland Presbyterian Church Investment Loan Program, Inc. as they may be adopted from time to time by its Board of Directors. The Cumberland Presbyterian Church Investment Loan Program, Inc. may terminate any depository account upon sixty (60) days written notice to the church organization.

Loans Receivable - Amounts that have been loaned are included on the Statement of Financial Position as loans receivable. There are twenty-four loans outstanding at December 31, 2018.

Loans receivable are collectible primarily through monthly payments based on up to a twenty-five-year amortization period. Interest rates, as determined by the board, are based on the Prime Interest Rate as reported in the Wall Street Journal plus 1.5% per annum. On loans originated for $500,000 or less, the interest rate will be adjusted triennially. On loans originated for more than $500,000, the interest rate will be adjusted annually for the term of the loan.

The composition of loans is as follows:

Loans receivable (secured by real estate)	$ 6,384,475
Less: allowance for loan losses	(850,000)
	$ 5,534,475

NOTES CONTINUED

Note E - Investment Loan Program - Continued

A summary of changes in the allowance for loan losses is as follows:

Balance at beginning of year	$	750,000
Provision charged to operations		100,000
Balance at end of year	$	850,000

Estimated receipts of principal payments for the five years subsequent to 2018 are:

Year ending December 31,		Amount
2019	$	424,809
2020		439,225
2021		456,258
2022		451,367
2023		1,382,607
	$	3,154,266

Note F - Funds Held in Trust

The Discipleship Ministry Team leader of the Ministry Council is responsible for certain funds held in trust for outside groups. Funds invested by the executive director in Investment Loan Program amounted to the following as of December 31, 2018:

P.R.E.M.	$	214,073

The General Assembly Corporation is responsible for funds held in trust for certain committees and commissions. These funds are shown as liabilities in the Statement of Financial Position of the General Assembly Corporation. Activity in these funds for the year ended December 31, 2018, is as follows:

	Nominating Committee		Committee on Judiciary
Balance January 1, 2018	$ 6,341	$	3,249
Our United Outreach	2,677		8,721
Disbursements	(2,702)		(8,841)
Balance December 31, 2018	$ 6,316	$	3,129

NOTES CONTINUED

Note F - Funds Held in Trust - Continued

	Committee on Theology and Social Concerns	Commission on Chaplains
Balance January 1, 2018	$ 15,281	$ 8,732
Our United Outreach	3,249	9,247
Disbursements	(3,294)	(9,374)
Balance December 31, 2018	$ 15,236	$ 8,605

Note G - Insurance Program

The Cumberland Presbyterian Group Health and Life Insurance Program is a fully insured, experience-rated plan with a policy year ending on the last day of February. Any excess of premium over medical claims and other Program expenses is retained by the insurer; excess losses are not carried forward as a charge against the experience for subsequent policy years, but are absorbed by the insurer. The Program is the responsibility of the Board of Stewardship, Foundation, and Benefits.

The Program has one Investment Loan Program account and one account in the Endowment Program. Both are used as a stabilization reserve to provide some protection against unexpected medical claims volatility. The balance at December 31, 2018 of the Investment Loan Program account is $92,189. The balance at December 31, 2018 of the Endowment Program account is $1,791,330.

Note H - Concentrations of Credit Risk Arising from Cash Deposits in Excess of Insured Limits

The Center maintains its cash balances in a financial institution located in Memphis, Tennessee. The balances are insured by the Federal Deposit Insurance Corporation up to $250,000 as of December 31, 2018. At various times throughout the year, there were balances that exceeded these FDIC limits. Cash and cash equivalents classified as securities and investments are items held in equities backed by the Federal Government. These equities, while backed by the Federal Government, are not insured by the Federal Deposit Insurance Corporation. At December 31, 2018, a total of $166,740 exceeded the FDIC limits.

NOTES CONTINUED

Note I - Real Estate

Real estate assets of both the Ministry Council and the Historical Foundation are held for investment and are therefore not depreciated. These assets amounted to the following at December 31, 2018:

Property Location	Ministry Council	Historical Foundation	Total
San Francisco, California	$ 51,818	$ -	$ 51,818
Birthplace Shrine Chapel, Dickson County, Tennessee	-	21,500	21,500
McAdow Home, Dickson County, Tennessee	-	17,255	17,255
Total	$ 51,818	$ 38,755	$ 90,573

Note J - Combined Statement of Activities Expenses

The total expenses of various Agencies are included in the Combined Statement of Activities as follows:

Expense Description	Agencies
Our United Outreach	Our United Outreach
General Assembly Corporation	General Assembly Corporation
Ministry Council	Ministry Council
Shared Services	Shared Services
Historical Foundation	Historical Foundation
Board of Stewardship, Foundation, and Benefits	Board of Stewardship, Foundation, and Benefits
Small Church Loan Program	Small Church Loan Program
Insurance Program	Insurance Program
Ministerial Aid	Ministerial Aid
Investment Loan Program	Investment Loan Program
Retirement Fund	Retirement Fund

Shared services costs consist of building, maintenance, computer and accounting services and are funded by Our United Outreach appropriations.

Inter-agency revenue and expense items for Our United Outreach have been eliminated on the combined statements of activity and functional expenses.

All assets of the Endowment Program are held in trust for external and internal agencies. The Program does not report net assets, and expenditures made from the Program are presented with changes in assets held in trust. Therefore, no statement of functional expenses information will be presented for the Program.

NOTES CONTINUED

Note K - Fair Value Measurements

Prices for closed-end bond funds and equity mutual funds are readily available in the active markets in which those securities are traded, and the resulting fair values are categorized as level 1.

Prices for mortgage backed securities, bond mutual funds, and real estate investment trusts are determined on a recurring basis based upon inputs that are readily available in public markets or can be derived from information available in publicly quoted markets and are categorized as level 2.

There is limited or no observable data for the prices of private investment entities that are held by the Center and the resulting fair values of these securities are categorized as level 3.

Fair values of assets measured on a recurring basis at December 31, 2018 are as follows:

		Fair Value Measurements at Reporting Date Using		
	Fair Value	Quoted Prices In Active Market for Identical Assets (Level 1)	Significant Other Observable Inputs (Level 2)	Significant Unobservable Inputs (Level 3)
December 31, 2018				
Mortgage backed securities	$ 16,656,607	$ -	$ 16,656,607	$ -
Equity mutual funds	1,251,562	1,251,562	-	-
Real estate investment trusts	5,521,099	-	5,521,099	-
Private investment entities	72,284,707	-	-	72,284,707
Total	$ 95,713,975	$ 1,251,562	$ 22,177,706	$ 72,284,707

Because of the multiple number and complexity of the calculations necessary, management does not believe it is practicable to estimate fair value of loans receivable, net of allowance for loan losses. Therefore, no adjustment has been made to the net carrying value of $7,359,182 listed on the Combined Statement of Financial Position.

NOTES CONTINUED

Note K - Fair Value Measurements - Continued

The following table provides information related to the previously mentioned investments that are valued based primarily on net asset value at December 31, 2018:

	Fair Value	Unfunded Commitments	Redemption Frequency (If Currently Eligible)	Redemption Notice Period
Private Investment Entities				
GT Emerging Markets (QP), L.P.	$ 6,318,102	None	Annual	90 Days
GT Offshore Fund, Ltd. (Class A)	9,217,555	None	Annual	90 Days
GT Offshore Fund, Ltd. (Class B)	10,002,969	None	Annual	90 Days
GT Institutional Fixed Income Fund	8,081,482	None	Annual	90 Days
GT ERISA Fund, Ltd. (Class A)	3,877,252	None	Annual	90 Days
GT ERISA Fund, Ltd. (Class B)	3,387,294	None	Annual	90 Days
GT Real Assets, L.P.	901,234	None	Annual	90 Days
GT Real Assets II, L.P.	830,155	None	Annual	90 Days
GT Special Opportunities III, L.P.	1,816,351	None	see note	see note
Palladian Partners VIII L.P.	1,870,919	None	Annual	90 Days
Palladian Partners IX L.P.	170,000	None	as realized	N/A
Headlands Capital Offshore, L.P.	1,261,201	None	Annual	90 Days
Midland Intl Equity QP Fund, L.P.	10,643,539	None	Quarterly	60 Days
Midland U.S. QP Fund, L.P.	12,553,523	None	Quarterly	60 Days
GT ILS Fund, LP	1,353,131	None	as realized	N/A
	$ 72,284,707			

The GT Special Opportunities III, L.P. provides for an annual redemption upon 90 days' notice after an initial lock-up period of eighteen months.

NOTES CONTINUED

Note K - Fair Value Measurements - Continued

The following table summarizes fair value by fund for investments in private investment entities that are valued based primarily on net asset value at December 31, 2018:

	Retirement Fund	Endowment Program	Total Fair Value
Private Investment Entities			
GT Emerging Markets (QP), L.P.	$ 1,921,115	$ 4,396,987	$ 6,318,102
GT Offshore Fund, Ltd. (Class A)	-	9,217,555	9,217,555
GT Institutional Fixed Income Fund LP	2,695,689	5,385,793	8,081,482
GT Offshore Fund, Ltd. (Class B)	-	10,002,969	10,002,969
GT ILS Fund, LP	366,601	986,530	1,353,131
GT ERISA Fund, Ltd. (Class A)	3,877,252	-	3,877,252
GT ERISA Fund, Ltd. (Class B)	3,387,294	-	3,387,294
GT Real Assets, L.P.	279,693	621,541	901,234
GT Real Assets II, L.P.	237,187	592,968	830,155
GT Special Opportunities III, L.P.	535,379	1,280,972	1,816,351
Palladian Partners VIII LP.	510,251	1,360,668	1,870,919
Palladian Partners IX LP.	45,000	125,000	170,000
Midland Intl Equity QP Fund, L.P.	3,028,357	7,615,182	10,643,539
Headlands Capital Offshore, L.P.	381,293	879,908	1,261,201
Midland U.S. QP Fund, L.P.	3,816,296	8,737,227	12,553,523
	$ 21,081,407	$ 51,203,300	$ 72,284,707

Assets measured at fair value on a recurring basis using significant unobservable inputs (Level 3):

Fair value at beginning of year	$ 74,824,663
Investments and distributions, net	(85,290)
Realized/unrealized gains (losses)	(2,454,666)
Fair value at end of year	$ 72,284,707

Net realized and unrealized gain on investments for Level 3 assets for the year are reported on the Combined Statement of Activity under Revenues, gains, and other support, with donor restrictions.

These investments without readily determinable values comprise approximately 61.34% of total assets at December 31, 2018.

All assets have been valued using a market approach.

NOTES CONTINUED

Note K - Fair Value Measurements - Continued

A description of the Private Investment Entities and the investment objectives is as follows:

GT Emerging Markets (QP), L.P. - This fund is organized as a "fund of funds" which seeks to achieve long-term capital appreciation through investments in limited partnerships, off-shore corporations, open-end mutual funds, closed-end mutual funds, commingled trust funds, and separately managed accounts that invest primarily in "emerging markets." Investments may also be made in industrialized nations such as the United States and Japan.

GT Offshore Fund, Ltd. / GT ERISA Fund, Ltd. - These are open-ended "umbrella" funds, incorporated as exempted companies in the Cayman Islands with multiple classes of Shares. Each class of share is separately valued and pursues its own clearly defined investment objective(s) and strategy(ies). These funds' overall investment objectives are as follows:

Class A is broadly diversified among multiple investment managers and multiple investment strategies. The strategies employed may include multi-strategy arbitrage, capital structure arbitrage, distressed debt, long/short equity or niche financing.

Class B seeks to achieve a superior rate of return exceeding that of the MSCI World Index with less volatility while minimizing market risk through a hedged approach. The primary investment strategy will be a long/short equity strategy. This class is broadly diversified among multiple investment managers and multiple long/short equity strategies.

GT Real Assets, L.P and GT Real Assets II, L.P. - These funds are organized as "funds of funds" investment vehicles+ that will pool and invest funds, generally through "Managed Investment Vehicles," for the purpose of generating attractive risk-adjusted returns by opportunistically investing in a broad spectrum of resources, real assets, and other investment strategies.

GT Special Opportunities, III, L.P. - This fund is organized as a "fund of funds" investment vehicle that will pool and invest funds, generally through "Managed Investment Vehicles," for the purpose of achieving a superior rate of return. The fund focuses on a very limited number of investment strategies that are considered to be opportunistic based upon prevailing market conditions. At times, the fund may only invest in one strategy and do so in a non-diversified manner, perhaps with only a single manager. The strategies sought by the fund will often be niche-focused. Accordingly, the risk level for the fund is anticipated to be extremely high.

Midland International Equity QP Fund, L.P. - This is an international equity fund which seeks to identify listed companies selling at a discount to intrinsic net worth on liquid stock exchanges of non-U.S. countries. The focus of this fund is long-term capital appreciation. This fund seeks to outperform the MSCI EAFE Index, net of fees and taxes, over a full market cycle.

Headlands Capital Offshore, L.P. - This is an offshore equity fund which seeks to outperform the broad U.S. equity market, net of fees and taxes over a full market cycle. The focus of this fund is long-term capital appreciation.

NOTES CONTINUED

Note K - Fair Value Measurements - Continued

<u>Midland U.S. QP Fund, L.P.</u> - This fund's objective is to outperform the broad U.S. equity market, defined as the Russell 3000 Index, net of fees and taxes, over a full market cycle. The fund seeks to compound capital at attractive rates through direct and indirect long-term ownership of publicly traded businesses domiciled in the United States.

<u>GT ILS Fund, L.P.</u> - This fund's objective is to invest in insurance-linked assets and securities that carry exposure to insurance risk. The fund seeks to achieve positive risk-adjusted returns over a long-term investment horizon with limited correlation to other asset classes.

<u>GT Institutional Fixed Income Fund L.P.</u> - This fund includes an investment in a private investment fund which invests primarily in closed-end bond funds.

<u>Palladian Partners VIII L.P. and Palladian Partners IX L.P.</u> - This fund includes investments in private investment funds which invest in a diversified set of strategies, carrying niche characteristics and implemented by smaller, well-aligned investor-operators.

Note L - Securities and Investments

Securities and investments at December 31, 2018 are as follows:

	Ministry Council	Historical Foundation	Investment Loan Program	Retirement Fund	Endowment Program	Total
Cash and cash equivalents	$ -	$ -	$ 3,713,093	$ 1,384,092	$ 329,514	$ 5,426,699
Mortgage backed securities			16,656,607			16,656,607
Equity mutual funds				573,936	677,626	1,251,562
Real estate investment trusts				883,151	4,637,948	5,521,099
Private investment entities				21,081,407	51,203,300	72,284,707
Real estate	51,818	38,755				90,573
	$ 51,818	$ 38,755	$ 20,369,700	$ 23,922,586	$ 56,848,388	$ 101,231,247

NOTES CONTINUED

Note M - Liquidity and Availability

Financial assets available for general expenditure, that is, without donor or other restrictions limiting their use, within one year of the balance sheet date, comprise the following:

Cash	$	550,416
Due from other agencies, boards, and divisions		4,668,731
Accounts receivable		5,789
Interest and dividends receivable		138,005
Securities and investments		17,590,421
Loans receivable		7,359,182
Total unrestricted financial assets		30,312,544
Less amounts not available to be used within one year:		
Investments in non-liquid securities		(13,247,523)
Loans receivable due in 12 months or more		(5,109,666)
Financial assets available to meet cash needs for general expenditures within one year	$	11,955,355

The amounts above do not include funds in the amount of $12,370,846 which have been designated by the General Assembly Corporation for specific purposes and are not intended for general expenditure. These additional funds could be made available if necessary.

Note N - Subsequent Events

Subsequent events were evaluated through June 18, 2019, which is the date the financial statements were available to be issued.

THE AGENCIES OF
THE CUMBERLAND PRESBYTERIAN CHURCH CENTER
OUR UNITED OUTREACH
STATEMENT OF FINANCIAL POSITION INFORMATION
DECEMBER 31, 2018

ASSETS

Endowment earnings receivable	$ 33,641
Endowments - held by Endowment Program	2,667,381
Total Assets	$ 2,701,022

LIABILITIES AND NET ASSETS

Liabilities:	
Cash borrowed from other agencies, boards, and divisions	$ 13,612
Due to outside church organizations	36,200
Total liabilities	49,812
Net Assets:	
Without donor restrictions	
Undesignated	354,298
With donor restrictions	
Perpetual in nature	2,100,361
Purpose restrictions	196,551
Net assets with donor restrictions	2,296,912
Total net assets	2,651,210
Total Liabilities and Net Assets	$ 2,701,022

See independent accountant's report.

THE AGENCIES OF
THE CUMBERLAND PRESBYTERIAN CHURCH CENTER
GENERAL ASSEMBLY CORPORATION
STATEMENT OF FINANCIAL POSITION INFORMATION
DECEMBER 31, 2018

ASSETS

Endowment earnings receivable	$ 5,594
Due from other agencies, boards, and divisions	618,827
Other assets	686
	625,107
Endowments - held by Endowment Program	429,929
Total Assets	$ 1,055,036

LIABILITIES AND NET ASSETS

Liabilities:	
Accounts payable	$ 694
Cash borrowed from other agencies, boards, and divisions	216,933
Due to other agencies, boards, and divisions	14,116
Funds held in trusts for others	33,286
Total liabilities	265,029
Net Assets:	
Without donor restrictions	
Undesignated	388,106
Designated	383,003
Net assets without donor restrictions	771,109
With donor restrictions	
Perpetual in nature	15,558
Purpose restrictions	3,340
Net assets with donor restrictions	18,898
Total net assets	790,007
Total Liabilities and Net Assets	$ 1,055,036

See independent accountant's report.

THE AGENCIES OF
THE CUMBERLAND PRESBYTERIAN CHURCH CENTER
MINISTRY COUNCIL
STATEMENT OF FINANCIAL POSITION INFORMATION
DECEMBER 31, 2018

ASSETS

Cash	$ 269,564
Accounts receivable	4,955
Endowment earnings receivable	169,226
Due from other agencies, boards, and divisions	2,492,705
Securities and investments	
Real estate	51,818
	2,988,268
Endowments - held by Endowment Program	15,869,052
Total Assets	$ 18,857,320

LIABILITIES AND NET ASSETS

Liabilities:	
Accounts payable	$ 6,607
Unearned subscriptions	8,215
Total liabilities	14,822
Net Assets:	
Without donor restrictions	
Undesignated	1,826,176
Designated	9,931,744
Net assets without donor restrictions	11,757,920
With donor restrictions	
Perpetual in nature	4,866,440
Purpose restrictions	2,218,138
Net assets with donor restrictions	7,084,578
Total net assets	18,842,498
Total Liabilities and Net Assets	$ 18,857,320

See independent accountant's report.

THE AGENCIES OF
THE CUMBERLAND PRESBYTERIAN CHURCH CENTER
SHARED SERVICES
STATEMENT OF FINANCIAL POSITION INFORMATION
DECEMBER 31, 2018

ASSETS

Cash	$ 204,595
Buildings and land	2,760,412
Less: Accumulated depreciation	(718,184)
Furniture and equipment	156,745
Less: Accumulated depreciation	(156,745)
Total Assets	$ 2,246,823

LIABILITIES AND NET ASSETS

Liabilities:	
Accounts payable	$ 239
Net Assets:	
Without donor restrictions	
Undesignated	204,356
Invested in buildings, land, and equipment	2,042,228
Net assets without donor restrictions	2,246,584
Total Liabilities and Net Assets	$ 2,246,823

See independent accountant's report.

THE AGENCIES OF
THE CUMBERLAND PRESBYTERIAN CHURCH CENTER
HISTORICAL FOUNDATION
STATEMENT OF FINANCIAL POSITION INFORMATION
DECEMBER 31, 2018

ASSETS

Cash	$	44,974
Endowment earnings receivable		19,410
Due from other agencies, boards, and divisions		176,476
Securities and investments		
Real estate		38,755
		279,615
Endowments - held by Endowment Program		1,558,407
Total Assets	$	1,838,022

LIABILITIES AND NET ASSETS

Liabilities:	$	-
Net Assets:		
Without donor restrictions		
Undesignated		176,900
Designated		44,362
Net assets without donor restrictions		221,262
With donor restrictions		
Perpetual in nature		1,230,329
Purpose restrictions		386,431
Net assets with donor restrictions		1,616,760
Total net assets		1,838,022
Total Liabilities and Net Assets	$	1,838,022

See independent accountant's report.

THE AGENCIES OF
THE CUMBERLAND PRESBYTERIAN CHURCH CENTER
BOARD OF STEWARDSHIP, FOUNDATION, AND BENEFITS
STATEMENT OF FINANCIAL POSITION INFORMATION
DECEMBER 31, 2018

ASSETS

Cash	$ 12,177
Endowment earnings receivable	36,611
Due from other agencies, boards, and divisions	317,454
	366,242
Endowments - held by Endowment Program	1,933,507
Total Assets	$ 2,299,749

LIABILITIES AND NET ASSETS

Liabilities:	$ -
Net Assets:	
Without donor restrictions	
Undesignated	366,242
Designated	29,973
Net assets without donor restrictions	396,215
With donor restrictions	
Perpetual in nature	1,647,741
Purpose restrictions	255,793
Net assets with donor restrictions	1,903,534
Total net assets	2,299,749
Total Liabilities and Net Assets	$ 2,299,749

See independent accountant's report.

THE AGENCIES OF
THE CUMBERLAND PRESBYTERIAN CHURCH CENTER
SMALL CHURCH LOAN PROGRAM
STATEMENT OF FINANCIAL POSITION INFORMATION
DECEMBER 31, 2018

ASSETS

Loans receivable, net of allowance for loan losses	$ 112,353
Due from other agencies, boards, and divisions	364,849
Total Assets	$ 477,202

LIABILITIES AND NET ASSETS

Liabilities	$ -
Net Assets:	
With donor restrictions	
Perpetual in nature	477,202
Total Liabilities and Net Assets	$ 477,202

See independent accountant's report.

THE AGENCIES OF
THE CUMBERLAND PRESBYTERIAN CHURCH CENTER
INSURANCE PROGRAM
STATEMENT OF FINANCIAL POSITION INFORMATION
DECEMBER 31, 2018

ASSETS

Accounts receivable	$ 834
Due from other agencies, boards, and divisions	92,189
Other assets	51,394
	144,417
Endowment Funds - held by Endowment Program	1,791,330
Total Assets	$ 1,935,747

LIABILITIES AND NET ASSETS

Liabilities:	
Accounts payable	$ 4,302
Net Assets:	
Without donor restrictions	
Undesignated	140,115
Designated	1,791,330
Net assets without donor restrictions	1,931,445
Total Liabilities and Net Assets	$ 1,935,747

See independent accountant's report.

THE AGENCIES OF
THE CUMBERLAND PRESBYTERIAN CHURCH CENTER
MINISTERIAL AID
STATEMENT OF FINANCIAL POSITION INFORMATION
DECEMBER 31, 2018

ASSETS

Cash	$	20,412
Endowment earnings receivable		32,750
Due from other agencies, boards, and divisions		308,999
		362,161
Endowment Funds - held by Endowment Program		3,185,921
Total Assets	$	3,548,082

LIABILITIES AND NET ASSETS

Liabilities	$	-
Net Assets:		
Without donor restrictions		
Undesignated		362,163
Designated		190,434
Net assets without donor restrictions		552,597
With donor restrictions		
Perpetual in nature		2,015,774
Purpose restrictions		979,711
Net assets with donor restrictions		2,995,485
Total net assets		3,548,082
Total Liabilities and Net Assets	$	3,548,082

See independent accountant's report.

THE AGENCIES OF
THE CUMBERLAND PRESBYTERIAN CHURCH CENTER
INVESTMENT LOAN PROGRAM
STATEMENT OF FINANCIAL POSITION INFORMATION
DECEMBER 31, 2018

ASSETS

Interest and dividends receivable, net of allowance for uncollectible interest		$ 88,047
Securities and investments		
Cash equivalents	$ 3,713,093	
Bonds and mortgage backed securities	16,656,607	
		20,369,700
Loans receivable, net of allowance for loan losses		5,534,475
Total Assets		$ 25,992,222

LIABILITIES AND NET ASSETS

Liabilities:	
Due to other agencies, boards, and divisions	$ 4,352,257
Notes payable to individual investors	3,309,926
Depository accounts held for church organizations	15,845,276
Total liabilities	23,507,459
Net Assets:	
Without donor restrictions	
Undesignated	2,484,763
Total Liabilities and Net Assets	$ 25,992,222

See independent accountant's report.

THE AGENCIES OF
THE CUMBERLAND PRESBYTERIAN CHURCH CENTER
RETIREMENT FUND
STATEMENT OF FINANCIAL POSITION INFORMATION
DECEMBER 31, 2018

ASSETS

Interest and dividends receivable, net of allowance for uncollectible interest		$ 8,213
Securities and investments		
Cash equivalents	$ 1,384,092	
Equity mutual funds	573,936	
Real estate investment trusts	883,151	
Private investment entities	21,081,407	
		23,922,586
Total Assets		$ 23,930,799

LIABILITIES AND NET ASSETS

Liabilities	$ -
Net Assets:	
Net assets available for benefits	23,930,799
Total Liabilities and Net Assets	$ 23,930,799

See independent accountant's report.

THE AGENCIES OF
THE CUMBERLAND PRESBYTERIAN CHURCH CENTER
ENDOWMENT PROGRAM
STATEMENT OF FINANCIAL POSITION INFORMATION
DECEMBER 31, 2018

ASSETS

Cash		$ 229,239
Interest and dividends receivable, net of allowance for uncollectible interest		41,745
Securities and investments		
Cash equivalents	$ 329,514	
Equity mutual funds	677,626	
Real estate investment trusts	4,637,948	
Private investment entities	51,203,300	
		56,848,388
Loans receivable, net of allowance for loan losses		1,712,354
		58,831,726
Less: Net endowments held in trust for internal agencies		(27,435,527)
Total Assets		$ 31,396,199

LIABILITIES AND NET ASSETS

Liabilities:		
Due to other agencies, boards, and divisions		$ 540,961
Endowments held in trust for external agencies		
Cumberland Presbyterian Children's Home	$ 4,424,341	
Memphis Theological Seminary	10,692,045	
Bethel University	2,901,814	
Other designated persons and organizations	12,837,038	30,855,238
Endowments held in trust for internal agencies		
Discipleship Ministry Team	2,035,856	
Missions Ministry Team	13,433,648	
Board of Stewardship, Foundation, and Benefits	1,933,507	
Our United Outreach	2,667,381	
General Assembly Corporation	429,929	
Communications Ministry Team	133,734	
Pastoral Development Ministry Team	265,813	
The Historical Foundation	1,558,407	
Insurance Program	1,791,330	
Ministerial Aid	3,185,922	27,435,527
Less: Net endowments held in trust for internal agencies		(27,435,527)
Total liabilities		31,396,199
Net Assets:		-
Total Liabilities and Net Assets		$ 31,396,199

See independent accountant's report.

THE AGENCIES OF
THE CUMBERLAND PRESBYTERIAN CHURCH CENTER
OUR UNITED OUTREACH
STATEMENT OF ACTIVITY INFORMATION
FOR THE YEAR ENDED DECEMBER 31, 2018

	Without Donor Restrictions	With Donor Restrictions	Totals
Revenues, gains, and other support:			
Contributions	$ 2,396,367	$ 52,269	$ 2,448,636
Endowment earnings	-	11,279	11,279
Income from oil royalties	13,001	-	13,001
Net realized and unrealized (loss) on investments	-	(63,066)	(63,066)
Net assets released from restriction	109,046	(109,046)	-
	2,518,414	(108,564)	2,409,850
Expenses:			
Program services	2,423,805	-	2,423,805
Management and general	27,676	-	27,676
Fundraising	92,044	-	92,044
Total expenses	2,543,525	-	2,543,525
Change in net assets	(25,111)	(108,564)	(133,675)
Net assets at beginning of year	379,409	2,405,476	2,784,885
Net assets at end of year	$ 354,298	$ 2,296,912	$ 2,651,210

See independent accountant's report.

THE AGENCIES OF
THE CUMBERLAND PRESBYTERIAN CHURCH CENTER
GENERAL ASSEMBLY CORPORATION
STATEMENT OF ACTIVITY INFORMATION
FOR THE YEAR ENDED DECEMBER 31, 2018

	Without Donor Restrictions	With Donor Restrictions	Totals
Revenues, gains, and other support:			
Our United Outreach	$ 191,717	$ -	$ 191,717
Contributions and gifts	290,695	-	290,695
Endowment earnings	22,355	-	22,355
Interest income	9,054	-	9,054
Other income	27,263	-	27,263
Net realized and unrealized (loss) on investments	-	(9,986)	(9,986)
Net assets released from restriction	(8,657)	8,657	-
	532,427	(1,329)	531,098
Expenses:			
Program services	215,382	-	215,382
Management and general	215,272	-	215,272
Fundraising	-	-	-
Total expenses	430,654	-	430,654
Change in net assets	101,773	(1,329)	100,444
Net assets at beginning of year	669,336	20,227	689,563
Net assets at end of year	$ 771,109	$ 18,898	$ 790,007

See independent accountant's report.

THE AGENCIES OF
THE CUMBERLAND PRESBYTERIAN CHURCH CENTER
MINISTRY COUNCIL
STATEMENT OF ACTIVITY INFORMATION
FOR THE YEAR ENDED DECEMBER 31, 2018

	Without Donor Restrictions	With Donor Restrictions	Totals
Revenues, gains, and other support:			
Our United Outreach	$ 1,225,579	$ -	$ 1,225,579
Contributions	-	823,765	823,765
Endowment earnings	(384,290)	67,376	(316,914)
Gifts - designated	1,908,766	-	1,908,766
Gifts - undesignated	156,501	-	156,501
Interest income	30,929	36,368	67,297
Registration fees	2,687	-	2,687
Rental income	-	-	-
Sales of materials, literature, etc.	138,285	-	138,285
Subscription income	27,743	-	27,743
Net realized and unrealized (loss) on investments	-	(369,024)	(369,024)
Net assets released from restrictions	862,061	(862,061)	-
	3,968,261	(303,576)	3,664,685
Expenses:			
Program services	3,532,674	-	3,532,674
Management and general	1,057,372	-	1,057,372
Fundraising	-	-	-
Total expenses	4,590,046	-	4,590,046
Change in net assets	(621,785)	(303,576)	(925,361)
Net assets at beginning of year	12,379,705	7,388,154	19,767,859
Net assets at end of year	$ 11,757,920	$ 7,084,578	$ 18,842,498

See independent accountant's report.

THE AGENCIES OF
THE CUMBERLAND PRESBYTERIAN CHURCH CENTER
SHARED SERVICES
STATEMENT OF ACTIVITY INFORMATION
FOR THE YEAR ENDED DECEMBER 31, 2018

	Without Donor Restrictions	With Donor Restrictions	Totals
Revenues, gains, and other support:			
Our United Outreach	$ 394,233	$ -	$ 394,233
Gifts	-	-	-
	394,233	-	394,233
Expenses:			
Program services	-	-	-
Management and general	437,030	-	437,030
Fundraising	-	-	-
Total expenses	437,030	-	437,030
Change in net assets	(42,797)	-	(42,797)
Net assets at beginning of year	2,289,381	-	2,289,381
Net assets at end of year	$ 2,246,584	$ -	$ 2,246,584

See independent accountant's report.

THE AGENCIES OF
THE CUMBERLAND PRESBYTERIAN CHURCH CENTER
HISTORICAL FOUNDATION
STATEMENT OF ACTIVITY INFORMATION
FOR THE YEAR ENDED DECEMBER 31, 2018

	Without Donor Restrictions	With Donor Restrictions	Totals
Revenues, gains, and other support:			
Our United Outreach	$ 71,679	$ -	$ 71,679
Contributions and gifts	7,609	64,337	71,946
Endowment earnings	-	6,573	6,573
Interest income	-	4,970	4,970
Sales of materials, literature, etc.	-	-	-
Net realized and unrealized (loss) on investments	-	(37,228)	(37,228)
Net assets released from restriction	166,978	(166,978)	-
	246,266	(128,326)	117,940
Expenses:			
Program services	87,788	-	87,788
Management and general	99,970	-	99,970
Fundraising	-	-	-
Total expenses	187,758	-	187,758
Change in net assets	58,508	(128,326)	(69,818)
Net assets at beginning of year	162,754	1,745,086	1,907,840
Net assets at end of year	$ 221,262	$ 1,616,760	$ 1,838,022

See independent accountant's report.

THE AGENCIES OF
THE CUMBERLAND PRESBYTERIAN CHURCH CENTER
BOARD OF STEWARDSHIP, FOUNDATION AND BENEFITS
STATEMENT OF ACTIVITY INFORMATION
FOR THE YEAR ENDED DECEMBER 31, 2018

	Without Donor Restrictions	With Donor Restrictions	Totals
Revenues, gains, and other support:			
Our United Outreach	$ 143,357	$ -	$ 143,357
Contributions and gifts	4,241	200	4,441
Endowment earnings	72,000	8,246	80,246
Interest income	11,216	-	11,216
Management service fees	56,278	-	56,278
Net realized and unrealized (loss) on investments	-	(109,410)	(109,410)
Net assets released from restriction	51,514	(51,514)	-
	338,606	(152,478)	186,128
Expenses:			
Program services	95,395	-	95,395
Management and general	264,092	-	264,092
Fundraising	-	-	-
Total expenses	359,487	-	359,487
Change in net assets	(20,881)	(152,478)	(173,359)
Net assets at beginning of year	417,096	2,056,012	2,473,108
Net assets at end of year	$ 396,215	$ 1,903,534	$ 2,299,749

See independent accountant's report.

THE AGENCIES OF
THE CUMBERLAND PRESBYTERIAN CHURCH CENTER
SMALL CHURCH LOAN PROGRAM
STATEMENT OF ACTIVITY INFORMATION
FOR THE YEAR ENDED DECEMBER 31, 2018

	Without Donor Restrictions	With Donor Restrictions	Totals
Revenues, gains, and other support:			
Contributions	$ -	$ 44,654	$ 44,654
Interest income	-	10,715	10,715
Net assets released from restriction	44,654	(44,654)	-
	44,654	10,715	55,369
Expenses:			
Program services	44,654	-	44,654
Management and general	-	-	-
Fundraising	-	-	-
Total expenses	44,654	-	44,654
Change in net assets	-	10,715	10,715
Net assets at beginning of year	-	466,487	466,487
Net assets at end of year	$ -	$ 477,202	$ 477,202

See independent accountant's report.

THE AGENCIES OF
THE CUMBERLAND PRESBYTERIAN CHURCH CENTER
INSURANCE PROGRAM
STATEMENT OF ACTIVITY INFORMATION
FOR THE YEAR ENDED DECEMBER 31, 2018

	Without Donor Restrictions	With Donor Restrictions	Totals
Revenues, gains, and other support:			
Premium revenue	$ 1,531,846	$ -	$ 1,531,846
Contributions	4,490	-	4,490
Endowment earnings	-	-	-
Interest income	9,701	-	9,701
Management service fees	-	-	
Net realized gain on investments	9,616	-	9,616
Net unrealized (loss) on investments	(49,553)	-	(49,553)
	1,506,100	-	1,506,100
Expenses:			
Program services	1,689,912	-	1,689,912
Management and general	27,468	-	27,468
Fundraising	-	-	-
Total expenses	1,717,380	-	1,717,380
Change in net assets	(211,280)	-	(211,280)
Net assets at beginning of year	2,142,725	-	2,142,725
Net assets at end of year	$ 1,931,445	$ -	$ 1,931,445

See independent accountant's report.

THE AGENCIES OF
THE CUMBERLAND PRESBYTERIAN CHURCH CENTER
MINISTERIAL AID
STATEMENT OF ACTIVITY INFORMATION
FOR THE YEAR ENDED DECEMBER 31, 2018

	Without Donor Restrictions	With Donor Restrictions	Totals
Revenues, gains, and other support:			
Contributions	$ -	$ 100	$ 100
Endowment earnings	122,948	13,608	136,556
Interest income	7,380	-	7,380
Net realized and unrealized (loss) on investments	-	(74,390)	(74,390)
Net assets released from restriction	127,555	(127,555)	-
	257,883	(188,237)	69,646
Expenses:			
Program services	258,088	-	258,088
Management and general	-	-	-
Fundraising	-	-	-
Total expenses	258,088	-	258,088
Change in net assets	(205)	(188,237)	(188,442)
Net assets at beginning of year	552,802	3,183,722	3,736,524
Net assets at end of year	$ 552,597	$ 2,995,485	$ 3,548,082

See independent accountant's report.

THE AGENCIES OF
THE CUMBERLAND PRESBYTERIAN CHURCH CENTER
INVESTMENT LOAN PROGRAM
STATEMENT OF ACTIVITY INFORMATION
FOR THE YEAR ENDED DECEMBER 31, 2018

	Without Donor Restrictions	With Donor Restrictions	Totals
Revenues, gains, and other support:			
Interest income	$ 958,653	$ -	$ 958,653
Interest expense	(618,348)	-	(618,348)
Net interest income	340,305	-	340,305
Provision for loan losses	(100,000)	-	(100,000)
Net interest income	240,305	-	240,305
Net (loss) on investments	(894,596)	-	(894,596)
	(654,291)	-	(654,291)
Expenses:			
Program services	55,000	-	55,000
Management and general	29,132	-	29,132
Fundraising	-	-	-
Total expenses	84,132	-	84,132
Change in net assets	(738,423)	-	(738,423)
Net assets at beginning of year	3,223,186	-	3,223,186
Net assets at end of year	$ 2,484,763	$ -	$ 2,484,763

See independent accountant's report.

THE AGENCIES OF
THE CUMBERLAND PRESBYTERIAN CHURCH CENTER
RETIREMENT FUND
STATEMENT OF ACTIVITY INFORMATION
FOR THE YEAR ENDED DECEMBER 31, 2018

	Net Assets Available for Benefits
Additions to Net Assets attributed to:	
Investment income:	
Interest and dividend income	$ 75,054
Management service fees	(17,443)
Net realized gain on investments	249,901
Net unrealized gain (loss) on investments	(944,290)
Net investment loss	(636,778)
Contributions:	
Contributions by participants	704,541
	67,763
Deductions from Net Assets attributed to:	
Participant withdrawals	1,322,792
Administrative expenses	4,041
Fundraising	-
Total deductions	1,326,833
Change in plan assets available for benefits	(1,259,070)
Net assets available for benefits at beginning of year	25,189,869
Net assets available for benefits at end of year	$ 23,930,799

See independent accountant's report.

THE AGENCIES OF
THE CUMBERLAND PRESBYTERIAN CHURCH CENTER
ENDOWMENT PROGRAM
SCHEDULE OF CHANGE IN ENDOWMENTS HELD IN TRUST
FOR THE YEAR ENDED DECEMBER 31, 2018

Change in Endowments held in trust:	
Revenues, gains, and other support:	
Contributions	$ 614,942
Interest and dividend income	313,386
Net realized gain on investments	316,711
Net unrealized (loss) on investments	(1,705,841)
	(460,802)
Disbursements to agencies	3,470,252
Management and general	-
Fundraising	-
Total expenses	
Change in endowments held in trust	(3,931,054)
Endowments held in trust at beginning of year	62,221,819
Endowments held in trust at end of year	$ 58,290,765
Represented by funds held in trust for others:	
Bethel University	$ 2,901,814
Cumberland Presbyterian Children's Home	4,424,341
Memphis Theological Seminary	10,692,045
Other designated persons and organizations	12,837,038
	30,855,238
Represented by funds held for The Agencies of	
The Cumberland Presbyterian Church Center:	
Discipleship Ministry Team	2,035,856
Missions Ministry Team	13,433,648
Board of Stewardship, Foundation, and Benefits	1,933,507
Our United Outreach	2,667,381
General Assembly Corporation	429,929
Communications Ministry Team	133,734
Pastoral Development Ministry Team	265,813
The Historical Foundation	1,558,407
Insurance Program	1,791,330
Ministerial Aid	3,185,922
	27,435,527
Endowments held in trust at end of year	$ 58,290,765

See independent accountant's report.

THE AGENCIES OF
THE CUMBERLAND PRESBYTERIAN CHURCH CENTER
OUR UNITED OUTREACH
STATEMENT OF FUNCTIONAL EXPENSES INFORMATION
FOR THE YEAR ENDED DECEMBER 31, 2018

	Program Expenses	Management and General	Fundraising	Total
Distribution to other agencies, boards, and divisions of The Cumberland Presbyterian Church:				
Bethel University	$ 119,464	$ -	$ -	$ 119,464
Board of Stewardship	143,357	-	-	143,357
Commission on Chaplains	9,247	-	-	9,247
Committee on Theology and Social Concern	3,249	-	-	3,249
Committee on Judiciary	8,721	-	-	8,721
Communications Ministry Team	296,272	-	-	296,272
Contingency Fund	11,946	-	-	11,946
Cumberland Presbyterian Children's Home	71,679	-	-	71,679
Discipleship Ministry Team	302,245	-	-	302,245
General Assembly Council	191,143	-	-	191,143
Historical Foundation	71,679	-	-	71,679
Legal Expense	-	25,000	-	25,000
Memphis Theological Seminary	137,145	-	-	137,145
Ministry Council	217,425	-	-	217,425
Missions Ministry Team	259,238	-	-	259,238
Nominating Committee	-	2,676	-	2,676
Pastoral Development Ministry Team	119,465	-	-	119,465
Program of Alternate Studies	30,105	-	-	30,105
Shared Service (Maintenance/Operations)	394,233	-	-	394,233
Shared Service (OUO Committee)	-	-	92,044	92,044
Unification Task Force	35,000	-	-	35,000
Property tax	2,192	-	-	2,192
Total Functional Expenses	$ 2,423,805	$ 27,676	$ 92,044	$ 2,543,525

See independent accountant's report.

THE AGENCIES OF
THE CUMBERLAND PRESBYTERIAN CHURCH CENTER
GENERAL ASSEMBLY CORPORATION
STATEMENT OF FUNCTIONAL EXPENSES INFORMATION
FOR THE YEAR ENDED DECEMBER 31, 2018

	Program Expenses	Management and General	Fundraising	Total
Computer	$ 585	$ -	$ -	$ 585
Conferences and events	28,908	-	-	28,908
Contract labor	312	-	-	312
Employee benefits	-	33,257	-	33,257
Equipment maintenance	3,807	-	-	3,807
Grants made	161,309	-	-	161,309
Insurance	1,858	-	-	1,858
Miscellaneous	541	-	-	541
Payroll taxes	-	4,527	-	4,527
Postage and shipping	359	-	-	359
Printing and publications	1,597	-	-	1,597
Retirement for Center employees	-	8,374	-	8,374
Salaries	-	173,641	-	173,641
Supplies	1,057	-	-	1,057
Travel	10,522	-	-	10,522
Total Functional Expenses	$ 210,855	$ 219,799	$ -	$ 430,654

See independent accountant's report.

49

THE AGENCIES OF
THE CUMBERLAND PRESBYTERIAN CHURCH CENTER
MINISTRY COUNCIL
STATEMENT OF FUNCTIONAL EXPENSES INFORMATION
FOR THE YEAR ENDED DECEMBER 31, 2018

	Program Expenses	Management and General	Fundraising	Total
Computer	$ 12,446	$ -	$ -	$ 12,446
Conferences and events	117,507	-	-	117,507
Consulting fees	6,800	-	-	6,800
Contract labor	30,773	-	-	30,773
Dues and subscriptions	4,070	-	-	4,070
Employee benefits	-	132,586	-	132,586
Grants made	2,627,118	-	-	2,627,118
Insurance	18,372	-	-	18,372
Legal fees	400	-	-	400
Miscellaneous	25,914	-	-	25,914
Missionary support	253,742	-	-	253,742
Office	3,525	-	-	3,525
Payroll taxes	-	31,078	-	31,078
Postage and shipping	35,236	-	-	35,236
Printing and publications	107,524	-	-	107,524
Purchases for resale	29,687	-	-	29,687
Retirement for Center employees	-	38,522	-	38,522
Salaries	-	886,264	-	886,264
Supplies	17,459	-	-	17,459
Telephone	2,493	-	-	2,493
Travel	208,530	-	-	208,530
Total Functional Expenses	$ 3,501,596	$ 1,088,450	$ -	$ 4,590,046

See independent accountant's report.

THE AGENCIES OF
THE CUMBERLAND PRESBYTERIAN CHURCH CENTER
SHARED SERVICES
STATEMENT OF FUNCTIONAL EXPENSES INFORMATION
FOR THE YEAR ENDED DECEMBER 31, 2018

	Program Expenses	Management and General	Fundraising	Total
Audit fees	$ -	$ 22,605	$ -	$ 22,605
Bank fees	-	12,310	-	12,310
Computer	-	2,666	-	2,666
Consulting fees	-	44,348	-	44,348
Depreciation	-	65,289	-	65,289
Employee benefits	-	17,968	-	17,968
Equipment maintenance	-	22,120	-	22,120
Insurance	-	11,379	-	11,379
Legal fees	-	76	-	76
Miscellaneous	-	80,000	-	80,000
Occupancy	-	85,685	-	85,685
Office expense	-	182	-	182
Payroll taxes	-	4,000	-	4,000
Postage and shipping	-	232	-	232
Property tax	-	1,005	-	1,005
Retirement for Center employees	-	2,614	-	2,614
Salaries	-	52,286	-	52,286
Supplies	-	1,723	-	1,723
Telephone	-	10,542	-	10,542
Total Functional Expenses	$ -	$ 437,030	$ -	$ 437,030

See independent accountant's report.

THE AGENCIES OF
THE CUMBERLAND PRESBYTERIAN CHURCH CENTER
HISTORICAL FOUNDATION
STATEMENT OF FUNCTIONAL EXPENSES INFORMATION
FOR THE YEAR ENDED DECEMBER 31, 2018

	Program Expenses	Management and General	Fundraising	Total
Archival acquisitions	$ 41,294	$ -	$ -	$ 41,294
Archival equipment	2,858	-	-	2,858
Birthplace shrine	9,338	-	-	9,338
Contract labor	2,813	-	-	2,813
Dues and subscriptions	2,425	-	-	2,425
Employee benefits	-	10,197	-	10,197
Insurance	3,646	-	-	3,646
Legal fees	184	-	-	184
Miscellaneous	427	-	-	427
Payroll taxes	-	6,243	-	6,243
Postage and shipping	157	-	-	157
Printing and publications	1,491	-	-	1,491
Purchases for resale	671	-	-	671
Retirement for Center employees	-	8,161	-	8,161
Salaries	-	81,612	-	81,612
Supplies	1,021	-	-	1,021
Travel	15,220	-	-	15,220
Total Functional Expenses	$ 81,545	$ 106,213	$ -	$ 187,758

See independent accountant's report.

THE AGENCIES OF
THE CUMBERLAND PRESBYTERIAN CHURCH CENTER
BOARD OF STEWARDSHIP, FOUNDATION AND BENEFITS
STATEMENT OF FUNCTIONAL EXPENSES INFORMATION
FOR THE YEAR ENDED DECEMBER 31, 2018

	Program Expenses	Management and General	Fundraising	Total
Computer	$ 1,262	$ -	$ -	$ 1,262
Dues and subscriptions	507	-	-	507
Employee benefits	-	60,529	-	60,529
Grants made	56,354	-	-	56,354
Insurance	3,657	-	-	3,657
Miscellaneous	221	-	-	221
Payroll taxes	-	7,850	-	7,850
Postage and shipping	1,509	-	-	1,509
Printing and publications	4,326	-	-	4,326
Retirement for Center employees	-	9,694	-	9,694
Salaries	-	193,869	-	193,869
Stewardship fees	3,540	-	-	3,540
Supplies	2,420	-	-	2,420
Travel and board meetings	13,749	-	-	13,749
Total Functional Expenses	$ 87,545	$ 271,942	$ -	$ 359,487

See independent accountant's report.

THE AGENCIES OF
THE CUMBERLAND PRESBYTERIAN CHURCH CENTER
SMALL CHURCH LOAN PROGRAM
STATEMENT OF FUNCTIONAL EXPENSES INFORMATION
FOR THE YEAR ENDED DECEMBER 31, 2018

	Program Expenses	Management and General	Fundraising	Total
Distribution to other agencies, boards, and divisions of The Cumberland Presbyterian Church:				
Investment Loan Program	$ 44,654	$ -	$ -	$ 44,654
Total Functional Expenses	$ 44,654	$ -	$ -	$ 44,654

See independent accountant's report.

THE AGENCIES OF
THE CUMBERLAND PRESBYTERIAN CHURCH CENTER
INSURANCE PROGRAM
STATEMENT OF FUNCTIONAL EXPENSES INFORMATION
FOR THE YEAR ENDED DECEMBER 31, 2018

	Program Expenses	Management and General	Fundraising	Total
Dues and subscriptions	$ 1,044	$ -	$ -	$ 1,044
Health insurance premiums	1,686,372	-	-	1,686,372
Payroll taxes	-	2,020	-	2,020
Postage and shipping	476	-	-	476
Retirement for Center employees	-	1,062	-	1,062
Salaries	-	26,406	-	26,406
Total Functional Expenses	$ 1,687,892	$ 29,488	$ -	$ 1,717,380

See independent accountant's report.

THE AGENCIES OF
THE CUMBERLAND PRESBYTERIAN CHURCH CENTER
MINISTERIAL AID
STATEMENT OF FUNCTIONAL EXPENSES INFORMATION
FOR THE YEAR ENDED DECEMBER 31, 2018

	Program Expenses	Management and General	Fundraising	Total
Financial assistance payments	$ 257,155	$ -	$ -	$ 257,155
Postage	933	-	-	933
Total Functional Expenses	$ 258,088	$ -	$ -	$ 258,088

See independent accountant's report.

THE AGENCIES OF
THE CUMBERLAND PRESBYTERIAN CHURCH CENTER
INVESTMENT LOAN PROGRAM
STATEMENT OF FUNCTIONAL EXPENSES INFORMATION
FOR THE YEAR ENDED DECEMBER 31, 2018

	Program Expenses	Management and General	Fundraising	Total
Audit fees	$ -	$ 6,700	$ -	$ 6,700
Legal fees	-	5,343	-	5,343
Miscellaneous	-	13,668	-	13,668
Office	-	2,696	-	2,696
Postage and shipping	-	725	-	725
Program management fees	55,000	-	-	55,000
Total Functional Expenses	$ 55,000	$ 29,132	$ -	$ 84,132

See independent accountant's report.

THE AGENCIES OF
THE CUMBERLAND PRESBYTERIAN CHURCH CENTER
RETIREMENT FUND
STATEMENT OF FUNCTIONAL EXPENSES INFORMATION
FOR THE YEAR ENDED DECEMBER 31, 2018

	Program Expenses	Management and General	Fundraising	Total
Contract labor	$ -	$ 4,041	$ -	$ 4,041
Participant withdrawals	1,322,792	-	-	1,322,792
Total Functional Expenses	$ 1,322,792	$ 4,041	$ -	$ 1,326,833

See independent accountant's report.

BETHEL UNIVERSITY

**FINANCIAL STATEMENTS
AND OTHER INFORMATION**

JULY 31, 2018 AND 2017

BETHEL UNIVERSITY

Table of Contents

	Page
INDEPENDENT AUDITOR'S REPORT	1 - 3
FINANCIAL STATEMENTS	
Statements of Financial Position	4
Statements of Activities	5 - 6
Statements of Cash Flows	7 - 8
Notes to Financial Statements	9 - 31
SUPPLEMENTARY INFORMATION	
Financial Responsibility Composite Score (unaudited)	32 - 33
University Key Financial Ratios (unaudited)	33 - 36
Unrestricted Net Assets Exclusive of Plant, Property, Equipment, and Related Debt and Obligation Under Financing Arrangement (unaudited)	37
OTHER INFORMATION	
Schedule of Expenditures of Federal Awards	38
Notes to Schedule of Expenditures of Federal Awards	39
INDEPENDENT AUDITOR'S REPORT ON INTERNAL CONTROL OVER FINANCIAL REPORTING AND ON COMPLIANCE AND OTHER MATTERS BASED ON AN AUDIT OF FINANCIAL STATEMENTS PERFORMED IN ACCORDANCE WITH *GOVERNMENT AUDITING STANDARDS*	40 - 41
INDEPENDENT AUDITOR'S REPORT ON COMPLIANCE FOR EACH MAJOR PROGRAM AND ON INTERNAL CONTROL OVER COMPLIANCE REQUIRED BY UNIFORM GUIDANCE	42 - 44
SCHEDULE OF FINDINGS AND QUESTIONED COSTS	45 - 46
SCHEDULE OF PRIOR YEAR FINDINGS AND QUESTIONED COSTS	47

Independent Auditor's Report

The Board of Trustees
Bethel University
McKenzie, Tennessee

Report on the Financial Statements

We have audited the accompanying financial statements of Bethel University (the "University"), which comprise the statements of financial position as of July 31, 2018 and 2017, and the related statements of activities and cash flows for the years then ended, and the related notes to the financial statements.

Management's Responsibility for the Financial Statements

Management is responsible for the preparation and fair presentation of these financial statements in accordance with accounting principles generally accepted in the United States of America; this includes the design, implementation, and maintenance of internal control relevant to the preparation and fair presentation of financial statements that are free from material misstatement, whether due to fraud or error.

Auditor's Responsibility

Our responsibility is to express an opinion on these financial statements based on our audits. We conducted our audits in accordance with auditing standards generally accepted in the United States of America and the standards applicable to financial audits contained in *Government Auditing Standards*, issued by the Comptroller General of the United States. Those standards require that we plan and perform the audit to obtain reasonable assurance about whether the financial statements are free from material misstatement.

An audit involves performing procedures to obtain audit evidence about the amounts and disclosures in the financial statements. The procedures selected depend on the auditor's judgment, including the assessment of the risks of material misstatement of the financial statements, whether due to fraud or error. In making those risk assessments, the auditor considers internal control relevant to the entity's preparation and fair presentation of the financial statements in order to design audit procedures that are appropriate in the circumstances, but not for the purpose of expressing an opinion on the effectiveness of the entity's internal control. Accordingly, we express no such opinion. An audit also includes evaluating the appropriateness of accounting policies used and the reasonableness of significant accounting estimates made by management, as well as evaluating the overall presentation of the financial statements.

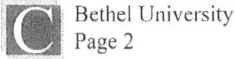
Bethel University
Page 2

We believe that the audit evidence we have obtained is sufficient and appropriate to provide a basis for our audit opinion.

Opinion

In our opinion, the financial statements referred to above present fairly, in all material respects, the financial position of Bethel University as of July 31, 2018 and 2017, and the changes in its net assets and its cash flows for the years then ended in accordance with accounting principles generally accepted in the United States of America.

Other Matters

Other Information

Our audits were conducted for the purpose of forming an opinion on the financial statements as a whole. The accompanying schedule of expenditures of federal awards, as required by Title 2 U.S. *Code of Federal Regulations* (CFR) Part 200, *Uniform Administrative Requirements, Cost Principles, and Audit Requirements for Federal Awards* (Uniform Guidance), is presented for purposes of additional analysis and is not a required part of the financial statements. Such information is the responsibility of management and was derived from and relates directly to the underlying accounting and other records used to prepare the financial statements. The information has been subjected to the auditing procedures applied in the audit of the financial statements and certain additional procedures, including comparing and reconciling such information directly to the underlying accounting and other records used to prepare the financial statements or to the financial statements themselves, and other additional procedures in accordance with auditing standards generally accepted in the United States of America. In our opinion, the information is fairly stated, in all material respects, in relation to the financial statements as a whole.

Disclaimer of Opinion on Supplementary Information

Our audits were conducted for the purpose of forming an opinion on the financial statements as a whole. The Schedules of Financial Responsibility Composite Score, University Key Financial Ratios, and Unrestricted Net Assets Exclusive of Plant, Property, Equipment, and Related Debt and Obligation Under Financing Arrangement, which are the responsibility of management, are presented for purposes of additional analysis and are not a required part of the financial statements. Such information has not been subjected to the auditing procedures applied in the audit of the financial statements and, accordingly, we do not express an opinion or provide any assurance on it.

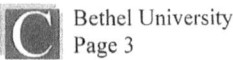
Bethel University
Page 3

Other Reporting Required by Government Auditing Standards

In accordance with *Government Auditing Standards*, we have also issued our report dated October 3, 2018, on our consideration of the University's internal control over financial reporting and on our tests of its compliance with certain provisions of laws, regulations, contracts, and grant agreements and other matters. The purpose of that report is solely to describe the scope of our testing of internal control over financial reporting and compliance and the results of that testing, and not to provide an opinion on the effectiveness of the University's internal control over financial reporting or on compliance. That report is an integral part of an audit performed in accordance with *Government Auditing Standards* in considering the University's internal control over financial reporting and compliance.

Crosslin, PLLC

Nashville, Tennessee
October 3, 2018

BETHEL UNIVERSITY
STATEMENTS OF FINANCIAL POSITION

ASSETS

	July 31,	
	2018	2017
Cash and cash equivalents	$ 1,595,343	$ 1,320,193
Perkins loan cash	5,935	64,895
Receivables:		
Contributions, net (Note B)	18,051,161	15,215,442
Students, net of allowances of $825,975 and $828,078, respectively	1,303,078	1,450,507
Perkins loans, net of allowances of $207,231 and $216,345, respectively	127,268	157,823
Other	73,805	70,930
Inventories	224,898	292,688
Prepaid expenses, deposits, and other assets (Note F)	373,792	254,041
Investments (Note C)	7,300,130	3,742,992
Beneficial interest in assets held by others (Note D)	3,828,845	3,710,652
Cash value life insurance	469,244	451,432
Property, buildings, and equipment:		
Land	260,851	260,851
Buildings and improvements	84,814,640	87,098,384
Equipment, furniture and automobiles	8,310,424	8,190,729
Library books	1,284,514	1,284,514
Construction in progress	284,437	274,289
	94,954,866	97,108,767
Less: Accumulated depreciation	(27,006,032)	(24,202,696)
Total property and equipment, net	67,948,834	72,906,071
Total assets	$ 101,302,333	$ 99,637,666

LIABILITIES AND NET ASSETS

Liabilities:		
Accounts payable and accrued liabilities	$ 2,413,920	$ 3,310,684
Accrued payroll and benefits	890,264	970,029
Deferred tuition revenue	2,673,907	3,331,149
Debt (Note E)	13,207,261	9,525,377
Obligation under financing arrangement, net (Note F)	45,850,701	46,460,584
Advances from the federal government	227,849	308,557
Total liabilities	65,263,902	63,906,380
Net Assets:		
Unrestricted	24,310,749	24,132,550
Temporarily restricted (Notes G and H)	838,101	838,973
Permanently restricted (Notes G and H)	10,889,581	10,759,763
Total net assets	36,038,431	35,731,286
Total liabilities and net assets	$ 101,302,333	$ 99,637,666

See accompanying notes to financial statements.

BETHEL UNIVERSITY
STATEMENTS OF ACTIVITIES

	Year Ended July 31, 2018			
	Unrestricted	Temporarily Restricted	Permanently Restricted	Total
Revenue, gains and other support:				
Regular tuition and fees	$47,910,370	$ -	$ -	$ 47,910,370
Degree completion tuition	3,617,772	-	-	3,617,772
Institutional scholarships and grants	(12,884,110)	-	-	(12,884,110)
Net tuition and fees	38,644,032	-	-	38,644,032
Bookstore income	772,207	-	-	772,207
Private gifts and contracts	5,021,147	29,667	11,625	5,062,439
Investment income	349,912	(1,069)	-	348,843
Unrealized gain on beneficial interests in assets held by others	-	-	118,193	118,193
Auxiliary fund revenues	7,396,145	-	-	7,396,145
Government grants	184,899	-	-	184,899
Other income	1,622,878	-	-	1,622,878
Net assets released from restrictions	29,470	(29,470)	-	-
Reclassification	-	-	-	-
Total revenue, gains and other support	54,020,690	(872)	129,818	54,149,636
Expenses:				
Education and general:				
Instruction	24,428,603	-	-	24,428,603
Academic support	2,373,637	-	-	2,373,637
Student services	11,507,207	-	-	11,507,207
Institutional support	11,181,719	-	-	11,181,719
Auxiliary enterprises	4,351,325	-	-	4,351,325
Total expenses	53,842,491	-	-	53,842,491
Net increase (decrease) in net assets	178,199	(872)	129,818	307,145
Net assets, beginning of year	24,132,550	838,973	10,759,763	35,731,286
Net assets, end of year	$24,310,749	$ 838,101	$ 10,889,581	$ 36,038,431

BETHEL UNIVERSITY
STATEMENTS OF ACTIVITIES -
Continued

	Year Ended July 31, 2017		
Unrestricted	Temporarily Restricted	Permanently Restricted	Total
$ 49,810,522	$ -	$ -	$ 49,810,522
5,541,903	-	-	5,541,903
(12,327,341)	-	-	(12,327,341)
43,025,084	-	-	43,025,084
1,101,073	-	-	1,101,073
4,208,952	534,636	267,275	5,010,863
458,650	-	-	458,650
-	-	157,938	157,938
7,146,440	-	-	7,146,440
166,127			166,127
1,394,994	-	-	1,394,994
1,763,359	(1,763,359)	-	-
6,948	(6,948)	-	-
59,271,627	(1,235,671)	425,213	58,461,169
26,320,892	-	-	26,320,892
2,557,504	-	-	2,557,504
12,398,579	-	-	12,398,579
12,047,878	-	-	12,047,878
4,688,387	-	-	4,688,387
58,013,240	-	-	58,013,240
1,258,387	(1,235,671)	425,213	447,929
22,874,163	2,074,644	10,334,550	35,283,357
$ 24,132,550	$ 838,973	$ 10,759,763	$ 35,731,286

See accompanying notes to financial statements.

BETHEL UNIVERSITY
STATEMENTS OF CASH FLOWS

	Year ended July 31,	
	2018	2017
CASH FLOWS FROM OPERATING ACTIVITIES:		
Increase in net assets	$ 307,145	$ 447,929
Adjustments to reconcile increase in net assets to net cash used in operating activities		
Non-cash:		
Allowance for doubtful student accounts, contributions and Perkins loans receivable	(181,310)	(615,710)
Loss on disposal of property and equipment	-	29,190
Unrealized gain on investments and beneficial interests in assets held by others	(609,868)	(337,337)
Non-cash contributions	-	(7,032)
Cash value life insurance	(17,812)	(451,432)
Depreciation and amortization	2,844,792	2,952,779
(Increase) decrease in:		
Contributions receivable	(2,665,626)	(3,102,437)
Student accounts receivable	149,532	477,213
Perkins loans receivable	39,669	52,040
Other receivables	(2,875)	847,447
Inventories	67,790	(32,030)
Prepaid expenses, deposits, and other assets	(119,751)	(10,465)
Increase (decrease) in:		
Accounts payable and student account deposits	(896,764)	(3,127,420)
Accrued payroll and benefits	(79,765)	526,484
Deferred tuition revenue	(657,242)	537,765
Advances from federal government	(80,708)	(38,367)
Contributions restricted for long-term investments	(11,625)	(267,275)
Total adjustments	(2,221,563)	(2,566,587)
Net cash used in operating activities	(1,914,418)	(2,118,658)
CASH FLOWS FROM INVESTING ACTIVITIES:		
Purchases of property, buildings and equipment	(930,147)	(1,743,917)
Proceeds from disposal of property and equipment	-	42,500
Net cash used investing activities	(930,147)	(1,701,417)
CASH FLOWS FROM FINANCING ACTIVITIES:		
Increase in annuity obligations	-	(385)
Proceeds from notes payable and line-of-credit	11,433,350	13,823,082
Payments on notes payable and line-of-credit	(7,751,466)	(9,845,401)
Repayments of financing arrangement and capital lease obligations, net	(632,754)	(612,547)
Contributions restricted for long-term investments	11,625	267,275
Net cash provided by investing activities	3,060,755	3,632,024

See accompanying notes to financial statements.

BETHEL UNIVERSITY
STATEMENTS OF CASH FLOWS - Continued

	Year ended July 31,	
	2018	2017
Net increase (decrease) in cash and cash equivalents	216,190	(188,051)
Cash and cash equivalents at beginning of year	1,385,088	1,573,139
Cash and cash equivalents at end of year	$ 1,601,278	$ 1,385,088
Supplemental disclosures of cash flow information:		
Interest paid	$ 1,963,120	$ 1,915,695
Building transferred to investment property	$ 3,042,592	$ -
Non-cash financing and investing activities:		
Purchases of property and equipment	930,147	1,743,917
Amount financed through capital leases, accounts payable, debt, or received through donations	(333,000)	-
Total paid for property and equipment	$ 597,147	$ 1,743,917

See accompanying notes to financial statements.

BETHEL UNIVERSITY
NOTES TO FINANCIAL STATEMENTS
JULY 31, 2018 AND 2017

A. <u>SUMMARY OF SIGNIFICANT ACCOUNTING POLICIES</u>

Organization and Business Purpose

Bethel University (the "University") is a private, residential, coeducational University affiliated with the Cumberland Presbyterian Church, dedicated primarily to educating students in the liberal arts and science while also offering select pre-professional programs, a graduate teacher education program, a master of business administration program, a master of criminal justice program, and a master of physician's assistant program. In addition to its traditional academic programs, the University also offers a degree-completion program. The University is accredited by the Southern Association of Colleges and Schools, Commission on Colleges, and its education emphasizes academic excellence, high achievement, intellectual and personal integrity, and participation in community life. Its Christian heritage finds expression in commitment to the values of personal growth, justice, community, and service.

Accrual Basis and Financial Statement Presentation

The financial statements of the University have been prepared on the accrual basis of accounting.

The University classifies its revenues, expenses, gains, and losses into three classes of net assets based on the existence or absence of donor-imposed restrictions. Net assets of the University and changes therein are as follows:

<u>Unrestricted net assets</u> - Net assets that are not subject to donor-imposed stipulations and net assets where donor-imposed stipulations have been met within the reporting period.

<u>Temporarily restricted net assets</u> - Net assets subject to donor-imposed stipulations that may or will be met by actions of the University.

<u>Permanently restricted net assets</u> - Net assets subject to donor-imposed stipulations that the University is required to maintain permanently. Generally, the donors of these assets permit the University to use all or a part of the income earned on related investments for general or specific purposes.

The amount of each of these classes of net assets is displayed in the statements of financial position and the amount of change in each class of net assets is displayed in the statements of activities.

BETHEL UNIVERSITY
NOTES TO FINANCIAL STATEMENTS
JULY 31, 2018 AND 2017

A. SUMMARY OF SIGNIFICANT ACCOUNTING POLICES - Continued

Use of Estimates in the Preparation of Financial Statements

The preparation of financial statements in conformity with accounting principles generally accepted in the United States of America requires management to make assumptions that affect the reported amounts of assets and liabilities, disclosure of contingent assets and liabilities at the date of the financial statements, and the reported amounts of revenues and expenses during the reporting period. The more significant areas include the recovery period for property and equipment, the allocation of certain operating expenses to functional categories, the collection of contributions receivable, and the adequacy of the allowance for doubtful student receivables. Management believes that such estimates have been based on reasonable assumptions and that such estimates are adequate. Actual results could differ from those estimates.

Contributions

The University reports gifts of cash and other assets as restricted support if received with donor-imposed stipulations that limit the use of the donated assets. When a donor-imposed restriction expires, *i.e.,* when the purpose of the restriction is accomplished, temporarily restricted net assets are reclassified to unrestricted net assets and reported in the statement of activities as net assets released from restrictions. The University has elected to report contributions received with donor-imposed restrictions as an increase to unrestricted net assets if the restrictions are met in the same fiscal year that the contributions are received.

The University reports gifts of land, equipment, and other assets as unrestricted support unless explicit donor-imposed stipulations specify how the donated assets must be used. Gifts of long-lived assets with explicit restrictions that specify how the assets are to be used and gifts of cash or other assets that must be used to acquire long-lived assets are reported as restricted support. Absent explicit donor-imposed stipulations regarding how long the long-lived assets must be maintained, the University reports expirations of donor-imposed restrictions when the donated or acquired long-lived assets are placed in service.

Contribution of services are recognized if the services received (a) create or enhance non-financial assets or (b) require specialized skills, provided by individuals possessing those skills and would typically need to be purchased if not provided by donation.

In the event a donor makes changes to the nature of a restricted gift, which affects its classification among the net asset categories, such amounts are reflected as reclassifications in the statements of activities.

BETHEL UNIVERSITY
NOTES TO FINANCIAL STATEMENTS
JULY 31, 2018 AND 2017

A. SUMMARY OF SIGNIFICANT ACCOUNTING POLICIES - Continued

Perkins Loan - Cash

As required by federal regulations, cash related to the Federal Perkins Loan Program is maintained in a separate bank account.

Student Accounts Receivable

The University records accounts receivable at their estimated net realizable value. An allowance for doubtful accounts is recorded based upon management's estimate of uncollectible accounts determined by analysis of specific student balances and a general reserve based upon agings of outstanding balances. Past due balances and delinquent receivables are charged against the allowance when they are determined to be uncollectible by management.

Notes Receivable - Students

Notes receivable from students at July 31, 2018 and 2017, totaled $127,268 and $157,823, respectively, net of allowances of $207,231 and $216,345, respectively. Student loans are granted by the University under the federally funded Perkins loan program. These funds are disbursed based upon the demonstration of financial need on the Perkins loan, at which time the loan will also begin accruing interest. Perkins loan amounts are then repaid through a third party billing service. Student loans are considered past due when payment has not been received within 30 days. At July 31, 2018 and 2017, student loans represented 0.13% and 0.16%, respectively, of total assets.

The allowance for doubtful accounts is established based on prior collection experience and current economic factors which, in management's judgment, could influence the ability of loan recipients to repay the amounts per the loan terms. Loan balances are written off only when they are deemed to be permanently uncollectible.

Contributions Receivable

Contributions receivable are recorded at their estimated fair value using a discount rate commensurate with the rate on U.S. Government Securities whose maturities correspond to the maturities of the contributions. Contributions receivable are considered to be either conditional or unconditional promises to give. A conditional contribution is one which depends on the occurrence of a specified uncertain future event to become binding on the donor. Conditional contributions are not recorded as revenue until the condition is met, at which time they become unconditional. Unconditional contributions are recorded as revenue at the time verifiable evidence of the promise to give is received.

BETHEL UNIVERSITY
NOTES TO FINANCIAL STATEMENTS
JULY 31, 2018 AND 2017

A. SUMMARY OF SIGNIFICANT ACCOUNTING POLICIES - Continued

Inventories

Inventories consist primarily of books and supplies and are stated at the lower of cost or market. Cost is determined using the average cost method.

Investments

Investments in marketable equity securities with readily determinable fair values and investments in debt securities are stated at their fair values in the statements of financial position. Fair value of investments is determined based on quoted market prices or using Level 2 or 3 inputs as described in Note I. All gains and losses (both realized and unrealized) and other investment income are reported in the statements of activities.

Property and Equipment

Property and equipment are recorded at cost at the date of acquisition or fair value at the date of donation in the case of gifts. Depreciation on property and equipment is calculated on the straight-line method over estimated useful lives of 20 - 40 years for buildings and improvements, 5 - 7 years for equipment and furniture, 5 years for automobiles, and 20 years for other property. Property held under capital leases are depreciated on the straight-line method based on the shorter of the estimated useful life of the property to the University or the life of the capital lease. Library books and repairs/renovations to buildings and equipment that do not add value or extend the useful life of the assets are expensed as incurred. Depreciation, operation, and maintenance charges are allocated to appropriate functional expense categories.

The estimate to complete construction in progress is $3,062,563 as of July 31, 2018.

Deferred Revenue

Deferred revenue consists primarily of charges and cash receipts collected prior to year-end for services rendered after year-end. These receipts pertain to upcoming tuition and fees.

BETHEL UNIVERSITY
NOTES TO FINANCIAL STATEMENTS
JULY 31, 2018 AND 2017

A. SUMMARY OF SIGNIFICANT ACCOUNTING POLICIES - Continued

Debt Issuance Cost

Costs incurred in connection with the issuance of the University's obligation under financing arrangement have been capitalized and are being amortized using the straight-line method. Effective August 1, 2016, The University adopted the provisions of FASB ASU 2015-03, *Imputation of Interest (Subtopic 835-30): Simplifying the Presentation of Debt Issuance Costs*. ASU 2015-03 requires entities to present issuance costs related to a recognized debt liability as a direct deduction from the carrying amount of the debt liability. The adoption required retrospective application. Unamortized debt issuance costs in the amount of $855,754 and $878,624 as of July 31, 2018 and 2017, respectively, have been netted against obligations under financing arrangement on the statement of financial position.

Advances from the Federal Government for Student Loans

The Perkins Loan Program is a campus-based program providing revolving loan funds for financial assistance to eligible postsecondary school students based on financial need. The Department of Education provides funds along with the University, which are used to make loans to eligible students at low interest rates. Refundable government advances for Perkins at July 31, 2018 and 2017 were $227,849 and $308,557, respectively.

Advertising Costs

Advertising costs are expensed as incurred and totaled approximately $488,620 and $1,343,236 for the years ended July 31, 2018 and 2017, respectively.

Tax Status

The University is exempt from Federal income taxes under §501(a) of the Internal Revenue Code ("IRC") as an organization described in IRC §501(c)(3). Accordingly, no provision for income taxes has been made in the accompanying financial statements. The University is not classified as a private foundation.

FASB Interpretation No. 48, *Accounting for Uncertainty in Income Taxes-an interpretation of FASB Statement No. 109*, codified in ASC Topic 740 clarifies the accounting for uncertainty in income taxes recognized in an entity's financial statements and prescribes a recognition threshold and measurement attribute for tax positions taken or expected to be taken on a tax return including the entity's status as a tax-exempt not-for-profit entity. Additionally, ASC 740 provides guidance on derecognition, classification, interest and penalties, accounting in interim periods, and disclosure. The University had no significant uncertain tax positions at July 31, 2018 or 2017.

BETHEL UNIVERSITY
NOTES TO FINANCIAL STATEMENTS
JULY 31, 2018 AND 2017

A. SUMMARY OF SIGNIFICANT ACCOUNTING POLICIES - Continued

Fair Value Measurements

Assets and liabilities recorded at fair value in the statements of financial position are categorized based on the level of judgment associated with the inputs used to measure their fair value. Related disclosures are included in Note I. Level inputs, as defined by Financial Accounting Standards Board Accounting Standards Codification ("ASC") 820, *Fair Value Measurements and Disclosures,* are as follows:

Level 1 - Values are unadjusted quoted prices for identical assets and liabilities in active markets accessible at the measurement date.

Level 2 - Inputs include quoted prices for similar assets or liabilities in active markets, quoted prices from those willing to trade in markets that are not active, or other inputs that are observable or can be corroborated by market data for the term of the instrument. Such inputs include market interest rates and volatilities, spreads and yield curves.

Level 3 - Certain inputs are unobservable (supported by little or no market activity) and significant to the fair value measurement. Unobservable inputs reflect the University's best estimate of what hypothetical market participants would use to determine a transaction price for the asset or liability at the reporting date.

Classification of Expenses

Expenses are classified functionally as a measure of service efforts and accomplishments. Direct expenses incurred for a single function are allocated entirely to that function. Joint expenses applicable to more than one function are allocated on the basis of objectively summarized information or management estimates.

Reclassifications

Certain reclassifications have been made to the 2017 financial statements in order for them to conform to the 2018 presentation.

BETHEL UNIVERSITY
NOTES TO FINANCIAL STATEMENTS
JULY 31, 2018 AND 2017

B. CONTRIBUTIONS RECEIVABLE

Contributions receivable at July 31, 2018 and 2017 consist of the following:

	2018	2017
Contributions receivable (present value)	$ 18,051,161	$ 15,385,535
Less: allowance for doubtful contributions	(-)	(170,093)
	$ 18,051,161	$ 15,215,442

Expected maturities of contributions receivable at July 31, 2018 are as follows:

Fiscal Year Ending July 31,	Amount
2019	$ 6,169,952
2020	2,232,718
2021	2,231,549
2022	2,219,510
2023	1,975,510
Thereafter	4,550,250
Total expected contributions	19,379,489
Less: allowance for net present value using a weighted average discount rate of 1.00%	(1,328,328)
Present value of contributions receivable	$ 18,051,161

- 15 -

BETHEL UNIVERSITY
NOTES TO FINANCIAL STATEMENTS
JULY 31, 2018 AND 2017

C. INVESTMENTS

The investments of the University are principally administered by the University or by the Board of Stewardship of the Cumberland Presbyterian Church, Inc. (the "Board"). The funds administered by the Board are co-mingled with funds of other agencies of the Church. The University's portion represents approximately 5.2% of the funds administered by the Board at July 31, 2018 and 2017. In fiscal year 2018, the University transferred a building with a book value of $3,065,463 to investment property, due to the building no longer being used for school activities. The investments of the University, including investment property with a book value of $3,688,273 and $472,810 as of July 31, 2018 and 2017, respectively, are invested as follows:

	2018	2017
Administered by the Board:		
Marketable equity and debt securities	$3,147,068	$3,064,954
Administered by the University:		
Marketable equity and debt securities	5,323	6,883
Certificates of deposits	100,743	100,492
Investment Property and Other	4,046,996	570,663
	$7,300,130	$3,742,992

D. BENEFICIAL INTEREST IN ASSETS HELD BY OTHERS

Beneficial interest in assets held by others represents arrangements in which a donor establishes and funds a perpetual trust administered by an individual or organization other than the University. The fair value of perpetually held trusts in which the University had a beneficial interest as of July 31, 2018 and 2017, was $3,828,845 and $3,710,652, respectively. The University records these trusts at estimated fair value. Income distributed to the University from the beneficial interest assets is temporarily restricted for scholarships.

BETHEL UNIVERSITY
NOTES TO FINANCIAL STATEMENTS
JULY 31, 2018 AND 2017

E. DEBT

The University has the following debt obligations at July 31, 2018 and 2017:

	2018	2017
Line-of-credit totaling $2,000,000 with Centennial Bank; bearing variable interest calculated as Prime Rate as published by The Wall Street Journal plus 1.00 % with a floor of 5.00%; collateralized by accounts receivable, equipment, and inventory. Line-of-credit consolidated and maturity date extended during fiscal 2018.	$ -	$1,999,861
Line-of-credit totaling $1,000,000 with Centennial Bank; bearing variable interest calculated as Prime Rate as published by The Wall Street Journal plus 1.00 % with a floor of 5.00%; collateralized by accounts receivable, equipment, and inventory. Line-of-credit consolidated and maturity date extended during fiscal 2018.	-	1,000,000
Line-of-credit totaling $3,000,000 with Centennial Bank; bearing variable interest calculated as Prime Rate as published by The Wall Street Journal plus 1.00% with a floor of 5.00%; (6.00% at July 31, 2018) line-of-credit matures and full payment due September 1, 2019; collateralized by accounts receivable, equipment, and inventory.	2,999,542	-
Note payable to City of Paris, bearing interest at 0.00%, with monthly principal payments of $8,663 due beginning on September 30, 2014, through final maturity on August 31, 2022.	424,462	528,413
Note payable to Carroll Bank & Trust, bearing interest at 5.25%, with the full principal balance maturing August 25, 2018; collateralized by certain real property. Paid in full June 22, 2018.	-	2,000,141

- 17 -

BETHEL UNIVERSITY
NOTES TO FINANCIAL STATEMENTS
JULY 31, 2018 AND 2017

E. DEBT - Continued

	2018	
Note payable to Carroll Bank & Trust, bearing interest at 5.25%, with the full principal balance maturing August 10, 2018; collateralized by certain real property. Paid in full June 22, 2018.	-	1,
Note payable to Carroll Bank & Trust, payable in monthly installments of $15,500 including interest of 5.50% through June 22, 2023, with a final payment of $2,237,634 due June 22, 2023; collateralized by certain real property.	2,496,109	
Note Payable to First Bank, bearing interest at 5.00%, with the full principal balance maturing August 31, 2017; paid in full on August 31, 2017.	-	
Note Payable to First Bank, bearing interest at 5.00%, with the full principal balance maturing November 6, 2018; collateralized by certain real property.	998,403	
Line-of-credit with a related party private company totaling $5,000,000, bearing interest at 5.00%, payable in monthly installments of interest only, continuing until July 31, 2021; at which time the balance is due; paid in full August 28, 2017.	-	2,
Line-of-credit with a related party private company totaling $5,000,000, bearing interest at 5.00%, payable in monthly installments of interest only, continuing until July 31, 2021; at which time the balance is due; $2,000,000 paid August 28, 2018.	4,000,000	
Note payable to Renasant Bank, payable in monthly installments of $13,609 including interest of 4.50% through August 12, 2018, with a final payment of $457,506 due September 12, 2018; collateralized by an agreement not to transfer or		

BETHEL UNIVERSITY
NOTES TO FINANCIAL STATEMENTS
JULY 31, 2018 AND 2017

E. DEBT - Continued

	2018	2017
Note payable to Renasant Bank, payable in monthly installments of $4,624 including interest of 5.425% (4.47% at July 31, 2018) through February 28, 2023, with a final payment of $110,188 due March 28, 2018; collateralized by an agreement not to transfer or encumber certain real property.	319,389	-
Line-of-credit with a related party private party totaling $1,500,000, bearing interest at 5.00%, payable in monthly installments of interest only, continuing until January 31, 2019; at which time the balance is due.	1,500,000	-
	$13,207,261	$9,525,377

The anticipated maturities of the University's notes payable are as follows:

Fiscal Year Ending July 31,	Amount
2019	$ 7,127,197
2020	3,158,980
2021	159,438
2022	159,438
2023	2,602,208
	$13,207,261

Interest Expense

For the years ending July 31, 2018 and 2017, Bethel University incurred interest expense of $1,963,120 and $1,915,748, respectively.

Compliance with Covenants

The Renasant Bank loan agreement contains a debt service coverage ratio that requires the University to maintain a debt coverage ratio of 1.25x, tested annually by the bank. Based on the University's calculations as of July 31, 2018, the University was in compliance with this covenant and ratio.

BETHEL UNIVERSITY
NOTES TO FINANCIAL STATEMENTS
JULY 31, 2018 AND 2017

F. OBLIGATIONS UNDER FINANCING ARRANGEMENT

On December 28, 2015, the United States Department of Agriculture (USDA) funded a Campus Facility Acquisition through a Rural Development Communities Facilities Loan with NCCD - Bethel Properties LLC, a separate legal entity independent of the University. The loan to NCCD - Bethel Properties LLC totaled $48,300,000, bearing a fixed interest of 3.25% with a repayment term of 40 years. NCCD - Bethel Properties LLC utilized the proceeds of the loan to lease certain University buildings, in which the University leased back from NCCD - Bethel Properties LLC. The University remits the lease payments to NCCD - Bethel Properties LLC, who in turn repays USDA. The monthly lease payments equal the monthly note payment. The agreement expires December 28, 2055. Due to easement and right of way concerns, substantially all of the McKenzie campus is incorporated into the lease, lease-back transaction ("financing arrangement"). Buildings held under the capital lease at July 31, 2018 totaled $57,998,848, net of accumulated depreciation of $8,962,584.

Minimum future lease payments under capital leases as of July 31, 2018, are as follows:

Fiscal Year Ending July 31,	Amount
2019	$ 2,161,908
2020	2,161,908
2021	2,161,908
2022	2,161,908
2023	2,161,908
Thereafter	69,864,089
	80,673,629
Less: Amount representing interest	(33,967,174)
Amount representing debt-refinancing costs, net	(855,754)
Present value of net minimum lease payments	$ 45,850,701

Annually, the University will incur amortization expense on debt-refinancing costs of $22,871, until the lease expires December 28, 2055.

Compliance with Covenants

The Sublease Agreement between NCCD - Bethel Properties LLC, as sublessor, and Bethel University, as sublessee, contains a covenant that requires the University to maintain a debt service coverage ratio of at least 1.0. This ratio is defined as earnings before interest, taxes, depreciation, and amortization divided by the annual lease payments due to NCCD – Bethel Properties LLC. Based on the University's calculations as of July 31, 2018, the University was in compliance with this covenant and ratio.

BETHEL UNIVERSITY
NOTES TO FINANCIAL STATEMENTS
JULY 31, 2018 AND 2017

G. <u>TEMPORARILY AND PERMANENTLY RESTRICTED NET ASSETS</u>

At July 31, 2018 and 2017, temporarily restricted net assets are available for the following purposes:

	2018	2017
Scholarships	$577,116	$578,235
Time restrictions and other	260,985	260,738
	$838,101	$838,973

At July 31, 2018 and 2017, permanently restricted net assets are as follows:

	2018	2017
Beneficial interest in assets held by others	$ 3,828,845	$ 3,710,652
Endowments	7,060,736	7,049,111
	$10,889,581	$10,759,763

The endowments represent nonexpendable funds that are subject to restrictions requiring the principal to be invested and only the income used as specified by the donors.

Net assets were released from donor restrictions by incurring expenses satisfying the restricted purposes. The following is a summary of the assets released from restrictions for the years ended July 31, 2018 and 2017:

	2018	2017
Institutional support expenditures	$29,470	$1,385,669
Scholarship and grant expenditures	-	377,690
	$29,470	$1,763,359

- 21 -

BETHEL UNIVERSITY
NOTES TO FINANCIAL STATEMENTS
JULY 31, 2018 AND 2017

H. ENDOWMENT

The University's endowment consists of individual donor-restricted funds established for a variety of purposes. As required by U.S. generally accepted accounting principles, net assets associated with endowment funds are classified and reported based on the existence or absence of donor-imposed restrictions.

Interpretation of Relevant Law

The Board of Trustees of the University has interpreted the applicable state laws as requiring the preservation of the original gift as of the gift date of the donor-restricted endowment funds absent explicit donor stipulations to the contrary. As a result of this interpretation, the University classified as permanently restricted net assets (a) the original value of gifts donated to the permanent endowment, (b) the original value of subsequent gifts to the permanent endowment, and (c) accumulations to the permanent endowment made in accordance with the direction of the applicable donor gift instrument at the time the accumulation is added to the fund. The remaining portion of the donor-restricted endowment fund that is not classified in permanently restricted net assets is classified as temporarily restricted net assets until those amounts are appropriated for expenditure by the University in a manner consistent with the standard of prudence prescribed by applicable state laws. In accordance with applicable state laws, the University considers the following factors in making a determination to appropriate or accumulate donor-restricted endowment funds:

- The duration and preservation of the fund
- The purposes of the University and the donor-restricted endowment fund
- General economic conditions
- The possible effect of inflation and deflation
- The expected total return from income and the appreciation of investments
- Other resources of the University
- The investment policy of the University

BETHEL UNIVERSITY
NOTES TO FINANCIAL STATEMENTS
JULY 31, 2018 AND 2017

H. ENDOWMENT - Continued

Changes in Endowment Net Assets

	Temporarily Restricted	Permanently Restricted	Total
Endowment net assets, August 1, 2016	$ 646,080	$10,334,550	$ 10,980,630
Reclassification	(6,948)	-	(6,948)
Investment return:			
Investment income	-	-	-
Net appreciation (realized and unrealized)	-	157,938	157,938
Total investment return	-	157,938	157,938
Contributions	-	267,275	267,275
Appropriation of endowment assets for expenditure	-	-	-
Endowment net assets, July 31, 2017	639,132	10,759,763	11,398,895
Investment return:			
Investment income	-	-	-
Net appreciation (realized and unrealized)	-	118,193	118,193
Total investment return	-	118,193	118,193
Contributions	-	11,625	11,625
Appropriation of endowment assets for expenditure	-	-	-
Endowment net assets, July 31, 2018	$ 639,132	$10,889,581	$ 11,528,713

BETHEL UNIVERSITY
NOTES TO FINANCIAL STATEMENTS
JULY 31, 2018 AND 2017

H. ENDOWMENT - Continued

Return Objectives and Risk Parameters

The University has adopted an investment and spending policy for endowment assets that attempt to provide a predictable stream of funding to programs supported by its endowment while seeking to maintain the purchasing power of the endowment assets. Endowment assets include those assets of donor-restricted funds that the University must hold in perpetuity or for a donor-specified period(s). Under this policy, as approved by the Board of Trustees, the endowment assets are invested with an overall total return objective as established for each time horizon: 1) Short Term, 2) Intermediate, and 3) Long Term according to the funding needs of the University. The returns will be compared with the generally accepted indices, *i.e.*, the S&P 500, certain Bond Indices, MSCI EAFE stock indices, and an index of U.S. Treasury Bills depending on the time horizon in place. At July 31, 2018 and 2017, the endowment assets consist of investments in certificates of deposit, marketable debt and equity securities, and beneficial interests in assets held by others.

Strategies Employed for Achieving Objectives

To satisfy its rate-of-return objectives, the University relies on a total return strategy in which investment returns are achieved through both capital appreciation (realized and unrealized) and current yield (interest and dividends). The University targets an investment allocation based on the three time horizons described above and that places emphasis on diversification of assets within prudent risk constraints.

Spending Policy and How the Investment Objectives Relate to Spending Policy

During fiscal year 2009, the University's Board of Trustees adopted a spending policy, which is based on the "Total Return" concept of determining the amount available for distribution. Total Return takes into consideration all of the elements of long-term investment return. The appropriate spending amount is based on the projected long-term Total Return of the funds, less an estimate of future inflation. The goal of the Total Return approach is to provide for a level of current income that protects the future purchasing power of the fund, thereby providing for increasing amounts of future income. The University anticipates that this percentage will be in the range of 3 to 5% of market value based on historical measurements of Total Return and Inflation. The market value of the fund will be noted each year on a specific date and a three-year rolling average market value will be established. The rolling three-year market value will be multiplied by the approved spending percentage which will be set annually.

BETHEL UNIVERSITY
NOTES TO FINANCIAL STATEMENTS
JULY 31, 2018 AND 2017

I. FAIR VALUES OF FINANCIAL INSTRUMENTS

Required disclosures concerning the estimated fair values of financial instruments are presented below. The estimated fair value amounts have been determined based on the University's assessment of available market information and appropriate valuation methodologies. The following table summarizes required fair value disclosures under ASC 825, *Financial Instruments*, and measurements at July 31, 2018 and 2017 for the assets and liabilities measured at fair value on a recurring basis under ASC 820, *Fair Value Measurements and Disclosures*:

	Carrying Amount	Estimated Fair Value	Fair Value Measurements Using		
			Level 1	Level 2	Level 3
July 31, 2018					
Assets:					
Investments:					
Cash and cash equivalents	$ 362,942	$ 362,942	$362,942	$ -	$ -
Certificates of deposits	100,743	100,743	100,743	-	-
Equity funds:					
U.S. Equities	93,773	93,773	93,773	-	-
Venture Capital	3,054,399	3,054,399	-	-	3,054,399
Investment Property	3,688,273	3,688,273	-	-	3,688,273
Total Investments	$7,300,130	$7,300,130	$577,458	$ -	$6,742,672
Beneficial interests in trusts	$ 3,828,845	$ 3,828,845	$ -	$ 3,828,845	$ -
Liabilities:					
Debt and financing arrangement	$59,057,962	$65,674,894	$ -	$ -	$ -

BETHEL UNIVERSITY
NOTES TO FINANCIAL STATEMENTS
JULY 31, 2018 AND 2017

I. FAIR VALUES OF FINANCIAL INSTRUMENTS - Continued

	Carrying Amount	Estimated Fair Value	Fair Value Measurements Using		
			Level 1	Level 2	Level 3
July 31, 2017					
Assets:					
Investments:					
Cash and cash equivalents	$ 196,383	$ 196,383	$196,383	$ -	$ -
Certificates of deposits	100,492	100,492	100,492	-	-
Equity funds:					
U.S. Equities	121,856	121,856	121,856	-	-
Venture Capital	2,851,451	2,851,451	-	-	2,851,451
Investment Property	472,810	472,810	-	-	472,810
Total Investments	$3,742,992	$3,742,992	$418,731	$ -	$3,324,261
Beneficial interests in trusts	$3,710,652	$3,710,652	$ -	$3,710,652	$ -
Liabilities:					
Debt and financing arrangement	$55,985,961	$62,258,702	$ -	$ -	$ -

Changes in Level 3 assets are as follows:

	Fair Value Measurements Using Significant Unobservable Inputs (Level 3)	
	2018	2017
Beginning Balance	$3,324,261	$3,103,038
Purchases and sales, net	197,231	221,223
Transfer of fixed asset	3,065,463	-
Donated assets	155,717	-
Ending Balance	$6,742,672	$3,324,261

BETHEL UNIVERSITY
NOTES TO FINANCIAL STATEMENTS
JULY 31, 2018 AND 2017

I. FAIR VALUES OF FINANCIAL INSTRUMENTS - Continued

The following methods and assumptions were used to estimate the fair value of each class of financial instruments:

Cash equivalents, receivables, accounts payable and accrued payroll and benefits, deferred revenue and advances from the Federal government for student loans

The carrying values of these items approximate their fair values due to the short maturities of these instruments.

Investments

Fair values are based on quoted market prices, where available, and Level 2 and 3 inputs. The carrying amounts and the fair values of the University's investments are presented in Note C.

Notes payable and obligations under financing arrangement and capital leases

For fixed rate debt, fair value was estimated using discounted cash flow analyses based on the University's current incremental borrowing rates for similar types of borrowing arrangements.

J. FUND RAISING ACTIVITIES

The University conducts fundraising activities each year. The total cost of these activities for fiscal years 2018 and 2017, was $325,099 and $670,030, respectively.

K. RETIREMENT PLAN

The University's full-time employees may participate in a retirement plan administered by the Branch Banking and Trust Company (BB&T). The University makes payments to the plan by withholding an employee-elected percentage from the employee's salary with the University matching the employee's deduction up to five percent (5%). Total matching contributions were made by the University for fiscal years 2018 and 2017, of $468,331 and $521,024, respectively.

BETHEL UNIVERSITY
NOTES TO FINANCIAL STATEMENTS
JULY 31, 2018 AND 2017

L. CONCENTRATION OF RISKS

Concentration of Risk

The University generates revenue predominantly from tuition and fees, investment income, gifts, auxiliary enterprises and contributions. In planning and budgeting during a fiscal year, significant reliance is placed on meeting tuition, gift, auxiliary, investment earnings and contribution goals in order for the University to sustain successful operations. In the event that enrollment or gifts and contributions significantly decrease in any one year, operations could be adversely affected.

Financial instruments that potentially subject the University to concentrations of credit risk and market risk consist principally of cash equivalents, investments, and student receivables.

The University, in connection with its activities, grants credit to students that involves, to varying degrees, elements of credit risk. The maximum accounting loss from credit risk is limited to the amounts that are recognized in the accompanying statements of financial position as student accounts receivable at July 31, 2018 and 2017.

The University also has two bank deposits in excess of those insured under regulatory insurance limits.

M. OPERATING LEASES

The University leases office and classroom space for satellite campuses for programs offered through its College of Professional Studies, office space for University services, and an activities space for a University athletic program. These leases expire at various dates through fiscal year 2024. Minimum future rental payments under non-cancelable operating leases as of July 31, 2018 are as follows:

Fiscal Year Ending July 31,	Amount
2019	$1,163,388
2020	247,165
2021	96,000
2022	49,800
2023	45,600
Thereafter	11,400
	$1,613,353

- 28 -

BETHEL UNIVERSITY
NOTES TO FINANCIAL STATEMENTS
JULY 31, 2018 AND 2017

M. OPERATING LEASES - Continued

Operating lease payments under the non-cancelable leases totaled $1,334,358 and $1,409,902 for the years ended July 31, 2018 and 2017, respectively.

On August 10, 2011, the University entered into a ten (10) year lease, which expires August 31, 2021, with a related party. The building leased provides office space for University services to students. Operating lease payments under the non-cancelable lease totaled $50,400 for each of the years ended July 31, 2018 and 2017, respectively.

N. FUNCTIONAL ALLOCATION OF EXPENSES

During the years ended July 31, 2018 and 2017, the University allocated the cost of certain professional fees and the operation and maintenance of physical plant, including depreciation and amortization expense of $2,844,792 and $2,952,779 respectively, over the cost of providing instruction, academic support, student services, institutional support, and auxiliary enterprises as follows:

	2018	2017
Instruction	$3,776,777	$4,249,648
Academic support	366,975	412,923
Student services	1,779,068	2,001,816
Institutional support	1,728,746	1,945,193
Auxiliary enterprises	672,735	756,965
Total operation and maintenance of physical plant	$8,324,301	$9,366,545

O. LITIGATION AND CONTINGENCIES

The University is a defendant in legal actions from time to time in the normal course of operations. It is not currently possible to state the ultimate liability, if any, in these matters. In the opinion of management, any resulting liability from these actions will not have a material adverse effect on the financial position of the activities of the University.

BETHEL UNIVERSITY
NOTES TO FINANCIAL STATEMENTS
JULY 31, 2018 AND 2017

P. RELATED PARTY TRANSACTIONS

During fiscal years 2018 and 2017, the University had an agreement with a company owned by a member of the University's faculty. Under the agreement, the company developed and is maintaining the following online programs of study for the University:

- Master of Business Administration
- Master of Arts in Education
- Master of Science in Criminal Justice
- Bachelor of Science in Organizational Leadership
- Bachelor of Science in Criminal Justice
- Bachelor of Science in Emergency Services Management
- Associates of Arts
- Associates of Science
- Dual Enrollment

Specifically, the company is responsible for developing course work, producing lectures and graphic presentations, and maintaining student records. Fees under the agreement range from $129 to $269 per student, per course. The most recent agreement was executed effective April 1, 2018 for three (3) years, and automatically renews for an additional term of one (1) year unless terminated in accordance with the agreement. Total fees incurred during fiscal years 2018 and 2017 were $5,005,500 and $5,944,319, respectively.

During fiscal years 2018 and 2017, the University entered into an agreement with a company co-founded by a member of the Board of Trustees. Under the agreement, the company was granted rights as the University's exclusive technology supplier for the Registered Nurse to Bachelor of Science in Nursing (RN to BSN) online program of study. The company has developed a learning management system (LMS) that is used as a platform for online curriculum delivery for the Colleges of Arts and Sciences and Health Sciences. The curriculum is developed by and remains the property of the University. Additionally, the company provides online support for students and faculty and has developed a process within the LMS to obtain other analytical data. Fees under the agreement are $50 per user per class and $25 per user per lab for licensing rights to the product, including all enhancements, modifications, and new releases or modules. The agreement was executed March 9, 2015 and shall continue for five (5) years, which will automatically extend for an additional two (2) years unless terminated in accordance with the agreement. Total fees incurred during fiscal years 2018 and 2017 were $738,900 and $743,075 respectively.

BETHEL UNIVERSITY
NOTES TO FINANCIAL STATEMENTS
JULY 31, 2018 AND 2017

P. RELATED PARTY TRANSACTIONS - Continued

The University entered into a line-of-credit with a private company owned by a member of the Board of Trustees. Total outstanding balance as of July 31, 2018 was $4,000,000 (See Note E).

The University entered into a line-of-credit with a private party who is a member of the Board of Trustees. Total outstanding balance as of July 31, 2018 was $1,500,000 (See Note E).

At various times throughout the fiscal year, the University transacts business with a related party as part of the normal business operations of the University.

The University entered into leasing arrangements with related parties as described in Note M.

Q. SUBSEQUENT EVENTS

The University has evaluated subsequent events through October 3, 2018, the issuance date of the University's financial statements, and has determined that there are no subsequent events requiring disclosure, except the subsequent payment of certain debt as disclosed in Note E.

SUPPLEMENTARY INFORMATION

BETHEL UNIVERSITY
SUPPLEMENTARY INFORMATION
YEAR ENDED JULY 31, 2018

FINANCIAL RESPONSIBILITY COMPOSITE SCORE (UNAUDITED)

As explained on the United States Department of Education's website (https://studentaid.ed.gov/sa/about/data-center/school/composite-scores),

> Section 498(c) of the Higher Education Act of 1965, as amended, requires for-profit and non-profit institutions to annually submit audited financial statements to the Department to demonstrate they are maintaining the standards of financial responsibility necessary to participate in the Title IV programs. One of many standards, which the Department utilizes to gauge the financial responsibility of an institution, is a composite of three ratios derived from an institution's audited financial statements. The three ratios are a primary reserve ratio, an equity ratio, and a net income ratio. These ratios gauge the fundamental elements of the financial health of an institution, not the educational quality of an institution.
>
> The composite score reflects the overall relative financial health of institutions along a scale from negative 1.0 to positive 3.0. A score greater than or equal to 1.5 indicates the institution is considered financially responsible.
>
> Schools with scores of less than 1.5 but greater than or equal to 1.0 are considered financially responsible, but require additional oversight. These schools are subject to cash monitoring and other participation requirements.

For the fiscal years ended July 31, 2016, 2017, and 2018, management calculated the University's financial responsibility composite scores as follows:

BETHEL UNIVERSITY
SUPPLEMENTARY INFORMATION
YEAR ENDED JULY 31, 2018

FINANCIAL RESPONSIBILITY COMPOSITE SCORE (UNAUDITED) - Continued

Ratios:	2016		2017		2018	
Primary Reserve Ratio:	0.0356		0.1044		0.1725	
Expendable Net Assets		$ 2,099,357		$ 6,054,601		$ 9,290,219
Total Expense		$ 58,903,145		$ 58,013,240		$ 53,842,491
Equity Ratio:	0.3571		0.3586		0.3558	
Modified Net Assets		$ 35,283,357		$ 35,731,286		$ 36,038,431
Modified Assets		$ 98,805,150		$ 99,937,666		$ 101,302,333
Net Income Ratio:	0.1549		0.0212		0.0033	
Change in Unrestricted Net Assets		$ 10,799,211		$ 1,258,387		$ 178,199
Total Unrestricted Revenue		$ 69,702,356		$ 59,271,627		$ 54,020,690
Strength Factor Scores:						
Primary Reserve strength factor score	0.3564		1.0437		1.7254	
Equity strength factor score	2.1426		2.1517		2.1345	
Net Income strength factor score	3.0000		2.0615		1.1649	
Composite Score:						
Primary Reserve Weighted Score	0.1426		0.4175		0.6902	
Equity Weighted Score	0.8570		0.8607		0.8538	
Net Income Weighted Score	0.6000		0.4123		0.2330	
Total Composite Score (Rounded):	1.6		1.7		1.8	

UNIVERSITY KEY FINANCIAL RATIOS

The financial health of the University can be evaluated through the use of ratios. The following ratios are customarily utilized by higher education institutions to measure financial condition. There are four fundamental financial questions addressed by analysis of four core ratios.

- Are resources sufficient and flexible enough to support the mission? - Primary Reserve Ratio
- Do operating results indicate the institution is living within available resources? - Net Operating Revenues Ratio
- Does asset performance and management support the strategic direction? - Return on Net Assets
- Are financial resources, including debt, managed strategically to advance the mission? - Viability Ratio

When combined, these four ratios deliver a single measure of the University's overall financial health, referred to as the Composite Financial Index. The following charts analyze the aforementioned ratios for the fiscal year ended July 31, 2016, 2017, and 2018:

BETHEL UNIVERSITY
SUPPLEMENTARY INFORMATION
YEAR ENDED JULY 31, 2018

UNIVERSITY KEY FINANCIAL RATIOS (UNAUDITED) - Continued

Composite Financial Index

The Composite Financial Index (CFI) is calculated based upon the values of its four component ratios: 1) Primary Reserve, 2) Net Operating Revenue, 3) Return on Net Assets, and 4) Viability Ratio. Once each of the four ratios is calculated, further weighting is conducted to measure the relative strength of the score and its importance in the composite score. The CFI combines the four core ratios identified below into a single score. The combination, using a prescribed weighting plan, allows a weakness or strength in one ratio to be offset by another ratio result. The CFI reflects a picture of the financial health of the institution at a point in time.

COMPOSITE FINANCIAL INDEX (CFI)

FY16	FY17	FY18
3.0	0.7	0.7

Primary Reserve Ratio

The Primary Reserve Ratio is intended to address the question of sufficiency and flexibility for support of the mission. The ratio measures the financial strength of the University by comparing expendable net assets, which includes those assets the University can access and spend quickly to meet obligations, to total expenses at the end of every fiscal year. This ratio identifies the University's financial strength and flexibility by identifying how long the University can function by using reserves without the generation of any new net assets. A primary reserve ratio of .40 or 40% is advisable, implying that the university has the ability to cover over 4 ½ months of expenses. Key items that can impact this ratio include principal payments on debt, using net assets to fund capital construction projects, endowment returns, and total operating expenses. Although not reaching the benchmark, the University's ratio is trending in a positive direction.

PRIMARY RESERVE RATIO   **EXPLANATION**

FY16	FY17	FY18	
$22,874,163	$24,132,550	$24,310,749	+ unrestricted net assets EOY
$ 2,074,644	$ 838,973	$ 838,101	+ temporarily restricted net assets EOY
$74,163,753	$72,906,071	$67,948,834	-- land, building, and equipment, net of depreciation EOY
$49,314,303	$55,464,585	$52,090,203	+ long-term debt EOY
$58,903,145	$58,013,240	$53,842,491	total expenses
0.00	0.13	0.17	Ratio
0.01	0.98	1.30	strength factor
0.0	0.3	0.5	weighted value

- 34 -

BETHEL UNIVERSITY
SUPPLEMENTARY INFORMATION
YEAR ENDED JULY 31, 2018

UNIVERSITY KEY FINANCIAL RATIOS (UNAUDITED) - Continued

Net Operating Revenues Ratio

The Net Operating Revenues Ratio is intended to indicate if the University is living within its available resources. The University needs to generate some level of surplus over long periods of time because operations are one source for reinvestment in future initiatives. Short-term deficits may occur as a result of strategic decisions. It is when deficits are unplanned or unmanaged and occurring as a result of core operations that evaluation of operations is necessitated. A positive ratio indicates the University is in good financial condition. An organization should establish a target percentage, and establishing a benchmark should be in line with operating growth. A ratio of 2 to 4 percent indicates the University operated within its means and should be maintained over time; however, fluctuations from year to year are normal. A large ratio identifies an operating surplus and a stronger financial position. While a negative ratio indicates an operating loss for the year, universities need to be careful about too large of a positive ratio, indicating under spending on mission critical initiatives.

NET OPERATING REVENUES RATIO (%):
Using Change in Unrestricted Net Assets

FY16	FY17	FY18	EXPLANATION
$10,799,211	$ 1,258,387	$ 178,199	change in unrestricted net assets
$69,702,356	$59,271,627	$54,020,690	total unrestricted revenue
15.5	2.1	0.3	ratio
10.00	1.63	0.25	strength factor
1.0	0.2	0.0	weighted value

Return on Net Assets Ratio

The Return on Net Assets Ratio is intended to assess if the asset performance and management support the strategic direction. The ratio measures whether the University is financially better off than in the previous year by measuring total economic return or the level of change in total net assets. This ratio is the most comprehensive measure of growth or decline in wealth over time. There is not a specific threshold; however, 3 to 4 percent is a generally acceptable real rate of return. An improving trend in this ratio indicates the university is increasing its net assets and is likely to be in a position to set aside financial resources to strengthen its future financial flexibility. Key items that may impact this ratio include changes in the net operating revenue ratio, endowment returns, capital gifts and grants, capital transfers, and endowment gifts. This indicator can be greatly impacted when borrowing money for a capital project and when the capital item is added to Net Assets. Looking at the trend will even out the anomalies.

BETHEL UNIVERSITY
SUPPLEMENTARY INFORMATION
YEAR ENDED JULY 31, 2018

UNIVERSITY KEY FINANCIAL RATIOS (UNAUDITED) - Continued

Return on Net Assets Ratio - Continued

RETURN ON NET ASSETS RATIO (%)

FY16	FY17	FY18	EXPLANATION
$10,368,546	$ 447,929	$ 307,145	change in net assets
$24,914,811	$35,283,357	$35,731,286	total net assets BOY
41.6	1.3	0.9	ratio
10.00	0.63	0.43	strength factor
2.0	0.1	0.1	weighted value

Viability Ratio

The Viability Ratio is intended to address the question of whether financial resources are being strategically managed to advance the mission of the University. It measures availability of expendable net assets for coverage of debt should the University be required to settle its obligations as of the date on the balance sheet. A 1:1 ratio is desired, indicating adequate net assets to meet obligations. This ratio is one of the most basic determinants of clear financial health and is regarded as governing the University's ability to assume new debt. A ratio of 1.25 or greater indicates a strong creditworthy University with sufficient resources to satisfy debt obligations; however, each university should identify the ratio that is right for its mission specific needs. A viability ratio that falls below 1:1 hinders the university's ability to respond to adverse condition, to secure external capital, and to have flexibility to fund new objectives. Key items that may impact this ratio include principal payments on debt, using net assets for capital construction projects, issuance of new debt, and endowment returns. Although not reaching the benchmark, the University's ratio is trending in a positive direction.

VIABILITY RATIO

FY16	FY17	FY18	EXPLANATION
$22,874,163	$24,132,550	$24,310,749	+ unrestricted net assets EOY
$ 2,074,644	$ 838,973	$ 838,101	+ temporarily restricted net assets EOY
$74,163,753	$72,906,071	$67,948,834	-- land, building, and equipment, net of depreciation EOY
$49,314,303	$55,464,585	$52,090,203	+ long-term debt EOY
$49,314,303	$55,464,585	$52,090,203	long-term debt EOY
0.00	0.14	0.18	ratio
0.00	0.33	0.43	strength factor
0.0	0.1	0.1	weighted value

- 36 -

BETHEL UNIVERSITY
SUPPLEMENTARY INFORMATION
YEAR ENDED JULY 31, 2018

UNRESTRICTED NET ASSETS EXCLUSIVE OF PLANT, PROPERTY, EQUIPMENT, AND RELATED DEBT AND OBLIGATION UNDER FINANCING ARRANGEMENT (UNAUDITED)

The Southern Association of School and Colleges, Commission on Colleges (SACSCOC), has various core requirements for meeting standards. One such requirement is Standard 13.1 requiring, among other things, the University to present a statement of financial position of unrestricted net assets, exclusive of plant assets and plant-related debt, which represents the change in unrestricted net assets attributable to operations. The chart below is provided to meet this SACSCOC requirement. Although the University's net unrestricted assets, excluding plant, property, equipment, and related debt is negative, the trend over the past three fiscal years is positive, indicating the University has taken measures to strengthen its financial stability.

**Statements of Financial Position of
Unrestricted Net Assets, Exclusive of Plant
Assets and Plant-Related Debt**

	July 31,		
Restatement of Net Assets without plant and plant-related debt	**2018**	**2017**	**2016**
Unrestricted Net Assets	$ 24,310,749	$ 24,132,550	$ 22,874,163
Less: property, plant, and equipment, net	(67,948,834)	(72,906,071)	(74,163,753)
Add: plant-related debt	47,919,661	48,464,433	49,499,301
URNA not including plant and debt	**$ 4,281,576**	**$ (309,088)**	**$ (1,790,289)**

OTHER INFORMATION

BETHEL UNIVERSITY
SCHEDULE OF EXPENDITURES OF FEDERAL AWARDS
YEAR ENDED JULY 31, 2018

Federal Grantor/Pass-through Grantor/ Program or Cluster Title	Federal CFDA Number	Federal Expenditures
U.S. Department of Education - Direct Awards		
Student Financial Assistance - Cluster: (1)		
Federal Direct Student Loans Program (Note C)	84.268	$41,548,484
Federal Perkins Loan Program (Note B)	84.038	334,499
Federal Work-Study Program (Note D)	84.033	153,649
Federal Supplemental Educational		
Opportunity Grants Program (Note D)	84.007	284,934
Federal Pell Grant Program	84.063	10,564,596
Total Student Financial Assistance - Cluster		52,886,162
U.S. Department of Education - Pass-through Program from:		
Special Education: Grants to States		
Tennessee Teachers Assistants Grant	84.027A	25,000
Total U.S. Department of Education		52,911,162
Total Expenditures of Federal Awards		$52,911,162

(1) Tested as a major program

See independent auditor's report.

BETHEL UNIVERSITY
NOTES TO SCHEDULE OF EXPENDITURES OF FEDERAL AWARDS
YEAR ENDED JULY 31, 2018

A. BASIS OF PRESENTATION

The accompanying schedule of expenditures of federal awards is presented in accordance with the requirements by Title 2 U.S. *Code of Federal* Regulations (CFR) Part 200, *Uniform Administrative Requirements, Cost Principles, and Audit Requirements for Federal Awards* (Uniform Guidance), on the accrual basis of accounting consistent with the basis of accounting used by the University in the preparation of its financial statements.

The University has elected not to use the 10-percent de minimis indirect cost rate allowed under the Uniform Guidance.

B. FEDERAL PERKINS LOAN PROGRAM - CFDA #84.038

The outstanding loan balance for the Federal Perkins Loan Program at July 31, 2018 was $127,268, net of the allowance for uncollectible loans of $207,231. Total loan disbursements for the program for the year ended July 31, 2018, were $0. Other disbursements include an expenditure for repayment of fund capital in the amount of $80,708.

C. FEDERAL DIRECT LOANS PROGRAM - CFDA #84.268

During the fiscal year ending July 31, 2018, the University processed $41,548,484 of new loans under the Federal Direct Loans program (which includes subsidized and unsubsidized Stafford Loans, Parents for Undergraduate Students, and Supplemental Loans for Students)

D. MATCHING FUNDS

The University received a waiver from the U.S. Department of Education and elected not to provide matching funds for the Federal Supplemental Educational Opportunity Grants program during the fiscal year ended July 31, 2018. The University received a waiver from the U.S. Department of Education and elected not to provide matching funds for the Federal Work Study program during the fiscal year ended July 31, 2018.

Independent Auditor's Report on Internal Control Over
Financial Reporting and on Compliance and Other Matters
Based on an Audit of Financial Statements Performed in
Accordance with *Government Auditing Standards*

The Board of Trustees
Bethel University
McKenzie, Tennessee

We have audited, in accordance with the auditing standards generally accepted in the United States of America and the standards applicable to financial audits contained in *Government Auditing Standards* issued by the Comptroller General of the United States, the financial statements of Bethel University (the "University"), which comprise the statements of financial position as of July 31, 2018, and the related statements of activities and cash flows for the year then ended, and the related notes to the financial statements, and have issued our report thereon dated October 3, 2018.

Internal Control Over Financial Reporting

In planning and performing our audit of the financial statements, we considered the University's internal control over financial reporting (internal control) to determine the audit procedures that are appropriate in the circumstances for the purpose of expressing our opinion on the financial statements, but not for the purpose of expressing an opinion on the effectiveness of the University's internal control. Accordingly, we do not express an opinion on the effectiveness of the University's internal control.

A *deficiency in internal control* exists when the design or operation of a control does not allow management or employees, in the normal course of performing their assigned functions, to prevent, or detect and correct misstatements on a timely basis. A *material weakness* is a deficiency, or a combination of deficiencies, in internal control such that there is a reasonable possibility that a material misstatement of the entity's financial statements will not be prevented, or detected and corrected on a timely basis. A *significant deficiency* is a deficiency, or a combination of deficiencies, in internal control that is less severe than a material weakness, yet important enough to merit attention by those charged with governance.

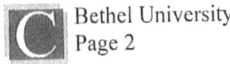
Bethel University
Page 2

Our consideration of the internal control was for the limited purpose described in the first paragraph of this section and was not designed to identify all deficiencies in internal control that might be material weaknesses or significant deficiencies. Given these limitations, during our audit we did not identify any deficiencies in internal control that we consider to be material weaknesses. However, material weaknesses may exist that have not been identified.

Compliance and Other Matters

As part of obtaining reasonable assurance about whether the University's financial statements are free from material misstatement, we performed tests of its compliance with certain provisions of laws, regulations, contracts, and grant agreements, noncompliance with which could have a direct and material effect on the determination of financial statement amounts. However, providing an opinion on compliance with those provisions was not an objective of our audit, and accordingly, we do not express such an opinion. The results of our tests disclosed no instances of noncompliance or other matters that are required to be reported under *Government Auditing Standards*.

Purpose of this Report

The purpose of this report is solely to describe the scope of our testing of internal control and compliance and the results of that testing, and not to provide an opinion on the effectiveness of the University's internal control or on compliance. This report is an integral part of an audit performed in accordance with *Government Auditing Standards* in considering the University's internal control and compliance. Accordingly, this communication is not suitable for any other purpose.

Crosslin, PLLC

Nashville, Tennessee
October 3, 2018

Independent Auditor's Report on Compliance For Each Major
Programs and on Internal Control Over Compliance
Required by Uniform Guidance

The Board of Trustees
Bethel University
McKenzie, Tennessee

Report on Compliance for Each Major Federal Program

We have audited Bethel University's (the "University") compliance with the types of compliance requirements described in the *OMB Compliance Supplement* that could have a direct and material effect on the University's major federal programs for the year ended July 31, 2018. The University's major federal program is identified in the summary of auditor's results section of the accompanying schedule of findings and questioned costs.

Management's Responsibility

Management is responsible for compliance with federal statutes, regulations, and the terms and conditions of its federal awards applicable to its federal programs.

Auditor's Responsibility

Our responsibility is to express an opinion on compliance for each of the University's major federal programs based on our audit of the types of compliance requirements referred to above. We conducted our audit of compliance in accordance with auditing standards generally accepted in the United States of America; the standards applicable to financial audits contained in *Government Auditing Standards*, issued by the Comptroller General of the United States; and the audit requirements of Title 2 U.S. *Code of Federal Regulations* (CFR) Part 200, *Uniform Administrative Requirements, Cost Principles, and Audit Requirements for Federal Awards* (Uniform Guidance). Those standards and the Uniform Guidance require that we plan and perform the audit to obtain reasonable assurance about whether noncompliance with the types of compliance requirements referred to above that could have a direct and material effect on a major federal program occurred. An audit includes examining, on a test basis, evidence about the University's compliance with those requirements and performing such other procedures as we considered necessary in the circumstances.

We believe that our audit provides a reasonable basis for our opinion on compliance for the major federal program. However, our audit does not provide a legal determination of the University's compliance.

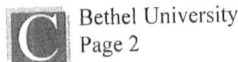
Bethel University
Page 2

Opinion on the Major Federal Program

In our opinion, the University complied, in all material respects, with the types of compliance requirements referred to above that could have a direct and material effect on its major federal program for the year ended July 31, 2018.

Report on Internal Control Over Compliance

Management of the University is responsible for establishing and maintaining effective internal control over compliance with the types of compliance requirements referred to above. In planning and performing our audit of compliance, we considered the University's internal control over compliance with the types of requirements that could have a direct and material effect on each major federal program to determine the auditing procedures that are appropriate in the circumstances for the purpose of expressing an opinion on compliance for each major federal program and to test and report on internal control over compliance in accordance with the Uniform Guidance, but not for the purpose of expressing an opinion on the effectiveness of internal control over compliance. Accordingly, we do not express an opinion on the effectiveness of the University's internal control over compliance.

A *deficiency in internal control over compliance* exists when the design or operation of a control over compliance does not allow management or employees, in the normal course of performing their assigned functions, to prevent, or detect and correct, noncompliance with a type of compliance requirement of a federal program on a timely basis. A *material weakness in internal control over compliance* is a deficiency, or combination of deficiencies, in internal control over compliance, such that there is a reasonable possibility that material noncompliance with a type of compliance requirement of a federal program will not be prevented, or detected and corrected, on a timely basis. A *significant deficiency in internal control over compliance* is a deficiency, or a combination of deficiencies, in internal control over compliance with a type of compliance requirement of a federal program that is less severe than a material weakness in internal control over compliance, yet important enough to merit attention by those charged with governance.

Our consideration of internal control over compliance was for the limited purpose described in the first paragraph of this section and was not designed to identify all deficiencies in internal control over compliance that might be material weaknesses or significant deficiencies. We did not identify any deficiencies in internal control over compliance that we consider to be material weaknesses. However, material weaknesses may exist that have not been identified.

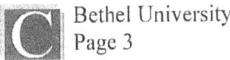
Bethel University
Page 3

The purpose of this report on internal control over compliance is solely to describe the scope of our testing of internal control over compliance and the results of that testing based on the requirements of the Uniform Guidance. Accordingly, this report is not suitable for any other purpose.

Crosslin, PLLC

Nashville, Tennessee
October 3, 2018

BETHEL UNIVERSITY
SCHEDULE OF FINDINGS AND QUESTIONED COSTS
YEAR ENDED JULY 31, 2018

I. SUMMARY OF INDEPENDENT AUDITOR'S RESULTS

Financial Statements

Type of auditor's report issued: <u>Unmodified</u>

Internal control over financial reporting:

- Material weakness(es) identified? ____Yes _X_ No
- Significant deficiency(ies) identified? ____Yes _X_ None Reported

Noncompliance material to financial statements noted? ____Yes _X_ No

Federal Awards

Internal control over major program:

- Material weakness(es) identified? ____Yes _X_ No
- Significant deficiency(ies) identified? ____Yes _X_ None Noted

Type of auditor's report issued on compliance for major program: <u>Unmodified</u>

Any audit findings disclosed that are required to be reported in accordance with 2 CFR 200.516(a)? ____Yes _X_ No

BETHEL UNIVERSITY
SCHEDULE OF FINDINGS AND QUESTIONED COSTS
YEAR ENDED JULY 31, 2018

I. SUMMARY OF INDEPENDENT AUDITOR'S RESULTS - Continued

Major Programs:

CFDA Number	Name of Federal Program	Amount Expended
SFA Cluster:		
84.063	Federal Pell Grant Program	$10,564,596
84.268	Federal Direct Student Loans Program	41,548,484
84.038	Federal Perkins Loan Program	334,499
84.007	Federal Supplemental Educational Opportunity Grants Program	284,934
84.033	Federal Work-Study Program	153,649

Dollar threshold used to distinguish between type A
and type B programs $1,587,335

Auditee qualified as low-risk auditee   ___Yes _X_ No

II. FINANCIAL STATEMENT FINDINGS

   A. Material Weakness in Internal Control

      None Reported.

   B. Compliance Findings

      None Reported.

III. FINDINGS AND QUESTIONED COSTS FOR FEDERAL AWARDS

   None Reported.

BETHEL UNIVERSITY
SCHEDULE OF PRIOR YEAR FINDINGS AND QUESTIONED COSTS
YEAR ENDED JULY 31, 2018

The University had no prior audit findings related to the testing of its federal award programs.

**CUMBERLAND PRESBYTERIAN
CHILDREN'S HOME**

FINANCIAL STATEMENTS
AND
AUDITORS' REPORT

DECEMBER 31, 2018

CUMBERLAND PRESBYTERIAN CHILDREN'S HOME

TABLE OF CONTENTS

	Page
Independent Auditors' Report	1
Statement of Financial Position	3
Statement of Activities	4
Statement of Cash Flows	5
Statement of Functional Expenses	6-7
Notes to the Financial Statements	8-15
Supplemental Information	
Schedule of Board of Stewardship Endowments	17-18

HANKINS, EASTUP, DEATON, TONN & SEAY
A PROFESSIONAL CORPORATION
CERTIFIED PUBLIC ACCOUNTANTS

Members:
AMERICAN INSTITUTE OF CERTIFIED PUBLIC ACCOUNTANTS
TEXAS SOCIETY OF CERTIFIED PUBLIC ACCOUNTANTS

902 NORTH LOCUST
P.O. BOX 977
DENTON, TX 76202-0977

TEL. (940) 387-8563
FAX (940) 383-4746

Independent Auditors' Report

Cumberland Presbyterian Children's Home
Denton, Texas

We have audited the accompanying financial statements of Cumberland Presbyterian Children's Home (a nonprofit organization), which comprise the statement of financial position as of December 31, 2018 and the related statements of activities and cash flows for the year then ended, and the related notes to the financial statements.

Management's Responsibility for the Financial Statements

Management is responsible for the preparation and fair presentation of these financial statements in accordance with accounting principles generally accepted in the United States of America; this includes the design, implementation, and maintenance of internal control relevant to the preparation and fair presentation of financial statements that are free from material misstatement, whether due to fraud or error.

Auditor's Responsibility

Our responsibility is to express an opinion on these financial statements based on our audit. We conducted our audit in accordance with auditing standards generally accepted in the United States of America. Those standards require that we plan and perform the audit to obtain reasonable assurance about whether the financial statements are free of material misstatement.

An audit involves performing procedures to obtain audit evidence about the amounts and disclosures in the financial statements. The procedures selected depend on the auditor's judgment, including the assessment of the risks of material misstatement of the financial statements, whether due to fraud or error. In making those risk assessments, the auditor considers internal control relevant to the entity's preparation and fair presentation of the financial statements in order to design audit procedures that are appropriate in the circumstances, but not for the purpose of expressing an opinion on the effectiveness of the entity's internal control. Accordingly, we express no such opinion. An audit also includes evaluating the appropriateness of accounting policies used and the reasonableness of significant accounting estimates made by management, as well as evaluating the overall presentation of the financial statements. We believe that the audit evidence we have obtained is sufficient and appropriate to provide a basis for our audit opinion.

Opinion

In our opinion, the financial statements referred to above present fairly, in all material respects, the financial position of Cumberland Presbyterian Children's Home as of December 31, 2018, and the changes in its net assets and its cash flows for the year then ended in accordance with accounting principles generally accepted in the United States of America.

Hankins, Eastup, Deaton, Tonn & Seay

Hankins, Eastup, Deaton, Tonn & Seay
Denton, Texas
June 24, 2019

Page left blank intentionally

CUMBERLAND PRESBYTERIAN CHILDREN'S HOME

STATEMENT OF FINANCIAL POSITION
DECEMBER 31, 2018

ASSETS:

Cash and cash equivalents	$ 231,604
Due from Board of Stewardship	62,330
Other receivables	122,142
Prepaid expenses	4,000
Land, buildings and equipment, net	3,369,218
Other long-term investments	8,411,029
TOTAL ASSETS	**$ 12,200,323**

LIABILITIES AND NET ASSETS:

Liabilities:	
Accounts payable	$ 57,416
Accrued liabilities	80,307
Line of credit - First United Bank	250,000
Total Liabilities	387,723
Net Assets:	
Without donor restrictions:	
Undesignated	3,205,342
Invested in property and equipment	3,369,218
	6,574,560
With donor restrictions:	
Perpetual in nature	5,206,392
Subject to purpose or use restrictions	11,357
Time-restricted for future periods	20,291
	5,238,040
Total Net Assets	11,812,600
TOTAL LIABILITIES AND NET ASSETS	**$ 12,200,323**

See Accompanying Notes to the Financial Statements.

CUMBERLAND PRESBYTERIAN CHILDREN'S HOME

STATEMENT OF ACTIVITIES
FOR THE YEAR ENDED DECEMBER 31, 2018

	Without Donor Restrictions	With Donor Restrictions — Purpose or Use Restrictions	With Donor Restrictions — Not Subject to Appropriation	2018 Total
Revenues, Gains and Other Support:				
Contributions and grants	$ 773,908	$ -	$ 401	$ 774,309
CPS revenue	670,787	-	-	670,787
Counseling & treatment services	146,174	-	-	146,174
Denominational support	65,423	-	-	65,423
Income on long-term investments	66,203	212	31,078	97,493
Oil and gas royalties	2,117	-	-	2,117
Rents	61,770	-	-	61,770
Subtotal	1,786,382	212	31,479	1,818,073
Net assets released from Restrictions	276,471	-	(276,471)	-
Total Revenue, Gains and Other Support	2,062,853	212	(244,992)	1,818,073
Expenses and Losses:				
Program services:				
Children's residential program	1,713,461	-	-	1,713,461
Family residential program	102,351	-	-	102,351
Counseling & treatment services	132,948	-	-	132,948
Administration	487,456	-	-	487,456
Chaplain	20,128	-	-	20,128
Development	57,484	-	-	57,484
Total Expenses	2,513,828	-	-	2,513,828
Losses:				
Unrealized losses on investments	224,640	2,831	186,152	413,623
Total Expenses and Losses	2,738,468	2,831	186,152	2,927,451
Change in net assets	(675,615)	(2,619)	(431,144)	(1,109,378)
Net assets at beginning of year	7,250,175	34,267	5,637,536	12,921,978
Net assets at end of year	$ 6,574,560	$ 31,648	$ 5,206,392	$11,812,600

See Accompanying Notes to the Financial Statements

CUMBERLAND PRESBYTERIAN CHILDREN'S HOME

STATEMENT OF CASH FLOWS
FOR THE YEAR ENDED DECEMBER 31, 2018

Cash Flows from Operating Activities:	
Change in net assets	$ (1,109,378)
Adjustments to reconcile change in net assets to net cash provided by operating activities:	
Depreciation	194,569
(Increase) Decrease in receivables	(52,299)
(Increase) Decrease in prepaid expenses	(2,744)
Increase (Decrease) in accounts payable/accrued liabilities	37,708
Unrealized losses (gains) on investments	413,623
Contributions restricted for long-term investment	(401)
Net Cash Provided (Used) by Operating Activities	(518,922)
Cash Flows from Investing Activities:	
Purchase of fixed assets	(22,084)
Investment withdrawals	368,135
Net Cash Provided by Investing Activities	346,051
Cash Flows from Financing Activities:	
Line of credit proceeds	375,000
Payments on line of credit	(225,190)
Proceeds from contributions restricted for investment in endowment	401
Net Cash Provided by Financing Activities	150,211
Net Increase in Cash and Cash Equivalents	(22,660)
Cash and Cash Equivalents at Beginning of Year	254,264
Cash and Cash Equivalents at End of Year	$ 231,604
Supplemental Data:	
Interest paid during the year	$ 4,325

See Accompanyin Notes to the Financial Statements.

CUMBERLAND PRESBYTERIAN CHILDREN'S HOME

STATEMENT OF FUNCTIONAL EXPENSES
FOR THE YEAR ENDED DECEMBER 31, 2018

	Program Services			
	Children's Residential Program	Family Residential Program	Counseling & Treatment Services	Total
Salaries and Wages	$ 984,223	$ 44,899	$ 93,752	$ 1,122,874
Employee Benefits	83,626	3,815	7,966	95,407
Payroll Taxes	141,614	6,460	13,489	161,563
Total Salaries and Related Expenses	1,209,463	55,174	115,207	1,379,844
Basic care and hygiene	14,938	245	-	15,183
Groceries	61,887	1,664	25	63,576
Recreational activities and dining out	42,010	623	389	43,022
Family assistance	602	4,582	-	5,184
Medical and dental care	1,968	-	-	1,968
Enrichment	13,679	1,111	-	14,790
Utilities and internet	93,146	5,657	-	98,803
Property, liability insurance	43,331	-	-	43,331
Building/grounds R&M	63,488	24,535	-	88,023
Supplies, postage, printing	6,858	43	-	6,901
Computer software, maintenance	10,239	175	-	10,414
Staff recruitment/training	5,721	-	5,701	11,422
Special events	-	-	-	-
Vehicle expenses	3,361	-	-	3,361
Travel	20,993	-	626	21,619
Rental/lease expense	340	-	-	340
Legal and professional fees	14,778	-	-	14,778
Dues and subscriptions	278	-	210	488
Public relations/advertising	-	-	75	75
Board expense	3,308	-	-	3,308
Interest/finance charges	75	-	89	164
Other	2,910	857	475	4,242
Total Expenses Before Depreciation	1,613,373	94,666	122,797	1,830,836
Depreciation	100,088	7,685	10,151	117,924
TOTAL EXPENSES	$ 1,713,461	$ 102,351	$ 132,948	$ 1,948,760

The accompanying notes are an integral part of this statement.

	Supporting Services				Total
Chaplain	Development	Administration	Total		Total Expenses
$ 9,241	$ 11,867	$ 170,904	$ 192,012		$ 1,314,886
785	1,008	14,521	16,314		111,721
1,330	1,707	24,591	27,628		189,191
11,356	14,582	210,016	235,954		1,615,798
-	-	-	-		15,183
-	-	-	-		63,576
164	115	5,742	6,021		49,043
-	-	-	-		5,184
-	-	-	-		1,968
1,852	-	-	1,852		16,642
-	-	36,128	36,128		134,931
-	-	14,386	14,386		57,717
62	155	22,558	22,775		110,798
335	21,664	13,839	35,838		42,739
350	1,003	13,049	14,402		24,816
77	89	6,042	6,208		17,630
-	1,170	-	1,170		1,170
-	124	2,294	2,418		5,779
-	583	1,936	2,519		24,138
-	-	6,262	6,262		6,602
-	3,127	70,471	73,598		88,376
16	247	2,825	3,088		3,576
-	5,745	54	5,799		5,874
-	-	7,417	7,417		10,725
58	81	6,308	6,447		6,611
1,404	558	4,179	6,141		10,383
15,674	49,243	423,506	488,423		2,319,259
4,454	8,241	63,950	76,645		194,569
$ 20,128	$ 57,484	$ 487,456	$ 565,068		$ 2,513,828

CUMBERLAND PRESBYTERIAN CHILDREN'S HOME

NOTES TO FINANCIAL STATEMENTS
DECEMBER 31, 2018

NOTE A - SUMMARY OF SIGNIFICANT ACCOUNTING POLICIES

Organization and Nature of Activities

Cumberland Presbyterian Children's Home (CPCH) is a nonprofit organization originally chartered in Kentucky in 1904 and moved to Denton, Texas in 1932. Its purpose is to provide long-term residential basic child care for children between the ages of 3 and 17. CPCH is licensed to care for up to 40 children. CPCH's primary sources of revenue are income from child care, donations and income from long-term investments.

Basis of Presentation

The financial statements are prepared on an accrual basis of accounting in accordance with accounting principles generally accepted in the United States of America. Revenues and related assets are recognized when earned, and expenses are recognized when the obligation is incurred. They are presented in accordance with the provisions of Financial Accounting Standards Board ("FASB") ASU No. 2016-14, "Not-For-Profit Entities".

FASB ASU 2016-14 establishes standards for general-purpose external financial statements for nonprofit organizations, including a statement of financial position, a statement of activities, a statement of functional expense and a statement of cash flows. FASB ASU 2016-14 requires the classification of net assets and its revenues, expenses, gains and losses into three categories, if applicable, based on existence or absence of donor-imposed restrictions. The categories are "without donor restrictions" and "with donor restrictions".

Accordingly, net assets of CPCH and changes therein are classified and reported as follows:

Net assets without donor restrictions – Net assets that are not subject to donor-imposed stipulations. Included in this classification are net assets earmarked by the Board for future purposes.

Net assets subject to purpose or use restrictions – Net assets subject to donor-imposed stipulations that specify a use that is more specific than broad limits relating to purposes under which CPCH operates.

Net assets not subject to appropriation or expenditure – Net assets subject to donor-imposed restrictions that must be maintained permanently by CPCH. Generally, the donors of these assets permit CPCH to use all or part of the income earned on any related investments for the specific donor purpose.

Public Support and Revenue

In the absence of a donor's explicit stipulation or circumstances surrounding the receipt of a contribution that make clear the donor's implicit restriction on use, contributions are reported as revenues or gains without donor restrictions, which increase net assets without donor restrictions. All donor-restricted contributions are reported as either net assets subject to purpose restrictions or net assets not subject to appropriation or expenditure, depending on the nature of the restriction. When a restriction expires (that is, when a stipulated time restriction ends or purpose restriction is accomplished), such restricted net assets are reclassified to net assets without donor restrictions and reported in the statement of activities as net assets released from restrictions.

CUMBERLAND PRESBYTERIAN CHILDREN'S HOME

NOTES TO FINANCIAL STATEMENTS
DECEMBER 31, 2018

Unconditional promises to give are recorded as received. Contributions receivable due in the next year are recorded at their net realizable value. Contributions receivable due in subsequent years are recorded at the present value of their net realizable value, using interest rates applicable to the years in which the promises are received to discount the amounts. There were no unconditional promises to give at December 31, 2018.

Contributions of donated noncash assets are recorded at their fair values in the period received. Contributions of donated services that create or enhance nonfinancial assets or that require specialized skills, are provided by individuals possessing those skills, and would typically need to be purchased if not provided by donation, are recorded at their fair values in the period received. Although individuals volunteer their time and perform a variety of tasks that assist the Foundation, these services do not meet the criteria for recognition as donated services.

Income Taxes

CPCH is exempt from Federal income taxes under Section 501(c)(3) of the Internal Revenue Code. In addition, CPCH has been determined by the Internal Revenue Service not to be a private foundation within the meaning of Section 509(a)(1) and 170 (b)(1)(A)(vi) of the Code.

Fixed Assets

All acquisitions of property and equipment in excess of $5,000 and all expenditures for repairs, maintenance, or improvements that significantly prolong the useful lives of the assets are capitalized. Prior to 1/1/13 CPCH used an acquisition cost threshold of $1,000 but increased the threshold to $5,000 at that date in order to reduce the administrative costs of recording and tracking items of furniture and equipment. Purchases of property and equipment are recorded at cost. Donations of property and equipment are recorded as support at their estimated fair value at the date of gift. Such donations are reported as unrestricted support unless the donor has restricted the donated asset to a specific purpose. Assets donated with explicit restrictions regarding their use and contributions of cash that must be used to acquire property and equipment are reported as restricted support. Absent donor stipulations regarding how long those donated assets must be maintained, CPCH reports expirations of donor restrictions when the donated or acquired assets are placed in service as instructed by the donor. CPCH reclassifies temporarily restricted net assets to unrestricted net assets at that time. Property and equipment are depreciated using the straight-line method over the estimated useful life of assets.

The class lives of the more significant items within each property classification are as follows:

Vehicles	5 years
Equipment	5 to 10 years
Furniture and fixtures	5 to 10 years
Buildings	20 to 40 years

Investment Securities

Investments in marketable securities with readily determinable fair values and all investments in debt securities are valued at their fair values in the statement of financial position. Unrealized gains and losses are included in the change in net assets.

CUMBERLAND PRESBYTERIAN CHILDREN'S HOME

NOTES TO FINANCIAL STATEMENTS
DECEMBER 31, 2018

Estimates

The preparation of financial statements in conformity with generally accepted accounting principles requires management to make estimates and assumptions that affect the reported amounts of assets and liabilities at the date of the financial statements and the reported amounts of revenues and expenses during the reporting period. Accordingly, actual results could differ from those estimates.

Cash and Cash Equivalents

For purposes of the statement of cash flows, CPCH considers all highly liquid investments with a maturity of three months or less to be cash equivalents.

NOTE B – INVESTMENTS

Investments in equity securities with readily determinable fair values and all investments in debt securities are measured at fair value. All non cash contributions are recorded at fair value at the date of receipt. Stock is recorded at the average of the high and low selling price on the date received. Investments sold are recorded at amount received on the trade date.

Investment income and realized gains and losses are reported as increases in unrestricted net assets unless the donor placed restrictions on the income's use. The change in fair value between years along with realized gains or losses are reflected in the statement of activities in the year of the change.

Some investments are held and managed by the Board of Stewardship, Finance and Benefits of the Cumberland Presbyterian Church, while other investments are held in an investment brokerage account in the name of CPCH, and are managed by investment managers of the brokerage firm. No single investment exceeds five percent of CPCH's net assets.

NOTE C – ENDOWMENTS

CPCH's endowments consist of 88 individual donor-restricted funds established by individual donors for a variety of purposes. Net assets associated with endowments are classified and reported based on the existence or absence of donor-imposed restrictions.

A reconciliation of the beginning and ending balances of endowment funds is as follows:

Balance, 12/31/17	$ 4,826,647
Contributions	401
Earnings	18,942
Investment gains (losses)	(102,194)
Distributions	(262,687)
Balance, 12/31/18	$ 4,481,109

CUMBERLAND PRESBYTERIAN CHILDREN'S HOME

NOTES TO FINANCIAL STATEMENTS
DECEMBER 31, 2018

Funds with Deficiencies

From time to time, the fair value of assets associated with individual donor restricted endowment funds may fall below the level that the donor requires CPCH to retain as a fund of perpetual duration. CPCH did not have any net deficiencies of this nature as of December 31, 2018.

Return Objectives and Risk Parameters

CPCH has adopted investment and spending policies for endowment assets that attempt to provide a predictable stream of funding to programs supported by its endowment while seeking to maintain the purchasing power of the endowment assets. Under this policy, as approved by the board of trustees, the endowment assets are invested in equity securities, fixed-income securities and short-term reserves with asset allocation within defined acceptable ranges, while assuming a moderate level of investment risk. CPCH expects its endowment funds, over time, to provide an average rate of return sufficient to provide operating funds as needed. Actual returns in any given year may vary from this amount.

Strategies Employed for Achieving Objectives

To satisfy its long-term rate-of-return objectives, CPCH relies on a total return strategy in which investment returns are achieved through both capital appreciation (realized and unrealized) and current yield (interest and dividends). CPCH targets a diversified asset allocation that places a greater emphasis on equity-based investments to achieve its long-term return objectives within prudent risk constraints.

Spending Policy and How the Investment Objectives Relate to Spending Policy

CPCH has no written spending policy that commits it to annual distributions from any of the endowment's fund balances. CPCH normally appropriates for distribution each year sufficient earnings needed to fund its operating budget. Accordingly, over the long term, CPCH expects the current spending policy to allow its endowment to continue to grow. This is consistent with CPCH's objective to maintain the purchasing power of the endowment assets held in perpetuity or for a specified term as well as to provide additional real growth through new gifts and investment return.

NOTE D – FAIR VALUE OF FINANCIAL INSTRUMENTS

CPCH's financial instruments, none of which are held for trading purposes, include cash, securities and receivables. CPCH has estimated fair value of financial instruments in accordance with requirements of SFAS No. 157. The estimated fair value amounts have been determined by CPCH, using available market information and appropriate valuation methodologies. However, considerable judgment is necessarily required in interpreting market data to develop the estimates of fair value. Accordingly, the estimates presented herein are not necessarily indicative of the amounts that CPCH could realize in a current market exchange. The use of different market assumptions and estimation methodologies may have a material effect on the estimated fair value amounts. The carrying amount of cash and cash equivalents, and receivables approximated fair market value at December 31, 2018 because of their relatively short maturity and market terms. The fair value of long term investments at December 31, 2018 is determined based on quoted market values for U.S. government securities, fixed income securities and equity securities.

CUMBERLAND PRESBYTERIAN CHILDREN'S HOME

NOTES TO FINANCIAL STATEMENTS
DECEMBER 31, 2018

NOTE D – FAIR VALUE OF FINANCIAL INSTRUMENTS (CONT'D)

Financial instruments are considered Level 1 when their values are determined using quoted prices in active markets for identical assets that the reporting entity has the ability to access at the measurement date. Level 2 inputs are inputs other than quoted prices included within Level 1, such as quoted prices for similar assets in active or inactive markets, inputs other than quoted prices that are observable for the asset, or inputs that are derived principally from or corroborated by observable market data by correlation or other means.

Financial instruments are considered Level 3 when their values are determined using pricing models, discounted cash flow methodologies or similar techniques and at least one significant model assumption or input is unobservable. Level 3 financial instruments also include those for which the determination of fair value requires significant management judgment or estimation.

In accordance with these definitions, the following table represents CPCH's fair value hierarchy for its investments measured at fair value as of December 31, 2018:

	Quoted Prices for Active Markets for Identical Assets (Level 1)	Significant Other Observable Inputs (Level 2)	Total
Equity securities	$ 6,538,081	$ -	$ 6,538,081
Fixed income securities	-	1,619,053	1,619,053
Certificate of deposit	-	253,895	253,895
Total	$ 6,538,081	$ 1,872,948	$ 8,411,029

The estimated fair value of investments was determined by CPCH in accordance with its investment policy. Estimated fair value is determined by CPCH based on a number of factors, including: comparable publicly traded securities, the costs of investments to CPCH, as well as the current and projected operating performance. Changes in unrealized appreciation or depreciation of the investments are recognized as unrealized gains and losses in the statement of activities. Because of the inherent uncertainty of these valuations, the estimated values may differ from the actual fair values that may or may not be ultimately realized.

NOTE E - LAND, BUILDINGS AND EQUIPMENT

Land, buildings and equipment at December 31, 2018 consist of the following:

	Cost	Accumulated Depreciation	Book Value
Land	$ 23,477		$ 23,477
Buildings	5,870,217	$ 2,854,919	3,015,298
Campus infrastructure	583,513	307,690	275,823
Furniture & equipment	345,126	312,666	32,460
Vehicles	150,037	127,877	22,160
Total	$ 6,972,370	$ 3,603,152	$ 3,369,218

CUMBERLAND PRESBYTERIAN CHILDREN'S HOME

NOTES TO FINANCIAL STATEMENTS
DECEMBER 31, 2018

NOTE F – NET ASSETS SUBJECT TO PURPOSE, USE OR TIME RESTRICTIONS

Net assets subject to purpose, use or time restrictions are available for the following purposes or periods:

Lena Hart Educational Fund	$ 4,442
Humphrey Scholarship Endowment	1,375
Walker Trimble Scholarship Fund	2,859
David Long Memorial Fund	379
Sybil V. Cockerham College Fund	1,496
Eleanor Sargeant Endowment	806
For periods after December 31, 2018 - term endowment to be received in a future year – Naomi Locke Trust	20,291
Total	$ 31,648

NOTE G - OTHER LONG-TERM INVESTMENTS

	Total	Unrestricted	Purpose/Use Restrictions	Not Subject to Appropriation
Endowments held by the Board of Stewardship	$ 4,424,341	$ -	$ -	$ 4,424,341
Certificates of deposit – First United Bank	253,895	253,895	-	-
Mutual funds held by First National Bank – Virginia Ekiss Trust	360,057	-	-	360,057
Mutual funds held by Regions Bank – Laura Harpole Trust	92,466	-	-	92,466
Mutual funds held by Fairfield Natl. Bank - Naomi Locke Trust	20,291	-	20,291	-
Funds held at J P Morgan:				
Lena Hart Educational Fund	6,942	-	4,442	2,500
Humphrey Scholarship Endowment	4,856	-	1,375	3,481
Walker Trimble Scholarship Fund	11,139	-	2,859	8,280
David Long Memorial Fund	1,379	-	379	1,000
Sibyl V. Cockerham College Fund	3,496	-	1,496	2,000
Eleanor Sargeant Endowment	3,386	-	806	2,580
Operating Reserve	2,953,870	2,953,870	-	-
Funds held at Charles Schwab: Operating Reserve	2,151	2,151	-	-
4,000 shares Exxon-Mobil held by CPCH - Jessie DiCarlo Endowment	272,760	-	-	272,760
Total	$ 8,411,029	$ 3,209,916	$ 31,648	$ 5,169,465

CUMBERLAND PRESBYTERIAN CHILDREN'S HOME

NOTES TO FINANCIAL STATEMENTS
DECEMBER 31, 2018

NOTE H – NET ASSETS PERPETUAL IN NATURE

Net assets perpetual in nature are restricted as follows:

Investments in perpetuity, the income from which is expendable to support any activities of CPCH	$ 5,206,392
Total	$ 5,206,392

NOTE I – SUBSEQUENT EVENTS

Management evaluates subsequent events through the date of the report, which is the date the financial statements were available to be issued.

NOTE J – COMPONENTS OF INVESTMENT RETURN

Investment return for the year ended December 31, 2018, including interest and dividends on investments and interest earned on cash balances is summarized as follows:

Unrestricted investment return:	
Interest and dividend income:	
JP Morgan investments	$ 82,972
Exxon Mobil stock investment	12,920
Other	4,143
Unrealized gains (losses) on investments	(224,640)
Total unrestricted investment return (loss)	(124,605)
Restricted investment return:	
Interest income:	
Board of Stewardship investments	31,078
Other	212
Unrealized gains (losses) on investments	(188,983)
Total restricted investment return (loss)	(157,693)
Less investment management fees	(33,832)
Total Investment Return (Loss)	$ (316,130)

NOTE K – BANK LINE OF CREDIT

From time to time CPCH draws on a $250,000 line of credit established at First United Bank of Texas for working capital purposes. A total of $375,000 was borrowed on the line of credit during 2018, with $250,000 owed at the end of the year. Total interest paid during 2018 on the line of credit was $4,325.

CUMBERLAND PRESBYTERIAN CHILDREN'S HOME

NOTES TO FINANCIAL STATEMENTS
DECEMBER 31, 2018

NOTE L – LIQUIDITY AND AVAILABILITY OF FINANCIAL ASSETS

CPCH has $416,076 of financial assets at the statement of financial position date, consisting of cash in its operating bank accounts and investment accounts of $231,604 and receivables from the Board of Stewardship and from providing program services of $184,472. None of these financial assets are subject to donor restrictions, time restrictions or other contractual restrictions that make them unavailable for general expenditure within one year of the statement of financial position date.

Endowment funds consist of donor-restricted endowments. Income from donor-restricted endowments is restricted for specific purposes, with the exception of the amount available for general use. Donor-restricted endowment funds are not available for general expenditure.

The financial assets balance of $416,076 at 12/31/2018 represents approximately 60 days of normal operating expenses. As part of its liquidity management, the CPCH structures its financial assets to be available as its general expenses, liabilities and other obligations come due. Cash in excess of daily requirements is invested in certificates of deposit and various short-term and long-term investments, with most of the investments managed by JP Morgan.

NOTE M – FUNCTIONAL EXPENSES

The costs of program and supporting services activities have been summarized on a functional basis in the accompany statement of activities. The statement of functional expenses presents the natural classification detail of expenses by function. Accordingly, certain costs have been allocated among the program and supporting services benefited. Salaries and benefits are allocated based on estimates of time spent by personnel in each program or supporting activity. All other expenses are reported based on the program or supporting activity that benefits from the expense.

SUPPLEMENTAL SCHEDULE

CUMBERLAND PRESBYTERIAN CHILDREN'S HOME

SCHEDULE OF BOARD OF STEWARDSHIP ENDOWMENTS
DECEMBER 31, 2018

Donor-established Endowments:

	Balance
Merlyn & Joann Kitterman Alexander	$ 911
W.A. and Elizabeth Bearden Trust	10,366
Grace Johnson Beasley Memorial Endowment	24,135
Bethlehem CPC Memorial Endowment	3,945
Bridges Scholarship Fund	27,249
J.T. and Dorothy Britt Trust	7,299
Children's Home Endowment	210,547
Lavenia Campbell Cole Trust 20%	13,276
Lavenia Campbell Cole Annuity Endowment	53,916
Lavenia Cole Testamentary Trust 25%	438,284
Mrs. A.L. Colvin Memorial Fund	1,187
John W. and Eva Cox Trust Fund	20,207
Steve Curry Trust	354,707
Daniel Class, First Cumberland Presbyterian Church	20,868
Donnie Curry Davis Memorial	122,117
Mary Elberta Davis Memorial	13,030
Fred and Mattie Mae Dwiggins Memorial Trust	52,320
J.S. Eustis Memorial Trust Fund	8,260
Clester H. Evans, Sr., Trust	13,791
John M. Friedel Trust	14,265
Joyce C. Frisby Memorial Endowment	18,383
Vaughn and Mary Elizabeth Fults Trust	13,158
Garner-Miller Memorial Trust	8,261
James C. and Freda M. Gilbert Endowment	75,796
Henry and Jayne Glaspy Memorial Fund	5,385
Rev. W.J. Gregory Memorial	67,686
Glenn Griffin Endowment	28,855
Rev. and Mrs. Henry M. Guynn Memorial	2,998
Chad Harper Endowment	13,620
Newsome and Imogene Harvey Endowment	1,665
Clarence & Lula Herring Endowment	3,940
Kenneth and Clara Holsopple Trust	34,877
George and Lottie M. Hutchins Trust	741,752
Norma K. Johnson Memorial Library	7,444
P.F. Johnson Memorial Endowment	12,357
Robert and Genevie Johnson Endowment	3,621
Mr. and Mrs. Robert L. Johnson	7,786
Violet Louise Jolly Endowment	786
Eulava Joyce Memorial Trust	6,497
Ruth Cypert and Harlie Klugler Memorial Fund	13,083
Blanche R. Lake Endowment	9,429
Wade P. Lane/Maude Dorough Memorial Trust	6,206
Adolphus M. Latta Memorial Trust	33,487
Mr. and Mrs. Robert F. Little Endowment Fund	23,661
Charles E. and Addie Mae Lloyd Endowment Fund	14,750
Tony and Ann Martin Endowment	2,823
Mrs. Lucille (Lucy) Mast Endowment	2,869

CUMBERLAND PRESBYTERIAN CHILDREN'S HOME

SCHEDULE OF BOARD OF STEWARDSHIP ENDOWMENTS (CONT'D)
DECEMBER 31, 2018

Donor-established Endowments:

	Balance
W.B. and Azales McClurkan, Sr. Memorial	$ 12,611
Williams J. McCall Memorial Trust	6,497
McEwen Church Trust	4,992
McKinley and Barnett Families Endowment	556,937
J.C. McKinley Endowment	12,303
Velma McKinley Trust	12,303
Mary McKnight Memorial Trust	7,395
Kenneth and Mae Moore Endowment Fund	4,594
Operational Trust Fund	96,652
Bert and Pat Owen Endowment	1,022
Hamilton & Merion Parks Family Trust #3	12,416
Joe Parr Trust Fund	51,074
Martha Sue Parr Endowment	1,043
Mary M. Poole Endowment Fund	624,877
Jack and Mary Proctor Memorial Trust Fund	41,663
SQ&K Maurine Proctor Trust	3,690
Mary Acena Prewitt Trust Fund	58,899
Rev. and Mrs. Joe Reed Memorial	3,225
Marguerite D. Richards Endowment	16,594
Agnes Durbin Richardson Trust	19,683
Pat N. & Essie H. Roberts Memorial	38,419
Frances Benefield Roberts Trust Fund	1,522
Rev. and Mrs. John A. Russell Memorial	2,971
John Ann and Mary Shimer	9,780
Rev. W.B. and Lydia Snipes Memorial Trust	22,345
Don M. & Nancy Tabor Endowment Trust	22,483
Townsend Trust Fund	25,075
Hattie A. Wheeless Fund	12,899
Whitfield Family Endowment	7,865
Porter and Hattie S. Williamson Memorial Trust	111,879
Helen Wynn Endowment Fund	12,388
Maxie and Will Young Memorial Endowment	13,543
Dixie Campbell Zinn Memorial Trust	4,071
Dr. John P. Austin Endowment	18,786
Total	$ 4,424,341

**Memphis Theological Seminary
of the Cumberland Presbyterian Church
Financial Statements
July 31, 2018 and 2017**

MEMPHIS THEOLOGICAL SEMINARY OF THE CUMBERLAND PRESBYTERIAN CHURCH

Table of Contents — *July 31, 2018 and 2017*

	Page
Independent Auditor's Report	3

Financial Statements

Statements of Financial Position	5
Statement of Activities	6
Statement of Functional Expenses	7
Statements of Cash Flows	8
Notes to the Financial Statements	9

Supplementary Information

Schedule of Expenditures of Federal Awards	20

Non-Financial Section

Independent Auditor's Report on Internal Control over Financial Reporting and on Compliance and Other Matters Based on an Audit of Financial Statements Performed in Accordance with *Government Auditing Standards*	22
Independent Auditor's Report on Compliance for a Major Program and on Internal Control over Compliance Required by the Uniform Guidance	24
Schedule of Findings and Questioned Costs	26
Summary Schedule of Prior Audit Findings	27

CANNON WRIGHT BLOUNT

INDEPENDENT AUDITOR'S REPORT

To the Board of Trustees
Memphis Theological Seminary of the Cumberland Presbyterian Church
Memphis, Tennessee

Report on the Financial Statements

We have audited the accompanying financial statements of Memphis Theological Seminary of the Cumberland Presbyterian Church (a nonprofit organization), which comprise the statement of financial position as of July 31, 2018, and the related statements of activities, functional expenses, and cash flows for the year then ended, and the related notes to the financial statements.

Management's Responsibility for the Financial Statements

Management is responsible for the preparation and fair presentation of these financial statements in accordance with accounting principles generally accepted in the United States of America; this includes the design, implementation, and maintenance of internal control relevant to the preparation and fair presentation of financial statements that are free from material misstatement, whether due to fraud or error.

Auditor's Responsibility

Our responsibility is to express an opinion on these financial statements based on our audit. We conducted our audit in accordance with auditing standards generally accepted in the United States of America and the standards applicable to financial audits contained in *Government Auditing Standards*, issued by the Comptroller General of the United States. Those standards require that we plan and perform the audit to obtain reasonable assurance about whether the financial statements are free from material misstatement.

An audit involves performing procedures to obtain audit evidence about the amounts and disclosures in the financial statements. The procedures selected depend on the auditor's judgment, including the assessment of the risks of material misstatement of the financial statements, whether due to fraud or error. In making those risk assessments, the auditor considers internal control relevant to the entity's preparation and fair presentation of the financial statements in order to design audit procedures that are appropriate in the circumstances, but not for the purpose of expressing an opinion on the effectiveness of the entity's internal control. Accordingly, we express no such opinion. An audit also includes evaluating the appropriateness of accounting policies used and the reasonableness of significant accounting estimates made by management, as well as evaluating the overall presentation of the financial statements.

We believe that the audit evidence we have obtained is sufficient and appropriate to provide a basis for our audit opinion.

Opinion

In our opinion, the financial statements referred to above present fairly, in all material respects, the financial position of Memphis Theological Seminary of the Cumberland Presbyterian Church as of July 31, 2018, and the changes in its net assets and its cash flows for the year then ended in accordance with accounting principles generally accepted in the United States of America.

CANNON WRIGHT BLOUNT PLLC   756 RIDGE LAKE BLVD   MEMPHIS TN 38120

PHONE 901.685.7500   FAX 901.685.7569   WWW.CANNONWRIGHTBLOUNT.COM

Other Matters

Other Information

Our audit was conducted for the purpose of forming an opinion on the financial statements as a whole. The accompanying schedule of expenditures of federal awards, as required by Title 2 U.S. *Code of Federal Regulations* (CFR) Part 200, *Uniform Administrative Requirements, Cost Principles*, and *Audit Requirements for Federal Awards*, is presented for purposes of additional analysis and is not a required part of the financial statements. Such information is the responsibility of management and was derived from and relates directly to the underlying accounting and other records used to prepare the financial statements. The information has been subjected to the auditing procedures applied in the audit of the financial statements and certain additional procedures, including comparing and reconciling such information directly to the underlying accounting and other records used to prepare the financial statements or to the financial statements themselves, and other additional procedures in accordance with auditing standards generally accepted in the United States of America. In our opinion, the information is fairly stated, in all material respects, in relation to the financial statements as a whole.

Other Reporting Required by *Government Auditing Standards*

In accordance with *Government Auditing Standards*, we have also issued our report dated November 13, 2018, on our consideration of Memphis Theological Seminary of the Cumberland Presbyterian Church's internal control over financial reporting and on our tests of its compliance with certain provisions of laws, regulations, contracts, and grant agreements and other matters. The purpose of that report is solely to describe the scope of our testing of internal control over financial reporting and compliance and the results of that testing, and not to provide an opinion on the effectiveness of Memphis Theological Seminary of the Cumberland Presbyterian Church's internal control over financial reporting or on compliance. That report is an integral part of an audit performed in accordance with *Government Auditing Standards* in considering Memphis Theological Seminary of the Cumberland Presbyterian Church's internal control over financial reporting and compliance.

Report on Summarized Comparative Information

We have previously audited Memphis Theological Seminary of the Cumberland Presbyterian Church's 2017 financial statements, and we expressed an unmodified audit opinion on those audited financial statements in our report dated November 8, 2017. In our opinion, the summarized comparative information presented herein as of and for the year ended July 31, 2017, is consistent, in all material respects, with the audited financial statements from which it has been derived.

Memphis, Tennessee
November 13, 2018

MEMPHIS THEOLOGICAL SEMINARY OF THE CUMBERLAND PRESBYTERIAN CHURCH

Statements of Financial Position *July 31, 2018 and 2017*

ASSETS

	2018	2017
Cash and cash equivalents	$ 2,980,258	$ 2,442,549
Investments, at fair value	11,632,087	11,202,716
Tuition and fees receivable, net of allowance of $108,554 in 2018 and $89,146 in 2017	25,649	50,000
Pledges receivable, net of discounts on pledges and allowance	95,962	460,261
Other receivables	301,391	159,164
Capital assets, net of accumulated depreciation	3,601,972	3,124,753
Cash value of life insurance	27,703	31,970
Land held for sale	27,448	27,448
Other assets	73,017	38,763
Total assets	$ 18,765,487	$ 17,537,624

LIABILITIES AND NET ASSETS

	2018	2017
Liabilities		
Accounts payable and accrued expenses	$ 316,269	$ 375,061
Line of credit	950,000	910,000
Note payable	2,543,779	1,588,012
Total liabilities	3,810,048	2,873,073
Net Assets		
Unrestricted		
Board designated	81,118	125,290
Other unrestricted	2,390,308	2,378,689
Temporarily restricted	5,521,437	5,413,312
Permanently restricted	6,962,576	6,747,260
Total net assets	14,955,439	14,664,551
Total liabilities and net assets	$ 18,765,487	$ 17,537,624

See independent auditor's report and notes to the financial statements

MEMPHIS THEOLOGICAL SEMINARY OF THE CUMBERLAND PRESBYTERIAN CHURCH

Statement of Activities

For the Year Ended July 31, 2018
(with summarized comparative totals for the year ended July 31, 2017)

	Unrestricted	Temporarily Restricted	Permanently Restricted	2018 Total	2017 Total
Operating Revenues and Support					
Tuition and fees, net of scholarships of $380,284 and $420,331	$ 1,610,703	$ -	$ -	$ 1,610,703	$ 1,718,815
Contributions and grants	820,511	1,126,829	168,507	2,115,847	3,006,514
Other revenue and support	91,162	-	-	91,162	150,818
Net assets released from restrictions	1,441,551	(1,441,551)	-	-	-
Total operating revenues and support	3,963,927	(314,722)	168,507	3,817,712	4,876,147
Expenses					
Educational program services					
Instruction	1,674,356	-	-	1,674,356	1,900,920
Library	297,394	-	-	297,394	361,995
Student services	266,337	-	-	266,337	290,504
Financial leadership for ministry	102,688	-	-	102,688	65,576
Program for alternative studies	131,022	-	-	131,022	105,404
Academic support	123,100	-	-	123,100	122,457
Supporting services					
Institutional support	1,159,343	-	-	1,159,343	1,064,921
Development and fundraising	719,809	-	-	719,809	554,817
Total expenses	4,474,049	-	-	4,474,049	4,466,594
Increase (decrease) in net assets from operations	(510,122)	(314,722)	168,507	(656,337)	409,553
Non-operating revenues and expenses					
Investment income	527,078	419,866	281	947,225	1,270,806
Change in net assets	16,956	105,144	168,788	290,888	1,680,359
Net assets, beginning of year	2,503,979	5,413,312	6,747,260	14,664,551	12,984,192
Reclassifications of net assets	(49,509)	2,981	46,528	-	-
Net assets, beginning of year - as restated	2,454,470	5,416,293	6,793,788	14,664,551	12,984,192
Net assets - end of year	$ 2,471,426	$ 5,521,437	$ 6,962,576	$ 14,955,439	$ 14,664,551

See independent auditor's report and notes to the financial statements

MEMPHIS THEOLOGICAL SEMINARY OF THE CUMBERLAND PRESBYTERIAN CHURCH

Statement of Functional Expenses

For the Year Ended July 31, 2018
(with summarized comparative totals for the year ended July 31, 2017)

		Educational Program Services				Supporting Services			2018	2017
	Instruction	Library	Student Services	Financial Leadership for Ministry	Program for Alternative Studies	Academic Support	Facilities Operations	Security Services	Institutional Support	Development and Fund Raising	Total	Total
Salaries and Wages	$ 1,063,069	$ 87,850	$ 187,048	$ 72,309	$ 71,818	$ 90,446	$ -	$ -	$ 431,706	$ 221,563	$ 2,372,060	$ 2,603,386
Benefits	173,592	14,958	16,217	1,360	13,525	22,591	-	-	88,775	53,314	427,032	483,607
Professional Development	18,074	200	89	250	-	560	1,877	-	563	-	21,613	24,563
Travel/Auto Expense	22,968	2,042	1,526	3,229	8,488	1,505	1,141	-	5,785	3,159	49,843	39,589
Office Supplies and Expense	13,634	56,014	8,521	4,612	1,805	2,591	3,668	-	41,554	58,297	190,696	207,396
Consultants / Professional	3,433	-	1,668	-	-	-	-	59,896	181,350	2,654	248,810	148,233
Special Events	23,622	-	2,121	2,435	28,474	-	(191)	-	32,449	47,464	136,565	200,125
Student / Covenant Groups	29,628	-	-	-	-	-	-	-	-	-	29,628	33,875
Repairs and Maintenance	165	416	-	-	-	-	74,644	-	2,486	-	77,711	114,628
Utilities	-	-	-	-	-	-	66,875	-	-	-	66,875	71,137
Insurance Expense	-	-	-	-	-	-	96,969	-	-	452	97,421	103,138
Property Taxes	-	-	-	-	-	-	19,565	-	-	-	19,565	20,395
Other Expense	22,240	751	6,606	8,507	1,090	-	(14,364)	-	80,767	24,069	129,666	153,573
Interest Expense	-	-	-	-	-	-	119,024	-	-	-	119,024	76,657
Capital Campaign Expense	-	-	-	-	-	-	-	-	-	299,480	299,480	35,440
Depreciation	-	-	-	-	-	-	188,060	-	-	-	188,060	150,852
Allocation of Facilities Operations & Security	303,931	135,163	44,209	8,318	5,822	5,407	(746,219)	(59,896)	293,908	9,357	-	-
	$ 1,674,356	$ 297,394	$ 266,337	$ 102,688	$ 131,022	$ 123,100	$ -	$ -	$ 1,159,343	$ 719,809	$ 4,474,049	$ 4,466,594

See independent auditor's report and notes to the financial statements

MEMPHIS THEOLOGICAL SEMINARY OF THE CUMBERLAND PRESBYTERIAN CHURCH

Statements of Cash Flows — *For the Years Ended July 31, 2018 and 2017*

	2018	2017
Cash Flows from Operating Activities		
Change in net assets	$ 290,888	$ 1,680,359
Adjustments to reconcile change in net assets to net cash provided by (used in) operating activities:		
Depreciation	188,060	150,852
Capital gains on investments	(823,220)	(1,155,210)
Bad debt expense	17,749	18,000
Discount on pledges	(17,825)	(20,129)
Changes in operating assets and liabilities:		
Tuition, fees and other receivables	(135,625)	140,717
Pledges receivable	382,124	275,046
Other assets	(34,254)	4,674
Accounts payable and accrued expenses	(58,792)	71,702
Net cash provided by (used for) operating activities	(190,895)	1,166,011
Cash Flows from Investing Activities		
Purchases of investments	(175,837)	(472,585)
Reinvestments of investment earnings	(50,410)	(69,070)
Sale of investments	620,096	766,706
(Increase) decrease in cash surrender value of life insurance	4,267	4,722
Purchases of property and equipment	(665,279)	(121,681)
Net cash flows provided by (used for) investing activities	(267,163)	108,092
Cash Flows from Financing Activities		
Increase (decrease) in line of credit	40,000	810,000
Proceeds from issuance of note payable	2,600,250	-
Principal payments on notes payable	(1,644,483)	(59,321)
Net cash flows provided by financing activities	995,767	750,679
Net increase in cash and cash equivalents	537,709	2,024,782
Cash and cash equivalents, beginning of year	2,442,549	417,767
Cash and cash equivalents, end of year	$ 2,980,258	$ 2,442,549
Supplemental Disclosure:		
Interest paid during the year	$ 116,967	$ 76,095

See independent auditor's report and notes to the consolidated financial statements

MEMPHIS THEOLOGICAL SEMINARY OF THE CUMBERLAND PRESBYTERIAN CHURCH
Notes to the Financial Statements *July 31, 2018 and 2017*

Note 1 – Organization and Purpose

The Memphis Theological Seminary of the Cumberland Presbyterian Church (the "Seminary") is an ecumenical Protestant seminary serving the Mid-South region from its campus in Memphis, Tennessee. Memphis Theological Seminary of the Cumberland Presbyterian Church provides postgraduate theological education to clergy and church leaders of the parent denomination and qualified students from other denominations. Memphis Theological Seminary of the Cumberland Presbyterian Church is governed by a Board of Trustees elected by the General Assembly of the Cumberland Presbyterian Church.

Note 2 – Significant Accounting Policies

Financial Statement Presentation

Memphis Theological Seminary of the Cumberland Presbyterian Church prepares its financial statements in accordance with accounting principles generally accepted in the United States of America, which involves the application of accrual accounting. Under generally accepted accounting principles, Memphis Theological Seminary of the Cumberland Presbyterian Church reports information regarding its financial position and activities according to three classes of net assets as follows:

> Unrestricted Net Assets — Net assets that are not subject to donor-imposed stipulations. Unrestricted net assets may be designated for specific purposes by action of the Board of Trustees or may otherwise be limited by contractual agreements with outside parties.
>
> Temporarily Restricted Net Assets — Net assets whose use by the Seminary is subject to donor-imposed stipulations that can be fulfilled by actions of the Seminary pursuant to those stipulations or that expire by the passage of time.
>
> Permanently Restricted Net Assets — Net assets subject to donor-imposed stipulations that they be maintained permanently by the Seminary. Generally, the donors of these assets permit the Seminary to use all or part of the investment return on these assets.

Contributions

Contributions received by Memphis Theological Seminary of the Cumberland Presbyterian Church are recorded as unrestricted, temporarily restricted, or permanently restricted support depending on the existence and/or nature of any donor restrictions. Temporarily restricted net assets are reclassified to unrestricted net assets upon satisfaction of the time or purpose restrictions.

Investment Valuation and Income Recognition

Investments are reported at fair value. Fair value is the price that would be received to sell an asset or paid to transfer a liability in an orderly transaction between market participants at the measurement date. See Notes 3 and 4 for discussion and computation of fair value.

Unrealized holding gains and losses are included in current year revenue and support as a component of investment income. Realized gains and losses are computed using the specific identification method.

Capital Assets

All acquisitions of property and equipment and expenditures for repairs and maintenance that prolong the useful lives of assets in excess of $1,000 are capitalized at cost. Expenditures for normal repair and maintenance are expensed to operations as they occur. Depreciation is provided through the straight-line method over the assets' estimated useful lives which range from three to ten years for equipment, fifteen years for library books and twenty-five to forty years for buildings.

Cash Equivalents

Cash equivalents are defined as short term, highly liquid investments that are both readily convertible to known amounts of cash and are so near maturity that they present insignificant risk of changes in value because of changes in interest rates.

MEMPHIS THEOLOGICAL SEMINARY OF THE CUMBERLAND PRESBYTERIAN CHURCH
Notes to the Financial Statements *July 31, 2018 and 2017*

Note 2 – Significant Accounting Policies (continued)

Use of Estimates in the Preparation of Financial Statements

The preparation of financial statements in conformity with generally accepted accounting principles requires management to make estimates and assumptions that affect the amounts reported in the financial statements and accompanying notes. Actual results could differ from those estimates.

Income Taxes

Memphis Theological Seminary of the Cumberland Presbyterian Church is a not-for-profit organization that is exempt from income taxes under Internal Revenue Code Section 501(c)(3) and is also exempt from state income taxes. The Seminary is generally no longer subject to federal and state audit for tax years prior to the year ended July 31, 2015.

Donated Property, Equipment and Services

Donations of property and use of property are recorded as support at their estimated fair value at the date of donation. Such donations are reported as unrestricted support unless the donor has restricted the donated asset to a specific purpose. No property was donated in 2018 or 2017.

Donated services are recognized as contributions if the services (a) create or enhance non-financial assets or (b) require specialized skills, are performed by people with those skills, and would otherwise be purchased by the Organization. There were no contributed services recorded in 2018 or 2017.

Functional Allocation of Expenses

The cost of providing the various educational programs and supporting services has been summarized on a functional basis in the statement of functional expenses. Accordingly, certain costs have been allocated among the programs and services benefited.

Subsequent Events

Memphis Theological Seminary of the Cumberland Presbyterian Church evaluated all events or transactions that occurred through November 13, 2018, the date Memphis Theological Seminary of the Cumberland Presbyterian Church approved these financial statements for issuance.

Note 3 – Fair Value Measurement

FASB ASC Subtopic 820-10 *Fair Value Measurements,*(formerly SFAS No. 157), defines fair value as the exchange price that would be received for an asset or paid to transfer a liability in the principal or most advantageous market for the asset or liability in an orderly transaction between market participants at the measurement date. SFAS No. 157 established a three-level fair value hierarchy that prioritizes the inputs used to measure fair value. This hierarchy requires entities to maximize the use of observable inputs and minimize the use of unobservable inputs.

The three levels of inputs used to measure fair value are as follows:

- Level 1 – Quoted prices in active markets for identical assets or liabilities.
- Level 2 – Observable inputs other than quoted prices included in Level 1, such as quoted prices for similar assets and liabilities in active markets; quoted prices for identical or similar assets or liabilities in markets that are not active; or inputs that are observable or can be corroborated by observable market data.
- Level 3 – Unobservable inputs that are supported by little or no market activity and that are significant to the fair value of the assets or liabilities. This includes certain pricing models, discounted cash flow methodologies and similar techniques that use significant unobservable inputs.

MEMPHIS THEOLOGICAL SEMINARY OF THE CUMBERLAND PRESBYTERIAN CHURCH

Notes to the Financial Statements *July 31, 2018 and 2017*

Note 3 – Fair Value Measurement (continued)

The estimated fair value of Memphis Theological Seminary of the Cumberland Presbyterian Church's financial instruments has been determined by management using available market information. However, considerable judgment is required in interpreting market data to develop the estimates of fair value. Accordingly, the fair values are not necessarily indicative of the amounts that Memphis Theological Seminary of the Cumberland Presbyterian Church could realize in a current market exchange. The use of different market assumptions may have a material effect on the estimated fair value amounts.

The carrying amounts of cash and cash equivalents, net receivables, cash value of life insurance, payables, accrued liabilities, and debt are a reasonable estimate of their fair value, due to their short term nature, method of computation and interest rates for current debt.

All financial assets that are measured at fair value on a recurring basis (at least annually) have been segregated into the most appropriate level within the fair value hierarchy based on the inputs used to determine the fair value at the measurement date.

The following table sets forth by level, within the fair value hierarchy, the Seminary's financial instruments at fair value as of July 31, 2018:

	Total	Level 1	Level 2	Level 3
Investment securities				
Cash/cash equivalents	$ 318,889	$ 318,889	$ -	$ -
Money market funds	2,269	2,269	-	-
Bonds and bond funds	6,202	6,202	-	-
Common and preferred stocks	181,601	181,601	-	-
Real estate investment funds	843,339	-	843,339	-
Mutual funds	302,039	302,039	-	-
Private investment entities	9,977,748	-	-	9,977,748
Total investments	$ 11,632,087	$ 811,000	$ 843,339	$ 9,977,748
Land held for sale	$ 27,448	$ -	$ -	$ 27,448

MEMPHIS THEOLOGICAL SEMINARY OF THE CUMBERLAND PRESBYTERIAN C

Notes to the Financial Statements — July 31, 2018

Note 3 – Fair Value Measurement (continued)

The following table sets forth by level, within the fair value hierarchy, the Seminary's financial instrume value as of July 31, 2017:

	Total	Level 1	Level 2	Leve
Investment securities				
Cash/cash equivalents	$ 110,737	$ 110,737	$ -	$
Money market funds	3,262	3,262	-	
Bonds and bond funds	22,698	22,698	-	
Common and preferred stocks	146,615	146,615	-	
Real estate investment funds	841,094	-	841,094	
Mutual funds	601,257	601,257	-	
Private investment entities	9,477,053	-	-	9,47
Total investments	$ 11,202,716	$ 884,569	$ 841,094	$ 9,47
Land held for sale	$ 27,448	$ -	$ -	$ 2

The private investment entities are investments entered into by the Board of Stewardship to achieve gr of return. They include funds whose inputs used to determine fair value are considered unobservab therefore Level 3 inputs.

The carrying value of the above land held for sale is based on expected recoverability at the tim Memphis Theological Seminary of the Cumberland Presbyterian Church uses appraised values information available to determine the carrying value. The inputs used to determine fair value are c unobservable and are therefore Level 3 inputs.

Transactions in Level 3 assets for the years ended July 31, 2018 and 2017, were as follows:

	2018	2017
Private investment entities		
Beginning balance	$ 9,477,053	$ 8,436,846
Change in allocation of investments	(383,013)	896,525
Reinvestments	448,090	94,174
Realized/unrealized gains (losses)	435,618	49,508
Ending balance	$ 9,977,748	$ 9,477,053
Land held for sale		
Beginning balance	$ 27,448	$ 27,448
Ending balance	$ 27,448	$ 27,448

MEMPHIS THEOLOGICAL SEMINARY OF THE CUMBERLAND PRESBYTERIAN CHURCH

Notes to the Financial Statements *July 31, 2018 and 2017*

Note 3 – Fair Value Measurement (continued)

Investment income was as follows for the years ended July 31, 2018 and 2017:

	2018	2017
Investment income	$ 124,005	$ 115,596
Realized investment gains	39,212	51,964
Unrealized investment gains	784,008	1,103,246
Net investment income	$ 947,225	$ 1,270,806

Note 4 – Endowments

Nearly all of Memphis Theological Seminary of the Cumberland Presbyterian Church's investments, which contain endowments, are managed by the Board of Stewardship, Foundation and Benefits of the Cumberland Presbyterian Church, Inc., and maintained in pooled investment accounts with other funds. The investments generally originate from gifts and contributions for which separate identifiable investment accounts are created that indicate the source of the funds and/or the purpose for which the funds are to be used. Many of these accounts are designated for monthly distributions to Memphis Theological Seminary of the Cumberland Presbyterian Church based on one-twelfth of 5% of the rolling average value. The Board of Stewardship, Foundation and Benefits, issues an aggregate amount to Memphis Theological Seminary of the Cumberland Presbyterian Church and charges the applicable accounts for their proportionate share. In addition, Memphis Theological Seminary of the Cumberland Presbyterian Church can request on an as needed basis, additional distributions that will be used for the purpose for which the account was created.

The Seminary has interpreted the Uniform Prudent Management of Institutional Funds Act ("UPMIFA") requiring a portion of a donor restricted endowment of perpetual duration be classified as permanently restricted assets. The amount of the endowment that must be retained permanently is in accordance with explicit donor stipulations as outlined in their respective endowment agreements. The Seminary has other endowment funds that are temporarily restricted by the donor as to purpose and are classified as temporarily restricted until they are expended on their respective purposes. Investment income and net appreciation on these permanently and temporarily restricted endowments is classified as temporarily restricted or permanently restricted if so directed by the donor in the respective endowment agreements or as unrestricted in the absence of donor instructions. The Seminary has other donated funds and board designated funds that are included in investments and are not restricted as to use. These funds, as well as investment income and net appreciation on these funds are classified as unrestricted. Expenditures (withdrawals) of the temporarily restricted and unrestricted funds are approved by management. The funds held by the Board of Stewardship, Foundation and Benefits of the Cumberland Presbyterian Church, Inc. are invested with the primary objective of providing a balance between capital appreciation, preservation of capital, and current income. This is a long-term goal designed to maximize returns without undue risk. The Board of Stewardship selects the investment portfolio where the endowments will be invested as described in the Investment Policy of The Cumberland Presbyterian Church Center, which outlines the asset allocations, permissible investments, and objectives of the portfolios.

MEMPHIS THEOLOGICAL SEMINARY OF THE CUMBERLAND PRESBYTERIAN CHURCH

Notes to the Financial Statements — July 31, 2018 and 2017

Note 4 – Endowments (continued)

Changes in endowment net assets for the years ended July 31, 2018 and 2017, were as follows:

	Unrestricted Board Designated	Unrestricted Other	Temporarily Restricted	Permanently Restricted	Total
Balance at July 31, 2016	$ 78,574	$ 1,696,067	$ 1,951,220	$ 6,546,696	$ 10,272,557
Investment return:					
Investment income	998	35,175	32,897	-	69,070
Change in market value	16,338	597,645	541,228	-	1,155,211
Total investment return	17,336	632,820	574,125	-	1,224,281
Contributions	100,000	104,006	-	268,579	472,585
Appropriation of endowment assets for expenditure	144,592	442,937	179,178	-	766,707
Reclassifications	73,972	(5,957)	-	(68,015)	-
Balance at July 31, 2017	125,290	1,983,999	2,346,167	6,747,260	11,202,716
Investment return:					
Investment income	419	25,188	24,803	-	50,410
Change in market value	6,740	421,136	395,063	281	823,220
Total investment return	7,159	446,324	419,866	281	873,630
Contributions	-	7,330	-	168,507	175,837
Appropriation of endowment assets for expenditure	8,707	375,219	236,170	-	620,096
Reclassifications	(42,624)	(6,885)	2,981	46,528	-
Balance at July 31, 2018	$ 81,118	$ 2,055,549	$ 2,532,844	$ 6,962,576	$ 11,632,087

Note 5 – Capital Assets

Capital assets are as follows at July 31, 2018 and 2017:

	2018	2017
Building and improvements	$ 4,014,225	$ 4,379,338
Furniture and equipment	924,566	903,709
Library books	1,907,852	1,885,318
Vehicles	19,099	44,014
	6,865,742	7,212,379
Less accumulated depreciation	4,619,744	4,747,257
	2,245,998	2,465,122
Land	712,508	208,650
Construction in progress	643,466	450,981
Capital assets, net	$ 3,601,972	$ 3,124,753

Depreciation expense for the years ended July 31, 2018 and 2017, was $188,060 and $150,852, respectively.

MEMPHIS THEOLOGICAL SEMINARY OF THE CUMBERLAND PRESBYTERIAN CHURCH

Notes to the Financial Statements *July 31, 2018 and 2017*

Note 6 – Concentration of Credit Risk

Memphis Theological Seminary of the Cumberland Presbyterian Church has cash equivalents invested by the Board of Stewardship, Foundation and Benefits. At July 31, 2018, these funds total $2,597,460 and are not insured by the Federal Deposit Insurance Corporation (FDIC).

In addition, Memphis Theological Seminary of the Cumberland Presbyterian Church maintains cash balances in accounts at a well-established financial institution located in Memphis, Tennessee. These balances are insured by the Federal Deposit Insurance Corporation up to certain limits. At July 31, 2018, Memphis Theological Seminary of the Cumberland Presbyterian Church had no uninsured balances.

Memphis Theological Seminary of the Cumberland Presbyterian Church's tuition and fees receivable are from students for which the majority receive some form of financial assistance. Management maintains an allowance for uncollectible based on periodic reviews of each individual student's account.

Note 7 - Pledges Receivable

Pledges receivable primarily represent pledges from numerous donors for a capital/comprehensive campaign totaling $297,472 and $379,596 at July 31, 2018 and 2017, respectively. Pledges receivable also include a pledge to offset the cost of a faculty member totaling $50,000 and $100,000 as of July 31, 2018 and 2017, respectively. These amounts have been discounted to present value using a rate of 3.07%. Management considered all pledges receivable at July 31, 2017, to be fully collectible; however, as of July 31, 2018, management has made an allowance for uncollectible amounts for the capital/comprehensive campaign.

The pledges, net of the discount, are due to be received as follows:

	2018	2017
Less than one year	$ 347,472	$ 308,396
One year to five years	-	171,200
Gross contributions receivable	347,472	479,596
Less: discount to present value	(1,510)	(19,335)
Less: allowance for doubtful pledges	(250,000)	-
Contributions receivable, net	$ 97,472	$ 460,261

Note 8 – Line of Credit

Memphis Theological Seminary of the Cumberland Presbyterian Church has a $1,000,000 unsecured revolving line of credit agreement with a local bank that matures December 2019. Borrowings outstanding under the agreement ($950,000 at July 31, 2018 and $910,000 at July 31, 2017) bear interest at the bank's prime rate (5.00 percent at July 31, 2018). The line is guaranteed by the Board of the Stewardship, Foundation and Benefits of the Cumberland Presbyterian Church.

MEMPHIS THEOLOGICAL SEMINARY OF THE CUMBERLAND PRESBYTERIAN CHURCH
Notes to the Financial Statements *July 31, 2018 and 2017*

Note 9 – Note Payable

Notes payable consist of the following at July 31, 2018 and 2017:

	2018	2017
Note payable, due in monthly installments of $15,777 bearing interest at 4.00% through October 2027 and a single balloon payment of the remaining unpaid balance in November 2027	$ 2,543,779	$ -
Note payable, due in monthly installments of $10,052 bearing interest at 3.85% through November 2025 and a single balloon payment of the remaining unpaid balance in December 2025	-	1,588,012
	$ 2,543,779	$ 1,588,012

The note payable is secured by property owned by the Seminary and located at 168 East Parkway South, Memphis, Tennessee.

Scheduled principal payments required for the years ending July 31 are as follows:

	Amount
2019	$ 89,118
2020	92,748
2021	96,527
2022	100,460
2023	104,553
Thereafter	2,060,373
Total notes payable	$ 2,543,779

Note 10 – Retirement Plan

Memphis Theological Seminary of the Cumberland Presbyterian Church sponsors a qualified defined contribution retirement plan for eligible employees as defined by the plan under IRC Section 403(b). Employees are eligible to participate in the plan immediately upon hire and contributions to the plan are vested immediately. Each participant in the plan may make voluntary contributions to the plan of up to the lesser of twenty percent (20%) of annual compensation received by the participant during the plan year, or the maximum allowed by law. Memphis Theological Seminary of the Cumberland Presbyterian Church matches participant's contributions to a maximum of 3.5%. Contributions to the plan by Memphis Theological Seminary of the Cumberland Presbyterian Church for the years ended July 31, 2018 and 2017, were $58,458 and $61,162, respectively.

MEMPHIS THEOLOGICAL SEMINARY OF THE CUMBERLAND PRESBYTERIAN CHURCH
Notes to the Financial Statements *July 31, 2018 and 2017*

Note 11 – Related Party Transactions

Memphis Theological Seminary of the Cumberland Presbyterian Church and the Board of Stewardship are separate corporations but both are affiliated with the Cumberland Presbyterian Church in that the governing board of the Church elects the members of the Board of Trustees of Memphis Theological Seminary of the Cumberland Presbyterian Church and the Board of Stewardship. There are no common board members between Memphis Theological Seminary of the Cumberland Presbyterian Church and the Board of Stewardship. Amounts due to and from the Board of Stewardship as of July 31, 2018 and 2017, are as follows:

	2018	2017
Seminary assets held by the Board of Stewardship:		
Seminary cash held	$ 2,597,460	$ 2,274,236
Seminary investments held	$ 11,442,105	$ 11,100,096
Other Receivables	$ 300,000	$ 148,612

Note 12 – Temporarily Restricted Net Assets

Temporarily restricted net assets consist of the following at July 31, 2018 and 2017:

	2018	2017
Endowment restrictions	$ 2,532,844	$ 2,346,167
Capital campaign restriction	109,648	839,276
Comprehensive campaign restriction	1,791,997	1,983,482
Faculty salary restriction	48,490	96,116
Financial Leadership/Thriving in Ministry	34,869	143,271
Center for Pastoral Formation	982,539	-
Other restrictions	21,050	5,000
	$ 5,521,437	$ 5,413,312

Note 13 – Concentration of Revenue

In the year ended July 31, 2018, approximately 26% of total operating revenues and support was received from one grantor. In the year ended July 31, 2017, approximately 32% of total operating revenues and support was received from one individual.

Note 14 – Future Operations

Memphis Theological Seminary of the Cumberland Presbyterian Church has sustained losses from operations in unrestricted funds in four of the last five fiscal years. Over this same period, tuition revenue has decreased due to declining student enrollment. Contributions over that period have fluctuated, but a significant portion of contributions have been restricted by the donors as to use other than for operations. Unrestricted contributions for the year ended July 31, 2018, increased from the prior year and management has reduced expenses for salaries and various other expenses. Therefore, the Seminary has experienced improvements in the results of operations for the year ended July 31, 2018; however, continued losses could still increase the use of unrestricted endowment funds and cause significant cash shortages. Management is committed to taking continued steps to increase enrollment, seek additional contributions, and bring expenses in line with revenues.

MEMPHIS THEOLOGICAL SEMINARY OF THE CUMBERLAND PRESBYTERIAN CHURCH

Notes to the Financial Statements *July 31, 2018 and 2017*

Note 15 – Commitment

In March 2017, Memphis Theological Seminary of the Cumberland Presbyterian Church entered into an agreement with an architectural firm to construct a building at a cost of $2,750,000. As of July 31, 2018, construction of the building had not begun. The construction cost is expected to be completely funded through contributions designated for the purpose of the project.

Note 16 – Reclassifications of Net Assets

During the fiscal year ended July 31, 2018, management determined that in the prior year, two of the Seminary's endowment funds had been classified incorrectly as unrestricted, temporarily restricted, or permanently restricted. These determinations were made on the basis of a review of the endowment documents. Reclassifications were made to correct the net asset presentation of these funds.

Supplementary Information

MEMPHIS THEOLOGICAL SEMINARY OF THE CUMBERLAND PRESBYTERIAN CHURCH

Schedule of Expenditures of Federal Awards *For the Year Ended July 31, 2018*

Federal Grantor/ Pass-Through Grantor/ Program or Cluster Title	CFDA Number	Total Expended
U.S. Department of Education Federal Family Education Loan Program	84.032	$ 1,684,358

Basis of Presentation

The accompanying schedule of expenditures of federal awards (the "Schedule") includes the federal award activity of Memphis Theological Seminary of the Cumberland Presbyterian Church under programs of the federal government for the year ended July 31, 2018. The information in this Schedule is presented in accordance with the requirements of Title 2 CFR U.S. *Code of Federal Regulations* Part 200, *Uniform Administrative Requirements, Cost Principles, and Audit Requirements for Federal Awards* (Uniform Guidance). Because the Schedule presents only a selected portion of the operations of Memphis Theological Seminary of the Cumberland Presbyterian Church, it is not intended to and does not present the financial position, changes in net assets or cash flows of Memphis Theological Seminary of the Cumberland Presbyterian Church.

Summary of Significant Accounting Policies

Expenditures reported on the Schedule are reported on the accrual basis of accounting. Such expenditures are recognized following the cost principles contained in OMB Circular A-21, *Cost Principles for Educational Institutions*, wherein certain types of expenditures are not allowable or are limited as to reimbursement. Memphis Theological Seminary of the Cumberland Presbyterian Church elected not to use the ten per cent de minimis indirect cost rate option.

Non-Financial Information

INDEPENDENT AUDITOR'S REPORT ON INTERNAL CONTROL OVER FINANCIAL REPORTING AND ON COMPLIANCE AND OTHER MATTERS BASED ON AN AUDIT OF FINANCIAL STATEMENTS PERFORMED IN ACCORDANCE WITH *GOVERNMENT AUDITING STANDARDS*

To the Board of Trustees
Memphis Theological Seminary of the Cumberland Presbyterian Church
Memphis, Tennessee

We have audited, in accordance with the auditing standards generally accepted in the United States of America and the standards applicable to financial audits contained in *Government Auditing Standards* issued by the Comptroller General of the United States, the financial statements of Memphis Theological Seminary of the Cumberland Presbyterian Church (a nonprofit organization), which comprise the statement of financial position as of July 31, 2018, and the related statements of activities, functional expenses, and cash flows for the year then ended, and the related notes to the financial statements, and have issued our report thereon dated November 13, 2018.

Internal Control over Financial Reporting

In planning and performing our audit of the financial statements, we considered Memphis Theological Seminary of the Cumberland Presbyterian Church's internal control over financial reporting (internal control) to determine the audit procedures that are appropriate in the circumstances for the purpose of expressing our opinion on the financial statements, but not for the purpose of expressing an opinion on the effectiveness of Memphis Theological Seminary of the Cumberland Presbyterian Church's internal control. Accordingly, we do not express an opinion on the effectiveness of Memphis Theological Seminary of the Cumberland Presbyterian Church's internal control.

A *deficiency in internal control* exists when the design or operation of a control does not allow management or employees, in the normal course of performing their assigned functions, to prevent, or detect and correct, misstatements on a timely basis. A *material weakness* is a deficiency, or a combination of deficiencies, in internal control, such that there is a reasonable possibility that a material misstatement of the entity's financial statements will not be prevented, or detected and corrected on a timely basis. A *significant deficiency* is a deficiency, or a combination of deficiencies, in internal control that is less severe than a material weakness, yet important enough to merit attention by those charged with governance.

Our consideration of internal control was for the limited purpose described in the first paragraph of this section and was not designed to identify all deficiencies in internal control that might be material weaknesses or significant deficiencies. Given these limitations, during our audit we did not identify any deficiencies in internal control that we consider to be material weaknesses. However, material weaknesses may exist that have not been identified.

Compliance and Other Matters

As part of obtaining reasonable assurance about whether Memphis Theological Seminary of the Cumberland Presbyterian Church's financial statements are free from material misstatement, we performed tests of its compliance with certain provisions of laws, regulations, contracts, and grant agreements, noncompliance with which could have a direct and material effect on the determination of financial statement amounts. However, providing an opinion on compliance with those provisions was not an objective of our audit, and accordingly, we do not express such an opinion. The results of our tests disclosed no instances of noncompliance or other matters that are required to be reported under *Government Auditing Standards*.

CANNON WRIGHT BLOUNT PLLC   756 RIDGE LAKE BLVD   MEMPHIS TN 38120

PHONE 901.685.7500   FAX 901.685.7569   WWW.CANNONWRIGHTBLOUNT.COM

Purpose of this Report

The purpose of this report is solely to describe the scope of our testing of internal control and compliance and the results of that testing, and not to provide an opinion on the effectiveness of the organization's internal control or on compliance. This report is an integral part of an audit performed in accordance with *Government Auditing Standards* in considering the organization's internal control and compliance. Accordingly, this communication is not suitable for any other purpose.

Cannon Wright Blount PLLC

Memphis, Tennessee
November 13, 2018

INDEPENDENT AUDITOR'S REPORT ON COMPLIANCE FOR A MAJOR PROGRAM AND ON INTERNAL CONTROL OVER COMPLIANCE REQUIRED BY THE UNIFORM GUIDANCE

To the Board of Trustees
Memphis Theological Seminary of the Cumberland Presbyterian Church
Memphis, Tennessee

Report on Compliance for a Major Federal Program

We have audited Memphis Theological Seminary of the Cumberland Presbyterian Church's compliance with the types of compliance requirements described in the *OMB Compliance Supplement* that could have a direct and material effect on Memphis Theological Seminary of the Cumberland Presbyterian Church's major federal program for the year ended July 31, 2018. Memphis Theological Seminary of the Cumberland Presbyterian Church's major federal program is identified in the summary of auditor's results section of the accompanying schedule of findings and questioned costs.

Management's Responsibility

Management is responsible for compliance with federal statutes, regulations, and the terms and conditions of its federal awards applicable to its federal program.

Auditor's Responsibility

Our responsibility is to express an opinion on compliance for Memphis Theological Seminary of the Cumberland Presbyterian Church's major federal program based on our audit of the types of compliance requirements referred to above. We conducted our audit of compliance in accordance with auditing standards generally accepted in the United States of America; the standards applicable to financial audits contained in *Government Auditing Standards*, issued by the Comptroller General of the United States; and the audit requirements of Title 2 U.S. *Code of Federal Regulations* Part 200, *Uniform Administrative Requirements*, *Cost Principles*, and *Audit Requirements for Federal Awards* (Uniform Guidance). Those standards and the Uniform Guidance require that we plan and perform the audit to obtain reasonable assurance about whether noncompliance with the types of compliance requirements referred to above that could have a direct and material effect on a major federal program occurred. An audit includes examining, on a test basis, evidence about Memphis Theological Seminary of the Cumberland Presbyterian Church's compliance with those requirements and performing such other procedures as we considered necessary in the circumstances.

We believe that our audit provides a reasonable basis for our opinion on compliance for the major federal program. However, our audit does not provide a legal determination of Memphis Theological Seminary of the Cumberland Presbyterian Church's compliance.

Opinion on a Major Federal Program

In our opinion, Memphis Theological Seminary of the Cumberland Presbyterian Church complied, in all material respects, with the types of compliance requirements referred to above that could have a direct and material effect on its major federal program for the year ended July 31, 2018.

Report on Internal Control over Compliance

Management of Memphis Theological Seminary of the Cumberland Presbyterian Church is responsible for establishing and maintaining effective internal control over compliance with the types of compliance requirements referred to above. In planning and performing our audit of compliance, we considered Memphis Theological Seminary of the Cumberland Presbyterian Church's internal control over compliance with the types of requirements that could have a direct and material effect on a major federal program to determine the auditing procedures that are appropriate in the circumstances for the purpose of expressing an opinion on compliance for a major federal program and to test and report on internal control over compliance in accordance with the Uniform Guidance, but not for the purpose of expressing an opinion on the effectiveness of internal control over compliance. Accordingly, we do not express an opinion on the effectiveness of Memphis Theological Seminary of the Cumberland Presbyterian Church's internal control over compliance.

A *deficiency in internal control over compliance* exists when the design or operation of a control over compliance does not allow management or employees, in the normal course of performing their assigned functions, to prevent, or detect and correct, noncompliance with a type of compliance requirement of a federal program on a timely basis. A *material weakness in internal control over compliance* is a deficiency, or combination of deficiencies, in internal control over compliance, such that there is a reasonable possibility that material noncompliance with a type of compliance requirement of a federal program will not be prevented, or detected and corrected, on a timely basis. A *significant deficiency in internal control over compliance* is a deficiency, or a combination of deficiencies, in internal control over compliance with a type of compliance requirement of a federal program that is less severe than a material weakness in internal control over compliance, yet important enough to merit attention by those charged with governance.

Our consideration of internal control over compliance was for the limited purpose described in the first paragraph of this section and was not designed to identify all deficiencies in internal control over compliance that might be material weaknesses or significant deficiencies. We did not identify any deficiencies in internal control over compliance that we consider to be material weaknesses. However, material weaknesses may exist that have not been identified.

The purpose of this report on internal control over compliance is solely to describe the scope of our testing of internal control over compliance and the results of that testing based on the requirements of the Uniform Guidance. Accordingly, this report is not suitable for any other purpose.

Cannon Wright Blount PLLC

Memphis, Tennessee
November 13, 2018

MEMPHIS THEOLOGICAL SEMINARY OF THE CUMBERLAND PRESBYTERIAN CHURCH

Schedule of Findings and Questioned Costs   *For the Year Ended July 31, 2018*

SECTION I - SUMMARY OF AUDITOR'S RESULTS

Financial Statements

Type of auditor's report issued:	*Unmodified*
Internal control over financial reporting:	
- Material weakness(es) identified?	___ yes __X__ no
- Significant deficiencies identified that are not considered to be material weaknesses?	___ yes __X__ none noted
- Noncompliance material to financial statements noted?	___ yes __X__ no

Federal Awards:

Internal control over major programs:	
- Material weakness(es) identified?	___ yes __X__ no
- Significant deficiencies identified that are not considered to be material weaknesses?	___ yes __X__ none noted
Type of auditor's report issued on compliance for major program:	*Unmodified*
Any audit findings disclosed that are required to be reported in accordance with 2 CFR section 200.516(a)?	___ yes __X__ no

Identification of major programs:

CFDA 84.032	U.S. Department of Education Federal Family Education Loan Program
Threshold for distinguishing type A and B programs:	*$750,000*
Auditee qualified as low risk auditee:	__X__ yes ___ no

SECTION II - FINANCIAL STATEMENT FINDINGS

There are no financial statement findings for the year ended July 31, 2018.

SECTION III - FEDERAL AWARD FINDINGS AND QUESTIONED COSTS

There are no federal award findings or questioned costs for the year ended July 31, 2018.

MEMPHIS THEOLOGICAL SEMINARY OF THE CUMBERLAND PRESBYTERIAN CHURCH
Summary Schedule of Prior Audit Findings — *For the Year Ended July 31, 2018*

There were no findings or questioned costs for the year ended July 31, 2017.

APPENDICES

REPORT OF THE CREDENTIALS COMMITTEE
(Appendix A)

The Credentials Committee certifies the list of commissioners on pages 5 and 6 of the Preliminary Minutes with the following change:

On the part of Minister Commissioners, Paul Lanz, West Tennessee Presbytery; Nate Matthews, del Cristo Presbytery; and Gin Soo Park, Cumberland East Coast Presbytery; are not present.

Enrollment as of 2:00 p.m. is certified as forty-six (46) ministers, forty-four (44) elders and twenty-five (25) youth advisory delegates.

Respectfully submitted,
Reverend Virginia Espinoza, Chair
Elder Larry Nottingham, Co-Chair
Elder Sally Sain
Youth Advisory Delegate Noah Jenkins

REPORT OF THE COMMITTEE ON
THEOLOGY AND SOCIAL CONCERNS/UNIFICATION TASK FORCE
(Appendix B)

I. REFERRALS

Referrals to this committee are as follows: The Report of the Unified Committee on Theology and Social Concerns and The Report of the Unification Task Force.

II. PERSONS OF COUNSEL

Appearing before this committee were: Reverend Edmund Cox (CPCA) and Reverend Mitch Boulton (CPC), representatives of Theology and Social Concerns; Reverend Perryn Rice (CPCA) and Reverend Steve Mosley, representatives of the Unification Task Force (CPC); Reverend Mike Wilkinson, president of the Ministry Council; Ms Edith Old, Director of Ministries; Ms. Charelle Webb, representative Ministry Council; and Reverend Jacqueline DeBerry, non-commissioner representing herself.

III. CONSIDERATION OF REFERRALS

A. UNIFIED COMMITTEE ON THEOLOGY AND SOCIAL CONCERNS

The committee considered the report, and after consultation with representatives of the Unified Committee on Theology and Social Concerns, the committee concurs in the report and makes the following recommendation:

RECOMMENDATION 1: That Recommendation 1 of the Report of the Unified Committee on Theology and Social Concerns, "that the UCTSC requests more time to consider other pertinent information from various perspectives in order to set forth a loving, Biblical and theological sound response," be adopted.

Our Committee acknowledges the diligent work done by the UCTSC on the subject of human sexuality. They have received and studied input from the members of the CPCA and the CPC and are requesting additional feedback. One opportunity for members of the denomination to address the UCTSC, either directly or by teleconference, is on August 24, 2019 (location TBD). Additional study papers may be submitted by October 1, 2019 to the UCTSC. Contact the chair of the UCTSC for further information. (www.cumberland.org\uctsc\)

The Committee adds this additional recommendation to encourage a timely conclusion by the UCTSC.

RECOMMENDATION 2: That the UCTSC return a response to the 190th General Assembly of the Cumberland Presbyterian Church.

B. UNIFICATION TASK FORCE

The committee considered the report, and after consultation with representatives of the Unification Task Force, the committee concurs in the report and makes the following recommendation:

RECOMMENDATION 3: That Recommendation 1 of the Report of the Unification Task Force, that this Proposed Plan for Union be adopted by the General Assemblies of the CPCA and the CPC; and that upon such approval, it be forwarded to the presbyteries of the CPCA and the CPC for ratification during the 2019-2020 year. Presbyteries will be instructed to submit a report of their vote to their respective General Assembly clerks in time to be announced by the 2020 General Assemblies," be adopted.

C. FURTHER ACTIONS++

The committee received a communication from the Ministry Council. After discussions with the Ministry Council and the Unification Task Force, action is not needed at this time.

The committee also heard from Reverend Jacqueline DeBerry at her request. She had some clarifying questions. The committee answered her questions to the best of our ability.

Respectfully Submitted,
Committee on Theological and Social Concerns/Unification Task Force

REPORT OF THE COMMITTEE ON MINISTRY COUNCIL
(Appendix C)

I. REFERRALS

Referrals to this committee are as follows: The Report of the Ministry Council, and The Memorial from Presbytery del Cristo Regarding a Denominational Day of Prayer and Fasting.

II. PERSONS OF COUNSEL

Appearing before this committee were: Mrs. Edith Old, Director of Ministries; Ms. Charelle Webb, Representative from Ministry Council; Reverend Pam Phillips-Burk, Pastoral Development Ministry Team; Reverend Steven Shelton, Communications Ministry Team; Reverend Elinor Brown, Discipleship Ministry Team; Reverend Milton Ortiz, Missions Ministry Team; Reverend Lynn Thomas, Global Cross-Cultural Ministries; and Reverend T. J. Malinoski, Evangelism and New Church Development Director.

III. CONSIDERATION OF REFERRALS

A. REPORT OF THE MINISTRY COUNCIL

We commend the members of the Ministry Council on their excitement and enthusiasm about their tasks, exceptional stewardship of all their resources, the creation of a cooperative and empowering environment, and the success of their hard work. We make the following recommendations:

RECOMMENDATION 1: That Recommendation 1 of the Report of the Ministry Council, "That the 189th General Assembly request presbyteries to call upon both lay and ordained Cumberland Presbyterians to start new communities of faith in their homes, neighborhoods, towns, cities, and local settings with the encouragement and support of their church session, presbyterial board of missions, presbytery, synod, and MMT for the purpose of extending the Gospel of Jesus Christ," be adopted.

RECOMMENDATION 2: That Recommendation 2 of the Report of the Ministry Council, "That the 189th General Assembly request presbyteries to promote and encourage all congregations to consider Beth-El Farmworker Ministry as a mission field for Cumberland Presbyterian church groups looking for short mission trip opportunities and experiences," be adopted.

RECOMMENDATION 3: That Recommendation 3 of the Report of the Ministry Council, "That the 189th General Assembly be called to pray during the General Assembly for our missionaries. Also, that the General Assembly prays that God continues to call churches and individuals to support these missionaries," be adopted.

(This prayer is suggested at the end of the commissioning ceremony. Youth Advisory Delegate Chandler Anderson has volunteered to offer this prayer.)

RECOMMENDATION 4: That Recommendation 4 of the Report of the Ministry Council, "That the 189th General Assembly request presbyteries to encourage all congregations to engage, promote, support, and participate in opportunities to grow the Kingdom of God in denominational ministries through the following: Explore denominational resources for Small Group Studies, Children and Youth Ministry, and Adult Bible Study; Pray for and support our missionaries through the Stott-Wallace Missionary Offering Fund; Visit and advocate for our Ministry Partners, Beth-El Farmworker Ministry, Project Vida, Coalition of Appalachian Ministries, and National Farm Workers Ministry; Encourage students to attend Bethel University and Memphis Theological Seminary; Support global and local mission opportunities," be denied.

RECOMMENDATION 5: That the 189th General Assembly request presbyteries to encourage all congregations to engage, promote, support, and participate in opportunities to grow the Kingdom of God in denominational ministries through the following: explore denominational resources for Small Group Studies, Children and Youth Ministry, and Adult Bible Study; pray for and support our missionaries through the Stott-Wallace Missionary Offering Fund; visit and advocate for our Ministry Partners, Beth-El Farmworker Ministry, Project Vida, Coalition of Appalachian Ministries, and National Farm Workers Ministry; encourage students to attend Bethel University, Memphis Theological Seminary, and the Program of Alternate Studies; and support global and local mission opportunities.

B. DECLARATION FROM HONG KONG PRESBYTERY

The Committee heard a report from our Commissioners from Hong Kong Presbytery on the declaration passed by the Hong Kong Presbytery concerning the increased Chinese pressure on the citizens of Hong Kong concerning the amendments to the Fugitive Offenders Ordinance. The Ministry Council Committee supports Hong Kong Presbytery as the presbytery defends the rights of the citizens.

RECOMMENDATION 6: That the 189th General Assembly pray for Hong Kong, China, Hong Kong Presbytery, and the churches in Hong Kong and especially the families of the Hong Kong Commissioners directly involved with this issue.

C. THE MEMORIAL FROM PRESBYTERY DEL CRISTO REGARDING A DENOMINATIONAL DAY OF PRAYER AND FASTING

RECOMMENDATION 7: That the Memorial from Presbytery del Cristo which states: "189th General Assembly of the Cumberland Presbyterian Church,

Believing that God, in creating persons, gives us the capacity and freedom to respond to God's mighty act of reconciling love accomplished in Jesus and that we are responsible for our choices and actions toward God, one another and the world;

Confessing that we rebel against God, reject our dependence, abuse the gift of freedom, willfully sin, both individually and collectively, and stand in need of God's redemption;

Rejoicing that God acts to heal the brokenness and alienation caused by our sin to restore us through the reconciliation of Jesus Christ and the outpouring the Holy Spirit calling every person toward repentance and faith;

Responding to God's acts of saving grace and forgiveness of sin, we make honest confession of sin against God, our brothers and sisters, and all of creation, amending the past so far as in our power through our choices, actions, and prayer;

Recalling that the renewal of believers is solely of God's grace, that when we trust in the Lord Jesus, we are recreated, born again, renewed in spirit, and made new persons in Christ who are empowered by the illuminating influence of the Holy Spirit to love and glorify God and to love and serve our neighbor;

Reminding all Cumberland Presbyterians that prayer is inseparable from the Christian life and to be a Christian is to pray and to join others in prayer and that we pray not primarily to receive from God but as an expression of our creaturehood and our dependence upon God as our Creator;

Guided by the primary purposes of prayer being to enter the presence of God, to experience anew God's judgement, grace, and power, to praise God and to invite God into our world and into our lives;

Declaring that the Cumberland Presbyterian Church, being nurtured and sustained by worship, by the proclamation and study of the word, and by the celebration of the sacraments, is commissioned to witness to all persons who have not received Christ as Lord and Savior;

Calls upon the 189th General Assembly of the Cumberland Presbyterian Church who is meeting concurrently with the 144th General Assembly of the Cumberland Presbyterian Church in America and;

Requests that a denominational day of Prayer and Fasting be set and observed by all members of the Cumberland Presbyterian Church at every level and in every nation to renew and revitalize us to bear witness to God's mighty act of reconciling love accomplished in Jesus Christ by which the sins of the world are forgiven.

Submitted by: Karen Avery, Presbytery del Cristo on March 15, 2019," be adopted.

Respectfully submitted,
The Ministry Council Committee

REPORT OF THE COMMITTEE ON JUDICIARY
(Appendix D)

I. REFERRALS

Referrals to this committee are as follows: The Report of the Permanent Committee on Judiciary; The Report of the Joint Committee on Amendments; and The Memorial from Nashville Regarding Sacrament of Baptism.

II. PERSONS OF COUNSEL

Reverend Geoff Knight, representative of the Permanent Judiciary Committee; Stated Clerk, and

Reverend Mike Sharpe appeared before the committee.

III. CONSIDERATION OF REFERRALS

A. REPORT OF THE PERMANENT JUDICIARY COMMITTEE

The committee concurs in the Report of the Permanent Judiciary Committee.

B. REPORT OF THE JOINT COMMITTEE ON AMENDMENTS

RECOMMENDATION 1: That Recommendation 1 of the Report of the Joint Committee on Amendments, "That the Preamble to the Constitution be amended by inserting the following paragraph between the first and second existing paragraphs: "Cumberland Presbyterian congregations are found around the world. While the mission of the church is the same everywhere, the forms and structures of the Constitution and Rules of Discipline do not always fit seamlessly with the cultures, traditions, and legal systems of some countries. In countries other than the United States the provisions of the Constitution and Rules of Discipline should be applied so far as possible, but the Constitution and Rules of Discipline are, at heart, documents which exist to promote spiritual objectives. If there are instances in which the letter of the Constitution and/or Rules of Discipline cannot be applied without compromising the mission of the church and the spiritual objectives identified in the Confession of Faith, it is the spirit of the law, rather than the letter, which must prevail."

That Constitution 3.03 be amended to read: "The authority of each level of church government is limited by the stated provisions of the Constitution. Although each judicatory exercises exclusive original jurisdiction over all the matters specifically belonging to it, the lower judicatories are subject to the review and appellate authority of the next higher judicatory."

That Constitution 3.35 be amended to read: "A particular church shall not sell, convey, lease, pledge, mortgage, or encumber its real property used for purposes of worship, nurture, or ministry without the written permission of the presbytery in which the particular church is located, transmitted through the session of the particular church. In granting its permission, the presbytery does not become a party to the church's agreement, nor a guarantor of any indebtedness."

That Constitution 7.06, which refers to the relationships of pastor, assistant/ associate pastor, stated supply, and interim pastor, be amended to read "A person shall enter into one of these relationships with a particular church only with the approval of the presbytery in the bounds of which the particular church is located. The church session shall bear responsibility for the selection of the person, and the presbytery's approval shall relate to the person's ministerial credentials, commitment to the theology and government of the Cumberland Presbyterian Church/Cumberland Presbyterian Church in America, and standing in his or her current presbytery, if any. The presbytery may authorize its board of missions or equivalent body to act on its behalf in examining the call and to give tentative approval to a relationship between a particular church and a minister, licentiate, or candidate, subject to formal approval at a meeting of the presbytery."

That Constitution 8.5(f) be amended to read "In general, to order with respect to the presbyteries, sessions, and churches under its care according to the government of the church, whatever pertains to their spiritual welfare and the edification of the church."

That Constitution 9.4 (d) be amended to read "Institute and review the work of denominational entities."

That Constitution 9.4(g) be amended to read "Take care that the lower judicatories observe the government of the church and exercise its review and appellate authority to redress what they may have done contrary to order."

That Constitution 9.4(m) be amended to read "Keep watch over the affairs of the whole church," be adopted.

C. THE MEMORIAL FROM NASHVILLE PRESBYTERY REGARDING SACRAMENT OF BAPTISM

It is the opinion of this committee that this memorial was directed inappropriately to the Permanent Judiciary Committee. Therefore, the Memorial from Nashville Presbytery which states:

"**WHEREAS the Confession of Faith, Section 5.18, states that the Sacrament of Baptism "symbolizes the baptism of the Holy Spirit and is the external sign of the covenant which marks membership in the community of faith", and**
WHEREAS the Confession of Faith, Section 5.21, states that "in administering the sacrament the pouring or sprinkling of water on the person by the minister fittingly symbolizes the baptism of the Holy Spirit", and
WHEREAS the General Assembly in 1968 granted a Memorial which allowed a minister to "perform the sacrament of baptism with the mode best suited to the specific situation" (Digest, page 18, 2.63d "interpretative"), and
WHEREAS the resulting practice of baptism over the years by Cumberland Presbyterian ministers is now so varied so as to have lost seemingly its connection to baptism as defined in the Confession of Faith, and has opened the door for practices not affirmed in the Confession such as "infant dedications" and repeating the sacrament (despite Section 5.19 of the Confession) under the guise of "believer's baptism",
THEREFORE BE IT RESOLVED that Nashville Presbytery memorializes the General Assembly to refer this Memorial to the General Assembly's Permanent Committee on the Judiciary to report back to the next General Assembly and to provide guidance and direction, particularly to presbyteries, on how to maintain and affirm the Confession of Faith in relation to the Sacrament of Baptism in actual practice.
Respectfully Submitted, Reverend Fred E. Polacek," be denied.

Respectfully submitted,
The Judiciary Committee

REPORT OF THE COMMITTEE ON CHAPLAINS/HISTORICAL FOUNDATION
(Appendix E)

I. REFERRALS

Referrals to this committee are as follows: The Report of the Board of Trustees of the Historical Foundation, The Report of the Commission on Chaplains and Military Personnel and The Report of the Evaluation Committee, Part II, Recommendations 7-11.

II. PERSONS OF COUNSEL

Appearing before this committee were: Ms. Susan Knight Gore, Archivist, Historical Foundation; Ms. Pat Ward, Board Representative, Historical Foundation; Navy Chaplain Lyman M. Smith (CAPT, CHC, USN), Director of the Presbyterian Council for Chaplains and Military Personnel, and Reverend Cassandra Thomas, representative to the Presbyterian Council for Chaplains and Military Personnel; Colonel David Lockhart, Chaplain at Fort Gordon Army Base, Augusta, Georgia; Reverend Tony Janner, retired Air Force Chaplain, member of the PCCMP; and Reverend Rickey Page, representative to the GA Evaluation Committee.

III. CONSIDERATION OF REFERRALS

A. REPORT OF THE BOARD OF TRUSTEES OF THE HISTORICAL FOUNDATION

The Committee appreciates the work being done by Archivist, Ms. Susan Knight Gore and the Board of Trustees of the Historical Foundation, and commends them for their dedication to the preservation of the records of the Cumberland Presbyterian Church in America and the Cumberland Presbyterian Church.

Church records and session minutes are of profound historical significance and importance. When the records of a congregation are lost, very little of that congregation's story may ever be recovered or recreated for preservation and research. Every effort must be made to secure congregational records before a church closes and the property is sold.

Preservation of materials is a critical issue for the Historical Foundation and the infiltration of water into the Archives makes it difficult to properly store and protect the Church's historical documents.

RECOMMENDATION 1: That Recommendation 1 of the Report of the Board of Trustees of the Historical Foundation, "that the General Assembly instruct presbyteries to obtain the session records of a congregation at the time the church is closed and then deposit them in the Historical Foundation," be adopted.

RECOMMENDATION 2: That the Center Interagency Team prioritize a permanent solution to the problem of water incursion into the Center building, especially in the portion of the building occupied by the Historical Foundation.

RECOMMENDATION 3: That presbyteries instruct their congregations to lift up the Denomination Day offering on the first Sunday in February as an important source of funding for the Historical Foundation and their work in preserving our history.

B. REPORT OF THE COMMISSION ON MILITARY CHAPLAINS AND PERSONNEL

The Committee reviewed the Report of the Presbyterian Council for Chaplains and Military Personnel, prepared and presented by members of the Cumberland Presbyterian Church who serve on the Council.

The Presbyterian Council for Chaplains and Military Personnel, also known as the Presbyterian Federal Chaplaincies, receives its support from four member denominations: Cumberland Presbyterian Church, Cumberland Presbyterian Church in America, Korean Presbyterian Church Abroad, and Presbyterian Church USA.

There are more chaplains today than there are pastors, yet there are still not enough chaplains to meet the needs of those employed by the military, prison system, and federal agencies. The PCCMP is working to make sure Presbyterian chaplains meet the highest standards for ordination and commissioning. As of March 4, 2019, the Cumberland Presbyterian Church in America had one chaplain on military active duty, and the Cumberland Presbyterian Church had four chaplains on military active duty, three chaplains in the military reserves with one more pending, two chaplain candidates, seven Veteran Affairs chaplains with two more pending, and 13 retired chaplains. The Moderator of the 189th General Assembly, Reverend Shelia O'Mara, is a retired military chaplain and the Vice-Moderator of the 187th General Assembly, Reverend Lisa Scott, recently accepted the position of Supervisory Chaplain at the Kansas City VA Medical Center, Kansas City, Missouri.

Presbyterian Chaplains will be present at Triennium this year, ministering to those in attendance and encouraging them to listen for God's call on their lives.

The Committee is grateful to the Commission on Military Chaplains and Personnel for the encouragement and support they provide to chaplains and to those whom they serve.

RECOMMENDATION 4: That Recommendation 1 of the Report of the Commission on Military Chaplains and Personnel, "that each Cumberland Presbyterian Church provide an opportunity for their congregations to receive an offering on the last Sunday of May, or another special day, to support our ministry through the PCCMP," be denied.

RECOMMENDATION 5: That Cumberland Presbyterian Church in America presbyteries and Cumberland Presbyterian Church presbyteries located in the United States encourage their congregations to provide an opportunity for their congregations to receive an offering on the last Sunday of May, or another special day, to support the ministry through the PCCMP.

RECOMMENDATION 6: That Recommendation 2 of the Report of the Commission on Military Chaplains and Personnel, "that individual congregations of the Cumberland Presbyterian Church and Cumberland Presbyerian Church in America determine and designate special days

through the year to hold up the chaplains and their families in the service to which they have been endorsed," be denied.

RECOMMENDATION 7: That Cumberland Presbyterian Church in America presbyteries and Cumberland Presbyterian Church presbyteries located in the United States determine and designate special days through the year to hold up the chaplains and their families in the service to which they have been endorsed.

C. REPORT OF THE EVALUATION COMMITTEE, PART II, (RECOMMENDATIONS 7-11)

The Evaluation Committee examined the work of the Historical Foundation and met with the Director of the Historical Foundation to discuss the function of the Foundation, the work that has been assigned to the Foundation, and the long-range plans for fulfilling the directives given to the Foundation by the General Assembly.

Consideration may need to be given to more cost-effective ways of housing the archival collection, while still providing researchers and historians access to church records. Foundational documents need to be reviewed and updated to reflect the Foundation's evolving role in a changing world.

Financial restraints prevent the Foundation from carrying out some of their plans for improving the work and function of the Historical Foundation.

RECOMMENDATION 8: That Recommendation 7 of the Report of the Evaluation Committee, "that General Assembly recommend that the Board of Trustees of the Historical Foundation review and/or revise the charter in light of the issues raised in this evaluation," be denied.

RECOMMENDATION 9: That General Assembly recommend that the Board of Trustees of the Historical Foundation review and/or revise the charter to make sure it is still accurate to the work of the Foundation.

RECOMMENDATION 10: That Recommendation 8 of the Report of the Evaluation Committee, "that the Board of Trustees of the Historical Foundation develop a long-range strategy to fulfill the requirements outlined in the Charter and include a transition strategy for replacing the Director and part time archivist," be denied.

RECOMMENDATION 11: That Recommendation 9 of the Report of the Evaluation Committee, "that the Board of Trustees of the Historical Foundation engage in leadership training. (It might be possible to partner with MTS who will be providing this training for its board.)," be denied.

RECOMMENDATION 12: That Recommendation 10 of the Report of the Evaluation Committee, "that the Board of Trustees of the Historical Foundation develop a job description for the director and part time archivist", be denied.

RECOMMENDATION 13: That Recommendation 11 of the Report of the Evaluation Committee, "that General Assembly revise funding strategies enabling the Historical Foundation to fulfill the requirements of the charter," be denied.

RECOMMENDATION 14: That the Board of Trustees of the Historical Foundation be encouraged to develop a long-range strategy, to include a succession plan along with updated job descriptions for all staff.

RECOMMENDATION 15: That we commend the Historical Foundation for their creative fundraising and for their excellent stewardship of the funds they receive, and that the General Assembly encourage the Board of Trustee of the Historical Foundation to develop funding strategies for helping the Foundation fulfill its mission.

RECOMMENDATION 16: That the General Assembly encourage individuals, congregations, and presbyteries to visit the Historical Foundation website, make use of the information available, and support the Foundation by donating through the link provided on their webpage. www.cumberland.org\hfcpc\

Respectfully submitted,
The Committee on Chaplains and Historical Foundation

REPORT OF THE COMMITTEE ON STEWARDSHIP/ELECTED OFFICERS/OUO
(Appendix F)

I. REFERRALS

Referrals to this committee are as follows: The Report of the Moderator; The Report of the Stated Clerk; The Report of the Board of Stewardship, Foundation and Benefits; The Report of the Our United Outreach Committee; The Report of the Place of Meeting Committee; and The Line Item Budgets Submitted by General Assembly Agencies.

II. PERSONS OF COUNSEL

Appearing before this committee were: Reverend Robert Heflin, Mr. Mark Duck, and Board Representative, Mr. Gary Tubb (Board of Stewardship); Reverend Cliff Hudson, and regional representatives: Colatta Edsell, Jeff McMichael and Bruce Hamilton (Our United Outreach Committee); Reverend Michael Sharpe, Stated Clerk; and Moderator of the 188th General Assembly, Reverend Jay Earheart-Brown. We wish to express our appreciation to the persons of counsel for their presentation.

III. CONSIDERATION OF REFERRALS

A. REPORT OF THE MODERATOR

Concurred in the moderator's report and expressed gratitude for Reverend Dr. Jay Earheart-Brown's service as moderator.

RECOMMENDATION 1: That Recommendation 1 of the Report of the Moderator, "that the 189th General Assembly formally express its appreciation for the life, ministry, and service of Reverend Buddy Pope as Vice Moderator of the 188th General Assembly, and that the clerk be instructed to send notice of our appreciation to Buddy's family at his earliest convenience," be adopted.

We agree with the moderator's assertion that our Constitution's description of advisory members is inadequate. The current language, in section 3.07, Judicatories of the Church, reads as follows:

"3.07 Other ministers [who are not members of the body] who are present in a meeting of presbytery or synod may or may not be seated by action of the body as advisory members, which if granted gives them the privilege to speak to any matter before the body. Persons so seated shall be introduced to the presbytery or the synod by the moderator."

We agree with the moderator's proposed constitutional amendment to current section 3.07 above to be replaced as follows:

"3.07 Every judicatory of the church has the prerogative to seat persons as advisory members, with full privilege of speaking to any issue before the judicatory, but no vote. The following persons shall be granted advisory membership in the stated judicatory:
a. Presbytery approved and installed assistant and associate pastors will be advisory members of the session they serve.
b. Elected officers of any judicatory (stated clerk, engrossing clerk, treasurer, etc.) and official representatives from any standing committee or board of the judicatory will be advisory members of that judicatory, if they are not members of the body, without the need to request permission to speak.

The following persons may be approved as advisory members of a judicatory, but are not required to be seated as such. Persons so seated shall be introduced to the judicatory by the moderator:

    a. In middle judicatories, visiting ordained Cumberland Presbyterian ministers from other presbyteries/synods.

    b. In middle judicatories, visiting elders from other presbyteries/synods.

    c. In any judicatory, youth advisory delegates elected to serve.

    d. Representatives from higher judicatories.

    e. Officers from the Cumberland Presbyterian Women's Ministry or other auxiliaries.

    f. Attorneys employed by the judicatory.

    g. Visiting ministers or leaders from other denominations with whom the judicatory is in partnership.

No judicatory should feel obligated to seat advisory members, but should grant this privilege in a way that serves the mission and ministry of the church. Persons who are not regular or advisory members of any judicatory may be granted permission to speak to the judicatory on majority vote or consent of the judicatory."

RECOMMENDATION 2: That Recommendation 2 of the Report of the Moderator, "that the General Assembly approve the proposed amendment to substitute a new section 3.07 for the existing 3.07 in the Constitution of the CPC/CPCA, and that the proposed amendment be forwarded to the Joint Committee on Amendments for their review and counsel," be adopted.

B. THE REPORT OF THE STATED CLERK

We commend the work of the Stated Clerk, Reverend Michael Sharpe, and the thoroughness of the actions described in his submitted report.

RECOMMENDATION 3: That Recommendation 1 of the Report of the Stated Clerk, "that the 189th General Assembly approve (with the changes of the CPYC date to June 21-26, 2020 and General Assembly to June 7-12, 2020 in Louisville, Kentucky) the following dates for the 2019-2020 Church Calendar:

CHURCH CALENDAR 2019-2020

July-2019

6	Children's Fest/Middle Schooler's Event, McKenzie, Tennessee
7	Outdoor Ministries Sunday
13	Program of Alternate Studies Graduation
13-27	PAS Summer Extension School, Bethel, McKenzie, Tennessee
16-20	Presbyterian Youth Triennium

August-2019

4	Bethel University Commencement
4-Sept 30	Christian Education Season
7-10	Youth Worker Retreat
18	MTS Fall Semester Begins (tentative)
18	Seminary/PAS Sunday
22	Bethel University Fall Semester Begins
25	MTS Fall Semester Begins (tentative)
28	MTS Opening convocation (tentative)
30	Bethel University Spring Convocation

September-2019

4	MTS Opening convocation (tentative)
8	Family Sunday
8	Senior Adult Sunday
12-15	Young Adult Ministry Council

15	Christian Service Recognition Sunday
15	International Day of Prayer and Action for Human Habitat
22	Seminary Sunday

October-2019

	Church Paper Month
	Clergy Appreciation Month
	Domestic Violence Awareness Month
6	Worldwide Communion Sunday
13	Pastor Appreciation Sunday
15	A Day at the Park
20	Native American Sunday

November-2019

	Any Sunday Loaves and Fishes Program
1	All Saints Day
3	World Community Sunday (Church Women United)
3	Bethel University Sunday
3	Stewardship Sunday
7-9	Symposium
10	Day of Prayer for People with Aids and Other Life-Threatening Illnesses
17	Bible Sunday
24	Christ the King Sunday

December-2019

	Any Sunday Gift to the King Offering
2	PAS Advisory Council
2-24	Advent in Church and Home
8	Bethel University Commencement
24	Christmas Eve
25	Christmas Day

January-2020

6	Epiphany
6	MTS Classes Begin
6-7	Stated Clerks' Conference
11	Human Trafficking Awareness Day
13	BU Spring Semester Begins
15	Deadline for receipt of 2019 Our United Outreach Contributions

February-2020

	Black History Month
1	Annual congregational reports due in General Assembly office
2	Denomination Day
2	Historical Foundation Offering
2	Souper Bowl Sunday
9	Our United Outreach Sunday
16	Youth Sunday
26	Ash Wednesday, the beginning of Lent
26–April 11	Lent to Easter

March-2020

Women's History Month (USA)
- 6   World Day of Prayer (CWU)
- 15   Children's Home Sunday
- 23-29   National Farm Workers Awareness Week

April-2020
- 5   Palm/Passion Sunday
- 9   Maundy Thursday
- 10   Good Friday
- 12   Easter
- 19   Earth Day

May-2020
- 1   Friendship Day (Church Women United)
- 7   National Day of Prayer
- 9   Bethel University Commencement
- 16   MTS Closing Convocation & Graduation
- 24   Memorial Day Offering for Military Chaplains & Personnel for USA churches
- 31   Pentecost
- 31   World Missions Sunday
- 31   Stott-Wallace Missionary Offering

June-2020
- 7-12   General Assembly
- 8-12   CPWM Convention
- 14   Cumberland Presbyterian Church Ministries Sunday
- 21   Unification Sunday
- 28-July 3   Cumberland Presbyterian Youth Conference, Bethel University, McKenzie, Tennessee

July-2020
- 5   Outdoor Ministries Sunday
- 9-12   Americas Youth Gathering 2020
- 11   Children's Fest/Middle Schooler's Event, Cookeville, Tennessee
- 11   Program of Alternate Studies Graduation
- 11-25   PAS Summer Extension School, Bethel, McKenzie, Tennessee
- 18   Children's Fest/Middle Schooler's Event, Cookeville, Tennessee

August-2020
- 1   Bethel University Commencement
- 2-Sept 30   Christian Education Season
- 5-10   Asian Youth Gathering 2020
- 16   Seminary/PAS Sunday
- 17   Bethel University Fall Semester Begins
- 25   Bethel University Convocation
- 26   MTS Fall Semester Begins (tentative)
- 27   MTS Opening convocation (tentative)

September-2020
- 13   Family Sunday
- 13   Senior Adult Sunday
- 20   Christian Service Recognition Sunday
- 20   International Day of Prayer and Action for Human Habitat

October-2020

        Church Paper Month
        Clergy Appreciation Month
        Domestic Violence Awareness Month

4   **Worldwide Communion Sunday**
11   **Pastor Appreciation Sunday**
18   **Native American Sunday**
20   **A Day at the Park**

November-2020

        Any Sunday Loaves and Fishes Program

1   **All Saints Day**
1   **Bethel University Sunday**
1   **Stewardship Sunday**
6   **World Community Day (Church Women United)**
15   **Day of Prayer for People with Aids and Other Life-Threatening Illnesses**
15   **Bible Sunday**
22   **Christ the King Sunday**
29- Dec 24   **Advent in Church and Home**

December-2020

        Any Sunday Gift to the King Offering

7   **PAS Advisory Council**
13   **Bethel University Commencement**
24   **Christmas Eve**
25   **Christmas Day,"** be adopted.

The stated clerk noted that in 2018, 202 congregations failed to submit their annual reports. It is important that statistics are as accurate as possible. Therefore, we recommend:

RECOMMENDATION 4: That all presbyteries remind local congregations of the importance and impact of submitting their annual reports.

C. THE REPORT OF THE BOARD OF STEWARDSHIP, FOUNDATION, AND BENEFITS

We commend the work of the Board and appreciate their hard work on behalf of ministers, churches, and all others they serve.

The committee concurred in the Report of the Board of Stewardship, Foundation and Benefits.

D. THE REPORT OF THE OUR UNITED OUTREACH COMMITTEE

RECOMMENDATION 5: That Recommendation 1 of the Report of the Our United Outreach Committee, "that General Assembly adopt the following Our United Outreach allocations for 2020:

The allocation is to be as follows:	$2,600,000.00	
Development Coordinator Office and OUO Committee		92,044.00
Unification Task Force		35,000.00
Sub-total	127,044.00	
(Amount to be allocated)	2,472,956.00	

Ministry Council	$ 1,236,478.00	50%
Bethel University	123,648.00	5%
Children's Home	74,189.00	3%
Stewardship	148,377.00	6%
General Assembly Office	197,836.00	8%
Memphis Theological Seminary/ Program of Alternate Studies	173,107.00	7%
Historical Foundation	74,189.00	3%
Shared Services	395,672.00	16%
Contingency	12,365.00	.5%
(Next four items total 1.5%)		
Comm. on Chaplains	14,356.00	.581%
Judiciary Committee	13,539.00	.548%
Theology/Social Concerns	5,045.00	.204%
Nominating Committee	4,155.00	.168%
	2,472,956.00	

Our United Outreach Goal $2,600,000.00," be adopted.

RECOMMENDATION 6: That Recommendation 2 of the Report of the Our United Outreach Committee, "that the OUO Committee request that General Assembly challenge churches to invite an OUO Representative or member of the OUO Committee to speak in their congregations," be denied.

Although the committee did not necessarily disagree with the OUO Committee's Recommendation 2, we felt the need to better express the importance for 2-way communication regarding OUO, the judicatories, and local churches and make the following recommendation:

RECOMMENDATION 7: That the presbyteries encourage churches to invite an OUO Representative or member of the OUO Committee to share a compelling case for OUO participation to the congregations, and encourage members to participate in ministries supported by OUO in order to increase understanding of uses of OUO funds.

E. THE REPORT OF THE PLACE OF MEETING

The committee concurs in the Place of Meeting Committee report.
Not included in the report, but discovered in our conversation with the Stated Clerk, it was communicated that the location of 190th General Assembly will be in Louisville, Kentucky (Cumberland Presbytery) – June 7-12, 2020.
In order to assist the Place of Meeting Committee find adequate facilities at the best rate, the committee makes the following recommendation:

RECOMMENDATION 8: To encourage presbyteries to extend an invitation to host General Assembly in future years, especially those that have not hosted in recent years.

F. LINE ITEM BUDGETS SUBMITTED BY GENERAL ASSEMBLY AGENCIES

The committee recognizes the uncertainty involved in preparing budgets, and expresses appreciation for the hard work of all the agencies that submitted budgets to the 189th General Assembly.
To achieve a better sense of surety, as well as providing better transparency, the committee makes the following recommendation:

RECOMMENDATION 9: Include, with the proposed Line Item Budget, the previous year's actuals for income and expenses.

Respectfully submitted,
The Stewardship/Elected Officers/OUO Committee

REPORT OF THE COMMITTEE ON CHILDREN'S HOME/HIGHER EDUCATION
(Appendix G)

I. REFERRALS

Referrals to this committee are as follows: The Report of the Board of Trustees of Memphis Theological Seminary, The Report of the Board of Trustees of Bethel University, the Board of Trustees of the Cumberland Presbyterian Children's Home,

II. PERSONS OF COUNSEL

Appearing before this committee were: Reverend Susan Parker, Interim President of Memphis Theological Seminary; Ms. Vanessa Midgett, member of the Board of Trustees of Memphis Theological Seminary; Reverend Kip Rush, Vice-Moderator of the Board of Trustees of Memphis Theological Seminary; Reverend Gloria Villa Diaz, member of the Board of Trustees of Memphis Theological Seminary; Mr. Michael Allen, member of the Board of Trustees of Memphis Theological Seminary; Reverend Rickey Page, member of the General Assembly Evaluation Committee; Reverend Michael Qualls, Director of the Program of Alternate Studies; Dr. Walter Butler, President of Bethel University; Reverend Mr. Robert Truitt, member of the Board of Trustees at Bethel University; Mrs. Courtney Banatoski, President & CEO of the Cumberland Presbyterian Children's Home; Mr. Sam Suddarth, member of the Board of Trustees of the Cumberland Presbyterian Children's Home; and Mrs. Hillary Castillo, Senior Director of Operations of the Cumberland Presbyterian Children's Home.

III. CONSIDERATION OF REFERRALS

A. THE REPORT OF THE BOARD OF TRUSTEES OF MEMPHIS THEOLOGICAL SEMINARY

1. Future Funding
God has blessed Memphis Theological Seminary over the course of its history with faithful Cumberland Presbyterians who give generously to see future Cumberland Presbyterian leaders receive a quality education. It is vital to the future of Memphis Theological Seminary that General Assembly, synods, presbyteries, churches, and members continue to pray for and financially contribute to continue the vital ministry it is doing.

RECOMMENDATION 1: That Recommendation 1 of the Report of the Board of Trustees of Memphis Theological Seminary, "that the General Assembly encourage Presbyteries to share the mission, vision and passion of MTS to train and sustain men and women for the Christian ministry and ask members to support the seminary with their financial resources and prayers," be adopted.

2. The Whosoever Will Bridge Program
In 2018, an anonymous donor created the "Whosoever Will Bridge Program." This program enables Bethel University graduates who then graduate with an M. Div. from Memphis Theological Seminary and then is called to serve full-time at a CP church to receive a stipend of $12,000 a year. This is a very generous gift meant to help and prepare future leaders in the CP to pursue their call to ministry and attend Bethel University and Memphis Theological Seminary.

RECOMMENDATION 2: That Recommendation 2 of the Report of the Board of Trustees of Memphis Theological Seminary, "that the Presbyteries inform all congregations of the Whosoever

Will Bridge program and provide probationers with the necessary information so they will be aware of this program," be denied.

RECOMMENDATION 3: That the Presbyteries inform all congregations and preparation for the ministry committees of each presbytery of the Whosoever Will Bridge program and provide probationers with the necessary information so they will be aware of this program.

3. Seminary/PAS Sunday

The Program of Alternate Studies has served the Cumberland Presbyterian Church by providing a quality education to ministers who were unable to pursue a seminary degree. This program has ensured that the CP church has educated ministers to lead churches in their respective gospel ministries.

RECOMMENDATION 4: That Recommendation 3 of the Report of the Board of Trustees of Memphis Theological Seminary, "that the third Sunday in August, (August 18, 2019)be included in the General Assembly Calendar as Seminary/PAS Sunday, and that Presbyteries encourage all churches to share information about MTS and PAS and receive a special offering on that day, or on a more convenient day of the session's choosing," be adopted.

4. Recognition of Dr. William "Bill" Rustenhaven, Jr.

The Cumberland Presbyterian Church is indebted to the faithfulness and leadership of the first director of the Program of Alternate Studies by the Reverend Dr. William "Bill" Rustenhaven, Jr., who died February 1, 2019. He invested in relationships with the students of PAS and made sure that all students were instructed with diligence and grace, and we are a better denomination for it.

RECOMMENDATION 5: That General Assembly give thanks to God for the life and ministry of Dr. William "Bill" Rustenhaven, Jr., who led the Program of Alternate Studies faithfully by "making a difference for the building of God's Kingdom and through his responsibility as participants in that Kingdom."

B. THE REPORT OF THE EVALUATION COMMITTEE, PART 1 (RECOMMENDATIONS 1-6)

1. The Mission of Memphis Theological Seminary

MTS allows the Cumberland Presbyterian Church to partner with the larger Christian community and participate in the ecumenical relationships that make up the body of Christ.

RECOMMENDATON 6: That Recommendation 1 of the Report of the Evaluation Committee, "that we affirm our need for an ecumenical seminary," be adopted.

2. Presidential Search

It is critical for MTS to hire the most qualified person for the position of president, regardless of denominational affiliation. However, the seminary needs a strong Cumberland Presbyterian presence in the administration and on the faculty.

RECOMMENDATION 7: That Recommendation 2 of the Report of the Evaluation Committee, "that General Assembly encourage Memphis Theological Seminary to strengthen the Cumberland Presbyterian presence in leadership and teaching at the seminary," be adopted.

3. The Interim President

Dr. Susan Parker has been the Interim President of MTS since August 2018. She is doing an excellent job leading and cultivating a spirit of transparency during this difficult season of change and transition at the seminary. Her experience as a strategic planner and fundraiser has helped bring needed direction to the institution.

RECOMMENDATION 8: That Recommendation 3 of the Report of the Evaluation Committee, "that we express our appreciation to Dr. Susan Parker for her leadership at Memphis Theological Seminary during this critical interim period," be adopted.

4. The Board of Trustees

The Board of Trustees' purpose is primarily to focus on the school's long-term viability and strategic vision. The size of the current board inhibits communication and participation. In an attempt to facilitate engagement and maximize the effectiveness of the Board of Trustees, we are recommending a reduction in the number of board members.

RECOMMENDATION 9: That Recommendation 4 of the Report of the Evaluation Committee, "that the Board of Trustees of Memphis Theological Seminary reduce the number of trustees from 24 to 14 by 2024 and that after any given trustee election the majority of members must be Cumberland Presbyterian," be denied.

A question arose regarding the process of reducing the number of trustees serving on the Board of Trustees. CPC Bylaw 10.06 states, "The corporation shall elect the twenty-four (24) directors of Memphis Theological Seminary as provided in its charter. The corporation shall elect the directors in such a manner that immediately following any election, there shall be eleven (11) directors who are members of denominations other than Cumberland Presbyterian Church." In order to make this reduction, we recommend 10.06 be changed.

RECOMMENDATION 10: That 10.06 of the Bylaws of the Cumberland Presbyterian Church General Assembly Corporation, *"The corporation shall elect the twenty-four (24) directors of Memphis Theological Seminary as provided in its charter. The corporation shall elect the directors in such a manner, that immediately following any election, there shall be eleven (11) directors who are members of denominations other than Cumberland Presbyterian Church"* be changed to *"The corporation shall elect the eighteen (18) directors of Memphis Theological Seminary as provided in its charter. The corporation shall elect the directors in such a manner, that immediately following any election, there shall be six (6) directors who are members of denominations other than Cumberland Presbyterian Church"* **to be presented to the 190th General Assembly.**

MTS received a grant to help with Board development through a program called "Wise Stewards," which includes a consultant. This will be a wise use of time by the Board, but it would be helpful to identify and recruit individuals with expertise in fundraising and finances.

RECOMMENDATION 11: That Recommendation 5 of the Evaluation Committee, "that the Board of Trustees and Memphis Theological Seminary leadership actively identify and recruit individuals with the skill set in fundraising and fiscal responsibility to serve on the Board of Trustees so that the denominational Nominating Committee can recommend candidates from pool of individuals with those skills to serve on the MTS Board," be adopted.

SACS is the accrediting agency that placed MTS on "warning" status due to their failure to demonstrate compliance with core requirements and standards of the principles of accreditation pertaining to institutional planning, quality enhancement plan, student outcomes, educational programs, staff for student support services, financial resources, financial documents, and financial responsibility.

RECOMMENDATION 12: That Recommendation 6 of the Evaluation Committee, "That the Board of Trustees and Memphis Theological Seminary leadership seek to employ a SACS consultant to help develop a strategic plan and move towards compliance in other areas mentioned in the SACS report to MTS," be adopted.

5. Assessment of the Relationship between the Seminary and the Presbyteries

For each member of the Committee on the Children's Home and Higher Education, this was an eye-opening experience. The serious realities of the financial challenges at MTS have caused us to be incredibly concerned for the future of our beloved seminary. In consulting with the president and members of the Board of Trustees, there are currently plans to address some of the problems MTS faces, which is encouraging. We understand that a strategic plan is in process of development, yet there are no action steps have been finalized and could not be presented to the committee. The current leadership should be commended for their work to bring stability to this situation. However, it is clear to the committee that these problems must be acknowledged by the General Assembly, the Board of Trustees, the faculty, and all who are affiliated with the seminary. The time for inaction and ignoring the facts must come to an end.

The discussions that we have had during this meeting of General Assembly have shown us all that there are many issues demanding immediate attention and accountability. We believe that many changes must take place at the seminary if it is to remain open and educate future ministers. Student enrollment must increase. Financial resources must be better raised and managed. Transparency must be committed to and maintained. In light of all these things, and many more not mentioned, the committee strongly recommends that the Evaluation Committee continue in their work to help identify and recommend actions to the General Assembly that will give MTS the best possible opportunity to become a viable and healthy institution again.

RECOMMENDATION 13: That Recommendation 7 of the Evaluation Committee, "that the Evaluation Committee continue to: (1) assess the relationship between Memphis Theological Seminary and the Presbyteries of the Cumberland Presbyterian Church; (2) monitor the financial solvency and stability of Memphis Theological Seminary in light of the concerns of both accrediting agencies. (MTS has until April 2, 2020 to show that their financial resources are adequate for long-term stability.); (3) assess the short and long-term goals of Memphis Theological Seminary. (MTS has until November 1, 2019 to develop a coherent and comprehensive institutional strategic plan.), (4) monitor progress made by MTS towards compliance with findings addressed in the ATS and SACs Report," be adopted.

C. THE REPORT OF THE BOARD OF TRUSTEES OF BETHEL UNIVERSITY

Bethel University has experienced a great deal of success and excitement in many aspects of the institution. As mentioned above (in Section A.2), BU has partnered with Memphis Theological Seminary and a private donor in the "Whosoever Will Ministry Bridge" program. President, Dr. Butler requested that we bring emphasis to this program and make churches and students aware of this program.

RECOMMENDATION 14: That the General Assembly urge the presbyteries and churches to pray for the staff, faculty, and students of Bethel University and encourage their students to consider attending Bethel University during their college search.

D. THE REPORT OF THE BOARD OF TRUSTEES OF THE CUMBERLAND PRESBYTERIAN CHILDREN'S HOME

The Cumberland Presbyterian Children's Home continues to serve children who have been removed from their homes as a result of abuse, neglect, various behavioral problems. The committee commends this excellent and crucial work among the most vulnerable in our society. The Children's Home provides wholistic care toward these children as they receive treatment and enter the foster care system. It is this care that demonstrates the love of Christ to those who have been abused.

RECOMMENDATION 15: That the General Assembly urge the presbyteries and churches to pray for the staff, families, and residents of the Children's Home and actively talk about the ministry of the Children's Home in their churches and ministries.

RECOMMENDATION 16: That the General Assembly urge presbyteries and in turn churches and other groups to continue support of the Children's Home with volunteer help, financial assistance, as well as celebrating Children's Home Sunday on March 15, 2020.

E. THE MEMORIAL FROM MISSOURI PRESBYTERY REGARDING THE PROGRAM OF ALTERNATE STUDIES

The Program of Alternate Studies has demonstrated great flexibility and concern for their students in the creation of their courses and workloads. Dr. Michael Qualls continues to improve the PAS program with many and evolving options for classes and creating community for future pastors to learn and grow into their pastoral ministries.

RECOMMENDATION 17: That the Memorial from Missouri Presbytery Regarding the Program of Alternate Studies, "WHEREAS the Cumberland Presbyterian Denomination was formed out of the Revival of 1800 resulting in the rapid creation of many churches on the frontier of western territories;

WHEREAS the newly created denomination leadership felt the urgent need to provide ministerial leadership required exceptions be made to educational requirements for ordination;

WHEREAS through the history of the denomination, there have been various routes of alternative education leading to ordination that did not require a traditional seminary educational degree;

WHEREAS those alternative education paths have produced ministers that were effective in spreading the gospel of Jesus Christ and serving the needs of the Church;

WHEREAS many called to the ordained ministry have been, and will continue to be bi-vocational pastors needing to maintain full-time employment outside the pulpit;

WHEREAS current educational theories have identified that adult learners respond to a variety of learning styles;

WHEREAS the current Program of Alternate Studies (PAS) is a certificate, non-degree awarding program requiring 35 courses;

WHEREAS the program length has made it difficult for some who attend PAS in response to their call to ministry to maintain their current employment;

WHEREAS many students in PAS are currently ministering to churches; and

WHEREAS it is the goal of PAS to provide an alternative educational pathway to ministry for the preparation of ministers in the Cumberland tradition,

Therefore be it RESOLVED, that alternative methods of education and assessment of learning should continue and be reviewed so that those called to ministry can be prepared in an alternative to seminary attendance;

Therefore be it RESOLVED, that instructors should use a variety of teaching and evaluation of learning methods that are compatible with alternative types of preparation for ministry;

Therefore be it RESOLVED, that PAS should explore granting credit for relevant pastoral experiences as they do for educational experience, including but not limited to creative expression and application of ministerial principles, alternate measures of assessment, independent study, and assessment of applied ministry activities on-site or through distance learning; and

Therefore be it RESOLVED, that it is encouraged that the directors of PAS evaluate the number of courses, consider combining courses and streamlining the curriculum, continue to offer weekend and on-line courses, and create a multi-year schedule of courses to afford ample opportunity for planning a satisfactory completion of the program.

I certify that this is a true copy of a memorial adopted by Missouri Presbytery on March 16, 2019.

Signed Larry Nottingham, Stated Clerk, Missouri Presbytery," be denied.

F. THE MEMORIAL FROM MISSOURI PRESBYTERY REGARDING THE REQUIREMENTS FOR RECOGNITION OF ORDINATION

The current PAS requirements for ministers seeking recognition of their ordinations from other denominations are sufficient and proper. It is important for all those seeking to be Cumberland Presbyterian ministers to understand and know the distinctives of our denomination as well as understand the history, polity, and sacramental practices of the Cumberland Presbyterians.

RECOMMENDATION 18: That the Memorial from Missouri Presbytery Regarding the Requirements for Recognition of Ordination, "WHEREAS there are ministers from another ecclesiastical body that desire to have their ordination recognized and become ministers in the Cumberland Presbyterian Church;

WHEREAS the constitution of the Cumberland Presbyterian Church (CP) currently states the following:

6.40 Recognition of Ordination

6.41 A minister of another ecclesiastical body who desires to become a minister in the Cumberland Presbyterian Church/Cumberland Presbyterian Church in America shall appear before the committee on the ministry of the presbytery in which he or she wishes to be received. The committee on the ministry shall investigate the following:

    a. Whether the minister has proper credentials from his or her ecclesiastical body;
    b. Whether the minister has a degree from a college and graduate school of theology;
    c. Whether the minister has a knowledge of the history, theology, and government of the Cumberland

Presbyterian Church/Cumberland Presbyterian Church in America;
d. Whether the minister seems fit for service as a minister in the Cumberland Presbyterian Church/Cumberland Presbyterian Church in America.

6.42 The committee on the ministry, if satisfied in each of the areas described in Section 6.41 may recommend to presbytery that the minister be received as an ordained minister in the Cumberland Presbyterian Church/Cumberland Presbyterian Church in America, upon giving affirmative answer to the questions put to licentiates at their ordination. Such procedure shall not exclude the opportunity for presbytery to examine the minister.

WHEREAS currently the Committee on the Ministry (COM) in Missouri Presbytery has been told that they are not to recommend recognition of the ordination until the minister of another ecclesiastical body has taken classes through the Program of Alternate Studies of CP History, CP Polity, Cumberland Presbyterian Theology I and Cumberland Presbyterian Theology II;

WHEREAS the COM has also been told that the minister must take two (2) of these courses on site at the Program of Alternate Studies (PAS) summer session;

WHEREAS the ministers already have a degree from a college and graduate school of theology and completing four classes at PAS would take a substantial period of time as well as at current fees cost the individual or the presbytery at least $1,480 in class fees, $163 in room and board plus travel expenses;

WHEREAS some of those wanting their ordination recognized are nearing or at retirement age;

WHEREAS there are CP churches that want the services of these ministers and want these ministers to provide all the sacraments granted ordained CP ministers;

WHEREAS there are opportunities other than PAS for a minister to experience CP culture and develop friendships throughout the denomination such as attendance at presbytery meetings, presbyterial retreats and denominational retreats or conferences;

Therefore be it RESOLVED, that the presbyterial COM should be allowed to individualize the program needed for each minister of another ecclesiastical body who is seeking to have their ordination recognized. This would be determined after a review of previous education, interview of the person and review of the individual circumstances leading to wanting the ordination recognized;

Therefore be it RESOLVED, that if formal coursework is needed, PAS should develop a course of study (not 4 courses) specifically for the minister seeking this recognition of ordination. This course of study should be offered as independent study, online study, weekend class, or at PAS summer session;

Therefore be it RESOLVED, that the presbyterial COM should make the minister, seeking to have their ordination recognized, aware of the various opportunities to experience CP culture and encourage attendance at PAS but that would not be a requirement for the ordination being recognized.

I certify that this is a true copy of a memorial adopted by Missouri Presbytery on March 16, 2019.

Signed Larry Nottingham, Stated Clerk, Missouri Presbytery," be denied.

Respectfully submitted,
The Committee on Children's Home/Higher Education

CHURCH CALENDAR 2019-2020

JULY 2019

6	Children's Fest/Middle Schoolers, Bethel McKenzie, Tennessee
7	Outdoor Ministries Sunday
13	Program of Alternate Studies Graduation
13-27	PAS Summer Extension School, Bethel, McKenzie, Tennessee
16-20	Presbyterian Youth Triennium

AUGUST 2019

4	Bethel University Commencement
4-Sept 30	Christian Education Season
7-10	Youth Worker Retreat
18	Seminary/PAS Sunday
22	Bethel University Fall Semester Begins
25	MTS Fall Semester Begins
28	MTS Opening convocation
30	Bethel University Fall Convocation

SEPTEMBER 2019

8	Family Sunday
8	Senior Adult Sunday
12-15	Young Adult Ministry Council
15	Christian Service Recognition Sunday
15	International Day of Prayer and Action for Human Habitat
22	Seminary Su8nday

OCTOBER 2019

	Church Paper Month
	Clergy Appreciation Month
	Domestic Violence Awareness Month
6	Worldwide Communion Sunday
13	Pastor Appreciation Sunday
15	A Day at the Park
20	Native American Sunday

NOVEMBER 2019

	Any Sunday Loaves and Fishes Program
1	All Saints Day
3	World Community Day (Church Women United)
3	Bethel University Sunday
3	Stewardship Sunday
7-9	Symposium
10	Day of Prayer for People with Aids and Other Life-Threatening Illnesses
17	Bible Sunday
24	Christ the King Sunday

DECEMBER 2019

	Any Sunday Gift to the King Offering
2	PAS Advisory Council
2-24	Advent in Church and Home
8	Bethel University Commencement
24	Christmas Eve
25	Christmas Day

JANUARY-2020

6	Epiphany
6	MTS Classes Begin
6-7	Stated Clerks' Conference Human
11	Trafficking Awareness Day BU
13	Spring Semester Begins Deadline for
15	receipt of 2019 Our United Outreach Contributions

FEBRUARY-2020

	Black History Month
1	Annual congregational reports due in General Assembly office
2	Denomination Day
2	Historical Foundation Offering Souper
2	Bowl Sunday
9	Our United Outreach Sunday
16	Youth Sunday
26	Ash Wednesday, the beginning of Lent
26-April 11	Lent to Easter

MARCH-2020

	Women's History Month (USA)
6	World Day of Prayer (CWU)
15	Children's Home Sunday
23-29	National Farm Workers Awareness Week

APRIL-2020

5	Palm/Passion Sunday
9	Maundy Thursday
10	Good Friday
12	Easter
19	Earth Day

MAY-2020

1	Friendship Day (Church Women United)
7	National Day of Prayer
9	Bethel University Commencement
16	MTS Closing Convocation & Graduation Memorial
24	Day Offering for Military Chaplains & Personnel for USA churches
31	Pentecost
31	World Missions Sunday
31	Stott-Wallace Missionary Offering

JUNE-2020

7-12	General Assembly, Louisville, Kentucky
9-11	CPWM Convention, Louisville, Kentucky
14	CPC Ministries Sunday
21	Unification Sunday
21-26	CPYC, Bethel University, McKenzie, Tennessee
28-July 3	Cumberland Presbyterian Youth Conference, Bethel University, McKenzie, Tennessee

www.ingramcontent.com/pod-product-compliance
Lightning Source LLC
Chambersburg PA
CBHW082107230426
43671CB00015B/2629